The AmeRícan Poet:
ESSAYS ON THE WORK OF TATO LAVIERA

The AmeRícan Poet:
ESSAYS ON THE WORK OF TATO LAVIERA

Edited by Stephanie Alvarez and William Luis

Copyright © 2014 by Center for Puerto Rican Studies. All rights reserved.

No part of this publication may be reproduced, distributed, or transmitted in any form or by any means, including photocopying, recording, or other electronic or mechanical methods, without the prior written permission of the publisher, except in the case of brief quotations embodied in critical reviews and certain other noncommercial uses permitted by copyright law.

Portions of "Tato in His Own Words—A Testimonio Based on Collected Interviews" were reprinted, with permission, from:
- Alvarez, Stephanie, William Luis and Edna Ochoa. 2010. An interview with Tato Laviera. *CENTRO: Journal of the Center for Puerto Rican Studies* 22(2): 34–49. © Center for Puerto Rican Studies.
- Hernández, Carmen Dolores. 1997. Tato Laviera. In *Puerto Rican Voices in English: Interviews with Writers*, ed. Carmen Dolores Hernández. 77–84. Westport: Praeger. © ABC-CLIO.
- Luis, William. 1992. From New York to the World: An interview with Tato Laviera. *Callaloo* 15(4): 1022–33. © The Johns Hopkins University Press.
- Martínez Diente, Pablo. 2006. 'Words without border': A bilingual conversation with Tato Laviera. *Afro-Hispanic Review* 25(2): 151–8. © Afro-Hispanic Review.

Library of Congress Cataloging-in-Publication Data

The AmeRícan poet : essays on the works of Tato Laviera / edited by Stephanie Alvarez and William Luis.
   pages cm
Includes bibliographical references and index.
ISBN 978-1-878483-66-9 (pbk. : alk. paper) — ISBN 978-1-878483-87-4 (ebook)
1. Laviera, Tato—Criticism and interpretation. 2. Puerto Rican literature--20th century--History and criticism. 3. American poetry—Puerto Rican authors—History and criticism. I. Alvarez, Stephanie, editor of compilation. II. Luis, William, editor of compilation.

PS3562.A849Z54 2013
811'.54--dc23
                    2012050061

Center for Puerto Rican Studies
Hunter College, CUNY
695 Park Avenue, E-1429
New York, NY 10065
centrops@hunter.cuny.edu
http://centropr.hunter.cuny.edu

Art Direction: Kenneth J. Kaiser

Printed in the United States of America on acid-free paper.

TABLE OF CONTENTS

Acknowledgements... ix

Foreword xi
STEPHANIE ALVAREZ

Introduction. The Life and Rebirths of Tato Laviera xv
WILLIAM LUIS

Photo Collection.. lvii

I. LANGUAGE, VOICE, AND MUSIC TO MATAO
The Poet as Earwitness: Reading Sound, Voice, and Music in Tato Laviera's Poetry 4
FRANCES R. APARICIO
Crazy Minds Think Alike: My Long Symbiotic Duet with Tato Laviera...................... 22
JUAN FLORES
Espanglish: Laviera's el nideaquínideallá Language in Fourteen Movements 46
EDRIK LÓPEZ

II. (RE)CREATING AND (RE)DEFINING HIS OWN SPACE(S)
Latinas Sing: Tato Laviera's Message for/About Women After Civil Rights Collapse.......... 66
SUSAN CAMPBELL
"Not Nowhere:" "Walking Bridges" in an AmeRícan Utopia............................... 82
ANALISA DEGRAVE
The New Accent in American Poetry: Tato Laviera's "AmeRícan"
in the Context of U.S. American Poetry...124
STEVEN P. SCHNEIDER
Insular Interventions: Tato Laviera's Dialogic Dialogue
with Luis Muñoz Marín and José Luis González 140
MARITZA STANCHICH

III. CREATIVE ACTS OF HEALING
Acts of Resistance: Creativity, Coalition and Consciousness in *King Of Cans* 158
JACQUELINE LAZÚ
Azucarao: Tato Laviera and the Poetics of Health Promotion........................... 176
GLENN MARTÍNEZ

TABLE OF CONTENTS, continued

Barrio, Body, Beat: Tato Laviera and the Holistic Rhythm of *Mestizaje* 188
ISRAEL REYES

La palabra, conciencia y voz: Tato Laviera and the Cosecha Voices Project
at The University of Texas—Pan American 204
STEPHANIE ALVAREZ and JOSÉ LUIS MARTÍNEZ

IV. AFRO-LATINIDADES
Speaking Black Latino/a/ness: Race, Performance, and Poetry in Tato Laviera,
Willie Perdomo and Josefina Báez 240
LAWRENCE LA FOUNTAIN-STOKES

"Kalahari" or the Afro-Caribbean Connection: Tato Laviera and Luis Palés Matos 258
ANTONIA DOMÍNGUEZ MIGUELA

V. TESTIMONIO
Tato in His Own Words—A Collaborative *Testimonio* 288
TATO LAVIERA and STEPHANIE ALVAREZ

VI. POEMS
i am a wise latina 328
la guarachera del mundo 330
piri 332
this-curso (epistle para un sabio) 336

VII. DRAMA
King of Cans 342

Works Cited 390

Contributors 406

Index 411

Photo Courtesy of Arte Público Press, University of Houston.

ACKNOWLEDGEMENTS

Special recognition is given to Edwin Meléndez, Xavier Totti, Noraliz Ruíz and other members of the Centro staff for their commitment to this project. Both Meléndez and Totti understood, rightly so, that this book should be published by the newly created Centro Press. We also acknowledge Hugo Paz and Andrea Zamora for their assistance in transcribing the interviews of the *testimonio*. We are also grateful for those who volunteered to blind review the essays. Many thanks to both Ruth Sánchez Laviera and Nancy True for assisting in confirming and clarifying various details needed for the book. In addition, Stephanie is grateful for the support of her family, first, her husband José Luis Martínez, for all of his encouragement throughout this project; and also her children Amaya, Tatiana, and Santiago, for their constant inspiration; and her father, Daniel Alvarez, for all his wisdom. Lastly, we thank Tato for his friendship, laughter, genius, and collaboration on this and so many other projects.

x

FOREWORD

STEPHANIE ALVAREZ

I was in the midst of writing my dissertation at the University of Oklahoma, Norman, in 2005. The topic was on the use of Spanglish in U.S. Latin@ literature. All of my "academic" training was in Spanish—focused on Latin American and Peninsular literatures. While taking coursework for my Ph.D. comprehensive exams, I remember coming across an advertisement for a summer mini-term course in Santa Fe, New Mexico, on Chicano literature. I was intrigued. I can honestly say that, as a Cubana born and raised in the United States, I was not exactly sure who was a "Chicana/o." The topic, combined with the fact that I could earn three credits in a short period of time, excited me. I asked the Chair of the Department of Modern Languages, at the time a Chicana/o, if I could take the course and have it count towards my degree. He said, "I don't see why not, but the Spanish section will need to approve it." The members of the faculty rejected my proposal because as I was told the class had nothing to do with Spanish. After that, I made it my mission to study U.S. Latina/o literature. I soon realized that I had been denied the opportunity to study the language, culture and literature of Latino/s in the United States and therefore deprived of the prospect to affirm my identity and place in our society.

Every essay I wrote after the initial denial was on the "Diaspora." I took an English course with Denise Chávez, who held a visiting appointment at the University of Oklahoma. That course would not count towards my degree, but it changed my life forever. One reading in particular, "How to Tame a Wild Tongue" by Gloria Anzaldúa, altered my destiny. In that so often cited essay from *Borderlands/La Frontera: The New Mestiza*, I came to understand that so many others and I had suffered linguistic terrorism. She opened the door for me to analyze this reality within my academic work and my own lived experiences. It became the centering theory for my dissertation. It was, of course, inevitable that these experiences would lead me on a path to Tato Laviera.

I recall the first time I read Tato's *La Carreta Made a U-Turn*. It was another one of those life-changing events. The words, the rhythm, the Spanish, the English, the Spanglish, the voice y *la política* resonated in me in ways like nothing else I had read in my entire life. It is no wonder that poems such as "my graduation speech" and "AmeRícan" are canonical poems. I am "brava," I know "esquina dudes," "juana bochisme," "machistas," "papotes" and so many other characters. I connected immediately to "the new rumbón," "the africa in pedro morejón," "the salsa of bethesda fountain," the *política* and walked around signing "se queda allí, se queda allí, se queda allí, es mi raíz."

In spring 2005, pregnant with twin girls, I immersed myself in the poetry of Tato as I wrote my dissertation. I also immersed myself in the music of Ismael Rivera. Every time I got in the car, Maelo was the CD of choice. Maelo was my musical and spiritual guide into Tato's unique cosmology. I discovered a Spanglish poetic world on the written page that had previously been kept hidden from me. Tato's poetry led to my own commencement, accepting and embracing "Spanglish to matao." I also discovered a dearth of scholarship that focused solely on Tato's work or any Latina/o poet. I wrote a chapter of my dissertation that focused on Tato, and submitted it to *CENTRO: Journal of the Center of Puerto Rican Studies*. The essay was accepted and published in Fall 2006, just as I began teaching at the University of Texas-Pan American (UTPA).

In Spring 2007, I received a number of hand-written messages in my mailbox to call "Mr. Laviera." I did not answer any of them. My initial reaction was that this poet was crazy and was calling to tell me "hermana, you got it all wrong." After many more messages—anyone who knows Tato knows he is persistent—and after laying my one-year-old twins down for a nap, I thought to myself, "I have about thirty minutes, let me get this over with and call this man." To my relief, Tato was thrilled with my publication. He went on to express his gratitude to me for my essay and helping him better understand his own work. He told me that he wanted to meet me within the next five years. He also added that he was now blind due to his diabetes. I hung up very happy. I called my dad. I told him of my conversation and mentioned how Tato wanted to meet in the next five years, and that I thought it was an odd request. My father, a Type 1 diabetic, suspected the reason was because the average life span of a diabetic on dialysis was five years. I quickly moved to bring Tato to campus that same semester.

In March 2007, Tato came to UTPA. If reading Tato had an impact on me, meeting him, watching him perform, and teaching with him completely changed me as person. He came to do a performance, lead a writing workshop, and participate in a poet-critic reading of my essay, all in one day, and was paid next to nothing. The following day, Tato, just hours after receiving dialysis, traveled unaccompanied to the Río Grande Valley. He also visited México for the first time and was astounded at the possibility of having one foot in each country at the same time as he stood on the bridge. For him it was the physical embodiment of his life's work. His visit impacted many people and led to numerous collaborations over the next few years. It led to the creation of Cosecha Voices. Cosecha Voices, the brainchild of Tato, discussed in one of the essays, is a collaborative project designed so that migrant farmworker students may document their experiences in print, oral and digital formats. Tato would spend three semesters at UTPA working with Cosecha Voices and the MFA program in English. At UTPA, like so many other places, Tato bestowed upon us many gifts of poetry, teaching, mentoring, drama, and friendship.

The summer after Tato's first visit, I contacted William Luis about publishing a collection of essays on Tato's work. He agreed, and William and I began to work together to bring the book to fruition. Originally, we were going to collect essays previously published on Tato. However, we realized the need for more new scholarship on Tato's work. Understanding the importance of Tato's life's work and the need for more scholarly books that focused on a single Latino/a author, we commissioned from both seasoned and up-and-coming scholars previously unpublished essays on Tato's writings. The response from the literary community was tremendous. Collecting these essays has been an honor, as each and every one of the contributors is committed to expanding the body of knowledge on Tato, his literature, and his *compromiso* to *la(s) comunidad(es)*. Tato has made an impact on each and every one who has contributed to this anthology and the too numerous to count people that read his work, saw one of his plays, worked with him or saw him perform. Unfortunately, Tato was right about meeting me within five years. Almost exactly five years after contacting me, Tato's health deteriorated quickly. He was hospitalized in late January 2013. He would remain hospitalized until his death November 1, 2013.

With this book we not only acknowledge Tato's importance as both an AmeRícan and American poet, but we also say *gracias*. *Gracias*, Tato, for giving voice to the many and varied experiences of so many Nuyoricans, Ricans, puertorriqueña/os, Latina/os, Americans (hyphenated or not) and all of humanity. *Hermano, este libro es para ti. Gracias por tu humanidad, amistad y generosidad.* So it is, Tato to matao. *Que en paz descanse.*

INTRODUCTION

THE BIRTH AND REBIRTHS OF TATO LAVIERA

WILLIAM LUIS

Para Ruth, hermana, madre y guía espiritual

Tato Laviera is one of the most important New York poets in recent memory. His work is a testament to his national and international reputation. In a career that spans more than thirty years, Laviera has published five major books of poetry: *La Carreta Made a U-Turn* (1979); *Enclave* (1981), Winner of American Book Award from the Before Columbus Foundation; *AmeRícan* (1985), whose title poem is the most published and anthologized ever written by a Puerto Rican poet in the United States; *Mainstream Ethics* (1989); and *Mixturao* (2008a). Laviera has written and produced twelve plays and published four: *The Spark* (2006b), *'77 PR Chicago Riot* (2007), *Bandera a Bandera* (2008b), and an act of *The King of Cans* (2012). He has also written a draft of a novel, *El Barrio*. Selections of his poems, plays, and novel have appeared in the *Afro-Hispanic Review*.

Laviera's literary career has not been a smooth and progressive transition from one publication to the other. Though every publication has been an overwhelming success, each stage has also been fraught with difficult moments. For some time now, Laviera had been legally blind; he suffered from diabetes and undergoes dialysis. Instead of accepting defeat, each fall had given him the necessary strength to overcome the challenges before him, as he rose to a higher and even stronger personal and literary plane.

Laviera is the prophet of his people, and his poetic destiny was already outlined in his classic *La Carreta Made a U-Turn*. In this first collection, Laviera rewrites René Marqués's canonical play, *La carreta* (1953), about the different stages of the Puerto Rican migration, first from the countryside to San Juan, then from San Juan to New York City, and after a series of tragic events in the metropolis, from New York back to Puerto Rico (Marqués 1991). Laviera's *La Carreta Made a U-Turn* suggests that the destiny of Puerto Ricans living in the United States is based not on a return to the paradisiacal island many have forgotten the reasons for leaving, but on remaining in the harsh and punitive New York City environment. This is a position other writers continue to underscore in their poems, from Miguel Piñero's "A Lower East Side Poem" to Mariposa's "Boricua Butterfly."

La Carreta Made a U-Turn contains the key to understanding all of Laviera's works, and it includes the seeds of what I call the Laviera Aesthetics. The opening poem "para ti, mundo bravo" serves as an introduction to Laviera's poetic world. In the first stanza the speaker shouts out to the world, announcing the presence of his poetic voice and desire to connect with his community, to speak to them about events that have become familiar to all of them. Here, the poetic voice defines his task as an observer, an ethnographer, or a historian documenting all things that take place within the immediate environment. The stanza reads as follows:

> in the final analysis
> i am nothing but a historian
> who took your actions
> and jotted them on paper (1979: 13)

The first four lines of this first collection describe the job of the poet, what he sees and writes and can be considered as Laviera's "ars poetica." However, it is interesting to note that the beginning of the poem starts with the ending, the "final analysis," a reference to a final outcome or when truth is known. But here I want to focus on the word "final" and finality as the outcome of a process, even though in the Laviera Aesthetics it is placed at the beginning. Therefore, the final also reverts back to its binary opposite, the beginning, and the poem highlights the concepts of beginnings and endings, for a beginning is a start of a process and the ending is the conclusion of that initial activity. But endings are also beginnings insofar as we, writers and critics alike, give meaning to the past not as an initial event that provided a first and limited impression of what will unfold before us, but as a conclusion of a process that gains insight from a contemporary and more recent perspective, which is later imposed on and attributed to that past. Beginnings and endings are inextricably intertwined. The concept of "in the final analysis" will always be present in the Laviera Aesthetics, as the poet moves to explain from a privileged or informed position what he observes about the past.

In this first poem, "para ti, mundo bravo," Laviera presents his métier as an observer, capturing what he sees emerging from his community: the suffering of his people, who at times wonder aimlessly without direction, struggling to survive in an hostile and unwelcoming environment. However, this mishap is what gives life to the poet and the poetic voice, and provides him with strength, purpose, and inspiration. Knowledge of the arduous daily life of Puerto Ricans and other Latinos/as surviving in an unfriendly and unfamiliar environment is enough to madden any sensible human being. Nevertheless, I want to concentrate on the candid and disarming tone of these early poems. If a hostile encounter were to take place between the poetic voice and his adversary, whoever that persona may be, the speaker would not meet violence with violence but with a book by Dostoevsky. This response is not to show that he is more knowledgeable or educated than his opponent, but to convey that books and the act of reading represent knowledge and growth, which "in the final analysis," a line that is repeated three times, including the start and end of the poem, is what makes the initial two antagonists richer, change the dynamics, and even produce a feeling of compassion between them.

The second poem, "even then he knew," attributes to the subject of the poem, Papote, a wisdom the poetic voice does not know he possesses. While "papote sat on the stoop"—a line that is repeated four times—other types of activities and conditions in the neighborhood are taking place, some of which have become a fixture of ghetto life: the social club playing music, a burned car, garbage in the streets, among others. However, the time and place are clear: It is one hot summer Sunday, not only because there is a reference to "Sunday garbage," but also because of the line that refers to the Pentecostal Church choir. Papote is also a fixture in his community, and the speaker tells the reader that Papote is uneducated, misinformed, and malnourished, and seems to be somewhat paralyzed; but he makes a decision, which is not to go anywhere. The unspecified "he" in the title of the poem refers to Papote who knew enough to be decisive, but also to the poetic voice who commands a certain insight to write a poem. I will say more about Papote later.

The use of language will always be a dominant characteristic of the Laviera Aesthetics. His "my graduation speech" already foretells his concerns about expressing himself in different languages: Spanish, English, and Spanglish. For he is a product of the three:

i think in spanish
i write in english
....
english or spanish
spanish or english

spanglish
now, dig this:

hablo lo ingles matao
hablo lo español matao
no sé leer ninguno bien
so it is, spanglish to matao
what i digo
¡ay, virgin, yo no sé hablar! (1979: 17)

Laviera's closing line of desperation, that he does not know how to speak, is unfounded, since he expresses himself eloquently in the poem. He communicates the frustration many of us feel when searching for the proper word while speaking any language. But there are other recurring themes in this first collection that will be carried on to the other books. Laviera's poems about Spanish themes in English are written for a predominantly English-speaking population that tends to romanticize the island and island culture. Such is the case of "savoring, from piñones to loíza," about Puerto Rican food and music. The poems that are written in Spanish are directed to a Spanish-speaking population in the Barrio or New York, but also in Puerto Rico. With his Spanish poems, Laviera wants to be on the same playing field as island poets; especially those who are willing to address issues important to Puerto Rican culture. Since there are not many island poets ready to discuss such delicate matters, Laviera becomes one of a handful of Puerto Rican poets eager to highlight issues others prefer to ignore. He tackles the myth of racial harmony many Puerto Ricans, both home and abroad, continue to perpetuate. Race, for Laviera, represents fertile ground; he documents and deconstructs this aspect of Puerto Rican culture.

In "el moreno puertorriqueño (a three-way warning poem)" Laviera expresses a concern that he will revisit in subsequent poems, the topic of racism in Puerto Rico and Puerto Rican culture. In the above-mentioned poem, the poetic voice questions the central idea of racial equality. When watching television soap operas, the Black characters are White actors with makeovers, none of whom he can identify with, and they seem to be making fun of him. The speaker even wonders if he lives in the past and is still a slave. The poem is also a tribute to Luis Palés Matos, who in the 1920s pioneered the *Negrismo* movement, which focused on stylized African images and rhythms (Palés Matos 1995). Though it is not difficult to criticize Palés Matos superficial understanding of the contributions

Africans made to Caribbean culture, his peers ostracized him for tainting with Black images Puerto Rican literature and culture. But Laviera refers specifically to Palés Matos "ñam ñam," a poem about cannibalism and the oral fixation of Africans, stuck in a primitive or infantile stage. Laviera pays tribute to the master poet and also distances himself from him to claim: "ñam ñam yo no soy / de la masucamba," which he repeats twice at the end of the poem. Though "masucamba" can be interpreted in many different ways, it is also considered to be a dance. The speaker negates any association with it, and becomes independent from the master poet but also from certain aspects of Puerto Rican society and culture.

While Laviera is a Nuyorican poet, a termed coined by Miguel Algarín and Miguel Piñero (1975), he recognizes that Nuyoricans or New Yorkers regardless of race do not live in isolation, for the city is known to be the home of many racial and ethnic groups. Laviera's poetry is concerned about other members of his community, Afro-Latinos/as and African Americans in particular. The black is present in poems such as "canción para un parrandero," "felipe luciano i miss you in africa," and "the africa in pedro morejón," among others.

Laviera feels an affinity with Puerto Ricans of all races, both on the island and mainland; however, he is also aware that Blacks occupy the lowest part of the social and racial strata of US society. In fact, the racial tension has brought Afro-Latinas/os to seek refuge in the African American community; moreover, African Americans have welcomed them. Arturo Alfonso Schomburg, Felipe Luciano, and Laviera himself are testaments to the cooperation between Afro-Puerto Ricans and African Americans. This perception is implicit in Laviera's recognition that race matters in the United States, allowing him to revisit similar concerns affecting Afro-Puerto Ricans back on the island. Later, Laviera tackles the problem of racism on the island with other poems like "Tesis de Negreza," based on Bobby Capo's well-known "Negro bembón." The poet reproduces the song, but he also offers a counter narrative, one that uncovers pride in his blackness. Laviera's communion with Blacks brings him closer to the African American community to which he also belongs.

Religion is an important component of the Laviera Aesthetics. In this first collection it appears with insistence in "excommunication gossip," and even tangentially in "orchard beach y la virgin del carmen." Religion is expressed as part of Puerto Rico's Catholic or Christian denominations. However, it is also an essential belief system Africans brought with them to the Americas during the period of slavery, and continues in the present with all followers, regardless of race. In "santa bárbara," who is syncretized with Changó in Regla de Ocha, the poetic voice attends a spiritual festivity, in which Blacks and Indians come back to life through spiritual possessions. The poetic voice, who is skeptical, is unwillingly possessed and becomes a believer. The poem highlights these important cultural and religious components of Puerto Rican and Latina/o life both at home and abroad, but it also marks the poetic voice and poet's spiritual initiation. For it is Laviera's spirituality that guides him through the maze of confusion, and he seeks clarity where others continue to find perplexity.

Laviera has the capability to move into a larger frame of reference that can encompass Spanish or Spanish-American writers and themes and their influence on his work. He illustrates this idea by writing a poem about the Nobel Laureate, Pablo Neruda, who was known for his political and social activism. Neruda had a profound understanding of the common man, which in his work takes center stage in "The Heights of Macchu Picchu" (Neruda 1990). In this epic poem, the poetic voice is immersed in the confusion of contemporary society, until he finds the physical structure of the Inca Empire. After marveling in its wonder, he focuses his attention on those who built it and been erased from history. Like the Nobel Laureate, in "the last song of neruda," the Nuyorican poet is concerned about the suffering of man within his immediate environment. With his poem, Laviera provides an identity to those who have become beggars of the Bowery and sleep in "warehouses":

> inside this assembly i shall declare
> that my poetry bleeded from prostatic
> cancer, and in exposing society's cancer
> i found the illumination of my thoughts,
> pero aun, the fallen are the purest of all (1979: 30)

In "the last song of neruda" Laviera shows his concern for those common people who have become marginal and dispensable in society. However, as in the case of Neruda, they have served as a source of inspiration for his poems.

Neruda also wrote love and sensuous poems, many of them dedicated to his wife Matilde.[1] "a sensitive bolero in transformation" is a sexual and sensual poem that focuses on the *senos* or breasts in a manner that recalls the hands that caresses the body in Neruda's "La infinita" ("The Infinite One"), which will take a lifetime to explore. Neruda's obsession with the breasts is also incorporated into Laviera's poem:

seno suave
                breasts caliente
                creates all the
                moods   all the
                feelings of my colors

seno   my third and fourth eyes

my longing is the   meñique
                anular
                del corazón
                índice
                pulgar
                fingers of a hand
                treat my breasts as sculptures
                choreographing the mental and
                spiritual ballet that would
                make his lips and then his
                body define me in my barest
                nudity to make the contact
                of harvesting flowless energy
                in space (1979: 39)

Like the master poet, Laviera is also obsessed with the breasts, a word he repeats ten times in Spanish (*seno*) and seven times in English.

As I have demonstrated above, an important component of the Laviera Aesthetics is to write love poems. However, there is another fundamental element that is present in "a sensitive bolero in transformation"; the poem proposes a different perspective, that of the woman, for it poeticizes the woman's body from the woman's point of view. As early as "a message to our unwed women", Laviera experiments with different voices; in this other poem a "you" of a judgmental community is transformed into a poetic "I," who has been given a voice to speak of her true feelings:

i am now a true woman
my child will not be called
illegitimate
this act was done with love
with passion
my feelings cannot be planned

i will not let their innocence
affect me
i will have him, coño,
because I want him
because I feel his breast
of life consoling
my hurt, sharing my grief,
if anybody does
not accept it
que se vayan pal ... me entienden
        pal ... lo oyen
        pal ... me escuchan. (1979: 37)

Here, Laviera uncovers the poetic "I" of a strong woman, who defies the societal norm and speaks about social and cultural concerns. She challenges the cultural norm by making her position public.

Some years later Sandra María Esteves crafted her much publicized "My Name is María Christina," about a Puerto Rican woman who represents the mother of a new wave of warriors.[2] But in "a message to our unwed women" Laviera already spoke about a poetic persona who gives birth to La Raza, that is, to a new cultural way of being.

Laviera provides a voice to women but also to inanimate objects. This idea to have others speak coincides with the task entrusted to testimonial literature, to give voice to those who have been denied a voice. In the Laviera Aesthetics it includes the Statue of Liberty: "lady liberty," the first poem in *Mainstream Ethics*, refers to one of the great symbols of US society, and it is arguably one of the best poems about the statue that sits atop Liberty Island. Laviera's composition is in dialogue with Frédéric Bartholdi, the architect of the statue, but also Emma Lazaruz, whose poem the "New Colossus" is inscribed in the base of Lady Liberty. Laviera's poem was written to commemorate the centenary celebration of the Statue of Liberty, an event that received much publicity throughout the country and in New York in particular. With this in mind, the first stanza captures the ambiance of the celebration, as tall ships dot the harbor's water, the television cameras focus on the event, and awac airplanes fly above. But the statue and its symbol have been eroded with time, and Lady Liberty even needs a transplant in order to survive, and bring her back to life. Indeed, Lady Liberty is alive and voices her discontent with the changing times that have denied liberty to all members of American society.

if you touch me, touch ALL of my people
who need attention and societal repair,
give the tired and the poor
the same attention, AMERICA,
touch us ALL with liberty,
touch us ALL with liberty. (1988: 9)

We should note that in the above stanza the word "touch" is repeated four times, the word "all" three times, the word "liberty" two times, and the word "America" one time. In its most basic form, America needs to touch many times or to touch all its people, as the next to the last stanza indicates:

so touch me,
and in touching me
touch all our people,
do not single me out,
touch all our people,
touch all our people,
all our people
   our people
      people (1988: 9–10)

The act of touching the breasts in "a sensitive bolero in transformation" is converted in "lady liberty" to touching her children or her people. Laviera provides a voice to the statue, and she worries about what her symbol means during the time of celebration. Laviera's concern for those who have been marginalized was already present in "the last song of neruda."

Music is another element present in the Laviera Aesthetics. Laviera's poems contain music, but they are also about music; music is sonorous, and music is also a cultural expression. Music is what immigrants and exiles carry with them when traveling abroad and setting roots in a different society and culture. It is the newcomer's connection to the past, and it establishes a link between the home and adopted country. "el sonero mayor" mixes the harsh life Ismael Rivera experienced with the music of his famous songs. In "the salsa of bethesda fountain," salsa is linked to Africa and Afro-Caribbean sounds, which for the speaker have been transformed into Puerto Rican *bomba* and *plena*, embodied in the African in all of us. The African presence is visible in "the africa in pedro morejón," as represented by the *guaguancó*, the *merengue*, the *guaracha*, and the mambo. Other poems that convey sounds and the music of instruments, in particular the conga, are "the new rumbón," "tumbao (for eddie conde)", and "summer congas (pregnancy and abortion)."

Music is part of the oral tradition, especially when referencing the Puerto Rican *declamadores*, for there is a poem entitled "declamación," about Jorge Brandon; and there is another one "la música jíbara," about *décimas* and music. As part of the mainland oral tradition, music is already audible with soapbox preachers, politicians, or hustlers, whose words are meant to entice or enchant the listener. The repetition of a refrain or a slogan is what the public remembers best. In poetry it is used as a vehicle to emphasis certain images or sounds, and Laviera does so by underscoring certain melodic words. This is clearly evident in the poem "tito madera smith," of *Enclave*.

Enclave continues to chronicle the life of the ghetto with poems such as "tito madera smith," a fast and smooth talking character, the quintessential hustler, who can transform himself in an instant to obtain his intended goal. The repetition of "he claims" (mentioned four times) and "do you know him" (repeated three times), culminates in the birth of his identity, which repeats the words "you can call him" ten times, emphasizing the musicality mentioned above:

> you can call him tito,
> or you can call him madera,
> or you can call him smitty,
> or you can call him mr. t.,
> or you can call him nuyorican,
> or you can call him black,
> or yo can call him latino,
> or you can call him mr. smith,
> his sharp eyes of awareness,
> greeting us in aristocratic harmony:
> "you can call me many things, but
> you gotta call me something. (1981: 26)

Certainly, Tito Madera Smith is a mixture of Spanish and English surnames, for he is tito, madera, smitty, mr. t., nuyorican, black, latino, and mr. smith. But above all, he is the speaker himself, as his "I" makes it clear at the end. As we read the poem, there are telling signs of the speaker's identity: He claims to translate Palés Matos, knows where Langston Hughes lived, is familiar with Santería, is black and prieto and from Santurce, and is very interested in *las mamitas*.

While it is not my intention to trace all the themes that are present in *La Carreta Made a U-Turn*, and study how they are transposed on to subsequent collections that define the Laviera Aesthetics, I do want to underscore some salient characteristics that are further developed in *Enclave*, and in some of Laviera's more recent writings. For example, "declamación," of *La Carreta Made a U-Turn*, in which Jorge Brandon appears prominently, closes Laviera's first collection. However, it is not accidental that Laviera begins *Enclave* with "jorge brandon," and this poem and character links both collections. In this second poem about the iconic figure, Brandon is present. However, he is only mentioned in the title; the poem does not refer to Brandon, but to poetry itself. In the first stanza, the speaker makes the following proclamation: "poetry is an outcry, love, affection, / a sentiment, a feeling, an attitude, / a song" (1979: 11). "jorge brandon," if you wish, is another component of Laviera's *arts poetica*, a meditation on poetry, of how the speaker conceives of this form of expression, which for him is unambiguously instinctual, "it is internal gut expressing intimate / thoughts upon a moment's experience." The process engages all your senses: "the smell of sand," "the mountain," "the recital," "to taste bitter memory," and "to feel." Above all, it is composed of an "attitude," an "experience," and "the soul."

There are other characters that are part of the ghetto landscape, like "juana bochisme," who knows everyone's business; "unemployment line," which describes the humiliating experience of having to struggle to receive what is his; and "bolita folktale," which chronicles five and one half hours of a numbers game in which don Julio played his number's dream, only to find out that he played Brooklyn and not Manhattan where the number won; and "serious dude," about a man who falls in love with a woman but does not care if she desires him or is committed to being with someone else. But if she wants to be with the poetic voice, he expects her other man to step aside.

Laviera's poetic personas have become a fixture in the New York City tapestry: Tito Madera Smith, Jesús Papote, Lady Liberty, all speak to particular aspects of the metropolitan city that has become Laviera's home. But there is an emphasis in another aspect of the Laviera Aesthetics, in poems written mainly, but not exclusively, in Spanish. In *Enclave*, these include "juana bochisme," "abandoned building," "maría ciudad," "compañera," "alicia alonso," "suni paz," "vaya carnal," "juana boria," and "homenaje a don luis palés matos." The latter is a continuation of "el moreno puertorriqueño (a three-way warning poem)" of his first collection. In this other poem the speaker identifies Palés Matos as Black: "pracutú-piriquín-prucú-tembandeando / el secreto máximo: que luis palés matos / también era grifo africano guillao de castellano" (1981: 67). Repeated twice, the poem ends with the three lines mentioned above. Undeniably, Palés Matos was responsible for making Blacks visible to Puerto Ricans, and he did so by imitating what he conceived to be the influence of African music in Puerto Rico and other Caribbean islands, as he conveys in "Danza negra," which features the famous refrain: "Calabó y bamboo / bambú y calabó." From this perspective, Laviera underscores the topic of race in Puerto Rico. For him, Palés Matos was not White, but rather he was a Black who passed for White, a well-kept secret Laviera reveals in his poem.

II

Enclave is remarkable because it confirms Laviera's reputation as a first-rate poet, and marks the direction his poetry will take. His second book also features one of the most significant poems in Laviera's work, one that ranks among the best poems written by any poet regardless of origin, ethnicity, or race. "jesus papote" is a composite of different early characters and contains important elements of the Laviera Aesthetics we have come to know. Jesús Papote, and in particular the nickname Papote, can be traced to the second poem, "even then he knew," found in *La Carreta Made a U-Turn*, which introduces Papote to the reader. Papote, as outlined above, becomes another entity of the ghetto environment. He suffers from malnourishment and lacks a formal education, and while there is movement around him, "he decides to go no where." However, Papote also points to another character, "tito madera smith," who is the antithesis of Papote; or with time Papote can be transformed into a Tito Madera Smith. Contrary to Papote, Tito Madera Smith is poetry in motion; his mouth is faster than his feet. But, as is to be expected, in the end characters like Papote and Tito Madera Smith do not fare well and have a limited future. We do know that in the decades of the sixties and seventies, Puerto Rican and Latino/a young men and women were victims of drug addiction and crime that plagued the ghetto, which claimed the lives and livelihood of many members of the Latino community.

Laviera's "jesús papote" responds to characters like Papote and Madera Smith insofar as their lives must come to an end in order to start anew and be reborn, in the words of Sandra María Esteves, into to a new race of warriors. While it is not my intention to recapitulate what I have written elsewhere about this remarkable poem (Luis 1997), I do want to focus on a few ideas that speak to the topic at hand. Those familiar with the poem know that Jesús Papote is a fetus with Christ-like qualities, as his given name suggests. In fact, he is the reincarnation of Christ, in the most humble of places, the Latino ghetto. However, in this second coming, the image of the Christ figure has been inverted or more correctly; it has been placed in a contemporary context, where Christ continues to be an outcast. In the original Biblical version, the Virgin Mary gave birth to a child that was not the son of Joseph, mother and husband were refused shelter, and the mother gave birth in a manger. In Laviera's version of the Christ story, Jesús Papote's mother is indeed an outcast: she is a prostitute with a strong drug addiction, does not know the father of her child, lives in an inhospitable environment, and the cold winter weather is foreign to the mild island climate she had come to know earlier. The opening stanza sets the background for the epic:

> ... brethren woman strung out deep
> cornered jungle streets eyes closed body
> crouched face tucked pregnant belly, sali-
> vating umbilical cord peddling multi-
> cut heroine sub-ghetto fortress chanting
> early winder 25 degree cold-frío shivering
> lacked attention lacked warmth born-to-be
> embryo asphyxiated 25 dollars powers pene-
> trating vein venas veins venas pouring
> rivers pouring up mountains muscles brain's
> tributaries. (1981: 12)

Jesús Papote is more than an individual; he is the embodiment of generations of Puerto Ricans and Latinos of mixed racial and cultural, backgrounds born, raised, and residing in New York City. In the first stanza, the birth is accentuated by "he was born," which is repeated eight times (not all of the phrases are reproduced in the following stanza):

> ....
> he was born son grand son great grand son
> he was born generations america puerto rico
> he was born europe africa 7 generations before
> he was born latest legacy family tree inheritor
> he was born he was born 20the century
> urban story greatest told abandonment
> concrete land new york city story of stories (1981: 13)

What follows is Jesús Papote's nine-month gestation journey, in which the fetus attempts to speak, guide, and give strength and inspiration to his mother. In this process he struggles to survive and keep his mother alive.

While the poem is not a treatise on when life begins, the poetic voice's "I" is born at the moment of conception:

> My name is jesús papote i live nine months gut soul
> i was addicted i was beaten i was kicked i was punched
> i slept in empty cellars broken stairways i was infect-
> ted i was injected spermed with many relations
> i ran from police jails i was high every day of life (1981: 14)

The poem outlines a nine-month expedition, recounting the months of gestation to birth. The refrain "My name is jesús papote" frames the stages of the mother's pregnancy, and the challenges associated with each month: "My name is jesús papote born holy saturday, easter / sunday march mother parading 3rd avenues' ...," "My name is jesús papote may month flowers she dis- / covered me making her green throwing up she wanted / abortion she took pill after pill ...," "My name is jesús papote june cold turkey center cold / turkey her system must contain itself...," "My name is jesús papote 4th of July celebration / plane ride across to puerto rico mountain house... / leo-mildness-august night tidal waves moving bells...," "My name is jesús papote september pregnant body new / york spells trouble once-again-racing-fast struggles...," "My name is jesús papote she october tried training / program cellar jobs she vowed not to use it again....," "My name is jesús papote november all souls day / grandma knocked on door oh no the prayers fell," "My name is jesús papote december christmas new / york city my inner cycle 9 months completed...." It is important to note that throughout the gestation period Papote's mother returns twice to Puerto Rico. First, she and the fetus are present on Easter Sunday; second, they travel in time for the 4th of July celebration. As I have indicated, the return trip to the island had already been outlined by Marqués's *La carreta*, which in Laviera's poem is accompanied by a vision of the idyllic island: "nights kissing early morning mango blossoms new sun / octapusing rays orange rainbows the ox-cart was your / solution your final triumph how beautiful you look" (1981: 17). As with the playwright's characters, in the poem the mother and fetus return to the island, and in the poem not once but twice. While every month has its own section, these two trips are special, for they are the only events that combine two months, in the first March and April, and in the second July and August, and they indicate an extended stay. The first trip is characterized by embarrassment and discord, and these and other factors force the mother to return to New York and attend to her drug addiction. The second visit is more harmonious, and the fetus encourages the mother to stay in Puerto Rico: "mamita don't go back give birth in island nativeness / tropical greetings nurturing don't go back don't / go back" (1981:17). As we know from Laviera's first collection of poems, *La Carreta Made a U-Turn*, and regardless of how the fetus feels, Laviera's carreta has to make a u-turn, for the island no longer offers solutions to the Puerto Rican diaspora.

It would be too simple or simplistic for these Puerto Rican characters to return to "island nativeness," to bask in the sun and eat native foods, as highlighted in Judith Ortiz Cofer's "Idea of Islands."[3] This returned journey is not realistic and responds more to a romantic and idealized vision of Puerto Rico, which was never part of the immigrants' reality before they left the island. René Marqués's *Cuentos puertorriqueños de hoy* (1981) narrates the harsh and even deadly conditions Puerto Ricans endured after Operation Bootstrap was put into effect. The attempt to industrialize the island forced many of them to abandon what could be appropriately considered an inferno. Regardless, there is no redemption without experiencing a fall, and for this reason Puerto Ricans must make a physical and symbolic u-turn and remain in New York City's inhospitable environment. The poetic voice must fall in order to be resurrected.

The resurrection is not just a physical act or a mere tragedy, but in Laviera's poem it takes place as part of the writing process, as suggested by my study of the line "in the final analysis" of "para ti, mundo bravo." Though we know that the act of writing follows the conversion, in which the writer looks back to see the origin of the journey and considers the present and future to understand where he is and where he will be going, Laviera's writing exhibits its own transformation and change. In the fourth stanza Jesús Papote's "I" emerges, and the speaker is aware that his birth is on Christmas day, thus allowing the reader to draw the analogy between Jesús Papote and Jesus Christ. However, at this stage in the poem he defines himself differently from the way he does after he undergoes the process of describing (through Laviera's writing) the nine-month journey. At the outset of the poem, Jesús Papote identifies himself as follows:

> my name is jesús papote i am born in oppression
> my death a deeper martyrdom unknown to pain to
> solitude to soledad to soledad's seven skins to
> darkness to darkness' mystery to mystery's spirit. (1981: 14)

The lines mentioned above indicate that he is no longer in the womb and is "born in oppression." They refer to a martyrdom associated with words like pain, solitude, and darkness. But later, there is a change. After describing the nine-month pregnancy period, at the moment of the birthing act, the poetic voice arrives at a different understanding of his life. The process unfolds subsequent to recounting the cycle of death and resurrection associated with the months of November and December. In November the grandmother's prayers are not answered, and the mother continues with her addiction. It is in November that death is present, as the phrase "death la muerte" is repeated ten times, and "death" twelve times. However, in December the poem shifts, from death to life, promising hope as expressed in the phrase "save him jesus," repeated four times. What follows in the next stanza, number seventeen, is Papote's actual participation in his own birth process, as he instructs his mother on what to do, he has become a midwife, in the process of producing his own life:

> Mami Mami push push i'm coming out celestial barkings
> Mami Mami push i don't want to die she slept
> Mami Mami push i want to live she slept cough
> Mami Mami i have the ability to love cough cough
> Mami Mami fight with me again she slept he slept
> Mami Mami i'm coming out out out push push push push
> Mami Mami can you feel me can you hear me push push
> push push empuja empuja cough cough push push push
> empuja empuja Mami cough cough push push i am fighting
> I am fighting push push nature nature i have a will
> to live to denounce you nature i am fighting by myself
> your sweeping breasts your widowing backbone
> yearnings your howling cemetery steps your
> death-cold inhuman palms Mami Mami wake up
> this is my birthday little mornings king
> david sang cough cough cough push push
> why do I have to eulogize myself
> nobody is listening i am invisible
> why tell me why do i have to be
> the one the one to acclaim that: (1981: 19)

If the stanza outlining the month of November is noteworthy because it insists on death, the one that follows, for the month of December, is full of life, conveyed by the word "push," repeated twenty-five times in Spanish and English. This Jesús Papote fights for his and his mother's life. He is a survivor and becomes a warrior before he is born; he has a will to fight and live in order to emerge from the womb and lead a productive life. The fight does not start at the moment of birth, but at the moment of conception and certainly while developing in the womb. However, as I mentioned above, the poem is born after the moment of birth, but the Jesús Papote who speaks at the end of the poem is different from the Jesús Papote who identifies himself as "born in oppression," and who experiences a death "unknown to pain," "to solitude to soledad to soledad's seven skins to / darkness to darkness' mystery to mystery's spirits" (1981: 14). This dark vision in which solitude is repeated three times, and darkness and mystery two times, corresponds to the events associated with the month of November more than with the jubilant birth that takes place in the month of December. If the poem were to be reorganized chronologically, Papote's negative vision of his existence would clash with his desire to live before and after the birthing process.

The Jesús Papote, the one who emerges after recounting the gestation period, is not surrounded by solitude or darkness but by a community of worshipers and caring people, expressed by the plural pronoun, in both Spanish and English, "We, nosotros," repeated sixteen times. The "We, nosotros" is not limited to the Hispanic or Latina/o communities but also comprises a cross-section of ethnic, racial, and national groups, which include "multi-ethnic black-brown-red in affirmations," "ghetto brothers black americans, indians / italians, irish, jewish, polish, ukranians / russians, german food and music lovers" (1981: 20), and "mathematicians," among others. These are the same multiethnic and racial communities Laviera pays "Ethnic Tributes" to in his third collection, *AmeRícan*.

Unlike the Jesús Papote who identifies himself with destruction at the outset of the poem, this other one is an integral part of the "We, nosotros" community of fellowship, who asks "permission," a word repeated six times, to articulate a noun in the language of origin, Spanish, which represents a Puerto Rican concept with universal meaning. The word in question negates accusation and expresses family, pride, reverence, and love, and brings blessing upon him and others, and this takes place when the poetic voice articulates the word *Bendición*.

With the pronunciation of *Bendición*, the only word written in upper case letters in the poem, Papote's mother awakens and comes to life; she experiences a rebirth and is transformed into a woman of action, ready to take charge of her own destiny. She breaks the umbilical cord, rises (physically and spiritually), and participates in the celebration of the (re)birth and arrival of her messiah Jesús (Jesus). It is befitting that the mother, who represents origin and traditions, displays Jesús Papote to the people, in a final paragraph full of images found in the liturgy: "jesús papote human legacy god the son at the right / hand holy spirit candles flowers incense wine water." It is indeed a time for celebration because Jesus has returned; and in so doing, he has been embodied as an outcast, an outcast of the outcast, a double outcast, that is, a Puerto Rican, an outcast of Puerto Ricans in the island and an outcast of mainstream citizens in the United States. In "jesús papote" birth and rebirth take place separately and simultaneously. The birth of Jesús Papote is initiated at the time of conception and his rebirth happens when he is born. However, Jesús Papote is a rebirth of Jesus, and this is also accompanied by the rebirth of the mother; from this perspective both are born of the same body, and the mother by giving birth also experiences a rebirth.

III

There is a relationship between the author and his work, between autobiography and (self) writing, as I have suggested at the outset of this introduction and highlighted in the poem "tito madera smith." The connection was made in an early interview I conducted with Laviera. When describing his childhood in Santurce, Puerto Rico, Laviera spoke about the musical era of Rafael Cortijo and Ismael Rivera, whose rhythms in one form or another find their way into Laviera's poems. This is particularly the case with "Negro Bembón" of *Mixturao*, in which the poet celebrates Cortijo and Ismael, but also challenges the meaning of the song they help to popularize.

In the interview Laviera makes a more direct connection between art and life when referring to the first poem that gave birth to his poetic talents, "even then he knew," which—as mentioned above—appears as the second poem of *La Carreta Made a U-Turn*. Laviera recalls the moment of the poem's inception:

> The first poems I wrote was "even then he knew," of *La Carreta Made a U-Turn*. An incredible thing happened. I was sick and there was a building they were fixing across the street from where I was living, on 7th Street. I was very ill that day. And this kid, I called him Papote, was sitting on the steps of the building at 1 o'clock when I came out; he was sitting there at 3 o'clock when I came out again. I looked out the window at 5 o'clock and he was there; *él estaba descalzo*. I looked at him and then *me cogió pena*. I said: "*Mira, espera allí.*" I went to get him

a sandwich and a soda. I came down the stairs and when I went out he was gone. He was there for five hours. So I went down and sat on the stairs and wrote my poem about that kid.... It was right there that "papote sat on the stoops ... and he decided to go no where." I showed my friend the poem and three hours later, *por el amor de Dios*, this guy, Sánchez was his name, came back and showed me a painting. It was destiny. I didn't want to meet him again because of my good luck. At 11:00 p.m. I had a painting and a poem about that kid. That was the calling. It was a concrete calling and there it emerged. This happened in July, 1966. (Luis 1992: 1024)

So, Laviera's epiphany that led to his initiation or birth into poetry came from a concrete situation, that of a young man he met while the future poet was recovering from an illness. He named his newfound friend "Papote," and when he went to join Papote, it was a coming together or the birth of Jesús (Laviera) and Papote.

There is another answer contained in the interview that is pertinent to this introduction to Laviera's work and the Laviera Aesthetics I share with the reader. This one also has to do with another moment of inception or beginning, when Laviera first arrived in New York in 1960. He recounts the experience in the following manner:

Yes, my coming to the United States was precipitated by my sister being eight months pregnant and my father not knowing about it. My mother wanted my sister to give birth in New York City, away from my father's anger. And when I left my house, I didn't know I was coming to the United States. I was on the plane and I had vivid images, which I included in the poem called "negrito" in *AmeRícan*. Once on the plane, I thought the US was all white, and I was scared I'd be the only Black person going there. I was totally terrified when the plane was landing. And in my poem called "negrito," I say:

> el negrito
> vino a nueva york
> vio milagros
> en sus ojos
> su tía le pidió
> un abrazo y le dijo,
> "no te juntes con
> los prietos, negrito." (1985: 41)

My uncle used to work in the airport, so my family came to meet me by the plane. When I came down from the plane, I saw these Black people, and I felt good. But my *tía política* grabbed my hand and said: "No te juntes con los prietos, negrito." It was the first thing that I was told, and here I'm thinking that there weren't going to be any Black people around. I responded: "Pero Titi." and she said: "No te juntes con los moyetos, negrito." "Pero Titi." "Si los cocolos te molestan, corre y si te agarran, baila." My family proceeded to take me to the Williamsburg area, which is all Black, and so my whole image changed; I didn't know what was going on. First I thought everyone was all white and then my *tía me dice eso* and proceeded to take me to an all Black area. I was totally shocked. Plus, I didn't know I was coming here and after six years my life was totally transformed. (Luis 1992: 1023–4)

Laviera's arrival in the United States marks a double birth (or rebirth), one associated with his life in the new country, and the other one with the beginning of his consciousness about race matters. Let us not forget that Laviera tells that this is a process that begins with his arrival and concludes six years later with his total transformation, but it is recounted from the present time of the interview.

Anyone familiar with Laviera's poetry understands the importance of race, whether it is present in the home or adopted country, whether it refers to Afro-Latinas/os, African Americans, Africans on the continent of Africa, or the strong presence of African religion and culture in Hispanic and Latino/a societies. Laviera's response shows that before he arrived in the United States, the future poet was aware of race and racial conditions in his home country, where he knew or was told he was Black, and abroad where he believed that there were no or few Blacks in the United States. Race and race matters will always be a touchstone for the Laviera Aesthetics. But for the moment I am interested in uncovering the initial moment of poetic creativity in Laviera's work, his birth as a writer, if you wish, but also as a way of understanding his rebirths. For if we follow closely "jesús papote," birth and rebirth can represent two different stages in a person's life, and they can also take place in the same time and space.

IV

In February 2010, I received a distressing message left on my home answering machine. A familiar voice, in a painful and subdued tone, pleaded for help. I immediately answered the call to investigate the nature of the message. Tato, barely audible, informed me that he had been removed from his apartment and was homeless. It was not clear what had happened, nor was I able to decipher the sequence of events. In a subsequent conversation he directed me to a recently published article David Gonzalez wrote for the *New York Times* (2010), which provided clarity and coherence to what Tato attempted to communicate to me in a fragmented manner. While I was aware that Tato suffered from diabetes, blindness, and underwent dialysis, Gonzalez explained that in December Tato was rushed to the emergency room, where he was diagnosed with water in the brain and required emergency surgery to install a shunt to drain the fluid. This, however, left him with partial paralysis in his left leg. Laviera had checked into a nursing home for physical therapy, but abandoned it for fear of becoming another empty body. Looking for help, he was able to secure the assistance of Lorraine Montenegro, the director of United Bronx Parents, who came to his rescue.

In conversations with Stephanie Alvarez, we began to mobilize the academic community to raise money and assist Tato find affordable and respectable housing. Emails began to circulate with electrifying speed, and money started to surface from foundations and individuals. Everyone felt a sense of urgency, and this was a worthy task that could not fail. More often than not we recognize the person after he expires, and it became imperative that we change this awful custom of "celebrating" our artists after they are gone. We should learn to appreciate the writer who is still with us. With the help of his community, Tato was able to recover.

On April 27, New York University student groups, in collaboration with community organizations, hosted a spectacular and filled-to-capacity tribute to Tato Laviera. Miguel Algarín opened the event, and Juan Flores emceed it. Notable Latino singers, artists, musicians, and poets contributed to the event. Nuyorican poets included Américo Casiano, Louis Reyes, Myrna Nieves, María Aponte, Sandra María Esteves, María Teresa Fernández (Mariposa), Nancy Mercado, José Ángel Figueroa, Jesús Papoleto Meléndez, Frank Pérez, Raúl Krios, Sery Colón and literary critics like Flores, Stephanie Alvarez, Edwin Meléndez, and yours truly. As a tribute to Tato, Alvarez, Flores, and I coauthored a parody of Laviera's "tito madera smith," which we retitled:

"Tato Madera Smith:"
he can sound like a viejita bochinchera in el barrio in one poem
and like a fetus in the womb begging for his mother to stay in puerto rico
in
another
do you know him?

> he can rap to a fly mamacita out of one side of his mouth
> and drink una tasita de café Bustelo out of the other
> do you know him?
>
> he can swim with alligators in the río bravo y grande by day
> and be maestro guru at the edimburgo poets café by night
> do you know him?
>
> he was homeless seeking shelter in the Bronx one day,
> and is resurrected to be here with us today
> do you know him?
>
> well we sure do!
>
> you can call him tato
> you can call him laviera
> you can call him smitty
> you can call him nuyorican,
> you can call him black,
> you can call him latino,
> you can call him many things, but
> you gotta know he's always with us!
>
> we love you tato.
> (Alvarez, Flores and Luis 2010: 7–8)

Tato, who sat on stage next to a statue of Santa Bárbara (Changó) on one side and Algarín on the other, was clearly moved by the celebration. He even felt inspired and mustered the strength to cancel the intermission and recite one of his own poems. He chose to perform, in his typical Nuyorican style, "nideaquinideallá," from his most recent collection, *Mixturao*. The event was a resounding success, and we were given the rare opportunity to applaud the talents of one of the best living poets of our time.

The East Harlem community found Tato a studio apartment in Taino Towers. The information was widely disseminated by a second *New York Times* article that provided additional information about Tato's living conditions. Gonzalez's May 2010 article confirmed that Tato lived in a studio apartment in Taino Towers, located on East 122 Street, in East Harlem or El Barrio, and that his sister, Ruth Sánchez, and his daughter, Ella, helped decorate it. Though he is blind, Tato navigates his way through the city and the social service agencies to secure the necessary assistance he receives. Many have stepped forward to help Tato: Ibrahim González, of WBAI radio; Gloria Quinones, activist lawyer in East Harlem; and City Councilwoman Melissa Mark-Viverito; and María Cruz, manager of Taino Towers. These people are also mentioned in the article.

There is another event that I want to share with the reader. In March 2012 I was awarded a Guggenheim Fellowship, and when I called Tato to discuss with him whether I should attend the Guggenheim reception at the New York Foundation, he insisted that I go, and the very same day of the event, May 9, coincided with his birthday. So he asked me to secure tickets for him and his assistant, and he further insisted that during my visit I say with him in Taino Towers. So, as it happened, we attended the Guggenheim reception, went out to dinner, and returned to his apartment to celebrate his birthday with his sister Ruth, his nieces, and many of his key supporters. There was music and, as it was to be expected, Tato recited some of his poems.

That same weekend, on May 11, I attended Música Nueva 5: Big Band Poetry Jam & Beyond, featuring Arturo O'Farrill and the Afro-Latin Jazz Orchestra, with recitals by New York poets like Sandra María Esteves, Caridad "La Bruja" De La Luz, and Laviera with musical arrangements. Tato recited "guarachera del mundo," a poem about the life of Celia Cruz, which poeticized her early history, her marriage, her singing style, and her universal message. Adam Kromelow arranged Tato's music. This event confirmed that Tato was indeed back, for Tato had undergone another rebirth.

The visit was marked by Ruth's request that an eye be painted on the ceiling of Tato's apartment, directly above the living room chair where he sits. This was a vision transmitted to her by her father that she wanted to fulfill. So we enlisted the help of a friend, Elizabeth, to paint the eye, which she did in her own artistic rendition. The eye that watches over Tato is painted with a white cornea; there is a blue-green iris, and a black pupil that reflects the island of Puerto Rico, painted in white. The top of the brown eyelid droops slightly over the cornea and is more pronounced than the bottom part. The brown and green eyelashes of a right eye flow across an absent face on the ceiling and to the center wall in different lengths, the longest ones caressing ever so slightly the pictures and awards that cover the wall. The end of the eyelashes curve at tips into palm trees leaves. There is also water, in the form of tears emanating from the corner of the eye and eyelid, dripping in a downward motion. An insignia accompanying the eye that eternally watches over Tato reads as follows: "Like Water And Wind / Movement Beyond Restriction," a phrase that captures the essence of Tato Laviera and his poetry. Both Tato and Ruth were touched by this rendition.

V

After writing this introduction to the anthology, a series of critical events have taken place in Tato's life that continue to speak to the title of this essay, "The Life and Rebirths of Tato Laviera." A little more than two years after receiving that dreadful telephone call from Tato in December 2010, I received another one while traveling in China in late January 2013, not from Tato but from his sister Ruth. Though I had disabled the roaming feature of my cell phone, I was surprised to see a call come in from Tato's cell number. I answered the call and heard a high distressing and frantic voice that belonged to Ruth, who explained to me that Tato was in the hospital. Ruth was not perturbed when I mentioned that she was calling Chengdu, China. As we talked, she proceeded to describe a series of events that began while Tato was receiving a scheduled dialysis treatment a week or so before. During the procedure, a staff member of the hospital observed that Tato was running a high fever. A doctor wanted to keep him in the emergency clinic for observation, but Tato refused to stay. Instead, he returned to his apartment in Taino Towers. When Ruth stopped by the apartment to visit him, Tato appeared to be sleeping, and she decided not to disturb him. The following day, she returned to his room and found Tato in the same position; he appeared to be unresponsive. Unable to wake him up, she called the ambulance and rushed him to the hospital. The doctors were never able to identify Tato's ailment or disease.

I stayed in touch with Ruth as often as I could while traveling first in the northwestern province of Xingjian and later in the southeastern province of Guangdong. After my return to the States on February 18th, Ruth and I have been on the phone almost every day, and at times as many as ten or more times a day, to help chart Tato's ailment and recovery. We were fighting against time because Tato's condition was deteriorating rapidly. Shortly after my return, Tato experienced two cardiac arrests and was on life support, and his body would not tolerate a third one. We knew that the doctors were exploring all the options in the material world, but Ruth and I were not satisfied with their response, so we journeyed into the spiritual realm, searching for answers in ancient knowledge, whose origins can be traced to African religions. This should not come as a surprise to readers of Tato's poetry. Consider, for example, poems like "santa bárbara," about the spiritual possession of the poetic voice. Also, Tato's Afro-Latino rhythms can be traced to the rumba and to the religious music used to communicate with the Orishas, mainly but not exclusively of Yoruba traditions. On more than one occasion, in his interviews Tato has stated that he is spiritual and has spiritual protections. Moreover, during the Tribute at New York University's

Kimmel Center to Honor Tato Laviera's recovery, or what I have called his rebirth, the statue of Santa Bárbara was present on stage with Tato and Algarín and oversaw the homage that memorable Tuesday, April 27. Tato is devoutly Catholic, as I have painstakingly described in my reading of "jesús papote," but he is also familiar with African religions in the New World. Ruth and I needed to explore all the means available to keep Tato with us.

Ruth had initiated the process by contacting a spiritual leader of the Dominican Republic living in New Jersey, a practitioner of Las 21 Divisiones, who, in her own words, claimed to be "la bruja de Balaguer" (Joaquín Balaguer's witchdoctor). I knew that each of Cuba's leaders had his own personal *Babalao* or *Palero*, and that Castro himself had been initiated while traveling in Africa, but I was amused to learn that Balaguer himself had his own spiritual leader. Well, it was she who placed Ruth in contact with practitioners of Haitian Vodun back in the country of origin. These and other events continued to confirm that New York (and the surrounding areas) were indeed Caribbean spaces.

The attempt to bring Tato back did not stop there, for Ruth was ready to do the impossible to save her brother's life. In fact, Ruth, as the older sister, considers Tato to be more than a brother, but a son, since she also helped to raise him. We also contacted a well-known *Palero* in Miami, and it was he who first revealed to us Tato's ailment. Tato was not suffering from his diabetic condition, but from something someone close to him did, someone who wanted to harm him. The reader can imagine the reason, which is material for and the subject of many television soap operas and telenovelas. The sickness was so great that the person called upon to cure him would have to stare Death in the face to reclaim Tato's body. This *Palero* was an intrepid, powerful, and confident man, but he would have to make the long journey by car, and the price for the many tasks to be performed appeared to be out of our immediate reach. However, he was willing to advise anyone else we contacted, but the person involved had to be a *Palero*, since more than anyone else, the *Palero* deals with things belonging to the underworld.

Ruth turned her sights closer to home and searched for someone in her immediate environment. As it so happens, unbeknownst to her, she found someone known to Tato, a Puerto Rican musician who also admired Tato's work. This young *Palero* took time from his busy schedule and his family to attend to Tato's health. His *Prenda* (which houses a deity) confirmed that Tato could be saved. However, in the process of cleansing Tato, he was forced to do the same to protect his family, and he unexpectedly became ill. Time continued to march forward at a rapid pace. While waiting for him to recover and contact her, Ruth was given the name of another

Palero, someone who was more experienced, and who had been ordained in Cuba. Like the *Palero* who lives in Miami, he prescribed a necessary Cambio de Vida (change of life), a unique ceremony that entails using a doll that represents the sick person and transferring the state of the patient to the doll. This and other rituals included the use of animals, which are employed to purify the person. Since the performance of the rituals, Tato's condition had been slowly improving. To be on the safe side, as soon as a close friend, a *Babalao*, was available, Ruth summoned his help; he was none other than Celia Cruz's spiritual advisor, for Ruth had been Celia's hairdresser. This formidable Cuban *Babalao*, who was also Celia's *Padrino*, traveled from Los Angeles to rescue Tato. He consulted Orula, the Orisha of divination, and performed the indicated ceremonies. The doctors were baffled by Tato's ailment and even more so by his cure. One even said to Ruth, "I don't know what you are doing, and don't want to know, but keep doing it." With the help of this and the other spiritual advisors, Tato's life was prolonged. We believed that he would be saved and return to a normal life, though with some diminished abilities. Our expectations were partially realized. With the extended time, we saw small miracles along the way, for this other Jesús was a miracle worker.

In one early March conversation, Ruth said to me, "Prepare yourself to come to New York at a moment's notice;" it was apparent that Tato's health had worsened. During this period, we were even discussing a celebration, rather than a funeral, with music, speakers, and readings. We even considered burial locations in the Bronx, where Celia Cruz and all the great musicians were resting, and a more preferable location in Manhattan, overlooking the Hudson River. However, with the execution of the initial rituals at the hands of the young *Palero*, Tato became stable, and I was able to plan my trip with a greater margin of time.

I traveled to New York, from March 20 to 24, to be with Tato and help Ruth. Upon my arrival, I took a taxi from LaGuardia airport directly to Mt. Sinai Hospital. Ruth and I met at the entrance of the hospital, and we both rode the elevator to the ninth floor. I found Tato resting on his back, and daytime medical workers were present to attend to an infected trachea. It so happened that the they believed that the tracheotomy was being attended to properly, but Ruth, who became Tato's Guardian Angel, had noticed otherwise, and she called for a specialist to examine him. Ruth was right, there was an infection, and she asked me to digitally record the doctor cleaning the incision. Though doctors are experts in their field, Ruth positioned herself as a vocal member of the team that oversaw Tato's health, and she lobbied effectively for her brother's care. A physician and long-time friend of the family guided Ruth through the labyrinth of medical procedures and decisions. Ruth also organized a group of friends and family to keep Tato company throughout his stay in the hospital. Ruth did not want to leave her brother alone, mainly due to his blindness and inability to talk.

Most of my time in New York was spent visiting Tato and helping Ruth. I soon recognized that Tato had many friends from different walks of life, something that is visible in his poetry with the array of characters marching through his poems. I was familiar with a small group I had met in previous trips, but as soon as the word spread that Tato was ill, everyone wanted to visit him. I became very close to Tato's family and helpers, and especially to his daughter Ella and Juan Flores, who were always by his side. Tato is indeed a very special and spiritual person, and even in his weakened state, I learned from him. While spending time with him, I searched inward in ways I had not done before to communicate with Tato. One afternoon, while caressing his shoulder, I placed my forehead next to his, then after a few minutes I pulled back and whispered to him: "You don't have to thank me, we do it because we all love you." Tato suddenly opened his eyes and greeted me with a big smile unlike any other one I had seen before, as if to say: "You understood what I said to you." And I did! Needless to say, the experience reduced me to tears. As someone who was raised in the Lower East Side and does not cry, the days I spent with Tato and Ruth were marked by many tearful moments. Tato did communicate with us with the help of a mentalist or medium, who in a previous visit saw his aura outside of his body, but this time she found him more centered in himself. We learned that Tato was appreciative of our efforts and that we were doing what we were expected to do. He found himself at peace and did not want us to be sad, because our unhappiness also affected him. Tato also made it clear that Ruth was "la luz y la protagonista" (the light and the protagonist) of his care and salvation. Ruth had accepted the challenge as if her own salvation depended on it. She is a remarkable person, and she did everything in her power to save her brother. Like Tato, she also became my spiritual inspiration. The final evening before my departure, Juan, Ruth, Nancy, and I celebrated with champagne the life of Jesús Abraham Tato Laviera.

The more I thought about Tato's condition, the more I felt the need to incorporate this most recent stage of his life into my essay. I began to think about how "jesus papote" and the fast approaching Easter weekend and Resurrection Sunday would shed light on his work and physical condition. After all, "jesús papote" alludes to Easter and Christmas, and it pertains to the births of the poetic voice. There were two clear interpretations of Tato

Laviera as persona of his own poem of life. The first one follows closely the death and resurrection of Christ. Tato's illness would claim his tired body, and he would resurrect in the next world. Tato's "disease" began to consume his body. I do not mean to suggest that Tato is an embodiment of Christ, but his condition shows that many, if not all of us, in one way or another mirror Christ's life. This is particularly the case as we experience physical and spiritual deaths and resurrections. I would go further and state that there are some special people whose lives are much closer to that of Christ. After all, Tato Laviera's given name is Jesús Abraham Laviera and his poetic persona, "jesus papote," is a Christ-like figure. In this reading, I waited to see if Tato "resurrected" on, before, or after Easter Sunday, especially since in his poem Easter Saturday represented the time of conception. This is perfectly understandable to me since the poem attempts to parody a popular notion of the birth of Christ. If Christ was born on December 25th, which coincides with the secular Winter Solstice, then the time of conception was initiated sometime in late March, around Easter weekend.

The second interpretation also takes into account the concept of death and resurrection. Tato is in a comatose state, but from this condition he will be resurrected in *El reino de este mundo* (The Kingdom of This World), to use the title of Alejo Carpentier's novel about slaves who, with the help of their African religion, successfully rebelled against their masters in Saint Domingue. This resurrection is closer to the life of Lazarus, whom Christ revived from the dead. In the case of Tato, in some respects Tato had died physically: while receiving dialysis, he suffered two heart attacks and a diffibulator had to be employed to bring him back to life. Tato was in a coma-like state, even though he had minimal body movements and made facial expressions. So I waited to see what would happened as Easter came and went, and the farther we got from Easter, the more I was convinced, regardless of what anyone said, that Tato would remain with us and resurrect in this world. I believed that Tato's life already had been played out in "jesús papote," and the poem contained an outcome related to his present physical and spiritual condition. But I asked myself, what type of close reading should I do of the poem in light of the events that were transpiring? The doctors were far from being optimistic, and one even suggested that Ruth consider Hospice Care, which clearly meant the physical end to Tato's life. As everyone knows, no one has ever left a Hospice Center alive (so far as I know). Shortly after my visit, Tato had to be rushed to surgery because he had an infected gall bladder.

While I was tempted to read the poem through the eyes of the doctors and Tato's present condition, a close reading of the poem clearly indicated the physical birth or rebirth of the poetic voice. According to the poem, the fetus Jesús Papote is alive in the womb of a mother who is addicted to drugs; she represents a type of death, but her son is strong, he has a strong voice and his determination keeps her alive. Equally important, he is born or reborn on Christmas Day. And the poem outlines many births, including that of the mother, and the many births of Jesús Papote, and by extension Jesús Laviera. Therefore, believing in this interpretation of the poem, in the present we are witnessing a rebirth or a resurrection of our Jesús Tato Laviera. During this other birth or rebirth, Tato will emerge with a different voice, a more spiritual one, in the company of many of his friends, and we will observe the unfolding of a miracle. When he finally comes back, he will not ask for the blessing of his grandmother or mother, but from his sister Ruth, who has been transformed into Tato's mother, for she was instrumental in raising him in New York. Tato is already surrounded by his friends, as he has received substantial support from his community. We anxiously await his return.

Indeed, Tato Laviera's life imitates poetry or poetry sets the foundation for life to take its course, for both poetry and life are inextricably intertwined. Just like his characters who find a voice to speak about their own conditions, Tato experienced downfalls and resurrections, or as I indicate with the title of this introduction, birth or rebirths. Laviera is Jesús Papote, the poetic voice who encountered death at the outset of the poem and in the month of November, and the one who is reborn, when he receives the blessing of his community, and he in turn gives life and meaning to its existence. He does so through his writings and as a friend and a spiritual consultant. After his tragic downfall, the Latino/a community united to help Laviera, and he was reborn and during this other birth its members gathered around him and he asked for their *Bendición*.

For Laviera is a savior, and he has become a savior of his own people. Laviera is Jesús Laviera, Jesús Papote, and, like his character, a symbol of Jesucristo. I want to read "jesús papote" as an autobiographical poem, not one written about his past, but about the paths his life will take in the present and future. The poet talks about a birth that he describes as a fall, dominated by the elements associated more with death than birth, and a birth that is also a rebirth, a second coming, not so much the one proclaimed by orthodox religions, but by the individual, the one that speaks to the Jesús Papote we all carry within. The tragedy in Laviera's life has allowed me to revisit his masterpiece poem and see how the present helps to read the past and understand how that initial event has unfolded in the present, for past and present are intimately linked.

I will make one final observation about the use of pronouns in the poem. Allow me to recapitulate some previously mentioned ideas. Though Laviera refers to the speaker's "I" in its various manifestations, the poem also addresses him in the third person "he" and his mother as "she." However, these pronouns are later displaced by the plural "we, nosotros" rendered in Spanish and English, repeated sixteen times. Then, the speaker requests permission to utter the sacred word, for in Christian orthodoxy the "word was made flesh," and the poetic voice asks for his Bendición. It is after this benediction that we experience a transformation in the poem. The final stanza starts with the pronoun "she," which refers to Papote's mother, but this "she" is not the same "she" or mother prior to the blessing. The mother has also undergone her own death and salvation, or birth and rebirth. In this other incarnation, external forces, such as drugs and the violence of others, but also the violence she directed toward her own body, no longer control her. It is as if she had shed the shackles of slavery—the shackles that have chained her soul, her will, and spirit. After her transformation, she becomes an active and productive member of society. The poem ends with the following stanza:

> she woke up she saw she startled she warmed she
> protected she cried she broke the umbilical cord
> she got up to follow the bells the bells the bells
> cats dogs vagabonds all followed the tinkle tinkle
> of the bells christmas bells nativity flowing bells
> faith hope and charity bells 1980 jesus christ and
> jesús papote midnight ecstasy of bells church steps
> door opens organ stops up the aisle she exclaimed
> hand holy spirit candles flowers incense wine water
> and finally the people grandmother she offered jesús
> papote to the people miracle cherubims flautists
> dancing and singing rejoice rejoice eternity smiles
> oh night divine oh night divine she knelt she smiled
> jesús papote's presence in the dignity of our lives. (1981: 21)

What the poem offers is a rewriting of the fall and resurrection or the birth and rebirth of Christ. As we know, in this other version, Jesus is Jesús Papote, and the Israelites are now Puerto Ricans. But we also have a rewriting of the trinity, not only in terms of the Father, Son, and Holy Ghost, but also when referring to Mary, Joseph, and Jesus. In this other rewriting, Joseph, the male figure is missing and is substituted by the grandmother. That is, there are two women, now two powerful women at that, and the Christ child, which make up a new trinity. The mother has awakened, she has liberated herself from her past, and the grandmother, a strong maternal figure, has remained supportive and constant throughout the birthing process. The mother presents Papote to the public. It is significant that the mother presents the child to the public, because the pronoun "she" is repeated in this last stanza twelve times. The number twelve closes a cycle and suggests the beginning of a new one.

VI

Nota Bene: On Friday, November 1, 2013, precisely at 8:06 Central Time, Ruth, afflicted by the news she would share with me, called to tell me that Tato passed away. Tato died approximately nine months after he became ill and around 9:00 PM Eastern Time, and was buried on the 9th of November. Nine is important in Tato's life. He was born on May 9th, migrated to New York at the age of nine, and was hospitalized on the 9th floor of Mount Sinai Hospital. In passing, Tato has shed the shackles of the material world and has resurrected into the spiritual one.

On November 6 I flew to New York to help Ruth with the final touches of the church service and burial arrangements. In reality, everything and been decided, and I was there to support Ruth. The celebration of Tato's life, as he wanted it to be, was a joyous and festive occasion. The Friday service was held at St. Peter's Church on 54th Street and Lexington Avenue in Manhattan, known as the Jazz Church to many musicians who have departed, and Father Fabián (of Argentine descent) presided over the service, which included communion. The event, which lasted approximately four hours, featured the testimonies from family and friends, who spoke eloquently about their relationships with Tato. Musicians, who accompanied Tato's recitals, played two musical compositions from Tato's *King of Cans*, and many poet friends read Tato's poems. The highlight of the service took place towards the closing moments. Claudio Fortuna and his group unexpectedly appeared at the back of the church drumming and singing an African based rendition of the "Ave María." The sounds and voices captivated everyone as the members of the group made their way down the isle and surrounded Tato's casket. While Ruth had mentioned to me that she had hired a group to perform the "Ave María," I was expecting something more solemn, but I realized that she had something else in mind; she brought African music and culture into the Catholic world. It was simply spectacular. The event was reminiscent of carnival or of the Cuban "Día de Reyes" (Three Kings Day) festivity as Pierre Toussaint Frédéric Miahle captured in one of his drawings (ca. 1855). Everyone, including the priest, broke out into a dance step to the beat of the African drums, and we all participated in a communal *despedida* to Jesús Tato Laviera.

The burial procession began at the Ortiz Funeral Home on 103rd Avenue the following day. A few of us, who desired to do so, were able to see Tato one final time. He wore his iconic Panama hat; he looked tranquil and rested peacefully. Those in attendance made our way to Woodlawn Cemetery in the Bronx, known as the final resting ground to many Hispanics and Latinas/os from New York. Upon departure we drove by Tato's Taino Towers apartment, parked in front, and honk the horns in a final farewell. We also thanked the workers for taking care of Tato while he lived there.

As it should be, Tato is "buried" in a Communal Mausoleum, on the top level or shelf, the highest point possible and near a window. Ruth did not want him near the ground level but next to the tall ceiling, to facilitate his continual upward movement. Family and friends gathered before the casket was raised to give one final testimony before placing him in his final resting place. Just as it was evident in "jesús papote," in this other "birth" or "rebirth" Ruth presented Tato to his community. In life the community was by his side, at his bedside at Mt. Sinai Hospital, at the service in St. Peter's Church, and at the burial in Woodlawn Cemetery. Tato has always been with his community and his community has always been with him. Tato has every reason to rest in peace. I (we) now ask for his *Bendición*, "BEN...DI...CI...ON."

VII

Laviera is a recognized poet but he is also an established and much supported playwright, and he has authored twelve plays, some of which have been performed throughout the United States, in cities like Chicago, New York, Washington D.C., and Philadelphia. His plays and place of stage include:

- *Olú Clemente*, Shakespeare Festival, Delacorte Theatre, New York (1978).
- *Piñones*, Musical performed at Nuyorican Poet's Café, New Federal Theatre, New York, Chicago's 11th Street Theatre, Washington D.C., New Jersey, Philadelphia (1979).
- *La Chefa*, New Federal Theatre, Henry St. Settlement, New York (1981).
- *Becoming Garcia*, New Federal Theatre, New York (1983).
- *AmeRícan*, Teatro 4, El Museo del Barrio, New York (1983), tour of twenty colleges and community organizations in 1985.
- *Here We Come*, Teatro 4, Shakespeare Festival, Circle Repertory Theatre, New York (1986).
- *Base of Soul in Heaven's Café*, New Federal Theatre, Shakespeare Festival, Circle Repertory Theatre, New York (1987).

- *King of Cans*, Red Carpet Theatre, Broadway 96, New York (2001).
- *Mixturao*, St. Marks Church, Henry Street Settlement, New York (2004).
- *The Spark*, Batey Urbano, Chicago (2006).
- *'77 PR Chicago Riot*, Batey Urbano, Chicago (2007).
- *Bandera a Bandera*, Batey Urbano, Chicago (2008b).
- *King of Cans*, Red Carpet Theatre, New York (2012).

Of these plays only five have been published: *The Spark* (*Afro-Hispanic Review* 25.2, Fall 2006), the first of a four-part drama, commemorating the 40th anniversary of the Puerto Rican riots in Chicago, narrating the 1966 disturbance against the abuse by police and city officials; *'77 PR Chicago Riot* (*Afro-Hispanic Review* 26.2, Fall 2007), the second play of a four-part drama, highlighting the 1977 riot in Humboldt Park during the Puerto Rican Day Parade in Chicago; *Bandera a Bandera* (*Afro-Hispanic Review* 27.2, Fall 2008), the third play of a four-part drama about Puerto Ricans in the Chicago Humboldt Park community; and a selection of *King of Cans* (*Afro-Hispanic Review* 31.1, Spring 2012), highlighting the lives of six homeless characters who comprise a can-picking workforce. Since loosing his sight, Tato has dedicated himself to writing more plays. The dialogues and descriptions of his characters originate from the conversations he hears on a daily basis.

Laviera has also ventured into the genre of the novel and has drafted *El Barrio*, about the colorful yet tragic characters who live and survive in this major Puerto Rican enclave. His characters resemble those already known to his poems and plays and express themselves in similar ways. In so doing, Laviera provides an archaeology of this sector of New York City and its people. A selection of this novel, which comprises more than six hundred pages in draft form, was published (*Afro-Hispanic Review* 29.1, Spring 2012), and begins with the following description:

> Every single morning at sunrise in East Harlem, at 6 o'clock in the morning, appeared the dawning shadow of Jesusa wearing her ultimate, constant luto, dressed in black with a see-through mantilla veil covering her face. Jesusa, in her long black dress and black boots, would come down her building stoop with definite, slow steps, so slow as not to harm the early pigeons parading in front of garbage cans. She would walk slowly, in definite, desired steps along the back of Lexington Avenue towards 105th Street, as early morning passerby and onlookers would say her name—"¡Jesusa! Buenos días, Jesusa!" She never addressed her audience, she never addressed anyone. (Laviera 2010: 207)

We anxiously await the publication of what promises to be an important addition to a substantial body of works.

VIII

It is mainly with his plays that the activist Laviera also makes a stage appearance. This should not come as a surprise to those who know the person Laviera. Laviera has had ample community organizational experience, beginning with a Youth Organizer for the Little Star of Broome, in 1968, and continuing in other positions as Manhattan Coordinator, United Bronx Parents Summer Feeding Program, from 1971–1973; as Associate Director of Community Services, Neighborhood Service System, 1972–1974; and as Executive Director, from 1974-1980. Laviera has also held many community consultant positions. But it is in the latter position that Tato's life intersects with mine. Tato and I had talked about having attended Seward Park High School, but there was another connection. As I was going through my deceased mother's papers before Tato became ill, I found her work identification card. On the front side there is a vibrant picture of her, with a beautiful smile. The card identifies her as an employee of the Association of Community Service Centers, located on 152 Avenue D, New York, New York, 10009. Name: Petra Santos; Signature: contains her name in script. On the backside there are three lines, with the following categories: File No., S.S. No., and Executive Director, signed by Jesus Abraham Laviera. When I found the ID, I immediately called Tato to tell him, and his response was "No way, bro." My mother was in charge of the Movimiento Hispano Unido, which trained recent immigrants to operate sewing machines, under the auspices of Mobilization for Youth.

Tato's activism enriches his works. He draws on his experience in support of his community to write about what surrounds him; he is a defender of those who are down and out, for they too are members of his society. As a dark-skinned Latino, Tato Laviera is also able to identify with those who are even more marginal than he, as is made evident in the characters he describes in *King of Cans*. And his political activism becomes transparent, for example, in *The Spark* and the *'77 PR Chicago Riot*. Laviera has become the poetic voice of his community's inhabitants, for they are also in search of a way to express themselves, and they have found a voice in Tato Laviera.

IX

The articles contained in the present anthology discuss important dimensions of what I call the Laviera Aesthetic. The co-editors commissioned works by emerging and established scholars, all authorities in their own right on the works of Laviera. They are unpublished essays, and were written exclusively for the anthology.

Stephanie Alvarez and José Luis Martínez's "La palabra, conciencia y voz: Tato Laviera and the Cosecha Voices Project at University of Texas—Pan American" documents Laviera's work with college and middle school migrant farmworker students. With Tato's love, guidance, and boisterous voice, he was able to get them to express themselves orally and for the first time in writing, as they conveyed their migrant experiences. Laviera was compassionate but also demanding, and students had to adjust to his New York style of doing things. Above all, Laviera taught them the power of language as he drilled into them "*La lengua es la ametralladora de la libertad*" and "Cada palabra es universo. Cada síííííílaba es una ex-pre-sión. Cada letra es un sonido sin fin." Alvarez and Martínez reproduce some of the skits the students put together, which revealed their isolation within the US society and educational system. These improvised performances also gave them confidence to express themselves. The Cosecha Voices project was so successful that there were activities in cities outside of McAllen, and included performances at the Nuyorican Poet's Café and Taller Boricua, as well as Kalamazoo College and the University of California-Irvine among others. The experience showed Laviera's resolve to touch as many people as possible, to learn to believe in themselves, and express themselves with self determination. Laviera did this by relying on the same tools he shared with others; he traveled on his own, fearless and determined to share his talents and enthusiastically embrace his mission in life.

Francis Aparicio's article, "The Poet as Earwitness: Reading Sound, Voice and Music in Tato Laviera's Poetry," studies the oral tradition as belonging to but also separate from the written one. For her, sounds, music, and rhythms present in Laviera's poems represent a path to recovering an oppositional space that challenges the arrogance of dominant Western culture. Aparicio relies on Sound Studies or Sound Theory "that will allow us to understand history and our world from the vantage point of sounds and their social, cultural and human meanings." She further adds: "If writing in the Western tradition has reduced the spoken word to 'a word without voice,' Laviera's poetry inverts this effect and indeed returns sound and audibility to poetry." Aparicio reviews Laviera's poetry and focuses on cultural tropes and racial otherness in US society by referencing music, clichés, voice, gossip, and other speech acts.

Susan Campbell's "Latinas Sing: Tato Laviera's Message to/About Women After Civil Rights Collapse" takes into account Martín Barbero's position that considers a literature that exists in the real world. She gathers poems in which the female voice speaks, and speaks with determination, as a liberated woman after the Civil Rights era. She also studies poems about men and their treatment of women, uncovering the hypocrisy of traditional Hispanic culture. Campbell concludes as follows: "Laviera emerges from the tradition of the Civil Rights struggle to underline a radical feminist concept that considers the protection of gender difference to be essential to the goal of greater racial and class-based equality." After the collapse of the Civil Rights struggle, a new activism that includes gender equality is born.

Analisa DeGrave's "'Not Nowhere:' 'Walking Bridges' in an AmeRícan Utopia" reads the concept of utopia within its etymological meaning as "'both 'good place' and 'no place,'" to suggest Laviera's *AmeRícan* represents "a complex interplay of affirmation and negation, hope and impossibility, and a geography in which "somewhere" is quite possibly located "off the map." She observes that words like "Nuyorican," "AmeRícan," and "nideaquínideallá" are utopian, for they are "not nowhere" or "not neither," but located somewhere outside of the United States and Puerto Rican mainstream. These and other words and poems are like "walking bridges," producing a movement that displaces motion in one direction, then in the opposite, and it is in this going back and forth that knowledge and awareness is created. The "walking bridge" also connects all people, in particular those who are colonized and are considered to be of minority status. And as is evident in Steven Schneider's essay of this collection, she sees a connection, a "walking bridge," if you wish, between Laviera and Whitman's "Song of Myself."

Antonia Domínguez Miguela compares the poetry of Luis Palés Matos with that of Tato Laviera. She observes Palés Matos's innovation in both theme and style, as the great Puerto Rican poet highlighted images that were considered outside the framework of Puerto Rican and Caribbean literatures and cultures at a time very few wanted to recognize the African presence in the same geographic space. When he rediscovers the Afro-Caribbean people, he creates a new poetic language. However, Palés Matos was ahead of his times, since the cultural elite preferred to emphasize their Spanish (European) heritage. Like Palés Matos, Laviera underscores the African component as a source of creativity and essential element of Puerto Rican culture. Nevertheless, Laviera's discovery is based on the racial conditions present in the United States, which allows him to understand how race unfolds in the island of Puerto Rico. Domínguez takes the reader on a voyage though Laviera's poems to best understand race in Laviera's works. Laviera does so though "tropicalizing" poetry, which allows the Nuyorican

Laviera to reconsider Puerto Rican national identity and assimilation into US culture. For both poets, the African element lends itself to undergo a process of cultural revival and resistance. If orality is important for both poets, in Laviera's case, the black or African component of his poetry enriches not only his Spanish, but also his English and his Spanglish.

Juan Flores's "Crazy Minds Think Alike: My Long Symbiotic Duet with Tato" revisits the initial encounter between critic and emerging poet, their longstanding relationship, and the shared work that brought them together. In this essay, Flores focuses on Laviera's language and in particular the linguistic ending of his words, which drop the intervocalic consonant in the final position, and leaves the "ao," as in the pronunciation of his most recent collection of poems, *Mixturao*. He considers it to be a part of Afro-Caribbean Spanglish, though for some speakers the consonant is fricative; in Afro-Caribbean speech like Laviera's, it is omitted. Basing his studies on Fernando Ortiz's conceptual sequence of transculturation, acculturation, deculturation, and transculturation, but also neoculturation, Flores describes a unique Afro-Spanish expression that he equates to the "ao." For Flores, the "ao" is a position of resistance against standard English and Spanish.

Lawrence La Fontain-Stokes's "Speaking Black Latino/a/ness: Race, Performance, and Poetry in Tato Laviera, Willie Perdomo, and Josefina Báez," traces the unfolding of Nuyorican poetry, in particular the part that that speaks to race and ethnic identities, through two generations of poets and its expansion to Cuban and Dominican cultures in a New York City experience that is transnational, multiethnic, and multiracial. He looks for a genealogy of the spoken word in African American culture, the Beat Generation, Walt Whitman, and the contributions made by Cuban, Dominican, and Puerto Rican immigrants from the nineteenth century to the present, artists who also contributed with their cultural traditions. The craft comes from Old World Europe through the Caribbean and from Africa. La Fontain-Stokes reads poems that underscore the importance of an Afro-Latino/a identity. In Laviera's case, it is a way of returning to an African mythic past and dialoguing with Puerto Rican and Cuban traditions; in Perdomo's, the poetic voice affirms his Puerto Ricanness to defend himself from being classified as an African American, but later realizing that he is both; in Báez, the speaker celebrates her "Dominicanish." According to La Fontain-Stokes, Báez's works are similar to but differ from those of the others in that "the performer fully incorporates dance, movement, and music to her presentation; she also offers a more dissonant narrative of Black Latino/a identity and culture."

Jacqueline Lazú researches one of Laviera's plays, *King of Cans* (2001), which premiered in El Barrio in 2001. She does so by first defining a

Nuyorican aesthetics, associated with Nuyorican writers. The play takes place in East Harlem as homeless people, with all the problems conveyed by that condition, work together to start their own business; they collect and sell cans. Though this may seem to be a meaningless task, for these workers, once they believe in their labor, they become relatively successful. The business reflects a microcosm of society, so Lazú suggests: "As the story develops they experience mutiny, love, deception, death, and success among their ranks." Lazú also uncovers how Laviera borrows biographical information to construct his characters: The Brain is modeled on Miguel Piñero; Reverend Sidewalk, on Pedro Pietri; and Latero, on the author. There is an attempt to infiltrate the organization, and Latero is imprisoned; his followers organize and triumph. The play is based on the socioeconomic conditions of a community of those who suffer most. For Lazú, the play is infused with Brechtian techniques.

Edrik López's "Espanglish: Laviera's el nideaquínideallá Language in Fourteen Movements" also targets the linguistic act, which he proposes to be a form of code switching, but also a signifier with different significations. This is something that appears in the literature of Latinas/os; however, it was already present in his childhood as a song that mixed the two languages. López also incorporates into his study the use of calques, which are semantic interferences or literal translations, when one language comes into contact with another. Like Flores, López contemplates calques as a language of resistance practiced by members of subaltern communities. López takes us through a journey that includes Laviera's poems but also the work of critics and other Latina writers like Sandra Cisneros and Gloria Anzaldúa.

Glenn Martínez's "*Azucarao*: Tato Laviera and the Poetics of Health Promotion" tackles the deadly problem of type 2 diabetes, which affects many Latinos/as. Martínez informs the reader that "the body's inability to properly use insulin in transporting broken down sugars and starches from the blood into cells" can lead to "kidney failure, retinopathy, and neuropathy," and Latinos/as are one and one half times more likely to die than non-Latinos/as from the disease. As the leading Latino poet, but someone who also has diabetes, Laviera has become an activist and the creator of the "Diabetic Sugar Slam." He considers bilingualism as the expression of the self, which "goes beyond language and that at once subdues it and shows its inherent limitations." Based on an interview with Laveira, Martínez shows how the poet's denial of knowledge or of his own condition, led to his self-discovery. It was too late for him, but not for others. So, he turned his anger into constructive action. As Laviera discovered the stories of his community, his "I" also became a collective "we," which led to the creation of the Diabetic

Sugar Slam: "a performance art contest in which participants are asked to provide a three-minute testimony using rap, poetry, song, or storytelling about the dangers of sugar contents or how diabetes has affected a family member, a friend, or society in general."

Steven Schneider's "The New Accent in America: Tato Laviera's 'AmeRícan' in the Context of US American Poetry," takes a different position from those of other Laviera scholars. He proposes to read Laviera's poetry as a conversation with American poets, such as Walt Whitman, Langston Hughes, and Allen Ginsberg. Schneider writes: "Rather than being uninformed and unconnected to this line of American poets, Laviera's work and especially his often cited poem 'AmeRícan,' ... can be better understood and richly interpreted within the context of these poets whose search for an expansive 'American' identity are consistent with those of Laviera." Schneider reads Laviera's vision of America in Whitman"s "America," *Leaves of Grass*, and "Song of Myself;" he considers Laviera's use of the common person in Hughes's "Refugee in America," "American Heartbreak," "Democracy," "Mother to Son," and his essay "The Negro Artist and the Racial Mountain;" and Laviera's sense of political and social justice in Ginsberg's "America." All four poets write poems about their understanding of America.

Maritza Stanchich's "Insular Interventions: Tato Laviera's Dialogic Dialogue with Luis Muñoz Marín and José Luis González" explores the poetic conversation Laviera establishes with the two island writers, even though one of them, González, lived in Mexico. Laviera's "pamphleteering" and "against muñoz pamphleteering" shows "a deep sense of betrayal, especially when taken in the context of Laviera's overall body of work, which is so often marked by a celebration of, to use his neologism, *AmeRícan* affinity for and fidelity to New York." The Muñocista programs promoted by the Popular Democratic Party, whose slogan was land, liberty, and bread, became hollow words. But Muñoz never really understood the diaspora. With González, Stanchich studies "sin nombre" and "sin nombre the first." She draws attention to the notion that "ambiguous anonymity of no name/sin nombre suggests collective circumstances as well as lacking the patriarchal lineage designed for the express purpose of inheriting monetary or property wealth, here nonexistent." Laviera takes issue with González's criticism of the diaspora and its use of language, for this island writer prefers a more "correct" way of thinking and form of expression.

Israel Reyes's "Barrio, Body, Beat: Tato Laviera and the Holistic Rhythm of *Mestizaje*" considers Laviera's poetry as holistic, which brings together his community in the narrow and broader sense of the word. Reyes searches for the term in medicine, and in Laviera's poetry, it becomes "a site of negotiation between marginality and a reaffirmation of Puerto Rican cultural traditions and systems of spiritual belief." It does not divide mind and body but creates a pluralism that speaks to the health of the Nuyorican community. Framing his study with references to Juan Bruce Novoa's use of "interlingual," a term that mixes languages rather than respect their authenticity, for Laviera the two languages sustain "a dialogue with the island while confronting the harsh reality of the urban context." Laviera's holistic poetry promotes the health of his community and the larger one surrounding it and creates a larger site for cultural healing.

X

The anthology concludes with three sections that feature Tato's own voice. The first is a compilation of previously published interviews that have been worked as a *testimonio*, in which the transcriber suppresses the questions, allowing Tato to speak. Though the *testimonio* is a genre that was first popularized by Miguel Barnet's *Biografía de un cimarrón* (1966; *Biography of a Runaway Slave*), a narration divided into three historical moments in which Montejo's voice is heard, Barnet corrects his language so as not to bring attention to the folkloric elements of his speech. We have taken a different position and have decided to reproduce Tato's words in Spanish, English, and Spanglish, with his tendency to code switch. Barnet believed that reproducing the original transcription would be distracting to the reader; in the case of Laviera, we believe it to be necessary because as a writer, his *métier* is language itself. Moreover, the transcriptions of the published interviews appear to be consistent with Tato's writings in Spanish, English, and Spanglish. However, as would be expected with any published interview, we have corrected obvious typos. In this *testimonio*, Laviera talks about life, his past and present.

XI

The anthology ends with four of Tato's unpublished poems: "i am a wise latina," "guarachera del mundo," "piri," and "this-curso (epistle para un sabio);" and the play, *King of Cans*.

XII

I want to thank Edwin Meléndez and Xavier Totti for believing in this project. They had the courage and wisdom to embrace Tato's extensive body of work and this anthology. Tato and all of us have found a home at the Centro. I am grateful to Tato for introducing me to his family. During his illness Ruth welcomed me into their home. Ruth and Tato were the force behind the completion this significant body of scholarship.

NOTES

1 For his love poems see, for example, *Veinte poemas de amor y una canción* (1924) *desesperada* and *Los versos del capitán* (1966).
2 For an analysis of this and other poems, see Luis (1997).
3 This highly regarded poem is also available in Luis (2013).

lvi

PHOTO COLLECTION

Tato Laviera holding the finished manuscript of La Carreta Made a U-turn *(1979). Photo Courtesy of Arte Público Press, University of Houston.*

Tato Laviera and Nicolás Kanellos (1979).
Photo Courtesy of Arte Público Press, University of Houston.

Luis Meléndez, Tato Laviera and Elba Cabrera at Association of Hispanics Art (AHA), ca. 1979-80. From the Elba Cabrera Collection, Centro Library & Archives.

Tato Laviera with (left to right) his sister Ruth, daughter Ella and mother María in their apartment in Water Street, Lower East Side (1983). Photo courtesy of the Laviera family.

Tato and congresswoman Nydia Velazquez at Agüeybaná bookstore (1996). Photo Courtesy of Sery Colón.

Performing at the Nuyorican Café (2009).
Photo courtesy of Stephanie Alvarez.

Tato in South Padre Island, Texas (2009).
Photo courtesy of Stephanie Alvarez.

Tato, Juan Flores and José Luis Martínez. Edinburg, Texas (2009).

With Stephanie Alvarez at the Nuyorican Café (2009).
Photo courtesy of Stephanie Alvarez.

Frances Aparicio with Tato at Puerto Rican Studies Association Conference (2010).
Photo courtesy of Stephanie Alvarez.

Performing with the Hoops for Haití Quartet (2011).
Photo courtesy of Jorge Quevedo.

Performing at the Hoops for Haití event. Taíno Towers, NY (2011).
Photo courtesy of Jorge Quevedo.

With his friend Gary Cruz (2012).
Photo courtesy of Gary Cruz.

Tato and his beloved sister Ruth (2012).
Photo courtesy of Gary Cruz.

Tato celebrating his birthday with William Luis (May 9, 2012).
Photo courtesy of Dr. Page.

Tato performing in Edingburg, Texas (2009).
Photo courtesy of Silvia Solís.

1

—I—

LANGUAGE, VOICE, AND MUSIC TO MATAO

3

The Poet as Earwitness: Reading Sound, Voice and Music in Tato Laviera's Poetry

FRANCES R. APARICIO

"An inquiry into the auditory is also an inquiry into the invisible" (Ihde 1976).

Tato Laviera is a performance poet. His poetry is eminently oral and aural—that is, it was written ideally to be recited to a live audience of listeners and to be listened to, not merely read silently on the page. When Laviera became blind due to complications with diabetes, his most recent poetry, *Mixturao* (2008a), continues to be characterized by a high degree of references to sounds, voices, and music. After he couldn't record visual images within him, sounds became increasingly important to a writer who always was an "earwitness" (Schafer 1977: 8–9) to the world around him and, particularly, to the Puerto Rican community in New York and in the diaspora.[1]

Some years ago, Laviera came to visit one of my courses at University of Illinois at Chicago (UIC) as part of the activities for the P'alante Conference organized by the Puerto Rican student group on campus. I had not seen Tato for many years, since the 1990s at least, and I was nervous to see him again. Because of his blindness, I was not sure how or what to do to communicate well with him again. Despite my misgivings, he performed his poetry at UIC in front of almost 200 students in a large lecture hall. He succeeded in making them sing and recite call and response rhythms with him as he orchestrated their participation from the lectern in front of the room. While at times he would look back thinking that there were other students behind him, he performed his poetry with the unequaled fervor and passion of always. He captured and maintained the attention of the students with his unusual gift for singing, rhythms, and poetic memory.

Indeed, all critics who have written forewords for his poetry books have unanimously described him as a poet of sound, rhythm, and music. In 1979, Nicolás Kanellos wrote in his "Foreword" to *La Carreta Made a U-Turn*, Laviera's first poetry book, that his collection was dedicated to, among others, "the great salseros and jazz musicians who, long before the poets, conjugated the sounds of three continents into the heartbeat of a people." Kanellos also mentioned the "town poets, barroom singers, and front porch philosophers whose oral tradition has kept the culture ringing in the air to be captured once again and recreated on paper by modern troubadours like Tato Laviera" (1979: 7). Introducing *Enclave* to its reader, critic Juan Flores likewise foregrounded the musical, rhythmic and sonic elements that inform this poetic work: "When Tato raps, he fingersnaps. His poems are en clave, songs in the key of the many people with whom Tato Laviera seeks to strike up a rhythm, grounded most of the time on la bomba...." (1981: 5). Flores frames this poetry within the oral traditions of bomba, plena, and salsa in order to give meaning to the racially informed verses that populate this book. In *AmeRícan*, Wolfgang Binder described Laviera as "quite aware of his Afro-Caribbean traditions, both on a folk level—in music, dance and mythology" (1985: 5-6), but also as an "astute chronicler of street life, of street talk." He mentions Laviera's "unfailing ear for nuances, for double talk, verbal facades and revelations, rhythms and sounds in chismes, conversations, monologues..." (Binder 1985: 6). In his latest publication, *Mixturao* (2008a), William Luis likewise reaffirms the role of sounds and voices as central to the production of social meaning in Laviera's poetry: "This prophet speaks with one voice, but, more correctly, with many voices and sounds..." (2008a: 2). I have also participated in the canonizing of Tato Laviera's poetry as a writing of the oral elements of Afro-Puerto Rican and Afro-Caribbean cultures. I wrote in the 1990s:

> Laviera has been called a "chronicler of life in El Barrio" and rightly so. His poetic language is not influenced by the written, academic tradition of poetry, but instead it is informed by popular culture, by the oral tradition of Puerto Rico and the Caribbean, and by the particular voices spoken and heard in El Barrio. Gossip, refrains, street language, idiomatic expressions, interjections, poetic declamation, and African Caribbean music such as salsa, rhumbas, mambos, sones, and música jíbara (mountain music) are but some of the raw material with which Laviera constructs his poems. Though published in a written format, Laviera's poetry is meant to be sung and recited. (1998: 3076)

At that time these comments converged with the emergence of spoken word, performance poetry and poetry slams since the 1980s.

The epigraph to this essay serves as a framework from which to approach Laviera's poetry in new ways. While it is common knowledge that Laviera is an oral poet, it is also a fact that his poetry is rendered accessible through publications, through the printed word in a highly literate society. In the poem "word" (*Mixturao*), Laviera affirms the double discourse of his poetry as a genre to be both heard and read: "Poetry was meant to be heard/Poetry was meant to be read." While new Internet technologies have allowed us the privilege of accessing websites that reproduce videos through which we could potentially see Laviera performing his own poetry,[2] most academics and formally educated readers have otherwise become familiar with Laviera's poetry through the printed page. Reminding us of both the tensions and simultaneities between literacy and orality, Laviera's poetry potentially does trigger expressions of nostalgia for the oral cultures of the past, what Tony Jackson has described in the context of *A Passage to India* as "the kind of communality and intimacy that literate cultures perceive as what-has-been-lost in becoming, precisely, literate" (2006: 6). The scholarly references mentioned above, culled from the forewords and prefaces to Laviera's poetry collections, partly exemplify this kind of nostalgia, an emotion that could well be associated with the need for a sense of coherent community life amid the fragmentary conditions of colonialism for Puerto Ricans and other Latinas/os in the United States as racialized minorities. The sense of displacement that ensues from migration and from transnational movements, triggered and motivated by economic aspirations for a better life, may fuel the kind of nostalgia constructed through and within the realm of sounds, voices, and popular music.

While it is true, as Henry Louis Gates has written, that African American literature was born out of the needs of the slaves to create "a speaking subject" that will allow them to reclaim their humanity via writing as an expression of their faculty to "reason" (1988: 129), similarly so, Laviera's poetic speakers continuously remind us that this orality challenges dominant power dynamics, that it allows the poet and his readers to recognize U.S. Puerto Ricans and Latinas/os as full citizens and as complete human beings. Don Ihde reminds us in his discussion of sound and phenomenology that older traditions have indicated that vision "objectifies" and sound "personifies" (1976: 21). While we now know that this is not necessarily the case, it is a powerful binary that I would like to deploy to examine Laviera's poetry as an expressive art through which sound contests and challenges the dominant notions of U.S. Puerto Ricans as racialized minorities. Laviera's strong oral textures in his poetic work function as an alternative discourse from which to re-construct Puerto Ricans in the diaspora, making them more fully "human," a discourse that challenges the visual invisibility and the demonization/criminalization of Latinas/os in the U.S. popular imaginary, in media, and in official institutions. Yet the printing of Laviera's poems and their distribution within the publishers's networks make him an integral part of the U.S. Latino/a literary canon as well as insert his work within the spaces of modernity. In this context, a reading of Laviera's poetic works through the emerging theories of Sound Studies, voice, and popular music, will shed new light on this work so central to our understanding of the everyday experiences of the Puerto Rican diaspora in the United States.

Sound Theory or Sound Culture as an emerging, interdisciplinary field of study is revolutionary in the context of its politics, for it directly challenges the visual, dominant axes that have informed Western Culture since classical times. Don Ihde documents some of the more predominant verbal metaphors that have permeated European philosophy and literature, concluding that "visualism has been the dominant way of knowing the world" (1976: 6-8). Derrida's own emphasis on logocentrism equally reminds us of the primacy of the written sign over the aural/oral element. Ihde and other scholars of Sound Studies call for a "philosophy of listening" (1976: 15) that will allow us to understand history and our world from the vantage point of sounds and their social, cultural and human meanings. While Sound Theory incorporates natural science methodologies such as acoustics and sound measurement studies with other fields such as social science, material culture, technology, and the arts and humanities, Laviera's poetry is very appropriate as an object of analysis through sound. His poetry, which is performance poetry, gives body to music, which has been "erroneously made into a pure, disembodied experience by philosophy and phenomenology" (Ihde 1976: 59). If writing in the Western tradition has reduced the spoken word to "a word without voice," Laviera's poetry inverts this effect and indeed returns sound and audibility to poetry. The primacy of the aural and the audible in performance poetry and in spoken word poetry is directly associated in the contemporary context to the resistance and opposition on the part of working-class poets of color, in particular, who have found in the aural a more authentic representation of their life experiences. By serving as "earwitnesses," performance poets of color enact their own sense of authenticity as producers of knowledge about contemporary United States and their world. This role clearly associates sound and aurality with authenticity, thus contesting the objectifying effects of racialization in modernity. Let us explore then how Laviera's poetry explores the politics and the predominant role of voices and of gossip, and the centrality of popular music as an intertext, ancestral matrix, and a tool for "healing" the ills of modern life.

I. The Politics of Sound and Modernity

One of the strongest memories I have of growing up in Puerto Rico was when my sisters and I stayed overnight at my grandmother's small apartment in Río Piedras. I don't remember now whether it was at the end of the day or at dawn, but it definitely was during those transitory times between day and night, when we would clearly hear the *cuchilleros* (knife sharpeners) announcing their trade in my grandmother's neighborhood, as they hauled their small carts up and down the residential streets. I grew up in the late 1950s and throughout the 1960s, during the years when San Juan was experiencing its transitions into modernity in various scales, from the building boom in the city to the residential growth in the suburban areas of this capital city, to the increasing industrialization and the gradual integration of new technologies into our everyday lives. Sound Studies scholars may isolate the *pregones* of the *cuchilleros* as a metaphor for the gradual dwindling of these manual technologies in the face of the modernities of life imposed by United States capitalism as Puerto Rico became an important, new market. If it is true that, with the invention of the telephone, the phonograph, and the radio, "sound was no longer tied to its original point in space and in time" (Ihde 1976: 89) in modern times, modernity has definitely been characterized by rapid changes in technologies of information and communication that have profoundly transformed our ways of life. Sound scholars write about "schizophonia," the "split between an original sound and its electroacoustical transmission or reproduction" (Ihde 1976: 90), and about how "modern life has been ventriloquized," again referring to the revolutionary technologies that nowadays have been achieved in cell phones, iPods, and blackberries. The use of earphones, mostly seen in today's popular use of iPods as individuals commute to and from work, has led to the creation of "headspace" (Ihde 1996: 118), which atomizes the experience of listening to music as a private one, not as in a concert hall or in an outdoor folk music festival. Thus, Sound Studies scholars consider the material production and consumption of music, sound, noise, and silence and how these have changed throughout history and within different societies, but this is done from a much broader perspective than standard disciplines. Indeed, one of the most suggestive tensions in this field of Sound Studies is the exploration of the binary or juxtaposition between the visual and the sonic. If the visual somehow remits us to Western culture and its implicit value as modernity, then the oral/aural elements risk being associated with a part of a primitive culture or primal experience, although we clearly know that this is not the case, for sounds remain central elements of our modern lives. In the context of the printed word, the tensions and gray areas between the written word and the oral structures that have informed literary production throughout history have already been examined (Pratt 1977; Ong 1982). The fact that in *AmeRícan* Laviera defines grafitti in New York as "música silenciosa" [silent music] (1985: 52) suggests that the poet defines visual signifiers as a sound system, as music, but without the sound, as silent music. This sort of synesthetic symbolic language reveals the interconnections among the arts and suggests that Laviera's sensibilities as a poet transcend the categorical boundaries between and among the senses imposed by science and society.

In the following pages I will examine the social and cultural politics of sound, particularly of voice, gossip, and popular Afro-Caribbean music in Laviera's poetry. I will foreground poetry as a form of orature, that is, as an oral, artistic expression that is just as sophisticated as writing and that takes into consideration its "performative techniques, the complex social role of the performer/artists, or the significance of audience" (Elder 1990: 1). Laviera's poetic works not only challenge the arrogance of Western notions of sophistication and literacy, but also reveal the ways in which, as Walter Ong has aptly put it, "thought itself relates in an altogether special way to sound" (1982: 7). The close association between the sounds of and in poetry and the production of knowledge will be evident in this reading of Laviera.

II. On Voice, Gossip and Identity

As Aaron Fox has written about the role of voice in white, working-class culture in South Texas, "The voice is a privileged medium for the construction of meaning and identity and thus for the production of a distinctive class culture. Song and singing comprise the expressive apotheosis of this valued vocality, and song, in turn, is locally understood as a consciously elaborated discourse about (the) voice" (2004: 20). While Fox's study focuses on his ethnography of Lockhart, Texas, and of white, rural working-class everyday culture and the role of voice and music for this community, there are some interesting theoretical frameworks that can be applied likewise to Laviera's poetry, despite the latter's urban focus. Fox, for instance, states that the role of voice in rural, working-class culture "is deeply oral and voice-centered because the historical project of this culture is to respond to and resist the alienation and objectification that is at the heart of a class-based political economy" (2004: 42). The voice is also defined as "the principal domain of both practical and theoretical consciousness and the pivotal site of their encounter" (2004: 45). Fox introduces his book on country music in this Texas town as an example of a method that "joins the politics of the voice to a formal poetics of voicing" (2004: 45). In many ways, I would like to explore this method in Laviera's verses. I am particularly interested in examining the politics of the poems that write about and through street voices and speech. While a comprehensive reading of all of Laviera's poetry books did not yield any significant number of references to urban sounds and indeed revealed the predominance of visual imagery regarding life in the city, it is also true that references to aurality and the poet's constant exhortation for readers to become his listeners clearly suggest a gesture of creating community through the performance of his poetry. By foregrounding the voices of everyday Puerto Ricans in the Bronx and in working-class communities in the diaspora, Laviera clearly contests the visualism associated with Western civilization as well as reaffirms the oral traditions of Afro-Caribbean history and culture. Voice in Laviera's poetry definitely subverts the cultural and racial otherness that dominant U.S. society has imposed on this underprivileged minority sector.

The social meanings of orality are clear in the poem "ay bendito" (Laviera 1985: 45) and "juana bochisme" (Laviera 1981: 27–8). In "ay bendito," the title itself remits the readers to what has become an essentialized signifier of Puerto Ricanness: the "ay bendito" phrase that has historically and socially signaled the myth of docility and of religious fatalism among the island population yet simultaneously reflects the collective sense of empathy and generosity of the Puerto Rican people. Laviera contests and challenges this construct precisely by writing a poem that lacks any particular referential content and that is uniquely composed of fillers and interjections. The emptiness of content reveals a lack, an absence of referential meaning. Yet it is precisely through the act of performing these fillers and interjections—such as "ay bendito," "ay virgen," "fíjese," "pero, qué se puede hacer?," "ay, madre," and others—that these popular phrases and signifiers become the vehicles through which readers and listeners create a reflexive consciousness about these myths. Again, the performance itself of these fillers and signifiers, lacking a particular value as signifieds, foregrounds their special role as terms that denote a lack. The association with theories of culture as a deficit, so predominant in U.S. society, would yield a reading that would reinforce these stereotypes and dominant racialized constructions of Puerto Ricans as uneducated, unintelligent, and unproductive citizens. Working-class Puerto Rican voices have historically been perceived as silenced and have been erased from U.S. media and from state institutions, such as schools; they create a framework from which to understand the ironies of this particular poem.

In "juana bochisme," in contrast, phrases and fillers such as "ay virgen," "dios santo," "dicen que...," "tú sabes," "verdad?," "santa maría purísima," and "se me perdió el hilo" all appear as fillers within a more coherent narrative. Notice the title's use of a double discourse; "bochisme" refers both to "chisme" and to "bochinche," hidden under the signifier that refers to her last name or to her nickname. While "juana bochisme" in contrast to "ay bendito" develops a set of particular narratives and situations regarding relatives, friends, and neighbors, it revels indeed in the transnational extension of *radio bemba*, that is, of gossip. Midway through the poem the verses narrate a trail of gossip:

> y la victoria ascensor, me dijo manny parque
> que lo oyó de tito esquina que lo habían llamado de puerto rico te lo juro, lo que pasa en nueva york inmediatamente lo saben en manatí
> (1981: 27)
> [and victoria elevator, manny park told me
> that he heard it from tito corner who had received a phone call from puerto rico
> i swear, what happens in new york is immediately known in manatí].

The verses suggest the role of gossip, voice, speech, and urban space (notice people's last names) in establishing transnational networks (Manatí is a town in Puerto Rico) and lived experiences. Indeed, nowadays the use of cell phones has literally increased the volume and immediacy of verbal communications and exchanges between the island and the mainland. The melodramatic, criminal, and sexual plots and stories referenced in this long poem, the numerous references to people's names, and the fact that juana, the speaker, is constantly forgetting the details, create a poem that turn the reader into an aural listener, a voyeur of sounds who is privy to this conversation between juana and her friend.

Laviera, indeed, reclaims gossip as an appropriate matter for his poetry. If feminists and sociolinguists have already examined gossip as a "key human social activity" (Dunbar 1996 in Thornborrow and Morris 2004) and "important in establishing and maintaining social relations and norms within a group" (Thornborrow and Morris 2004: 248), Laviera extends this vindication of gossip and performs it throughout the poems mentioned above. Gossip, defined as "talk about an absent third party" (Thornborrow and Morris 2004: 249), has traditionally been undermined and criticized for being low status. Scholars such as Alexander Rysman, in "How the 'Gossip' Became a Woman" (1977) examined the gendered history of gossip and its association with women and indicate that the transgressive role of gossip is that it helps to create relations among women outside the institutional spaces of patriarchy. The stereotype of gossip functions as a divide-and-conquer device that prevents women from getting together. However, Karen Adkins, in "The Real Dirt: Gossip and Feminist Epistemology," is the one who goes farther in arguing for the centrality of gossip not only in informal social relations, but in the production of knowledge. Her article contests the view of gossip as "less authoritative women's knowledge" (2002: 215) and likewise examines the ways in which gossip is valuable only to those on the margins; these points lead to an analogous argument about separate-but-equal logic. Rather, she argues for the value of "connected knowing" among women and also gives some examples of how gossip is "embedded in traditional ways of knowledge making," including the production of scientific knowledge. She concludes that gossip "helps us make connections between seemingly unconnected ideas" and that "it helps us select out that to which we pay epistemic attention" (2002: 223). In this framework, Laviera's poems such as "ay bendito," "juana bochisme," and "callejerismos" [to be examined later] all attest to the analogous scholarly transvaluation of gossip mentioned above. Gossip then becomes an important tool for producing knowledge in local social networks and communities. For Laviera, working-class and working-poor Puerto Ricans in New York City do produce knowledge that challenges the dominant notions of knowledge production reproduced by academic and other social institutions. By being an "earwitness" to these voices and later reproducing them as his poetic matter, Laviera reclaims this particular social discourse that has been traditionally undermined as petty, low-status, and unimportant for society as a whole. The poet reminds us readers/listeners of the central role of gossip in the constitution of local communities and in their negotiations of power differences.

In *AmeRícan* (1985) there are a good number of poems that reproduce diverse voices. Each of them speaks to a different social situation, however, evincing the imaginative ways in which the Nuyorican poet deploys "voice" in very heterogeneous, ideological discourses. For instance, in "m'ija" (1985: 62), a poem in Spanglish, the poem reaffirms the sense of family ties for a Puerto Rican young woman during her birthday. Despite her reticence to celebrate this special day, her mother still plans a festivity for the close family, reinforcing the tight sense of belonging and community that family symbolizes. After the party, the young woman goes out dancing and runs into the man she desires, and the poem concludes with the suggestion that they spent the night together. The last lines of the poem, in Spanish, remind readers of the trust needed for gossip and friendships to be cemented: "te lo puedo contar a ti todo, para eso somos amigas" [i can tell you everything, that is why we are friends].

"brava" deals with a very different speaker: the Puerto Rican woman who speaks only English and is being pressured by those around her to speak in Spanish. She expresses her anger at others and threatens to use physical violence if she has to. She speaks of herself as "sabrosa" and "proud" and ironically goes on to use Spanish to threaten her interlocutors with physical violence in order to defend herself: "go ahead, ask me, on any street/corner that i am not puertorriqueña,/come dímelo aquí en mi cara/offend me, atrévete, a menos/que tú quieras que yo te meta/un tremendo bochinche de soplamoco/pezcozá that's gonna hurt you/in either language..." (Laviera 1985: 63). In this speech-act, Laviera inverts one of the common reactions among Latinas/os to the English-only ideologies in the United States. When asked to speak only English, many Latino/as have reacted by using four-letter words in public to express their anger at these nativist, Anglo-privileged ideologies and policies, as well as to remind others that they do know enough English to speak it. The use of Spanish among Latino/as in the United States cannot be interpreted as a lack of interest in integrating themselves into the fabric of U.S. society, but as an example of personal freedom to use the language that binds them together, to form a linguistic community that serves as a boundary with those others whom they may consider outsiders to the culture. The English-only policies enacted particularly since the 1980s have constructed Latino/as in the U.S. as totally resistant to speak and learn English, when in fact the opposite is true (Crawford 1992). So, when "brava" says "my spanish arrived / tú quieres que yo hable / en español" y le dije/all the spanish words/in the vocabulary, you / know which ones, las que / cortan, and then i proceded / to bilingualize it...," she is inverting the forms of resistance that Latino/as have deployed against English-only pressures. This time, however, the pressures are to speak Spanish, and as a result, "brava," a Puerto Rican woman, is defined as "not puertorriqueña" by others because of her lack of skills in Spanish. Laviera gives her a voice in order to render more complex the identity constructions that silence or mute English-speaking Latinos/as who are ultimately rendered as "vendidos" or "coconuts" because of their lack of Spanish. There are some interesting deconstructions functioning in this poem simultaneously. First, English-speaking Boricuas are not monolingual but can actually use Spanish if they have to. This particular case also signals the poet's attempt to question and deconstruct the homologies between nation and language. Second, there are the gender contradictions at play. "brava" is a woman who uses strong language and threatens with physical violence in order to defend herself and her pride, thus challenging patriarchal notions of feminine behavior in traditional, Catholic-informed cultures. Third, "brava" reminds her interlocutor that physical violence— the references to "soplamoco" and "pezcozá"—"is going to hurt in either language," thus reminding the listener/reader that actions transcend verbal signifiers in terms of the potential impact they can have on others.

"callejerismos" serves as an extension of these previous poems about street voices, popular speech, and working-class sounds. The title remits us to "street slang." The poem begins with the imperative verb, "óyeme" [listen to me], which is capitalized and repeated five times throughout the poem, including the last word of the poem. This use of the word as a leitmotif creates a particular rhythm related to breathing patterns in addition to establishing from the beginning the role of the reader as a someone listening to that voice. Indeed, the reader is interpellated as a listener. The repetition of "óyeme" is, most significantly, associated with the relationship of the physical body with language, voice, and sound. It is as if Laviera wanted to return the physicality of sounds and voices to the printed page.

The poem is mostly in Spanish with a number of concepts and terms in English. However, the content of the *bochinche* in this case is the reference to many of the controversies around Afro-Caribbean *farándula*, particularly salsa singers, the dancing of merengue in Latin America, and Mexican soap operas. The poem reminds us of a Latina/o version of newspaper or magazine gossip columns on Hollywood actors and actresses. The speaker in this poem is a free gossiper who is willing to speak publicly what others know privately but do not dare share: "no te atreves decir públicamente pero lo / hablas privadamente así que tranquilo" [you don't dare to say this in public but/you speak it privately, so take it easy] (2008: 57). There is the suggestion that this speaker may be a threat to others who prefer their talk to remain private. The binary public/private is again related also to the technology of writing, for the use of the alphabet led to reading as a private act (Jackson 2006: 4). Orality, speech, voices, sound, and music all reclaim the public nature of social life, thus instilling in speakers a sense of identity in view of the collective space and the local community to which they belong.

While there is mention that salsa music is a music that has been mediated by the industry, recorded and commercialized, it is the *chisme* around these interpreters, musicians, actors and actresses that creates a particular consciousness that this is part of the social history of the people as well. Perhaps by writing poems about the *farándula*, Laviera reclaims these individuals as part of *el pueblo*, cementing a sense of ownership of their lives, conflicts, and controversies, rather than allowing the industry and the media to monopolize the social meanings behind these figures. The poem includes a reference to the debates about the authorship of salsa music, whether it is Cuban or Puerto Rican. While Cuba is "el centro de la salsa" [the center of salsa], Laviera insists that "los puertorriqueños son los mejores arreglistas" [the best arrangers] (2008: 57). Other references include the value of Rubén Blades in salsa music, despite his interventions into acting and a political life in Panama, the importance of the merengue dance in the Caribbean and throughout Latin America, the conflict between Celia Cruz and Andy

Montañez over his visit to Cuba, the role of Mexican soap operas and their actors and actresses. Likewise, there are a number of references to the national tensions between Puerto Ricans and Mexicans, such as the mention of Carlos Santana's interpretation of Tito Puente's "Oye como va" in terms of a discussion about authorship, and of JLo and Selena. The poem's construction as a speech-act concludes with an exhortation to tune in again tomorrow in any corner to find out more gossip or "comentario" from this speaker. An interesting statement regarding how this voice does not have the diffusion of radio or television reveals once more the perceived limitations of oral speech. With no access to dominant media, these voices in the neighborhoods, in the local spaces, continue to recreate their own networks of communication and distribution of knowledge and information about what is of interest to them as individuals and as a local, Latina/o community. Here Laviera is reclaiming a sense of ownership over these controversies and famous individuals, for gossiping about them is in many ways a form of reclamation about authorship and authority, and a way of asserting a politics against the commodifying effects that the industry has imposed on them. Indeed, this leads us back to the historical return to Afro-Caribbean music as the "ancestral matrix" of Boricua culture that Laviera achieves in his early poetry.

III. Popular Music and the Printed Poem

In the last section of *La Carreta Made a U-Turn*, Laviera celebrates the genesis of his *mestizo*/mulatto racial and cultural heritage through the intertextual presence of Afro-Caribbean popular music in his poems. The title of this section, "El arrabal: nuevo rumbón" [The ghetto: a new type of rumba], is poetry constituted by musical discourse. This return to black roots through the popular structures of sound, through the memory and aural experience of listening to these sounds familiar to his community, are deeply connected to his attempt to reclaim poetry in its primary original role. Intertextuality with music represents one potential way of this poetic recovery: the traditional rumba is reconfigured into a "nuevo rumbón," a new path toward the social and poetic expression. The space of the ghetto acquires presence and identity in conjunction with the musical sounds that emerge from it, leading to a singular creative force. Laviera in this context proposes a "vernacular" discourse and texture that produces an "ancestral matrix" from which he can produce an autochthonous North American, AmeRícan creativity.

The return to the Puerto Rican African roots is inscribed in the poetry, in the rhythms and languages of the Caribbean, of the Nuyorican and of the African-American: the congas, the drums, the tumbao, the rumbas, the salsa music, the *sones*, *santería*, Ismael Rivera, Marvin Gaye, soul music, and spirituals, among other references. Laviera believes that poetry is a ritual that, along with music, serves as an artistic means through which we are cleansed or redeemed from the modern social ills. This role is clearly expressed in the poem "the new rumbón": "congas the biggest threat to heroin / congas make junkies hands healthier / las venas se curan ligero / con las congas conguito congas" (Laviera 1979: 39).

Salsa, on the other hand, represents a cultural model of *mestizaje*, synchretism, and transculturation. Given its transnational, transcultural and transracial history and dissemination, salsa music represents the integration of African-American, Latino/a, and North American rhythms and traditions of sound. Salsa is an amalgam of polyrhythmic structures, clave rhythms, repetitions, and antiphonal patterns derived from African musics; from U.S. jazz it has borrowed the harmonic patterns, the improvised solos, and the presence of the brass instruments; from the Latino/Hispanic tradition it has kept the lyrical themes and the strophic structures, not to mention the heterogeneous folkloric and popular musical genres and forms that inform salsa's compositions since the 1970s.

Laviera's readers cannot escape the semiotic intertextuality and the discursive heteroglossia that permeates his poetry, all of it informed by the cultural and racial meanings of Afro-Caribbean popular musics. One finds different linguistic strata, such as words and sounds in African languages, in Spanish, in English, hummings, musical echoes, percussive rhythms, song lyrics, all of them interwoven in a semiotic intertextuality. Musical sounds are transmuted into the printed page in order to be read silently, hopefully without losing entirely their sonic and melodic identities. This process of inscribing music in poetry reveals the desire for an ideal reader who can recognize these musical elements within the poetic discourse.

The next to the last poem of *La Carreta* reveals the relationship between music and poetry, a dialectic tension that is likewise evident in future poems, such as "migración" and "bilingüe"—such as in *Mixturao* (2008a). In the poem dedicated to Ismael Rivera, the "sonero mayor," Laviera evinces the dialogic relationship between music and poetry. Laviera structures the text in a dual format on the space of the page, a method that he employs in many other poems throughout his works. The text to the left is the poetic voice who speaks about Ismael in third person, a voice that praises Ismael and comments on him. The right column, separated by quotation marks, is made up of fragments from Ismael's most popular songs and lyrics. The reader/listener familiar with said repertoire will automatically evoke the echoes of these melodies that are behind the lyrics. Laviera himself would sing these songs in a poetry reading. The poetic experience is then produced by the dialogue established between both voices, a sort of musical and verbal counterpoint. One stanza creates coherence and meaning from the next, thus revealing a poetic reading that is based on verses chained to each other:

el me dio, y le da
a muchos condenados en la tierra
su único momento
de placer y de alegría

"dime por qué me abandonaste
no me atormentes, amor, no me
mates, ten compasión dime
por qué" (1979: 83–4)

Laviera constructs a poetic figure of Ismael, Maelo, as most representative of "the downtrodden" [los de abajo], the street musician of Barrio Obrero: drug addict, prisoner, black, and poor. Laviera poetizes this sociological phenomenon, whereas the musical figures of the entertainment world become heroes and god-like figures for the people. The concert in honor of Maelo that took place in 1987 at the Coliseum Roberto Clemente was absolute evidence of this late sonero's popularity and charisma. The concert lasted more than twelve hours and was attended by children, the elderly, young people, and families, as well as the then-Governor of Puerto Rico. It was a sort of collective feast, a "new rumbón," a religious ritual that invoked the generous and popular spirit of Ismael Rivera. Music and religion continue to be closely related, even in a society as industrialized and urban as that of current Puerto Rico. Given the experiences and traumas of displacement, Puerto Ricans in the diaspora hang on to these musical traditions and rewrite them, renewing in transnational circuits their sense of vitality within the urban context of that other island, New

York. While in some ways Laviera refers to other sorts of music in his other poetic works, such as rock as in "john forever" (1981: 60–1), cello music in "suni paz" (1981: 58), and all forms of national musical forms in Latin America in "hispano" (1988: 47), he still predominantly continues to celebrate and reaffirm the spiritual, healing power of Afro-Caribbean musical rhythms and forms, such as the Puerto Rican bomba in "bomba para siempre"—the last poem in *Enclave* (1985). In this poem Laviera reiterates the phrase "se queda allí" [there it remains] as a reminder of the lasting presence of bomba in Puerto Rican culture. Even in its renewed forms and current recoveries of bomba, the rhythms continue to signify the historical continuity of blackness in the constructions of Puerto Rican identity by generations in the past, present and future.

IV. Conclusion

If "writing disembodies language" (Jackson 2006: 8), then Laviera's poetry, informed and structured around speech acts, oral formulas, and the preeminence of popular music, offer the written word a return to its sonic manifestations. Given the central role of orality, aurality, voice, gossip, sounds, and popular music, there is no doubt that Laviera's readers cannot read his poetry on the page without sounding out in their minds the rhythms and sonic elements of this language. Walter Ong reminds us that "reading a text means converting it to sound, aloud or in the imagination, syllable-by-syllable in slow reading or sketchily in the rapid reading common to high technology cultures. Writing can never dispense with orality" (1982: 8). Yet as Don Ihde has written, "There are vast differences between hearing voices and reading words" (1976: x). In "word" Laviera exhorts his readers/listeners, in a sort of ars poetica, to read poetry both silently and also aloud. Each mode offers a different experience to the reader. The silent mode leads to "total self-absorption," is intellectually probing, and creates a sense of "dignified silence" and intimacy ("intimate"). The oral reading returns poetry to the body of language, to the "consonants physically/muscling personal/voices integrated...." He exhorts us to read in both ways, not sacrificing one for the other: "So read deep in/So read out loud." At a poetry reading in Calvin College in 1998, Laviera told the students that "every word is a universe, every syllable is an expression, and every letter is an endless sound" (Vásquez 1998). His poetry performances attest to these principles that have guided Laviera's poetry writing. We have seen this, for instance, in the renowned poem "asimilao," in which Laviera focuses on the loss of the letter "d" to trace a genealogy of blackness erased from the standard versions of linguistic history and etymology. This archaeology of race, triggered by the absence or presence of one letter in a word, reveals the talent with which Laviera manipulates language in order to deconstruct the dominant narratives about race, gender, class and culture in the United States and in Puerto Rico. His poetic performances come alive precisely in the interstices between the printed, visual word and its oral/aural enactment. Poetry is well and alive for Laviera, and it is a gift of sound that will survive future changes in technology and social experience.

NOTES

[1] Here I use the term "earwitness," just as Sound Studies scholars such as Schafer have. Literary writers from the past have become authentic sources for documenting the sounds of their times. In this sense, Laviera's poetry can also be read as a similar source for our contemporary times (Schafer 1977: 8–9).

[2] YouTube has a couple of poetry readings by Tato Laviera, including one at Texas A&M University. The electronic journal *Encrucijada*, at Dartmouth College, also includes a poetry reading by Laviera in video format.

21

Crazy Minds Think Alike: My Long Symbiotic Duet with Tato Laviera

JUAN FLORES

I remember vividly when Tato Laviera came to my office and presented me with a copy of *La Carreta Made a U-Turn*. It was late 1979; the book, his first, had just come out, and he was beaming with pride. Who can forget that huge smile, that effervescent personality when he fills a space? He dropped the book on my desk and said, "I want you to read this." Emphasis on the "you." So that was my subway reading that evening on the way home from the Centro [Center for Puerto Rican Studies], which in those days was located at John Jay College, before the move to Hunter College. In those thirty minutes or so I read the book through, getting to the last page just as the train was pulling into my stop in Brooklyn. I had not expected much, to be frank, not because of Laviera in any way, but because of the several new poetry books I had read those days most were pale imitations of Pedro Pietri, with a little Víctor Hernández Cruz or Sandra María Esteves thrown in. It was pretty predictable, however laudatory the idea of young Ricans finding poetic expression might be.

But as I walked up the stairs to the street I thought, no, this is different. There is an original, fresh voice here, and thematics and messages that are different, and important. I was, actually, excited. I could not wait to share my impressions with Laviera. I called him (this was before email) and asked if he could come back to my office the next day. So we met again, same place, same time. But this time we talked for hours, on into the evening, and got to know each other. I told him that I was busy working on an article, for the (pretty prestigious) journal *Daedalus*, which was pulling together a special issue on four "minority groups," which included Puerto Ricans, and they got the Centro to come up with two articles, one on political economy and migration, the other on culture and identity. I was responsible for the latter of these and would collaborate with the Centro researchers on sociolinguistics. My part would be on the issues of assimilation, cultural resistance, and other pertinent factors—in other words, identity. As I was talking with Laviera and going over with him some of the things I deeply appreciated about his writing, I suddenly realized that his work contained the seeds of the thoughts I was then working through for my piece of the *Daedalus* article (Flores, Attinasi and Pedraza 1981): the whole question of cultural identity, migration, and the formation of community. Even the title, *La Carreta Made a U-Turn*, with its ingenious reflection on the direction(ality) of cultural movement and change (the surprising "u-turn" and its challenge to the unidirectional sensibility of the literary work referred to, René Marqués's play *La carreta*), even the title meshed perfectly with my lines of thinking, to the point that I ended up using the same title for the article: "*La Carreta Made a U-Turn*" (Flores, Attinasi and Pedraza 1981).

Of course, it was not just the title, either. From Laviera's book and our conversations I developed a whole perspective on issues of Americanization and "assimilation resistance" (as they called it back then) that was new and challenging, both to mainstream U.S. social science and wishful assimilationist ploys of all sorts, but also to the smug, facile cultural nationalism of the Puerto Rican intellectual and political elite. Like Laviera, I liked that "plague on both houses" and love for the people stance, and I was glad to assume it in such good company. We were really in synch, a remarkable symbiosis.

La Carreta Made a U-Turn belongs to the so-called Nuyorican modality. Freely bilingual in style and conception, it was written by a young Puerto Rican who grew up in the streets of New York City. The poems are filled with that biting defiance and strident pride that erupted on the literary landscape in 1973 with *Puerto Rican Obituary* by Pedro Pietri. Laviera's is another voice responding to the oppression and misery that have been the lot of most Puerto Ricans since their proverbial oxcart pulled up to Ma Liberty's Golden Door. Mass unemployment; inadequate and distorted education; rampant prejudice and injustice; high crime rates and drug abuse that are systematically fostered by the very society that condemns them; social isolation, whether behind bars or in depressed, run-down neighborhoods—these are and promise to remain the most evident thematic sources of Puerto Rican cultural works in the United States.

To expose and denounce such negative conditions, writers like Laviera draw vital inspiration from the struggle to resist the conspiring forces of assimilation and exclusion, forced incorporation and endemic inequality. Their main recourse is the spirit of national, or "ethnic," affirmation that has been the other face of the colonial history of the Puerto Rican people, both on the Island through the centuries and over the decades as immigrants in the United States. Symbols of indigenous and slave opposition to Spanish rule are held up against the leveling effects of cultural imperialism, as is the militant courage of the Puerto Rican Nationalists, from Pedro Albizu Campos to Lolita Lebrón. These strains of the national legacy, though, most commonly appear in direct interaction with complementary expressive resources available in the immediate North American setting. Among the poets, this admixture is most evident in the bilingual technique itself, with its characteristic switching between colloquial Puerto Rican Spanish and a variety of urban American English, the latter often the dominant literary idiom. The effect is generally suggestive of contemporary Black and Chicana/o poetry, but always with a distinctively Puerto Rican reference and expressive quality.

What makes Laviera's work particularly interesting is that in it, this Nuyorican potential finds unusually sustained realization, and that, as the title indicates, contemporary Puerto Rican experience in the United States is evoked by a direct response to the classic dramatization of the migration process in the national literature. *La carreta*, which traces the archetypal Puerto Rican journey from rural origins to the San Juan slums to the South Bronx, is a drama written in 1953 by René Marqués, one of the Island's foremost modern authors. Marqués's death in 1979—the same year that Laviera's book was published—signaled the close of an era in Puerto Rican letters. In his thirty productive years, Marqués worked in a wide variety of literary forms—often with greater artistic success than in *La carreta*—and expressed a range of notions about Puerto Rican politics and culture. But it was *La carreta* that became widely familiar to Puerto Rican and international audiences and came to be extolled for over a generation as the classic literary rendition of recent Puerto Rican history.

In *La carreta*, the entire migration experience is presented as a process of abrupt moral and cultural deterioration. By the time we meet them in their dilapidated Bronx tenement, the "typical" *jíbaro* family, extended around the matriarch Doña Gabriela, has been so traumatized by their collision with a hostile, technocratic Anglo-Saxon society that their only hope for salvation is a return to the Island and the resumption of peasant life on the land. The "oxcart," guiding symbol of the play and an abiding reminiscence of abandoned national roots, must be restored to its natural place in a world uncontaminated by inhuman modernity and incompatible foreign values. The final vision of a regained life of decency on the sacred soil never fails to capture the minds and hearts of Puerto Ricans of all ages, especially the thousands who have lived through that disillusioning migration process firsthand.

Laviera, who was raised as a child of *La carreta*, picks up where Marqués left off; his book, though not written in dramatic form, may be read as the "fourth act" sequel to Marqués's work. It is anything but a faithful continuation, though, since Laviera's task went beyond that of merely filling in the twenty-five years that elapsed since Marqués wrote his influential play. For Laviera, *La carreta* is not only old-fashioned but fundamentally misleading. In fact, Marqués is considered to have steered the metaphorical Puerto Rican oxcart in the wrong direction, and *La Carreta Made a U-turn* is an attempt to set it back on the course of real historical and cultural experiences. As the "Nuyorican" corrective to an imposing national self-image, Laviera's poetry thus provides a focus for critical insights into the problems of Puerto Rican identity and assimilation in contemporary U.S. society.

The most obvious of these problems is the perennial question of return to the Island, or more generally, of the direction in which Puerto Rican migrants are headed. Laviera recognizes that, even with the substantial return migration of the past decades, going back "home" has not been the typical fate of Puerto Ricans who have come to the United States or of their offspring born here. Nor should nostalgia for the "old country" be taken uncritically as their inherent disposition or aspiration. For the most part, Puerto Ricans are here to stay, as Laviera suggests in the rather irreverent homage to his own boyhood that begins the volume:

> papote sat on the stoop
> miseducated   misinformed
> a blown-up   belly   of malnutrition
> papote sat on the stoop
> of an abandoned building
> he decided to go nowhere. (1979: 14)

This is the first, most evident meaning of the "u-turn": the oxcart, rather than pointing to the long-lost byways of Puerto Rico—Marqués's own reversal of direction—is proceeding ever more deeply into the thick of North American life. Laviera titles the first part of his collection "Metropolis Dreams," a deliberate reference to the final act of *La carreta*, "La metrópoli," where the nightmarish urban reality is ultimately transcended in the dream of return to the native land. Laviera's "dreams," on the other hand, are intrinsically bound up with the metropolitan nightmare, and Puerto Rico no longer harbors any such physical or emotional release—at least not in the melodramatic, provincial, retrogressive way that Marqués suggests. The thought of return migration by now, for the likes of Laviera, hardly conjures the illusion of pastoral bliss that brought Doña Gabriela and her daughter, Juanita, to their final affirmation of life. As Laviera puts it in his bilingual poem "my graduation speech":

i want to go back to puerto rico
but i wonder if my kink could live
in ponce, mayagüez and carolina

tengo las venas aculturadas
escribo en spanglish
abraham in español
abraham in english
tato in spanish
"taro" in english
tonto in both languages (1979: 17)

One of the many ironies about *La Carreta Made a U-Turn* is that it is, indeed, a return to Puerto Rico. The very structure of the book suggests that direction, proceeding as it does from the metropolis to "El Arrabal" (the slum), and from English to Spanish as the prevalent poetic idiom. In fact, there is throughout a closer familiarity with the Island and the Spanish language than is common in Nuyorican writing. But this is surely because Laviera spent his early boyhood in Puerto Rico, moving to New York in 1960. In that, he is different from many of his literary peers and even from such relative "old-timers" as Piri Thomas and Pedro Pietri.

But what binds this work with most others written by Puerto Ricans in the United States is that the view of Puerto Rico is conditioned by formative years lived in New York. As a result, the Puerto Rico to which the Nuyorican oxcart returns is markedly different from the Puerto Rico of the official culture. Laviera's Puerto Rican roots lead neither to the folkloric *jíbaro*, content under the Commonwealth, nor to the glorified pantheon of the national elite—two sources of patriotic pride that are so prominent in Marqués and his works. Rather, going back to Puerto Rico evokes the popular culture of an Afro-Caribbean island, the birthplace of musical and poetic forms like *la bomba, la plena, la décima*, and *el seis*. It is a culture of the slave and peasant masses, the culture of a colonial people who have known not only misery and submission—and pious "decency"—but also joy, creativity, and struggle. All these strains of subordinate indigenous expression are invoked and affirmed in *La Carreta Made a U-Turn*.

Yet these expressions are also transformed, since they are in constant reciprocity with the currents and crosscurrents of cultural life in urban United States. Laviera calls his symbolical return to the Island "Nuevo Rumbón," a new path, since it clashes sharply with the dominant cultures of both societies: the elitist Hispanophile tradition of Puerto Rico and the chauvinist White Anglo-Saxon Protestant core of North American values and identity. Posed against both European legacies is the African culture base shared by Caribbean and American Blacks. Thus Laviera in "the salsa of bethesda fountain" finds hostility and estrangement in North American society, as was the case in the works of earlier Island-based authors like Marqués, José Luis González, and Pedro Juan Soto. But the young Puerto Rican writers also give voice to a strong sense of cultural unity and solidarity with American Blacks:

a blackness in spanish
a blackness in english
mixture-met on jam session in central park,
there were no differences in
the sounds emerging from inside (1979: 67)

Stylistically, this Afro-Caribbean orientation is present in the hovering influence of Palés Matos, who established African rhythmic possibilities as a core element of Puerto Rican poetry. Laviera's indebtedness to Palés Matos, especially in his poems in Spanish, is conscious and explicit, though he generally adapts, rather than merely imitates, his model. The lines from "tumbao (for eddie conde)" are an example:

> pito que pita
> yuca que llama
> salsa que emprende
> llanto que llora
> última llamada sin fuego
> tumba que la tamba
> tumba que la bamba baja
> que pacheco se inspira
> que ismael la canta
> oh!   y el baquiné (1979: 62–3)

"el moreno puertorriqueño" is also within the Afro-Caribbean tradition. Like most of Laviera's verse, this fascinating "three-way warning poem," as he calls it, is meant to be declaimed, and it relies for full impact on oral presentation.

Laviera's appeal to the non-European roots of colonial cultures, while sometimes veering toward a clichéd spiritualized Africanism, is by no means uncritical or merely escapist. Africa is a source and reference point, not a sacred hermitage: a sympathetic connection to Africa must also be a questioning one if it is to align with present-day realities. Laviera makes this clear in the pensive "the africa in pedro morejón":

> yes, we preserved what was originally african,
> or have we expanded it? i wonder if we have
> committed the sin of blending? but i also hear
> the AFRICANS love electric guitar clearly mis-
> understanding they are the root,
> or is it me who is primitive?
> damn it, it is complicated. (1979: 57)

"the american dollar symbol," the poem continues, "that's african; / the british sense of royalty, that's african; / the colors in catholic celebrations, / that's african" (1979: 57–8). And in the closing lines, the appealing mythologies preached by his Afro-Cuban friend seem to dash against the sobering reality of the New York ghetto:

> this high-priest, pedro, telling me all of this
> in front of an abandoned building. (1979: 58)

No remote ideals or easy ways out can alter the immediate stage-setting of Puerto Rican life in New York. However much pride and inspiration may be gained from national origins and the Afro-Caribbean heritage, the "abandoned building" is always hauntingly there, the inevitable backdrop and immediate historical circumstance in which those counter-traditions are really at work. Here, in the land of "broken English dreams," as Pietri called it, is where the *carreta* now sits, where masses of Puerto Rican workers have come to live with little prospect of either advancement or return to Puerto Rico.

Laviera is also keenly aware of the political impetus that set the crowded exodus in motion—for him, Marqués and the postwar migration are both products of the Luis Muñoz Marín era in Puerto Rican history. Muñoz Marín, at the helm of Island politics from 1940 through 1964, and the father of Operation Bootstrap and the Free Associated State (Commonwealth), kindled the false sense of freedom, mobility, and progress that impelled the oxcart to the benevolent North. In "something i heard," Laviera comments bitterly on the hypocrisy of this influential political rhetoric:

> on the streets of san juan
> muñoz marín stands on top
> of an empty milk box
> and brings his land, liberty,
> bread message to a people
> robbed of their existence.
> napoleon's father attentively
> listened as muñoz said, "inde-
> pendence is just around the
> corner."
>
> napoleon' father took it
> literally, he went around
> the corner and found a donkey
> tied to a pole. (1979: 28)

He lashes out "against muñoz pamphleteering" in another poem, that "hollow sepulcher of words, / words i admired from my mother's eyes, / words that i also imbedded as my dreams" (1979: 29). And in direct reference to the migration, Laviera writes: "Inside my ghetto i learned to understand / your short range visions of where you led us, / ... your sense of stars landed me in a / north temperate uprooted zone" (1979: 29). The populist promises of Muñoz Marín, his patriotism divested of the demand for independence, formed the ideological program for Marqués and *La carreta*—"el concepto del vocablo PATRIA," as Laviera puts it, "que Luis Muñoz le dio a los carreteros" (1979: 86).

From all of these angles and with recurrent irony, Laviera anatomizes the Puerto Rican cultural experience in New York. He reflects critically on all that would give false solace to his uprooted compatriots, as in the memorable "song of an oppressor," directed against the magnetic television novela *Simplemente María*, which keeps his poor working-class mother in a state of sentimental hypnosis:

mami, you sit so calmly
looking at your novelas ...
mami, tears of sacrifice sanctify
your delicate face, valley of tears
in your heart
mami, i love you
this spirit of love gives me rancor
and hatred, and i react to the song
simplemente maría... (1979: 42)

And after all, is not *La carreta* itself like a novela par excellence, a heartrending melodrama of the Puerto Rican migration?

But perhaps Laviera's most penetrating commentary is the very linguistic range and modulation of the poetry itself. Between the English poems that begin the book and the Spanish poems that end it, bilingual switching and blending are employed with consistent dexterity. The overall impression, despite the strategic shift from one language to the other, is one of almost undelectably fluid transition, and from the standpoint of either language tradition, of a qualitative expansion of idiomatic resources. As recent studies of Chicano/a literature show, bilingual writing entails more than merely utilizing the aggregate of expressive possibilities in each of the vernaculars, as if the options were simply between two fixed vocabularies. More than a poetic device, code switching corresponds directly to the generalized linguistic practices of Puerto Ricans and Chicanos/as whose experiences gave rise to, and are in turn recaptured in, the representative works of each new generation of writers.

In *La Carreta Made a U-Turn*, moreover, as in much Nuyorican writing, bilingual usage is also a matter of thematic concern in its own right, central to what is being said and not merely a device. Laviera's "my graduation speech" is an excellent example, at once an enactment of the linguistic dilemma of Puerto Ricans in the United States and a telling commentary of it. At first glance the poet-persona seems only to be confirming that the jarring clash between Spanish and English has left Puerto Ricans hopelessly inarticulate and illiterate in either language and even in their makeshift "Spanglish." The poem ends:

hablo lo ingles matao
hablo lo español matao
no se leer ninguno bien
so it is, spanglish to matao
what i digo
        ¡ay, virgen, yo no sé hablar! (1979: 17)

But a closer look suggests that this cynical castigation of his linguistically crippled countrymen and of the educational system responsible for such an outcome—since it is, after all, his "graduation speech"—is only its most evident intention. The entire poem, in fact, rather than degenerating into sheer nonsense or incoherent rambling, is a carefully structured argument that demonstrates a wealth of expressive potential and a rigorous logical ability. Prefacing his self-mocking "speech" with the succinct paradox, "i think in spanish i write in english," the speaker then offers possible "resolutions" to the conflict—return to Puerto Rico or deliberate gravitation toward one or the other language. Each is rejected, the second not only because his voice does not fit neatly into either exclusive idiom, but also because such a choice would only limit his linguistic virtuosity. Furthermore, the poem illustrates that the apparent contradiction between thought and language ("i think in spanish i write in english") can be and is contravened in the course of actual conceptualization and verbalization, Thus "¡ay, virgen, yo no sé hablar!" at the close must be understood ironically: the reader is by now aware that the speaker knows what he is saying and can say what he thinks, in both languages and in a wide array of combinations of the two.

Laviera is not claiming to have ushered in a "new language," the tendency at times in the more magniloquent pronouncements of the "Nuyorican renaissance." Rather, his intention is to illustrate and assess the intricate language contact experienced by Puerto Ricans in New York, and to combat the kind of facile and defeatist conclusions that stem so often from a static, purist notion of linguistic change. Laviera is emphasizing that the cultural decimation endured by Puerto Ricans in the United States, most glaringly evident in the bewildering, unequal clash between English and Spanish, has another side. Perhaps covertly that same process also involves an enrichment, or a shift of focus, that at the linguistic level serves to define the expressive resources available to the Puerto Rican poet in the United States.

From this critical and realistic perspective, then, Puerto Ricans in the United States are tending toward neither assimilation nor uncritical cultural preservation; they are neither becoming Americans nor continuing to be Puerto Ricans in any handed-down or contrived sense. Their historical position as a colonial people at the lowest level of the North American class structure makes either option unfeasible. But what is left is not simply confusion, or cultural anomaly, or a "subculture of poverty," as a wide spectrum of commentators, including René Marqués, Eduardo Seda-Bonilla, and Oscar Lewis conclude. It is a delicate balance, "a light touch," as Laviera calls a remarkable short poem. Although he casts illusions aside, he is still not disillusioned, but instead builds a new affirmation from the life he sees and feels around him:

> inside the crevice
> deeply hidden in basement land
> inside an abandoned building
> the scratching rhythm of dice
> percussion like two little bongos
> in a fast mambo.
>
> quivering inside this tiny ray
> of sun struggling to sneak in.

the echo of the scent attracted
a new freedom which said. "we are
beautiful anywhere, you dig?" (1979: 16)

After the *Daedalus* article came out we decided to take it on the road: any invitation to speak or present that either of us received, we'd only accept if it included the other. We traveled all over the nation, to Boston, to Chicago, to D.C., presenting our "duet" of poetry and historical/theoretical reflections about culture and identity as exemplified by the situation of Puerto Ricans in the United States, the "diaspora" (before that term gained currency).

And then, after Laviera had a chance to read and think about my article departing from his ideas, visions, and poetics in *La carreta*, Tato blessed me with a couple of poems. One was "tito madera smith," which he dedicated to me (to my great honor!) and which I will refer to further along. The other, of course, was "asimilao," that hilarious think-piece about the class and racial origins of assimilationist thinking (and acting). By the time he shared that one with me I was busy writing another essay as a follow-up to the *Daedalus* piece. Once again I named my essay after the title and a line in a Laviera poem, this time "asimilao." I called my article, quoting a full line, "'Qué assimilated, brother, yo soy asimilao':..." (Flores 1985). Here, even more than in my earlier writing, Laviera's ideas and unique voice provided me with the scaffold for my analysis of the spiritual and intellectual "journey" undertaken by Nuyoricans (and other diasporic communities of color) in structuring a new and different identity to differentiate that experience from the prevalent model of assimilation and easy Americanization, and yet also as different from merely "preserving" the culture of origin. Laviera and his ingenious poetic visions helped me recognize and formulate a different model, and different path of cultural transformation.

Such, then, are four moments of Nuyorican cultural interaction within the U.S. society, briefly summarized as the here-and-now, Puerto Rican background, reentry and branching out. Again, they are not necessarily to be taken as sequential stages in the manner in which I have presented them but as fields of experience joined by transitional phases of cultural awareness. How and to what extent these moments of sensibility relate to the advance of political consciousness is another, more complicated matter. It is clear, in any case, that Puerto Rico not only serves as an imaginary realm of cultural self-discovery, but must also be recognized as a nation whose political status looms large on the agenda of international relations. The quest for Puerto Rican identity in the United States thus remains integrally tied to the prospects of national independence or continued colonial subordination to or, as the official euphemism would have it, "association" with the United States. Generally speaking, the gathering of cultural consciousness on the part of the Nuyoricans inclines them toward the first of these options.

It will also be necessary, with further study, to elaborate the correspondences between the cultural geography outlined here and the multiple spatial directions of the Puerto Rican migration. I would only suggest that the spiritual movement back and forth between New York and Puerto Rico bears some significant correlation to the migratory circulation of Puerto Ricans in the ongoing exchange of workers for capital under colonial conditions. In the Puerto Rican case, neither the migration itself nor the cultural encounter with U.S. society is a one-way, either/or, monolithic event. Rather, it is one marked by further movement and the constant interplay of two familiar yet contrasting zones of collective experience.

Acknowledging that the structure of the Puerto Rican's coming-to-consciousness, which I present here as my own invention, actually dawned on me as I read Laviera. When considered in succession, his first three books take us through the entire journey, each volume giving voice to one of the passages from one moment to the next. The first, *La Carreta Made a U-Turn* focuses on the contrast between the New York here-and-now and the Puerto Rico of enchantment and cultural richness. The second book, entitled *En Clave* or *Enclave*, transports that meaning gathered from the national culture and establishes a distinctive place for it in the re-encountered New York setting. And the third, *AmeRícan*, is the branching out, the striking of sympathetic chords with other cultural groups on the basis of expansive Puerto Rican sounds and rhythms. The poet ranges widely in his "ethnic tributes," as he entitles a substantial part of the book, addressing and embracing many of the adjacent peoples in the crowded New York environs. One of the heartiest of these embraces is called "jamaican":

> reaches their guts into the Caribbean
> the second africa, divided by yemaya
> reaches their guts into the third world,
> marley-manley emerging people

reaches their guts into urban america,
reggae-reggae, modern english.
reaches their guts into ethiopia,
rastafarian celebrated deities.
reaches their guts into washington sq. park,
jamaican english, folkloric blackness,
reaches their guts into puerto ricans,
where we shared everything for free,
yeah, brother, very good, very, very
good, yeah, real good! (1985: 29)

Here is the young Puerto Rican re-fashioning New York City along Caribbean, Third World lines, or voicing resonantly his awareness that history is doing so.

Yet as is clear from the neologistic title "AmeRícan," Laviera is intent on reaching beyond the New York enclave. He seeks to stake a claim for Puerto Rican recognition before the whole U.S. society, especially as Puerto Ricans are by now clustered in many cities other than New York. He is goading the society to come to terms with the "Rican" in its midst, arguing through puns and ironic challenges that he will not be an American until he can say "Am-e-Rican" ("I'm a Rican") and be proud of it. He even diagnoses, in similar playful terms, the problem of assimilation. "assimilated?" he begins one poem, "que assimilated, brother, yo soy asimilao," and ends with a confident reference to the Black base of Puerto Rican popular culture, "delen gracias a los prietos / que cambiaron asimilado al popular asimilao" (1985: 54).

And in reaching across the United States, not assimilating but growing together with neighboring and concordant cultures, how could the Nuyorican poet fail to embrace the Chicano? Getting to Chicago, Houston, and Los Angeles, Laviera surely sensed what his characters felt during their stay in New York. Chicanos and Nuyoricans, concentrated at opposite ends of the country, branching out in different cultural directions, still exemplify a close cultural affinity.

Listen to Laviera, the Nuyorican, rapping to his Chicano brothers. Here again, in "vaya carnal," it is the poet affirming a new language mix, "Chicano-riqueño," and at the same time forging those deeper cultural links that unite Mexicans and Puerto Ricans beneath the "Hispanic" surface:

sabes pinche, que me visto
estilo zoot suit marca de
pachuco royal chicano air
force montoyado en rojo
azul verde marrón nuevo
callejero chicano carnales
eseándome como si el ése ése
echón que se lanza en las
avenidas del inglés con
treinta millones de batos
locos hablando en secreto
con el chale-ese-no-la chingues
vacilón a los gringos americanos,
¿sabes?, simón, el sonido del este
el vaya, clave, por la maceta
que forma parte de un fuerte
lingüismo, raza, pana, borinquen,
azteca, macho, hombre, pulmones
de taíno, de indios, somos
chicano-riqueños, que curado.
simón, qué quemada mi pana,
la esperanza de un futuro
totalmente nuestro,
tú sabes, tú hueles,
el sabor, el fervor del
vaya, carnal. (1981: 59)

That *Journal of Ethnic Studies* (Flores 1985) article, in turn, got Laviera going again, and he then extended on the "asimilao" poem with a new one, which he paired with "asimilao" in his thinking: "melao." Here he carried the reflections of "asimilao" about cultural changes within the United States into the international arena, by capturing the dynamic relation between working-class Black expression on the Island and that in the U.S. setting. What a dynamic, lively few lines. I remember how he would read that one publicly, enunciating and voicing slowly and carefully to bring out the full impact of his dramatic narration of changing Afro-Puerto Rican language over three generations of emigrant life: Melao, Melao's son

Melaito, and then Melaito's son. When he finished his recital there would be this amazing silence, a loud silence, because you could almost hear people thinking and letting the story sink in emotionally.

Aside from his prophetic sense of the complexities of diasporic cultural identities, what I found unique about Laviera's contribution was his emphasis on race and blackness, the distinctive perspective of the Afro-Puerto Rican in the United States and his relation to African Americans. I would talk this up a lot with him, and he was always receptive; it's clear that he dedicated "tito madera smith" to me because of my harping on this cultural convergence going on before our very eyes in the Nueva York environment. As time went by through the 1990s and 2000s, and my thinking turned increasingly toward the subjects of "diaspora" and "Afrolatinidad," that dimension of Laviera's writing took on increasing significance. So that finally, when in 2009 I was asked to say some words of tribute to Laviera at an event in his honor at the University of Texas Pan American in McAllen, Texas, I drafted up my third article on him, which I have incorporated into this essay. Its focus on Black Spanglish first dawned on me after I looked at his last poetry book, *Mixturao*, and how the final –ao was such a signature usage in Laviera's work throughout. I actually counted, and found a huge number of that word-ending in all of his books, and of course I always had in mind the way he talks, just like so many of the other Afro-Latinas/os I knew. Laviera took ownership of the –ao as a symbolic trademark, as it were, indicative of his Afro-diasporic identity. I got so immersed in this idea that when I was writing up that presentation I almost started calling him "Ta'o"! But not quite! Tato... is Tato!

Laviera calls his last book *Mixturao*. It makes me think of other lively words, like *asopao*, or *encebollao*, or *cansao*, or *jabao*, or some of Laviera's own poem titles like "asimilao," "craqueao," and "melao." That final –ao puts a charge into any word, old or new, everyday or highfalutin, a resonance of street, of blackness, and *afrocaribeñismo*. In Laviera's case, we are talking about Afro-Spanglish, the ultimate *mixturao*.

So what is with this ubiquitous –ao in Laviera's language? Building on Fernando Ortiz's influential theory of transculturation, Stephanie Alvarez regards it as "the linguistic symbol for not only resistance to acculturation, but also creative neoculturation. Both reside in the African component of Puerto Rican culture, on the Island and in the metropolis" (2006: 35). That is, the –ao not only expresses the intense mixing and fusing of the many ancestral strains of Caribbean cultural history but is also evidence of the neologistic, inventive creativity arising from that momentous process. As Alvarez reminds us, the idea of neoculturation indicates that the process involves not only mixing, and "acquiring another culture" (acculturation), as well as the "loss or uprooting of a previous culture" ("deculturation"), but the "creation of new cultural phenomena." Ortiz explains that, analogously to the reproduction of individuals, "the offspring always has something of both parents but is always different from each of them" (1995: 102–3). In other words, the –ao is not about just taking on another culture (Spanish in this case) but resisting it, and not about losing a previous culture (the African), but giving poetic stature to something new, the Afro-Caribbean Spanish vernacular.

Beyond that "original," neo-African transculturation or creolization, in Laviera's case we are also concerned with the new, transnational version of that process as implied in the use of Spanglish. –ao thus resonates to some extent with English, "ow," as perhaps most suggestively deployed in contemporary Latino letters in the title and protagonist of Junot Díaz' prize-winning novel *The Brief Wondrous Life of Oscar Wao* (2007). This bold allusion to Oscar Wilde is actually what might be called an "Afro-Spanglish" usage; Díaz is "wowing" us with an Afro-Spanish take-off on the very English yet defiantly off-beat Wilde. Retaining the intended chuckle, the inverse would be, "Nos está wildeando." Laviera himself refers to this re-semanticizing tactic as "afro-españolisao"; in the refrain of his homage poem to Palés Matos he says playfully (and "–ao-fully") of that renowned pioneer of Africanism in Puerto Rican poetry, "También era grifo africano guillao de castellano" (Laviera 1981: 66–7).

The –ao is everywhere in Laviera's work, by preliminary count surely the most frequent stylistic occurrence in all of his writing, not to mention his speech. Just to mention those I gathered in compiling a provisional concordance, and to evoke the remarkable colorfulness and wit so unmistakable about his voice, here are a few that I came up with: *eslembao, tumbao, colao, disgustao, babalao, encarcelao, agallao, pescao, bacalao, controlao, craqueao, enchulao, pasao, pasteurizao, homogenizao*. Even his own nickname, Tato, comes under the playful neocultural sway: though he never uses "Tao," at one point, in the poem "puertorriqueña," he toys with the literal meaning of the name: "'tá tó'", in other words, in the longer, non-transculturated form, "está todo" (1985: 67).

Laviera offers his most extended rationale for this phonological leitmotiv in the programmatic poem "asimilao." Here the anatomy of that single word shows up the multiple levels of creative resistance to the English "assimilated," and by obvious extension the whole ideology of assimilation that hounds the Nuyorican as a hybrid identity vis-à-vis both the American English and the white, middle-class Spanish usages. It starts with the English "assimilated," but immediately interrupts its weight and meaning first with a question mark, then with the colloquial "brother," and then by re-signifying the very process by answering in the colloquial Afro-Spanish, including the – ao: "yo soy asimilao." Some cultural change is happening to me, no doubt, but rather than acculturation it is neoculturation. The diagnosis runs very deep, and concludes with the idea that the very word "asimilao" is evidence of non-assimilation: "the sound LAO was too black / for LATED, LAO could not be / translated, assimilated, / no, asimilao, melao, / it became a black/ Spanish word..." (Laviera 1985: 54).

And then comes the next level or dimension of the neoculturalism: "asimilao" signals not only resistance against assimilation to English, that is, American English as used in mainstream social science with its melting-pot wish dreams, but against "standard," academically sanctioned Spanish as well and the privileged whiteness of which it is an expression. Square in the middle of the poem, and following "it became a black / Spanish word," there is a crucial turn, indicated by "but": "but / we do have asimilados / perfumados..." (1985: 54). "Asimilao" is thus a resistance against both the English word, "assimilated," and against the "correct," standard usage in Spanish, the past participle "asimilado." Along with the national/ethnic resistance there is also the class and cultural—read racial— thrust of the neocultural usage: those who use, and exemplify, the word "asimilado" are identified as "perfumados," a clear reference to social privilege and the elitist attitudes that go along with that status. Creating the Black Spanish identity, as epitomized in this one word, thus involves standing up to both the non- (or anti-) Spanish, and the non- (and anti-) Black. In both senses, it is the vernacular, "popular" experience that is being heralded. The "AO / de la palabra / principal," as pronounced at the end of the poem, rejects assimilation, that is, acculturation, in both directions, and in both senses it is Black people, "los prietos," who are to be thanked: "dénles gracias a los prietos / que cambiaron asimilado al popular asimilao" ["thank the blacks, who changed asimilado to the popular asimilao"] (1985: 54).

That "change" from "asimilado" to "asimilao" and more generally that all-powerful –ao usage, is referred to in technical linguistic terms as the "weakening of the intervocalic /d/." It is a widely recognized phenomenon in the annals of Spanish phonological research and analysis, and is sometimes attributed, at least in part and to some extent, to African influence on the Spanish language since the Middle Ages. In his exhaustive study, *A History of Afro-Hispanic Language* (2008), and prior to that in the chapter "The African Connection" of his widely used *Latin American Spanish* (1994), eminent scholar John Lipski establishes the –ao as one of the most common signs of Africanism within Spanish language history, though he is careful to acknowledge that the phenomenon is highly variable, and is more accurately seen as part of the broader one of weakening or deletion of syllable-final or word-final consonants, which has little or nothing necessarily to do with language contact. Scholarly work on the subject also tends to focus on the Spanish of the Americas, and especially the Andalusian influence on those variants, with much attention going to Caribbean Spanish, where that influence is paramount (Noll 2005: 96–110; Navarro Tomás 1950: 101–2; de Granda 1996: 94–108). It is important to emphasize the further insight that, whatever the degree of Africanism, or Andalucianism, in this particular linguistic development, and however ubiquitous and variable it may be, there seems to be strong consensus that it is most frequent in the vernacular, in what are sometimes referred to as "las capas más populares." Once again, in Laviera's terms, "cambiaron asimilado al popular asimilao."

Two further related points are pertinent to the relation between the technical scholarly discussion of –ao and its occurrence in Laviera's poetry. One is that the shift from -ado to –ao in Spanish is actually a further development of the "weakening" of /t/ to /d/ in the vernacularization of Latin to Spanish; -atus gradually became –ado. This is of special interest in the Spanglish re-creolizing process, as is evident even in "asimilao," where we move from "assimilated" to "asimilado" to "asimilao," that is, from English to standard Spanish to vernacular Spanish. Secondly, there are degrees of weakening or softening of the intervocalic /d/, from a more softly pronounced d to a /th/ (or often /r/) to a total deletion, or what is called phonetic zero. This is evident even orthographically, with –ao sometimes rendered –a'o so as to register that something is being occluded. Laviera's poetics, as articulated in "asimilao," seems to settle for nothing less than phonetic zero, the total suppression of that oppressive /d/. And let us not forget that the feminine version of this deletion is even more radical, involving as it does the elimination of both the /d/ and the final a, or the compression of the two a's into one highly accented one, as in, say, "asimilá," or even "ná" for "nada."

In less technical but perhaps more suggestive terms, Laviera's deployment of the –ao is referred to as "eye dialect." It is basically an orthographic practice, a handy definition being "the use of non-standard spellings (spellings considered incorrect) to create the effect of a dialectal, foreign, or uneducated speaker."[1] Generally, and especially among linguistic scholars, the practice of eye dialect and even the word itself tend to be discredited and frowned upon. The most common argument is that writing phonetically tends to generate or reinforce stereotypes and prejudice toward people considered less educated; and, indeed, dialect writing has historically been used to mock poor people, and most notably people of African descent. But there are also more complex reasons, as explained by linguistics professor Ricardo Otheguy in refreshingly articulate terms: "I find dialect-writing to be a little silly. Writing things like *wannacum* instead of *want to come* reveals that the writer thinks that *want to come* is actually meant to reproduce the way you say it, and since it obviously fails, an improvement is needed in the form of eye dialect. That is, eye dialect rests fundamentally in a misunderstanding. It supposes that conventional writing is somehow meant to represent pronunciation, and since it does not, a better, more phonetic writing is required, especially if it is meant to characterize the talk of people whose speech contains pronunciation features not sanctioned by the society. But conventional writing does not represent anybody's pronunciation, not even that of anchor men on their best linguistic behavior on TV, so one hardly needs to invent new writing to fit popular speech. Conventional writing never represents anybody's pronunciation in any language (even in Spanish or German), and the improvement wrought by eye dialect is illusory. It too fails to represent pronunciation."[2]

Interestingly, though, Otheguy is quick to recognize that his reaction to the term eye dialect is "unfortunately a purely technical one." He dismisses his own argument, so well put and well taken, as "deformación profesional, that is, the failure of the technician, in this case the linguist, to see the joy to the writer and the reader, and all in all it is therefore a wonderful thing from the literary and human standpoint, silly or not from the professional's point of view." In literary terms, then, which is how we need to appreciate Laviera, the use of eye dialect can be a powerful technique, and as he shows so well with his deployment of –ao, may carry an arsenal of cultural and political tools with which to counteract the authority of Eurocentric, elitist, and racist distortion. As far back as 1971 there was already a serious study, "Eye dialect as a literary device," and over the years an entire subfield of literary history and interpretation has flourished, amidst raging debates, dedicated to dialect writing (Browde 1971; Ives 1971).[3]

Beyond the literary resource that eye dialect may offer writers and readers, there is also the great "joy" and creative significance that it implies at a human level, which is also crucial to a full appreciation of Laviera. As linguistics scholar Ana Celia Zentella recognizes, "Eye dialect provides great insight into folk rendering of dialect, since it is the only way we have, in old texts, of knowing how things were pronounced."[4] As Zentella would be the first to acknowledge, and as her own research demonstrates so well, it is not only "old texts" to which this recovery effort needs to be applied, but in the validation of contemporary phonetic practices as well, as part of a larger community affirmation. The struggle to ascertain and uphold social identities among marginalized and stigmatized communities takes precedence over the rules and laws established by linguistic technicians, a point made with great clarity and magnanimity by linguistic expert Otheguy when he says,

> ...poets and laymen in general are entitled to identify something in their language as especially unique and the marker of a felt identity, even if it is not unique to them at all. So, for example, many Caribbean peoples identify syllable- or word-final /s/ weakening as "really" Caribbean, when it is in fact a very widespread phenomenon in many parts of Spain and the Americas. So if Tato, or someone studying his work, identifies the –ao from –ado as really significant for the poet or the critic in some way, and can spin a meaningful story from it, who is the linguistic technician to spoil the party?[5]

Laviera's –ao, then, is a linguistic validation of the notion that Puerto Rican, Nuyorican, and Afro-Latino communities are transgressors as regards to hierarchically established codes of value and authority. Laviera's poetics of eye-dialect is at the same time a transnational politics of intercultural sharing and human solidarity of the kind necessary for hemispheric change in the Americas. The opening stanzas of "Mixturao," the title poem of his new volume, give voice to that larger political and human agenda of the defiant, signature –ao:

> we-who engage in
> western hemispheric
> continental Spanish majority
> communally sharing linguistics
> in humanistic proportions
>
> we-who integrate
> urban America
> simmering each other's slangs
> indigenous nativizing
> our tongues' cruising accents
> who are you, English,
> telling me, "Speak only English
> or die" (2008a: 29)

NOTES

[1] See Wikipedia under "eye dialect" (http://en.wikipedia.org/wiki/Eye_dialect/).
[2] Ricardo Otheguy, personal email communication, 4 December 2008.
[3] Also helpful is Cohen Minnick (2004: 28–41).
[4] Ana Celia Zentella, personal correspondence, 9 December 2008.
[5] Ricardo Otheguy, personal email correspondence, 9 December 2008.

45

Espanglish: Laviera's el nideaquínideallá Language in Fourteen Movements

EDRIK LÓPEZ

A "Spanglish text" or a text in *espanglish*, as Tato Laviera would say, is a hybrid, mosaic-patterned text about the experience of speaking a language that does not belong here, but is arriving, and is in the process of becoming a language. The present article places in a conceptual relationship Laviera's poetry with two major texts on "writing subjects:" Gloria Anzaldúa's *Borderlands/La Frontera* (1987) and Roland Barthes' *Pleasure of the Text* (1975). It argues that while both Anzaldúa and Barthes are concerned with the body, they differ in the way that the body moves in and out, or works itself through language and writing. I take my lead from Laviera's approach to writing Spanglish and how the very "situatedness" of his body along racial, national and linguistic edges produces writing that leads away from any particular stricture on theorizing in scholarship. In this article, body-memories of language are pressed against theories of language. The paper examines other writers like Zora Neal Hurston and Sandra Cisneros. I argue that a more corporal and vital form of speaking about the body and theorizing about language formation is found in the poetry of Laviera than his academic theoretician counterparts. The body resists languaging. This article, in fourteen diverse sections, attempts to present various forms of the Spanglish Laviera points us toward while honoring the very language-recalcitrant ethos of its manifestation.

1

Tato Laviera tells the reader that a text in spanglish is about kinks: the knot before speaking, as sound attempts to become a sign: the stutters and struggles to affirm itself as language, the "*¡ay, virgen yo no sé hablar!*" of "my graduation speech."

i think in spanish
i write in english

i want to go back to puerto rico,
but i wonder if my kink could live
in ponce, mayagüez and carolina
//
si me dicen barranquitas, yo reply,
"¿con qué se come eso?"
si me dicen caviar, i digo,
"a new pair of converse sneakers."
ahí supe que estoy jodío
ahí supe que estamos jodíos
english or spanish
spanish or english
spanenglish
now, dig this:
hablo lo inglés matao
hablo lo español matao
no sé leer ninguno bien

so it is, spanglish to matao
what i digo
    ¡ay, virgen, yo no sé hablar! (1979: 7)

Laviera ends the poem stating he does not know how to speak, but speak the poem does, and seamlessly. Laviera teaches us that the paradox of the Spanglish text is that it speaks about not being able to speak. A condition also described by Gustavo Pérez Firmat in "Dedication," "...how to explain to you / that I / don't belong to English / though I belong nowhere else..." (1995: 3). It attempts to signify a phonetic, syntactic, and morphological impossibility, and in the process, making such impossibility not only possible, but possible in the highest form of speaking in the West: literary writing. What i digo: Spanglish is writing from the knot, the "I don't know how to speak" of two languages.

2

Chicana writer Sandra Cisneros reveals such possibilities in her novel *Caramelo*:

> Every night the blankets and pillows are brought out from the closet and my bed made. Father's glow-in-the-dark travel alarm clock watches over me from its crocodile box. Before I close my eyes, Father winds it and places it nearby so I won't be afraid.
> Father makes the same joke he always makes at bedtime. — *¿Qué tienes? ¿Sueño o sleepy?*
> —*Es que tengo sleepy*. I have sleepy, *Father*. (2002: 52)

Cisneros here pens one of the most prevalent forms of the Spanglish text, the seemingly simple switch between the English and Spanish language. Linguists refer to it as code-switching, one of a number of language contact-induced changes. Spanglish texts purposefully smooth this transition. On many occasions, they go easy on the tongue, preceding the switch with consonants or vowels in English that have a homonymic relationship in Spanish. The rounded, back, mid-open /o/ vowel glides naturally to the voiceless fricative /s/. All it takes is to lift the tongue to the hard palate and displace the same air being used. No awkward stop, no new breath: *o sleepy*.

In *Caramelo*, the family is in Mexico City, and they are hosting a party for Father's birthday. It is late at night, and Celaya is tired. The question the Father asks is specious and a bit absurd. It is play—between father and daughter—between languages. There is no real choice, no alternative, no denotative difference in the question's choices: *sueño o* sleepy. There is, however, a connotative difference: a choice of the signifier. The mark on the page and the voice of the father create a brief moment of aporia, "the same joke he always makes." The "o" signals the arbitrary moment in the choice between proper languages: the Spanglish text lacks any justifiable reason to choose between the two. *¡Ay, virgen, yo no sé hablar!*

Yet despite the signaled paralysis, both Laviera and Cisneros do speak. The text grants the circle of signification to complete its journey: sometimes traveling twice over—all that translation that is made in Spanglish texts—a glaring signal of insecurity. For Spanglish texts the *no sé* is not about the page itself, whereas *I can't speak* is something more corporeal.

3

After I moved to Florida from Puerto Rico in 1988, I remember only a few moments of angst related to speaking. "Él no puede hablar español. Él habla Spanglish," my mother said with a chuckle to one of the few Spanish speakers in the area, the first time I heard that word. I chuckled, too. Spanglish—a word conceived in paradox—is a funny word. Its very sound is a metonym for the way the tongue splits at the intersection between the two syllables, especially if you say it like my mother did, with Spanish phonemes: /es-pan-glish/. In fact, one of the first Puerto Rican stories written in all-out Spanglish, entitled "Pollito Chicken" (1981), makes fun of this very language. Although the author, island Puerto Rican Ana Lydia Vega, has since renounced her story, "Pollito Chicken" mocks the speech of diasporic Puerto Ricans who have left the island and have developed in her mind an unusual hybrid:

> Lo que la decidió fue el breathtaking poster de Fomento que vio en la travel agency del lobby de su building. El breathtaking poster mentado representaba una pareja de beautiful people holding hands en el funicular del Hotel Conquistador. Los beautiful people se veían tan deliriously happy y el mar tan strikingly blue y la puesta del sol—no olvidemos la puesta de sol a la Wintson-tastes-good—la puesta de sol tan shocking pink en la distancia . . .". (1981: 75)

Since I was born in Puerto Rico, I immediately recognized the reference of "Pollito Chicken" as the song by the same name that kids in Puerto Rico—I was one of them—were made to sing to learn the English translation for words we may encounter in our Free Associated State Puerto Rican lives. The song is very short and very catchy: *Pollito chicken, gallina hen, lápiz pencil, y pluma pen, ventana window, piso floor, maestra teacher, y puerta door.* Here a first memory of language in Puerto Rico: Spanglish developed in us long before we arrived in the States.

4

A calque, in its linguistic definition, is a type of "error" committed by a speaker of a second-language. As Sarah Thomason defines it in *Language Contact*, "a calque is a type of interference in which word or sentence structure is transferred without actual morphemes; sometimes called a loan translation. A calque is typically a morpheme-by-morpheme translation of a word from another language, as in German *über-setzen* 'translate' (literally 'across-set' from Latin *trans-*'across' *-lat-* 'carry'") (2001: 260).

For example, if in Spanish, in Puerto Rico, I have a "dolor de cabeza," I say in English, in the United States, that I have a "pain of head." A calque is an ultraliteral translation. It is too much algebra: taking that X = Y in the corresponding sentential order. Calquing is an interference feature in a subject's contact with what is usually a non-native language. At a linguistic level it involves "the importation of material and/or structures from one language into another . . . all interference is contact-induced change" (Thomason 2001: 267). The interference in the phrase "pain of the head" is a semantic interference, one dealing with the second degree (figurative level) of the English language, but it is not a structural interference—one that deals with the actual *grammar* of the language itself. Pain of head is understood, but not in the same way as a headache. Sandra Cisneros uses numerous calques in *Caramelo*.

> 1) Everyone hot and sticky and in a bad mood, hair stiff from riding with the windows open, the backs of the knees sweaty, a little circle of spit next to where my head fell asleep; "good lucky" Father thought to sew beach towel slipcovers for our new car. (2001: 17)
> 2) —What's the matter, Lala? ¿Estás "deprimed"? Father says, chuckling.
> It's an old joke, one he never gets tired of, changing a Spanish word into English, or the other way round, just to be a wise guy.
> I think to myself, *Yes, I'm* deprimida. *Who wouldn't be depressed in this family?* But I don't say this. (2001: 238)

In linguistics, calquing is an intriguing phenomenon because calquing requires a speaker who is not completely foreign to the target language, meaning that the calquing speaker is not a complete outsider. Nevertheless, the use of a calque exposes the degree to which the speaker is still "outside" the language. The speaker has denotative knowledge of the language; however, the speaker lacks connotative knowledge. The speaker lacks figurative speech. That is why "pain of the head" *sounds weird* to an English-only speaker, but not to those who also speak Spanish. The phrase does not have a dominantly understood connotation in the English language like "headache" does. In other words, what the calquing speaker lacks is a proper understanding of the metaphoric languages in English. *Calquing is the language of a speaker whose speech is too literal.* The real tongue creeping into language, disallowing metaphor: a language that has not left the body. Coincidentally, Gayatri Spivak once wrote that deconstruction is taking language as literally as one can. As she says in *Outside in the Teaching Machine*, "[I've] learned the extreme importance of an absolutely literal-minded reading: To follow the logic of the rhetoric—the tropology—wherever it might lead" (1993: 21).

However, there is a turn, a twist on calques, being done by Sandra Cisneros in the novel. The calquing speaker is actually "more inside" English than the monolingual. Without Spanish, "good lucky": *buena suerte*; "deprimed": deprimida (depressed); and "rule": *regla* (period), remain literal and lose their figurative meaning—and therefore, its *literary* meaning in English. The play with calques in *Caramelo* accomplishes a way to "slip" Spanish into English itself. In other words, the narrator's calques are subversive ways—in both senses of the term—to write "in English" Spanish phrases. It is a type of sub-alterity, where in the context of monolingual hegemony, the speaker submits to the monolingual at face value, by reproducing for the monolingual a false echo.

W.E.B. Du Bois and Anzaldúa have both referred to this form of sub-alterity as double or mestiza consciousness—the idea that marginalized people in colonial contacts cannot survive without speaking two languages at once. Through calques, Spanglish texts create a language of resistance. They move the space designated by linguists to calques, as error, and make the calquing speaker have a more intimate knowledge of the English language than the monolingual person. Spanglish texts accomplish a way to signal a new *choteo/* As in other practices by subaltern communities like the African-American signifyin' or the Cuban *guachafita*, Laviera and Cisnero's Spanglish texts show us a way to pretend to submit and speak only one language, literally speaking, of course.

5

All Spanglish texts are untranslatable. Sure, one could, in theory, inverse the Spanglish text to where any English is Spanish and vice versa. Turn Spanglish into *Espanglés*. Make "Pollito Chicken" into "Chicken Pollito" and have kindergarten kids in the United States sing every morning before naptime. Possible, if only the global order, the colonialism that defines the relation between English and Spanish—that tension that the spaces where Spanglish is spoken signifies—were only so easily reversible. For if you translate Spanglish texts, it is merely one calque after another. Therefore, the connotative colonial relationship is the untranslatable in both Cisneros and Laviera's Spanglish. As Laviera writes in *Mixturao*:

> **we-who** are at peace in continental
> inter-mixtures mutualities
> do hereby challenge
> united states isolationism
> anti-immigrant mono-lingual
> constitutional bullets
> declarations telling us to
> "speak only english or die"
> "love it or leave it"
> spelling big stick carcass
> translations universally excluded
> multi-lingual multi-cultural
> expressions "need not to apply"
> who are you, English,
> telling me, "Speak only English
> or die." (2008a: 30)

> which u.s. ethnic slang do you speak? (2008a: 26)

The struggle of Spanglish is not that it cannot speak but that it acts as a contrapuntal to the discourse that says *it should not* speak. By speaking, it refuses the historical violence positioning English as sole mediator of reality in the United States. The problem with the Spanglish text is not one with the signified—it is irrelevant that you are tired and need a nap—the problem is with the signifier; it is a phonetic problem: choose the wrong phoneme, and you may reveal yourself and be labeled a pseudo-ethnicity from one side of the border to being considered ignorant from the other. At its base, the problem with the Spanglish text is a problem with the signifier of the signifier. The tongue.

By speaking, Spanglish texts enact sacrilege: the equal, shared space in syntax moving toward a return as Corky Gonzales affirms in the canonical and epic Chicano/a poem "I am Joaquín," "I am the masses of my people and

I refuse to be absorbed. I am Joaquín" (1997: 266). Laviera, in what can be described as a Nuyorican epic poem, "jesús papote," reveals a similar vision:

> we, nosostros, respectful of spanish-english forms
> . . .
> we, nosotros, inside triangle of contradictions
> . . .
> We, nosotros, conceiving english newer visions
> . . .
> we, nosotros, oral poets transcending two european forms
> spanish dominance when spanish was strong
> english dominance when english was strong
> we digested both we absorbed the pregnancies (1981: 19–20)

As Laviera demonstrates, Spanglish has never been about the words themselves, but the shared space between the words. Spanglish is the juxtaposition of Spanish with English. Spanglish is the collision. The problem is what the shared space signifies to the regime of monolingualism: *there is another phonetic presence*. The problem with Spanglish is that it reveals the presence of another speaker, another body. It signals the shared space between different racialized bodies, whose historical colonial structure is replicated in language itself. Spanglish is a sign to language, culture and nation in the United States about the enduring presence of its historically denied colonial migrant. Laviera's poetry is a frenetic sound revealing through art the daily desire to be heard:

> bomba: puerto rican history for always, national pride
> bomba: cadera beats, afternoon heat, sunday beach:
> bomba: we all came in, negritos bien lindos:
> bomba: center space, intact beauty, rhythmic pride: (1981: 68)

6

If we were swapping stories today, I'd have mentioned the news report that the telephone company Sprint, in its billing letter in Spanish, threatens customers with phone cutoff unless their check is received by the end of the month. According to the news report, the Anti-Defamation League and the National Council of La Raza have filed complaints. Why? Because the billing letter in English is somewhat differently worded: "As a customer you are Sprint's number one priority. We . . . look forward to serving your communication needs for many years to come."

And, if the officer had more time, we might have arrived at an understanding that language, especially English, has been used as a racial weapon in immigration.'
. . . a Texas judge ordered the mother of a five-year-old to stop speaking in Spanish to her child. Judge Samuel Kiser reminded the mother that her daughter was a "full-blooded American." "Now, get this straight. You start speaking English to this child because if she doesn't do good in school, then I can remove her because it's not in her best interest to be ignorant. The child will only hear English." (Kumar 2000: 32)

7

Although the notion that bilingualism is psychologically harmful is scientifically unjustified, many people, including some scholars, still argue that multilingualism is a social handicap. One consequence of the 'melting pot' tradition in the United States is a widespread belief that immigrants must abandon their ethnic-heritage languages promptly and shift to English in order to become true Americans. This belief is held by many recent immigrants as well as by the offspring and descendants of immigrants, and it is also aimed at nonimmigrant nonnative English speakers, Native Americans, as well as (in particular) French and Creole speakers in Louisiana and Spanish speakers in the Southwest. Sometimes the belief has been elevated to public policy. Early in the twentieth century, for instance, a government policy of assimilating Native Americans to Anglo culture included vigorous—and largely successful—efforts to force them to abandon their native languages in favor of English; and the modern "'Official English'" movement in the United States has led to the adoption of English as the official language in over twenty states, an approach usually accompanied by efforts to eliminate bilingual education programs so as to encourage monolingualism in English. (Thomason 2001: 34)

8

In the great game of the powers of speech, we also play prisoner's base: one language has only temporary rights over another; all it takes is for a third language to appear from the ranks of the assailant to be forced to retreat: in the conflict of rhetorics, the victory never goes to any but the *third language*. (Barthes 1975: 50)

9

As a mode of writing, the Spanglish text does not escape the body. In *Tongue Ties* (2003), after dividing language into three forms—*lenguas, idiomas,* and *lenguaje*—Gustavo Pérez Firmat indirectly makes this case: "A tongue is language incarnate, as body part, an organ rather than a faculty. By calling our language a tongue, we highlight our bond to it, which is why we use possessives with lengua more often than with *lenguajes.... Lenguajes* can be native and *idiomas* can be national or regional, but only a lengua can be familial" (2003: 14). Put in such a manner then, the Spanglish text is a mode of writing that links ethnicity and race (the body) with language. It signals a resistance to language as a system to which you give your body: "If a *lengua* is corporal and *idioma* is locative, *lenguaje* is language detached from both person and place; that is, language as structure, as an abstract and rational system, somewhat like Saussure's *langue*" (Pérez Firmat 2003: 18). The Spanglish text is a lengua, a tongue, refusing to ignore the presence of the body in the act of writing the orality of a locale. Laviera phrases it in his poem, "spanglish," as "two dominant languages / continentally abrazándose" (2008a: 26). In doing so, text becomes the inverse of linguistics: it is bringing language to the body and not the body to Language. As Laviera shows us through his invocation of Langston Hughes, the Spanglish text is the act of not submitting the tongue for the structure.

he claims he can walk into east harlem
apartment where langston hughes gives
spanglish classes for newly-arrived
immigrants seeking a bolitero-numbers
career and part-time vendors of cuchi-
fritters sunday afternoon in central
park, do you know him? (1981: 24)

10

I remember being caught speaking Spanish at recess—that was good for three licks on the knuckles with a sharp ruler. I remember being sent to the corner of the classroom for "talking back" to the Anglo teacher when all I was trying to do was tell her how to pronounce my name. "If you want to be American, speak 'American.' If you don't like it, go back to Mexico where you belong."

"I want you to speak English. *Pa' hallar buen trabajo tienes que saber hablar el inglés bien. Qué vale toda tu educación si todavía hablas inglés con un 'accent,'*" my mother would say, mortified that I spoke English like a Mexican. At Pan American University, I, and all Chicano students were required to take two speech classes. Their purpose: to get rid of our accents.

Attacks on one's form of expression with the intent to censor are a violation of the First Amendment. El Anglo con cara de inocente nos arrancó la lengua. Wild tongues can't be tamed, they can only be cut out. (Anzaldúa 1987: 53–4).

11

NATIVIZATION. The phonological adaptation of a borrowed word to fit receiving-language structure. For instance, the name of the famous German composer Bach is often nativized by English speakers, with a velar stop /k/ replacing the German velar fricative /x/; other English speakers, often (but not always) those who know some German, retain the German fricative. (Thomason 2001: 272)

RENATIVIZATION. The phonological adaptation of a stolen word to fit the colonially displaced language structure. For instance, the name of the sea-side town of San Pedro, California, is often renativized by crazy, militant, probably postcolonial Latina/o speakers, with a short frontal vowel /e/ replacing the American long frontal /i:/. The actual natural English nativization of the Spanish name Pedro should not replace the vowel /e/, instead, English speakers normally aspirate the /e/: Pehdrou. The way it is now—Piiidrou—is something else: it is an intentional, phonological distancing of the word from its Spanish signifier.

This movement across texts is the very flow of Spanglish. This movement is a *perpetual translation*, using the literal meaning of the term: "from one form to another." The "absolute flow of becoming," the idea that things are always in a perpetual process of change—*moving*—opposes a view of the world by which things are fixed, by which things are naturally in a level of "being"—being American, being human, English being language—by which things have *settled*. Spanglish being spoken by diverse communities within the United States, despite their presence over generations, signals to them that we have not quite fully arrived. That we are still in the becoming. That in still becoming, we are resisting. That we are still migrants, or as Laviera says,

> LA VIDA es un inglés frío
>   un español no preciso
>   un spanglish disparatero
>   una insegurida de
>   incendios automáticos. (1981: 33)

The problem for *them* is that you must not be in the process. You must be established, settled. Here or there. There is no room for the transition, for movement, for perpetual translation. "What we are suffering from," Anzaldúa wrote in *Borderlands/La Frontera*, "is an absolute despot duality that says we are able to be only one or the other" (1981: 97). Spanglish is neither English nor Spanish. It is on the border of the two, and because of this

> This is her home
>   this thin edge of
>   barbwire. (1981: 13)

The problem with the becoming is that *they* don't know which way it is going. In other words, in what direction of the border is your loyalty? Spanglish, the *nideaquínideallá* language refuses to settle, that exposes its very movement between established regimes. Spanglish is the refusal to disavow the very language of the migrant, of her traveling tongue, her nomadic speech and hidden flights. Yet, Spanglish is also letting go of the "homeland".

In the chapter entitled "Spic Spanish?" of *Caramelo*, Celaya tells us how her father use to say sardonically that "Spanish was the language to speak to God and English the language to talk to dogs" (Cisneros 2002: 208). If this is the case, what is Spanglish, then? It could be language at its most human state—for it reveals the transformative power we have over language and not the other way around. That we can exercise a freedom at the phoneme, but only if we understand that language is not settled, that language is a becoming that does not aim at a final state, which does not flow into being. Spanglish signifies the scary thought to them that English in the United States is changing; that English, *como la vida*, is far from settled.

12

> Perhaps, in part, this fear comes from the conscious or unconscious knowing that English, for instance, is notorious for having a huge number of loanwords—by some estimates up to 75% of its total vocabulary, mostly taken from French and Latin. A large portion of these loanwords flooded into the language some time after the Normans conquered England in 1066, bringing their French language along with them. (Thomason 2001: 10)

English itself was (and still is) a Spanglish text. Laviera knows this, so does Cisneros; so do all who live at the seams. Laviera's Spanglish texts are writings that reveal the very process of their becoming—their seams in the morphemes, their intertexts in the syntax, and their interlanguages in their phonetic switches. They are texts that do not suffer when they arrive at the knots in the attempt to trace language backwards to its etymology, but find a basic freedom in the way the process of transculturation has transformed the dominant language in the same movement of transforming the language dominated. They are texts that have given up the illusion that what they are doing is locating the place where history has settled and can be discovered and dug up. Spanglish texts undermine the idea that the writing of decolonization is a backward process through the mother tongue. Spanglish is home. Here. There is no Spanglish back there.

> For the Mexico-Texan he no gotta lan',
> He stomped on the neck on both sides of the Gran',
> The dam gringo lingo he cannot spik,
> It twisters the tong and it make you fill sick.
> A cit'zen of Texas they say that he ees,
> But then, why they call him the Mexican Grease?
> Soft talk and hard action, he can't understan',
> The Mexico-Texan he no gotta lan'.
> If he cross the reever, eet ees just as bad,
> On high poleeshed Spanish he break up his had,

American customs those people no like,
They hate that Miguel they should call him El Mike,
And Mexican-born, why they jeer and they hoot,
"Go back to the gringo! Go lick at hees boot!"
In Texas he's Johnny, in Mexico Juan,
But the Mexico-Texan he no gotta lan'. (Paredes 1991: 102)

13

"When I saw poetry written in Tex-Mex for the first time," Anzaldúa wrote in *Borderlands/La Frontera*, "a feeling of pure joy flashed through me. I felt like we really existed as a people" (1987: 59–60). In *Borderlands*, language is the *affect* of the body. "For only through the body," she wrote, "through the pulling of the flesh, can the human soul be transformed. And for images, words, stories to have this transformative power, they must arise from the human body—flesh and bone..." (1987: 75). All of these writers in Spanglish, Laviera, Cisneros, Paredes and Anzaldúa, do write a writing that is "close" to the body. *Text* truly signifies *tissue* to them as Anzaldúa's language puts it as an amalgamation of body cells organizing towards an organ towards a system towards an organism: the text itself, the body, "flesh and bone." The joy in reading Chicana/o literature for Anzaldúa is being able to see her body and language as text before her. That is the same flash of joy I and so many others experience in reading (and hearing) Tato Laviera.

> *"Deslenguadas. Somos del español deficiente.* We are your linguistic nightmare, your linguistic aberration, your linguistic mestisaje, the subject of your burla. Because we speak with tongues of fire we are culturally crucified. Racially, culturally and linguistically *somos huérfanos*—we speak an orphan tongue." Shame. Low estimation of self. In childhood we are told that our language is wrong. Repeated attacks on our native tongue diminish our sense of self. The attacks continue throughout our lives. Chicanas feel uncomfortable in talking Spanish to Latinas, afraid of censure. Their language was not outlawed in their countries. (Anzaldúa 1987: 58)

Writing is healing for Anzaldúa: from a body that has been split, from a mother tongue that has been cut off—by the nation, by patriarchy, and *by her own mother*. That is why she can write that:

...being a writer feels very much like being a Chicana, or being queer—a lot of squirming, coming up against all sorts of walls. Or its opposite: nothing defined or definite, a boundless, floating state of limbo where I kick my heels, brood, percolate, hibernate and wait for something to happen. Living in a state of psychic unrest, in a Borderland, is what makes poets write and artists create. (1987: 72-3)

Laviera certainly experienced this—a citizen-but-not-quite-one, marginalized racially and linguistically in both countries—and thus lived in a Borderland, too, and that is why he moves, too, in his writing toward what Anzaldúa calls the Coatlicue state: "duality in life, a synthesis of duality, and a third perspective—something more than mere duality or a synthesis of duality. Coatlicue depicts the contradictory. . . .she is a symbol of the fusion of opposites: the eagle and serpent, heaven and the underworld, life and death, mobility and immobility, beauty and horror" (1987: 46-7). Coatlicue allows Anzaldúa to perceive the third ground she inhabits: "*soy un amasamiento*, I am an act of kneading, of uniting and joining" (1987: 81). *Now*, the migrant can speak. The pleasure of the Spanglish text is first a pleasure of the kneading of two languages, two tongues into "un amasamiento". Or rather, as Anzaldúa puts it, it is the pleasure of having not a mother tongue but a "forked tongue" (1987: 55). "This almost finished product seems an assemblage, a montage, a beaded work..." (1987: 66). The joy is the transformation enacted in the text to Spanglish: from an orphan tongue to a third language. Laviera demonstrates this third language does not solely belong to his ethnic enclave, but exits in other communities as well. His poem "vaya carnal" is a song of recognition to his Chicano/a relations: "sabes, pinche, que me visto / estilo zoot suit marca de / pachuco royal chicano air" (1981: 59).

14

The third space, the *third language*, is the space and language of the becoming. So the third space is not Spanglish—it is *not Spanglish*—but what Spanglish represents: the perpetual movement of language and body. For Spanglish cannot aim for being, cannot envy the oppressor, but must let go and give room for other bodies and languages in similar relations to English, (even Englishes within English), for other bodies and languages in their own third space. The third language is language that is not stuck in the argument between two spaces, but that is aware of the perpetual movement of things that disrupt arguments based on settled speech, dead speech. That is why Spanglish is a text that has not become language. As soon as it becomes language, Spanglish is no longer Spanglish.

It follows, then, Spanglish is not a "deformed" way of speaking, nor is highly conceptual academic English the pinnacle of language. The Becoming undermines English as language-being one, particularly linguistic migrants, must achieve, and constantly evaluate their "arrival" in the United States against those here who have English in them, somehow. The little story of how "English" changed dramatically with the Norman invasion in 1066 and what Spanglish (and Tagolish and Japlish or Ukrainglish) point to is the very change of English occurring in front of us. When Tato Laviera writes that he speaks the inglés and español "matao" or killed Spanish and killed English, he is almost touching on the very idea of killing the *Being* of English as heard in the Nuyorican poet Pedro Pietri:

> A Rican lost in New York A Rican in New York lost A New York lost Rican. And the more you walked in the opposite direction of tropical dreams and urban ambitions the more difficult it became to talk in Spanish or English. So *Spanglish* came to the rescue and we became **Out of Focus Nuyoricans** which is the same as being and not being lost. We followed the *piragüero* all the way to the Brooklyn Bridge and jumped and landed on the bar stool of a members only club in *El Barrio* where we read *El Diario*. A train became *el train* a truck became *el truck* a sandwich became *un sanwiche de* ham and cheese *con aguacate* please and *por favor cojelo con* take it easy *porque se me apago la boila del building y no tengo esteem*. ("El Passport," Pedro Pietri, in Maldonado 2004)

Celia Cruz's iconic phrase succinctly captures the intricate relation of language and body in Latino/a writing. She would say in concerts and recordings to her English-speaking audiences, "forgive me but my Inglish is not berry good-looking." Although a joke on trans-language misspeaks, Cruz's phrase reinforces the link between body and speech in Latina/o communities. It's no coincidence that *lengua* is both *tongue* and *language*, and an English that is not very good-looking speaks to the way the body resists absorption in the languaging process. The insight given by Cruz and by Laviera is that the body is language—it does not reside solely in the head. Their bodies and their languages exist in concrete cityscapes and that tongue/lengua that is the paint of their poems, songs, and literature, is sometimes battered and bruised. The product of which is *el inglés matao* or *not bery good-looking*.

– II –
(RE)CREATING AND (RE)DEFINING HIS OWN SPACE(S)

Latinas Sing: Tato Laviera's Message for/About Women After Civil Rights Collapse

SUSAN M. CAMPBELL

Poet, Tato Laviera inherits a legacy of local poetic resistance from the Civil Rights-inspired Nuyorican tradition. Much of his work recounts daily life in the Puerto Rican enclaves of New York City and points out social problems in the community. Of interest here is how Laviera's poetry functions as a contestatory but non-revolutionary art form in the decade of the 1980s in terms of the position of women. Laviera's messages about Nuyorican issues of bilingualism, ethnicity, and crime within the New York context were published just as the civil rights movements that addressed those same issues were collapsing. Likewise, his messages about/for Nuyorican women were contemporary with a surge in mainstream middle-class feminism in the 1970s and very early 1980s, and the subsequent failure of the Equal Rights Amendment in 1982. These facts may provoke an initial analysis that, as a civil rights-inspired/inspiring poet, Laviera arrived as the (political) party was ending.

If, however, the focus is on multiracial feminist groups, which began in the 1970s but gained momentum in the 1980s, Laviera's published poetry goes hand in hand. In this way, his work points to a "new," growing movement, thus fulfilling Jesús Martín Barbero's (1993) description of pointing toward new means of struggle: "The 1982 defeat of the ERA did not signal a period of abeyance for multiracial feminism. In fact, multiracial feminism flourished in the 1980's, despite the country's turn to the Right" (Thompson 2002: 345). To cite Angela Davis, "1981, with the publication of *This Bridge Called My Back*, was the year when women of color had developed as a 'new political subject,' due to substantial work done in multiple arenas" (Thompson 2002: 344).[1] Multiracial feminism was indeed a new means of struggle at that time since its goals were wider in scope than those of male-dominated Civil Rights movements and those of Anglo/American feminism. Laviera's poems run parallel to the multiracial women's movement as a new way to effect social change. He seems to have been inspired by their struggle as they formed their alliances, worked with Anglo/American feminist groups, collaborated with male-dominated civil rights groups and formed their own parties. He doesn't predict their work but writes along with them.

Tato Laviera publishes his first collection of poetry in 1979, the year before the election of Ronald Reagan symbolized a growing tide of conservatism. The 1980s[2] is a period that saw the ebb of social changes achieved through civil rights movements. In general terms, the notion of social change in the decade of the 1980s shifted toward a notion of personal achievement, which was a mantra of the Republican Party at the time. The responsibilities for lack of achievement shifted in kind to fall more solidly on the shoulders of individuals rather than on the structure of society. Along with the growth of multiracial feminism, this difference in political circumstance, the change from the Carter to the Reagan administration gives Nuyorican poetry from the 1980s special meaning, a new reading that distinguishes it from other Nuyorican poetry written from the late 1960s through the 1970s. Laviera's first four published works span the 1980s, a decade of increasing conservatism. Twenty years after publishing his fourth book, Laviera publishes *Mixturao and Other Poems* in 2008 and brings some new perspectives to his poetic commitment to the Nuyorican community.

The qualities of marginal voice and oblique, contestatory perspective take on new meaning when faced with the lowered expectations of social movements' potential to create social change on the basis of racial identity during the 1980s. Laviera innovated the Nuyorican genre during this period. New conditions obviate a new reading. Once the material situation has changed, that is, the Civil Rights movements linked to Nuyorican poetry have disintegrated, how is it most useful to read this poetry? What becomes the new scope and mission of its production and reading?

The shift in the political paradigm beginning in the 1980s swept aside the leftist movements that had been powerful for two decades before. This paradigm coincided with the prevalence of postmodern thought in literary criticism. Surprisingly, neither this political shift nor the tendency toward postmodern criticism has had a significant effect on the way Nuyorican poetry has been analyzed compared to other genres of literature. Critical thought on Nuyorican poetry, from the 1960s through to the present day, tends to maintain a modernist,[3] socially oriented focus. Attention is paid to this literature's power to raise the consciousness of its target audience by contesting the negative images and definitions of Puerto Ricans found in the dominant culture's social and civic discourse. This continued modernist focus may be due to the fact that much of Nuyorican poetry itself has maintained its contestatory, anti-hegemonic qualities throughout its existence despite the decline of leftist movements with which it shared its origins.

What can be quite useful to characterize Nuyorican poetry in the 1980s is Jesús Martín Barbero's important and subtle distinction between a vision of literature that is separate from the real world and literature that engages the world directly. From this dichotomy, Martín Barbero renders something more complex. His approach offers a way to see literature that engages in social struggle after the modernist Civil Rights movements have collapsed. Barbero cites modernist scholars such as Theodor Adorno and Max Horkheimer (Martín Barbero 1993: 54), who view culture as a top-down phenomenon in which consumers must uncritically accept what is provided them. Adorno and Horkheimer also criticize a cultural approach to real world problems as an evasion of the real world milieu. Martín Barbero then describes the limits of modernist analyses that might no longer be applicable to the current global era and those of postmodernist approaches that too often disregard the political, real-world functions of literature. Finally he highlights a third option:

> something radically different occurs when culture points to new dimensions of social conflict, the formation of new socio-political actors around regional, religious, sexual and generational identities. (1993: 209)

In *Communication Culture and Hegemony: From the Media to Mediations* (1993), Martín Barbero criticizes many Marxist literary theorists for ignoring the role of the receiver of a cultural product—the reader/listener in the case of poetry. While Martín Barbero supports the Marxist view of the manipulative quality of media, he problematizes this concept by adding that the receiver also creates his/her own conclusions.

In some of Laviera's poems about gender and romantic relationships, the poet fulfills what Martín Barbero would term "pointing toward a new means of struggle," that is, he points to an innovation in Nuyorican activism. Since Laviera also works as a playwright,[4] some of his poems develop as preliminary sketches of dramatic personae that are later incorporated into theatrical pieces. Laviera claims that he attempts to accomplish this in many of his poems about or through the perspectives of women (Campbell 2002).

An example of the myriad poems of this type is the triumphant lyric entitled "a message to our unwed women" (Laviera 1979), in which Laviera imitates the voice of a young Puerto Rican woman who is determined to allow her pregnancy to come to term despite the critical voices that surround her. Another is the implicitly critical portrayal of "juana bochisme" (Laviera 1981), a neighborhood gossip who defends her loose tongue with questionable rationalizations. In a similar vein, "olga pecho" (Laviera 1981), describes a woman who participates in her own destruction by gambling her monthly paycheck away. She is juxtaposed, however, on the same open page with "maria ciudad" (Laviera 1981), who raises her children alone, prays to the Orishas, works full time, and triumphs through her diligence and sacrifice.

In "enchulá" Laviera (1985) puts on the voice of a woman who learned that her desire for a serious romantic commitment brought her feelings of rejection and powerlessness so she now takes control by demanding "short range" relationships. Through making herself less available she is able, if not to have emotional intimacy, at least to have some control over her romantic relations. Finally, "compañero" captures the voice of a woman who demands some power in her relationship and respect from her partner. This poetic voice proposes a romantic partnership that will nurture them both as equals and serve as a basis for equality on other levels. When Laviera's female character says, "i am looking for equality, on all levels, personal, / family, societal" (1988: 33), she hints that their personal relationship can help foster societal relationships that are more equitable, or at least that this respect on a personal level must exist as a prerequisite for the society as a whole to change. As Laviera portrays individuals, each with his/her own strengths and weaknesses in any given poem, he builds a complex, heterogeneous vision of Nuyorican characters once these poems are seen together. This is a general truth in Laviera's poetry and also the case in his depiction of different women's relationships with men.

These last two works fit not only into the category of poems in which Laviera fashions a voice character, but also into a group in which he designs male-female romantic relationships. In this category, he focuses on degrees of mutual respect the couple shares and thus describes how they contribute to the greater cause of societal equality. Laviera provides numerous examples of poems that portray vignettes of romantic relationships that function at varying levels of well-being.

One case, the poem "machista" in the *Mainstream Ethics* (1988) collection, features a mainly Spanish-speaking man who unsuccessfully attempts to control a mainly English-speaking woman through what could be considered traditional or old-fashioned courtship. This language difference marks their varied levels of acculturation into mainstream American society. The male character appears to hold on to traditional Puerto Rican social conventions, while the female character has begun to identify herself with aspects of modern U.S. society, particularly mainstream Anglo-American feminism. In the view of feminist theorist, Becky Thompson, "[t]his feminism is white led, marginalizes the activism and world views of women of color, focuses mainly on the United States, and treats sexism as the ultimate oppression" (2002). Nevertheless, Anglo/American feminism had the capacity to stimulate some Puerto Rican women to take new political positions based on their gender identity. This is one case in which Laviera shows the cultural breadth of the Nuyorican community. The fact that the female character speaks mainly English hints that she is one Puerto Rican woman to whom Anglo-American feminism provides inspiration or a model of struggle. Her language and her focus on being a professional show that for her, the goals of mainstream Anglo/American feminism were inspiring. We can be sure of the heterogeneity of the Puerto Rican community in New York, which certainly included some women who identified with what mainstream feminism had to offer. As we will soon see, many Puerto Rican women had other feminist goals. The male character comments several times within the poem that he wants to "atraparla" (Laviera 1988: 30), but she rebukes him for his *machista* ways. He describes her with diverse terms like "black y qué / english morena, callejera, professional, / buena hija de arroz y habichuelas" (1988: 30). The first two verses express her modern, mainstream American qualities through the use of English "black, english professional" and "callejera" so she is a Black, streetwise New York professional. The second "arroz y habichuelas" expresses her Puerto Rican roots and potentially her mulata ethnicity.[5] An interesting point here is that as part of her mainstream American qualities, she is identified as Black. Her Puerto Rican identification as "arroz con habichuelas" is a more nuanced racial identity. Here it is important to remember the mainstream U.S. culture's binary construction of race, which includes a common consideration of mulattos and *mestizos* as almost undifferentiated, and most importantly racialized as non-white. On the other hand, the Puerto Rican myth of "the rainbow people" assumes a racial continuum rather than a binary construction and asserts that cultural identification supersedes racial identification (Rodríguez Morazzani 1996: 158). Throughout the verses the poetic voice emphasizes her dual influences. But through the female character's own comments quoted by the male character's voice, Laviera seems to support an Anglo-American, liberal, mainstream concept of feminism. In response to the male character's attempts to manipulate her, she replies,

> honey, i got too much on the ball,
> and i work too hard to sit down
> at seven o'clock and worry about
> your dull inactivities, tipo. (1988: 31)

It is her self-identification as an independent working woman that keeps her from succumbing to her suitor's machinations. She is proud of her work and her busy schedule. When she finds out that he has spent one hundred dollars on an evening out with her expecting a certain amount of influence over her in return, she responds by writing him a check for fifty dollars and ending their relationship. The money she earns by working pays for her dignity and independence. In this poem, the source of machismo is constructed as male, traditional, and Puerto Rican. The agent of change is a liberal, mainstream, Anglo-American feminist tradition that focuses special attention on women's economic independence through work outside the home. The poem clearly focuses blame for the relationship's failure on the male voice's sexist attitude, and seems to show the female voice that defends her independence on economic terms as an example of progress.

So it seems that Laviera accepts the notion that liberation for Puerto Rican women living on the mainland can come from liberal, mainstream, Anglo-American feminist traditions. In this poem, Laviera offers Anglo/American feminism as an option for some Puerto Rican women. The languages the characters speak bear upon the message the poem brings forth. This poem offers a scenario in which Anglo/American feminism conflicts with traditional Puerto Rican machismo. The female character's strength comes from her Anglo/American identification and the male character's worldview comes from his Puerto Rican identification. Laviera is well aware of Puerto Rican feminist traditions but has chosen to portray a Nuyorican woman in this poem who culls the influences of mainstream Anglo/American feminism rather than multiracial, Puerto Rican feminism.

While poems with heterosexual,[6] romantic themes stressing mutual respect or the lack of it appear throughout Laviera's work, the section, "Oro in Gold" in the *Enclave* (1981) compilation centers on sensual moments and love partnerships that possess the senses of equality and mutual respect lacking in "machista." The poems, "just before the kiss," "standards," "velluda: alliterated y eslembao," "the patria in my borinquen," "penetration (to sandra esteves/julia de burgos)," and "compañera" form a poetic whole that characterizes a complete vision of an ideal romantic relationship that would serve as a building block for greater societal harmony. It is here that Laviera shows the influence of multiracial feminism in his work. If the poem "compañero" hints at the link between equitable and loving personal relationships and parallel societal relationships, the "Oro in Gold" section spells out the connection. This is particularly significant in the context of Civil Rights collapse. The Young Lords Organization, an example of a group that fought for the rights of Puerto Ricans and saw itself as a brother organization to the Black Panthers, was never fully able to eradicate the gender-based prejudice within its ranks.

It is important to mention that throughout its existence, the Young Lords Organization fought race-based discrimination from an anti-capitalist position but suffered from a patriarchal orientation, which somewhat accelerated its demise. When women in the group proposed structural changes, they were incorporated, as can be seen in the organization's Point 5 of its Thirteen Point Platform, which is entitled, "We want equality for women. Down with machismo and male chauvinism" (Maristany 1983: 17). Many male Young Lords, however, continued to struggle with their old patterns of sexist behavior. The cultural plane of The Young Lords' tri-partite strategy to revolutionize daily life for Puerto Ricans in New York and beyond consisted in an effort to redefine Nuyorican identity in positive terms both in the realm of greater society and for the community, itself. Providing ideological guidance for Puerto Rican youth, with unprecedented support of Puerto Rican elders, the Young Lords fought Anglo-American hegemony on three planes: culturally with what they taught, with what they sang, and with what they wore; politically in that they recognized that the political system functioned against their interests; and physically in that they defended themselves against police brutality in Puerto Rican neighborhoods (Marre 1979). Strategies like this as well as those of other Civil Rights defenders like the Black Power movement in some ways served as inspiration for multiracial feminist groups.

The struggle that women waged for equality within Civil Rights organizations gave birth to multiracial feminist groups, tendencies that differ enormously from the liberal, mainstream feminism lauded in "machista." Rather than focusing on individual rights, economic equality with men, and a U.S. perspective, multiracial feminist groups focus on social justice and are heavily influenced by the Black Power movement and other race-based civil rights groups (Thompson 2002: 337). They have a framework for liberation on the multiple planes of race-class-gender-sexuality-nationality since they recognize "interlocking oppressions" (Thompson 2002: 337). In the 1980s, Laviera echoes these radical women's proposals to alter the structure of Civil Rights for a new struggle with a foundation of gender respect.

"just before the kiss," the first poem in the "Oro in Gold" section, is the most graphically sensual poem and also the tamest. This poem arouses and provokes through the voice of a lover reveling in the sensuality of a canela brown woman. The voice metaphorizes her to cocoa, cinnamon, arroz con dulce, and a host of other sweet things. This may remind the reader of many other works of literature and music that eroticize the medium brown skin of a mulata. This poem, however, plays with the racial essentialism of the sensual *mulata* archetype evident in the *negrista* movement of the 1920s and 1930s with poets like Luis Palés Matos, Emilio Ballagas, Nicolás Guillén, and José Zacarías Tallet. Without commenting on the pitfalls of racial stereotyping, Laviera sidesteps them. He includes, in the poetic voice's reverie, not only affection and admiration of the woman's body and affection, but also recognition and respect of her actions outside a sexual context. She is, "como canela brown warrior woman diplomática / with her terms" (1981: 47). This line conjures images of a woman able to defend herself and to adroitly articulate her needs. Laviera successfully presents the sensuality of the mulata woman without reducing her to the erotic object of lore and so subverts a patriarchal tendency in Latin American writing.

The poem "standards" emanates from the voice of a woman much like the independent female character in "machista." In "standards," she names her conditions for the potential relationship between her and her suitor. She requires respect, freedom, and sincerity in order to be his lover. Unlike in "machista," the relationship succeeds; a fact the reader learns through a progression of verbs that switch from future tense, "i will take...talk...caress," to present continuous, "seducing...scenting," and finally to the imperative, "touch, oh, touch, deep" (1981: 48). Aside from narrating a challenge met and promise kept, Laviera finishes the poem/sexual act with the word "libertad," implying that a good relationship built on respect and sensuality can liberate.

"velluda: alliterated y eslembao" follows "standards" and "just before the kiss" to form a trilogy of sensuality empowered by respect. These three poems with "standards" at the zenith depict sensual love as a dignifying act. Similar in style to other depictions of sex that degrade the female figure, these differ by shattering the traditional subject-gaze, object body dynamic.

With "the patria in my borinquen," Laviera departs from the vein of the "Oro in Gold" section by using the liberating sensual theme to describe a poetic voice's relationship with language and Puerto Rico. Laviera's trope on the romantic relationship as allegory for political power relations includes his own affair with patria and language. As a lover of patria and language, he admits experiencing a weak moment of machismo but patria is "strong enough to overcome all obstacles" (1981: 50) and so teaches him to change. Laviera returns to this theme of redemption in "Enrojo" in the *Mixturao* compilation. Here again, Laviera links the romantic, albeit a political relationship disguised as romance, with the overcoming of personal flaws that can impede social change.

Laviera's poem "penetration (to sandra esteves/julia de burgos)" intertextually salutes fellow Nuyorican poet, Sandra María Esteves' poem to Julia de Burgos, "A Julia y a mí" (1981). Laviera triumphantly lauds Esteves' and Burgos' efforts as poets, and as Puerto Rican women. The first three of the poem's five stanzas center on the hardship that Puerto Rican women have faced in the twentieth century, the early part through pinpointing moments in Burgos' writings and the latter part through Esteves' experiences. The last two stanzas celebrate Puerto Rican women's struggle to end their oppression. This poem can be counted among the numerous triumphal odes in Laviera's five volumes of poetry.[7] He empathizes with Puerto Rican women's strife, applauds Esteves' strength to overcome it and Burgos' posthumous victory in inspiring her. He names their goals: "patriotic confrontation" (1981: 51) and "puerto rican women's self-destiny" (1981:

52), that is to say, their struggle for rights from the perspectives of racial, national, and gender-based identification.

The full expression of respect, partnership, and sensuality culminate in "compañera (for susana)," the last poem in the "Oro in Gold" section of *Enclave* (1981). This last work inverts the thematic structure of "just before the kiss," the first in the section, which surges with sensuality and erotic charge and dedicates one line to mutual respect. Rather, "compañera" marches out the message of solidarity within the couple and in the community while dedicating three lines in the last stanza to sensuality. The verses "entre el don de un amor fiel, entre el cariño libre de mentiras,/ entre el beso firme y sensual" (1981: 53) follow a set of five stanzas about grass roots organizing in Puerto Rican communities. This collection of verse about sensuality, mutual respect, and change on a societal scale through personal building blocks comes to its climax by exalting political activism on a local level. In this last poem, social change is the orgasm while sensuality is only the foreplay.

In the poems featured here, Tato Laviera takes on poetic voices of women who, together, embody a heterogeneous Nuyorican identity. His work has been discussed and analyzed by intellectuals from the Americas and Europe, who mostly focus on the linguistic interplay of his poetry and the way he depicts the social conditions of Puerto Ricans in New York City. Some of his poems have become canonical examples of American literature. As a writer who represents the Nuyorican community to the nation and the world, Laviera has a great responsibility toward his male and female comrades. In William Luis's (1992) interview with him, national and world readers get an opportunity to look inside a local dynamic: Laviera's writing relationship with the Nuyorican community, based on a democratic interplay between representative and represented. When asked about strategies he takes to be accepted by his community, Laviera responds,

> I believe that politically I have to write about women. Of all the poems I have written, forty-one of them have characters which are exclusively women. *Yo estoy solito allá afuera with that.* And good characters, characters of women that I respect and that women use. I had to make sure that I have women that speak in my poetry by themselves and have a very feminine structure. There is also a black structure.... If I say I cover my angles, you know why, *porque la*

comunidad puertorriqueña es la comunidad más bochinchosa en el seno del mundo. If I don't please all of them, *me jodo*. I'm in trouble because they'll find some fault *porque tú no hiciste esto y porque tú no hiciste lo otro... No quiero pleito con la gente* mía. (1992: 1028)

When asked about the inspiration(s) of their work, many writers would opt for a strategic, self-protective or self-aggrandizing answer, particularly in an interview to be published and read by many. To William Luis's question, however, Laviera gives an immediate, sincere, and quotidian answer. His feet are being put to the fire. He is one representative of the Nuyorican community who is heard and read far outside his local milieu. He and his characters may stand in for any Nuyorican in the eyes of a poetry reader in California, Puerto Rico, Germany, or France. This honor carries great responsibility and one sees from this interview that many members of the Nuyorican community do what they can to assure Laviera represents them in a way they feel is right. The fact that Laviera has taken the trouble to count the number of poems with exclusively female characters indicates that he has felt the need to quantifiably defend his literary work. In interviewer William Luis's own writing, he affirms one contribution of Puerto Rican feminists in the U.S.: "I am referring to the contributions made by the women's movement in creating a sense of consciousness among both Puerto Rican male and female writers, leading them to challenge traditional Hispanic culture.... The gay and lesbian movement has had a smaller, but nevertheless significant, impact on writers as well" (1997: 39). In view of this insight into Laviera's relationship with the community he represents, he has written about and from the perspective of poor Nuyoricans, about and from the perspective of women, about and from a black perspective. Given the multiple plane focus of multiracial feminism—the paradigms of race-class-gender-sexuality-nationality—Laviera has touched on all of these but one. He has embodied many poetic voices but not that of a gay man or a lesbian. Perhaps with all the effort Laviera has made to represent Nuyoricans "well" in race, class, and gender terms, a push toward his positive depiction of a gay relationship was lacking. Perhaps among all the checks the Nuyorican community places upon Laviera's poetic production, they have not pushed toward reflecting gay Nuyorican culture. Perhaps Laviera, himself, with all the constraints he seems to feel on his work, has chosen not to include this perspective.

Twenty years after publishing his fourth book, *Mainstream Ethics* (1988), Laviera produces *Mixturao and Other Poems* (2008a). Generally speaking, he remains true to his style and subject matter. In the two-decade interval, some changes in theoretical framework seem to have influenced his writing. Between Laviera's work in the 1980s, and 2008, Luis mentions

> the emphasis on "hispano" of *Mainstream Ethics* and "Latino" of *Mixturao*.... Whereas "hispano" emphasized the Hispanic language, culture, and traditions, "Latino" is a communal acceptance of the adopted environment that produces a new and hybrid culture, based on the coming together of differences. (2008a: xv)

Between the "Oro in Gold" section of *Enclave* to the "Mujeres" and "Hombres" sections in *Mixturao*, Laviera has shifted his gender focus. This addition of a section specifically about men may mirror an academic shift from a focus on Women's Studies to one on Gender Studies, examining not only women and their difference but also men and their relationship to a perceived gender centrality and neutrality. We will see this "coming together of differences" exemplified in the way Laviera describes women's and men's negotiation of public space.

In, "Mujeres" and "Hombres," Laviera avoids using voice characters to carry his message. The exception is "Riqueña Hip-Hop," a defense of the dignity of the Puerto Rican flag, written from the perspective of a young Puerto Rican woman. Generally, however, he writes about women and about men in these sections. In this section, "Enrojo" is a description of a street scene and a treatise on men's and women's rights in public space. Here the male poetic voice expresses lascivious wishes about a woman walking down the street who is described with words like "pure," and "divinity;" she is seen as holding an "old-fashioned/cartera" in front of her curves with "espiritus/protectivos/jealously/guarding" her. She may feel the eyes on her and react by protecting herself from the gaze by covering her body with her bag. As she tries to cover herself, wishing to be free of the gaze on her, she finds that her wish to go unscrutinized won't be granted. Her rights do not extend to preventing the gaze of others. The poetic voice, on the other hand, expresses shame at his thoughts, feeling "ashamed-of-myself / enfermito," and ends the poem with a salute of recognition for all his, "continental / amigos in silence / tirando / piropos

/ atoloquedá" (2008a: 34–5). These *piropos* are not said out loud to the woman with the notebook; they are only thought. The poetic voice and the other men around gaze at the woman to the point that she is aware of it but they have learned that this behavior is unacceptable in society today. This social norm prevents them from saying the things they'd like to say. The poem shows a vignette of gender negotiation in which each party has limited freedom. This poem seems like a follow up of "the patria in my borinquen," in which Laviera admits to *machista* feelings and then says that his sense of national pride teaches him to be better. One could imagine the influence of multiracial feminism, which connects the goals of gender equity to ethnic and national liberation on the author.

In the "Hombres" section, all poems except "Militant" are dedicated to a specific man. In the cases of "Spanglish Carta," "Patriota," and "Preludio Barroquero," they are odes to fellow writers. In the case of "Consignas in Brutality," dedicated to Anthony Báez, who was the victim of police brutality, and "Carpetas in Your Dossier" dedicated to Ramón Bosque Pérez, who writes about and suffered from political persecution in Puerto Rico, they use one man's situation to comment on a generalized problem.

"Militant" is the only poem without a specific dedication, and it links, if not all the poems in the section, certainly "Consignas in Brutality" and "Carpetas in Your Dossier." The poem is a wakeup call to "brothers and sisters" (2008a: 46) of the Nuyorican community that some elements of society are preying upon the young. This "virus" comes in the form of those who try to initiate young people into lives of crime, induce them to use and sell drugs, hire them for pyramid scheme sales jobs, and market luxury items to them that they cannot afford. The poetic voice of the militant places blame on the elders in society who "wash our / hands like pontious pilate" (2008a: 47) and do nothing "to confront / the vultures destroying our future" (2008a: 47). The theme of responsibility resonates here as the militant reminds the elders of their obligation to protect "our children."

"Consignas in Brutality" mourns Anthony Báez, who died after being strangled in police custody in 1994 during the mayorship of Rudolph Giuliani. The poem reads like a street demonstration chant against police brutality with a call and response structure. The caller demands that the responders / the community react by coming together and raising their voices as one. Like the call in "Militant," intended to make community elders take responsibility for fighting the ills in society, here a protester calls on the community to do the same.

"Carpetas in Your Dossier" names the gentrification of El Barrio in Manhattan and increased street surveillance as the societal ills to be fought through awareness. The agents of these changes are described as spreading through the area like vermin, in the same way Puerto Ricans themselves had been described decades before. After characterizing the threat that gentrification and surveillance constitute to the community, the poetic voice warns the community to "abre los ojos" and arm themselves with "all your resources" (2008a: 53). These poems in the "Hombres" section call the Nuyorican community to vigilance and action. They demand that (not necessarily male) Nuyoricans protect younger generations and take responsibility by becoming the pillars that hold up their community. Protection and responsibility are traditional qualities expected in men. This is perhaps the reason why these poems are grouped under "Hombres," even though they contain no call to a specifically male audience. In addition, "Militant" specifically calls "brothers and sisters" (2008a: 46) to action. It is possible that when Laviera set out to portray men, protection and responsibility were the two qualities he perceived as being expected of them, valued in them, and thus defined them.

As a representative of the Nuyorican community, poet Tato Laviera positions himself as a speaker for and about both genders, for and about Puerto Rico and New York, for and about poor classes, for and about non-White ethnic groups. In this sense, Laviera carries on the messages of Civil Rights movements that had declined even before he published his first book, and then of multiracial feminism, which grew contemporary to his poetry. Much of his poetry, especially the "Oro in Gold" section in the *Enclave* compilation, is an example of Jesús Martín Barbero's (1993) notion of culture, which points toward new ways to effect social change, rather than retreating from the political or real-world realm. In "machista," he seems to espouse mainstream Anglo/American feminism's focus on liberation through economic independence as a possible inspiration for some Puerto Rican women. In the section "Mujeres" from *Mixurao and Other Poems*, Laviera shows a negotiation of rights in public space between men and a woman. He calls men to take responsibility and to protect others in the "Hombres" section. Perhaps his message is that men are measured along lines of responsibility and protection since these are the qualities expected of/respected in them as men. With much of his poetry outlined here, Laviera emerges from the tradition of the Civil Rights struggle and underlines a multiracial feminist concept that the rights of people of both genders are essential to the goal of greater racial, national, and class-based equality.

NOTES

[1] As Thompson (2002) states, multiracial feminism did grow in the 1980s, but it never had the broad impact on the nation that mainstream Anglo/American feminism had.

[2] Laviera's first four volumes of poetry are *La Carreta Made a U-Turn* (1979); *Enclave* (1981); *AmeRícan* (1985); and *Mainstream Ethics, (ética corriente)* (1988).

[3] I use the term modernist to refer to a political perspective that focuses on the struggle of alienated, marginalized groups to gain access to the rights enjoyed by the mainstream. This struggle is waged on a national level.

[4] Laviera has written a number of plays that have been produced off-Broadway, often at theaters with a particular Puerto Rican interest, like Teatro4. These plays have not been published in written form.

[5] In much Latin American literature, white rice mixed with dark beans, as in the dish arroz y habichuelas, symbolize the miscegenation of Europeans and Africans.

[6] While Laviera underlines the importance of respect between men and women in the context of romantic relationships as a base for social progress, he does not extend this understanding to sexual preference. He does not include in the struggle for social change any reference to acceptance of the relationships of LGBTQIA-identified people.

[7] When Laviera dedicates a poem to someone, he almost always does so by lavishing praise on that individual with the greatest unbridled enthusiasm.

"Not Nowhere:" "Walking Bridges" in an AmeRícan Utopia

ANALISA DEGRAVE

One of the recurring questions in utopian thought is the issue of difference in society. Is it possible to create a society of equity and justice among differing ethnicities and diverse political, economic, and religious perspectives? How does heterogeneity fit within the greater whole? Where would one find such a place? What is its name and who lives there? Famously coined by Thomas More in the early sixteenth century, the word, "utopia," points to some of these very tensions involved in creating a harmonious society—for, etymologically, it means both "good place" and "no place." From its beginnings, the concept of utopia has been bound to a complex interplay of affirmation and negation, hope and impossibility, and a geography in which "somewhere" quite possibly is located "off the map." The locus of home, hope, and belonging for U.S. Puerto Ricans also reveals a curious geography—from a nostalgic longing for a paradisiacal "Island," an affirmation of New York City as a new-found home, to more abstract geographic descriptors such as "in between," "here," or "neitherfromherenorfromthere"—the English translation of one of Tato Laviera's most recent poems.[1] Sometimes employed to identify Laviera and other U.S. Puerto Rican artists, community organizers, and scholars, the term "Nuyorican" has a paradoxical etymology similar to that of "utopia," as it describes someone whose identity is situated somewhere "in between" or on the "border."[2] Efraín Barradas explains: "[el] puertorriqueño que se autodenomina neorrican se declara distinto, nuevo: ni puertorriqueño por entero ni plenamente estadounidense" (1980: 15). In fact, one issue that regularly appears in Nuyorican/U.S. Puerto Rican works is that of identity. On the one hand, Puerto Ricans living in the United States are viewed within "mainstream" Anglo-America to be "otro minority group más," outsiders or on the "border." On the other, from the Puerto Rican islanders' perspective, they are not recognized as "verdaderamente boricuas" (truly—islander—Puerto Ricans) (Barradas 1980: 11, 15). As I will discuss in this essay, two neologisms coined by Laviera, "AmeRícan" and "nideaquínideallá," are also notably utopian in character. And, similar to the term "Nuyorican," these words reveal an etymology that highlights a complex and paradoxical geography and identity. In effect, the words, "Nuyorican," "AmeRícan," and "nideaquínideallá" stem from and straddle the paradox of being "somewhere," that is, as Juan Flores and George Yúdice assert, "not nowhere" (1993: 203) or being "someone" that, as Sandra María Esteves declares, is "Not Neither" (1994: 60). Linguistically, geographically, culturally and politically, the U.S. Puerto Rican/Nuyorican experience is located outside of the "mainstream" in both the United States and in Puerto Rico—on the border, a new variation on More's "no place."

As is underscored by their titles, the location of the ideal community is central in Laviera's *AmeRícan* (1985) and "nideaquínideallá" (2006a). Among other paradoxes of utopian dynamics, both terms suggest that the geographic location of home is not limited to one specific or officially recognized place.[3] This is not to say, however, that the liminal places or identities of "AmeRíca" or "nideaquínideallá" are off the map or "nowhere." In "Living Borders/ Buscando América: Languages of Latino Self Formation," Flores and Yúdice note that one of the manners in which Laviera and other Latino artists declare that the border is "not nowhere" is through "cultural remapping" where the "imposed border emerges as the locus of redefinition and re-signification" (1993: 202). Countering the idea that this space is marginal, empty, or off the map, Laviera draws attention to this so-called "nowhere" space outlining the identity of his community. He defines what his community is not, affirms what it is or wants to be, and seeks to forge for his community an identity where the dominant culture—whether through ambivalence or intolerance—says there is none. Places called "nideaquínideallá" and "AmeRícan" are placed on the map in Laviera's poetry.

Before examining Laviera's poems, however, it is vital to underscore that Laviera's map of an "AmeRícan" society or of a place called "nideaquínideallá" is distinct from many constructs of ideal spaces due to its insistence on an on-going process of creating a better society. Unlike most examples of utopian discourse, *AmeRícan*, is not defined through binaries, nor does it provide a specific political or ideological map for constructing the ideal community (Sargent 2000: 13).[4] In fact, Laviera's ideal society best corresponds to what Lyman Tower Sargent in "Utopian Traditions: Themes and Variations" refers to as a "critical utopia." According to Sargent's definition, a "critical utopia" is a process of constantly reworking the parameters of utopia; it is an approximation to a better world in a "self-reflective" way. A "critical utopia" recognizes that there will be "identifiable problems yet to be solved" (2000: 13). Different from the Marxist model of an ideal society, for example, "critical utopias" do not express the existence of an ultimate "resolution" or end to a historical process. This is perhaps the most elusive of utopian constructs as there is a call for unspecificity in an overall vision of the future.

In addition to the concept of "critical utopias" and the affirmation that "nowhere" is "somewhere," my analysis of Laviera's poetry is based on the metaphor of "walking bridges." The metaphor of "walking bridges" is highlighted by Laviera and Véronique Rauline in "Tato Laviera's Nuyorican Poetry: The Choice of Bilingualism" in their discussion of Nuyorican, Chicana/o, and Creole constructions of identity—"peoples whose history has been one of negation, uprooting, transplantation and exile" (1998: 147). Departing from the metaphor of "walking bridges" found in the poem "AmeRícan," Rauline and Laviera assert that the poetry of the latter rejects the "simplistic either / or alternative" of choosing a name and identity. They add that Laviera's poetry provides "an escape from the neither / nor (or in-between) downgrading reserved to those who refuse to be culturally maimed" (1998: 147). As the title of their essay indicates, Rauline and Laviera focus on the ways that the poet's use of language registers a reformulation of identity. While language is also an important dimension of Laviera's works, I frame my use of the metaphor of the "walking bridge" within the scope of the "critical utopia." Similar to the paradigm of the "critical utopia," the "walking bridges" in the title poem of *AmeRícan* underscore the notion of a "self-reflexive" approximation toward a more perfect society:

> AmeRícan   across forth and across back
> back across and forth back
> forth across and back and forth
> our trips are walking bridges!
>
> ....
>
> we stand, affirmative in action,
> to reproduce a broader answer to the
> marginality that gobbled us up abruptly! (1985: 94)

Apart from the general parameters of respect and love, which will be examined shortly, the "self-reflective" approximations of the "critical utopia" find their parallel in the trips taken by Laviera's literary travelers.

In fact, one of the central ideas that I propose in this essay is that *AmeRícan*'s poems represent models of practice in the formation of a new U.S. identity since Laviera's poetry suggests the need for critical analysis as well as alternative ways of reading, conceptualizing, and defining America. Akin to the absence of a final "solution" in the movement toward the ideal in the "critical utopia," Laviera's literary travelers have no "end" to their trips; they must be active and critical and constantly reflect on their circumstances—going "across forth and across back / back across." Unlike many constructions of ideal societies, which neatly define their borders and identities with binaries of "here" and "there" or "us" and "them," easy solutions are not available in "AmeRícan," nor in "nideaquínideallá" for that matter, and readers must take "walking bridges" going back and forth to formulate a "broader answer" to "marginality." "Marginality" (the "border" or "nowhere") and the "melting-pot" are not acceptable answers. Countering these unacceptable answers, Laviera adds to them, "reproducing" a broader solution to "nowhere." Located in the movements of this "critical utopia" of "walking bridges," Laviera shows us that a U.S. Puerto Rican identity exists even as it continues to evolve; it is "not nowhere," and it needs to be recognized in a way that goes beyond simplistic and limiting paradigms. The rejection of marginality is also underscored through the "walking bridges" of associations and "strategic resistance" outlined by the spectrum of voices in *AmeRícan*'s "Ethnic Tributes."[5] And, as with the "critical utopia," there is no ultimate solution in creating a better society in Laviera's "America," and the inhabitants of this new community must constantly undergo a process of "self-reflection" to avoid creating new polarizing discourses that would marginalize others, even if that "other" has historically marginalized communities on the fringe of the dominant cultural "core." In other words, while Laviera's poetry outlines specific examples and models of practice that are to be avoided, as I explain below in the section "Elusive 'Enemies,'" and is different from traditional utopian constructs, Laviera does not rigidly codify AmeRíca's "enemies." Consequently, he steers clear of a permanent polarization between "us" and "them" and provides "walking bridges" for future associations between the culturally dominant "core" and marginalized communities.

Countering "the monocultural dictates of the official public sphere" that U.S. Puerto Rican/Nuyorican's space is "nowhere" (Flores and Yúdice 1993: 203), Laviera's *AmeRícan* delineates the identity of his community.

In an ingenious play on the tensions of language, space, and identity, *AmeRícan* literally stresses—with a capital "R" and an accented "í,"—the role of difference in national identity within the United States. With these modifications of the very word, "American," Laviera underscores the need to redefine the role of difference in the construction of a new national identity in the United States. True to its utopian character, Laviera's literary constructions of an ideal society simultaneously reject certain aspects of the present and past to affirm those of a new and better world. In *AmeRícan*, one utopian construct, the "melting pot," is negated to make space for another that affirms racial, linguistic, and cultural specificity and strategic associations within America.

As suggested above, movement is key in the process of reformulating a new national identity. The importance of movement is evidenced in the continual act of going "across forth and across back / back across and forth back" (1985: 94) over the poetic "walking bridges" in *AmeRícan*. Two decades later, we find recognizable echoes of the "back and forth" movements in "nideaquínideallá," in which such approximations are described as "evolucionarios" and, fittingly, the "back and forth" process of *AmeRícan* continues to move. In "nideaquínideallá," both the poetic speaker's "nationality" and the movement through space through which this identity are forged demonstrate a similar self-reflective process of approximation as the words linked to "nationality" and movement/space/identity have, themselves, been "updated." In 1985, "AmeRícan" identity is created in a continual process of going "back and forth" between two identifiable places—America (Amer-) and Puerto Rico (-Rican). In 2006, however, the name, "nideaquínideallá," is more abstract and is not linked to any particular place—at least in nomenclature, yet the process of the creation of identity and belonging continues even as it has slightly changed, now simply, "backnforth" (Laviera 2006a: 173).

Critical Readers and Poetic Models of Practice

There is a certain Brechtian component to Laviera's poetry in that it requires active and critical readers. It is difficult to read his works passively, and, similar to Brecht's thought on art and society, Laviera creates a destabilizing discourse that forces the reader to come away from the text, ideally, thinking critically. We must move "back and forth" over his poetic "walking bridges" as the textual and ideological answers posed by the author's questions are not clear-cut. And in this respect, Laviera's poetry demonstrates two very pronounced areas of postmodern discourse; (1) there is no grand narrative in Laviera's "AmeRícan" as "solutions" are constantly reworked and redefined and (2) respecting the individual subjectivity of the colonized other is paramount. As we find later in "nideaquínideallá," definitions of identity, place, and language are difficult to define and, as I noted above, they are "evolucionario(s)." Engaged and challenged through stereotypes, humor, mimicry, orality, criticism, and word-play, readers find models of practice in *AmeRícan's* voices. Going "back and forth" and "backnforth" over its poetic "walking bridges," readers must think critically in imagining notions of a better world.

As is the case for other Nuyorican poets, for Laviera, poetry is a "contact sport" (Algarín and Holman 1994: 1); his work possesses a performative quality and is sociopolitical in nature. While humor plays an important and strategic role in *AmeRícan*, the poetry it includes is part of a serious, hard, and urgent "sport" that actively pushes toward "contact" between poetry and politics. In "From New York to the World: An Interview with Tato Laviera," William Luis discusses the form and content of Laviera's poetry:

> Readers familiar with Tato's poetry recognize that his poems are broad-reaching and respond to a diverse audience as represented by Nuyoricans, Chicanos, Caribbeans, Latin Americans, and Afro-Americans. His poetry is full of the music of bomba and plena, and of rap and preaching. However, it is also socially minded and historical in content. Indeed, his poems are a conglomeration of voices, songs, dialects, and cultures, producing a unique synthesis that is moving, instructive, and aesthetically appealing. (1992: 1022)

With the diversity of voices, dialects, and speech patterns he incorporates, it is clear that orality is a defining feature of Laviera's works. This oral quality is critical to the performative and participatory character of *AmeRícan* and "nideaquínideallá," as well as the ways in which the poet works to provoke an emotive and analytical response in his audience.[6]

In fact, one could argue that Laviera's work contains what Ernst Bloch refers to as the "utopian quality of art" (1988: xxxiii, xxxvi, 73, 107); in form and content, it seeks to engage his audience analytically and subjectively while projecting a revised notion of U.S. American identity. Although Laviera does not provide a concrete map on how to arrive at this new identity, as Theodor Adorno asserts in "Lyric Poetry and Society," perhaps any artistic work, including those that seem to represent a very overt escape from reality, could be considered utopian in that they "[proclaim] the dream of a world in which things would be different" (1974: 58). According to Bloch, however, depending on the ways an artist constructs her/his work, the vision of a better world is rendered as "abstract" (impossible) or "concrete" (approaching the realm of possibility) (1988: 73). One of the ways in which Laviera attempts to bridge the gap between his vision of a better world and real possibilities is by establishing a critical discourse that evaluates a perceived disorder in contemporary society (Pradeau 2000: 88). Through mimicry, humor, and overt criticism, "AmeRícan" outlines what is to be rejected in a new America—racial or cultural prejudice and "bad intentions." Pierre-François Moreau in *Le Récit Utopique* explains that one of the key elements of the modern utopia genre is the construction of a vision of a model place that "enunciates under what conditions such a social life is possible" (qtd. in Pradeau 2000: 88). Through its numerous sketches of different ethnic communities in the United States and by incorporating the oral speech patterns of this diverse community, "AmeRícan" points to the everyday lives of a variety of subjects, but with emphasis on minorities and their "strategic resistance" and associations, as the sphere in which real-life examples of and the initiating steps toward affirmation, resistance, love, and transformation take place. Laviera's poetic models of practice are firmly rooted in the real.

John Beverley and Marc Zimmerman in *Literature and Politics in the Central American Revolutions* argue that culture can be a fundamental tool in transforming society when it "[encodes] new forms of personal, national, and popular identity" and when it allows a heterogeneous public to identify itself with diverse subject positions of agency and responsibility (1990: ix, 2). One of the ways in which Laviera literally speaks to a heterogeneous audience is by writing in Spanish, English, and Spanglish. According to Laviera, "Being a Puerto Rican gives me the totality of having a universal mission to talk to different groups at different times. And the fact that I do it in Spanish and English allows me to talk to the entire continent" (Luis 1992: 1027). In terms of reception and circulation, writing in three languages theoretically allows him to reach a more linguistically heterogeneous audience. Furthermore, by articulating a new identity for the United States in Spanish and Spanglish, Laviera recognizes these languages as a legitimate and powerful means of discourse toward social transformation. Laviera has stated that his poetry registers the "voices" of "a thousand people in every syllable." In fact, he asserts that it is his obligation to return these voices to "his people": "It is my responsibility, as effectively as I can, to let the voices of my people, at any moment, integrate into me and I just give it back to them the way they give it to me" (Luis 1992: 1027). Spanglish, gossip, and the ingenious twists of street talk and jokes find their home in "AmeRícan." In addition to making us laugh and repeat the poems, the voices that we find in these poetic models of practice highlight the fact that the AmeRícan society projected in this work is addressed to and created by a variety of people—by those who sing with the music of Pedro Flores, "gospel boogie," or "bolero love songs," by those who "[speak] new words in Spanglish tenements," and by those who "[walk] plena-rhythms" (1985: 94–5). Whether the subject is a Spanglish-speaking prisoner, a Black Nuyorican, a reggae artist, or a devout Puerto Rican Catholic woman, AmeRícan affirms a variety of subject positions in its profile of a new and better society.

A recurring trope found in constructions of ideal societies is the act of identifying and codifying one's heroes/allies and enemies. In literary works that place utopia within the paradigm of nationhood, the enemy is often a (neo)colonial power or another country that is perceived to hinder the establishment of the ideal state. In other works, the enemy of utopia is internal. Often the identities of "us" and "them" are bound to the spatial binaries of "here" and "there." Whether external or internal or both, these enemies are juxtaposed to the utopian hero/community. In the case of *AmeRícan*, Laviera collects the voices and creates images of colonized and minority peoples from within the U.S. in order to confront cultural and colonial dominants on a national scale. Laviera creates "walking bridges" to branch out and connect colonized and minority peoples. As Juan Flores notes in reference to both "AmeRícan" and to the material interactions of cultures in New York City, the role of specificity and strategic association should not be confused with either "assimilation" or "cultural pluralism":

> Though characterized by the plurality and integration of diverse cultures, the process here is not headed toward assimilation with the dominant "core" culture, or even toward respectful coexistence with it. Rather, the individual and interweaving cultures involved are expressions of histories of conquest, enslavement and forced

incorporation at the hands of the prevalent surrounding society. As such, the main thrust in each case is toward self-affirmation and association with other cultures caught up in comparable processes of historical recovery and strategic resistance. (1993: 184–5)

As Flores asserts, while Laviera includes a "diversity" of cultures in his redefinition of America, any idea of a "happy" or unqualified multiplicity of cultures in the United States meets with a critical "resistance" in the poet's marked affirmation of conquered, colonized, and/or marginalized cultures within the U.S. Self-affirmation, "strategic resistance," and associations are also literally accented in the title of this work. Although this neologism represents a "reaching beyond the New York enclave," the word "AmeRícan," strikes an accent on the "Rícan"—the Puerto Rican in the American. By doing so, he "seeks to stake a claim for Puerto Rican recognition before the whole U.S. society...goading the society to come to terms with the 'Rícan' in its midst, arguing through puns and ironic challenges that he will not be an American until he can say 'Am-e-Rícan' ("I'm a Rícan") and be proud of it" (Flores 1993: 194). With this and other "accents," Laviera redefines the utopian contours of any traditional core U.S. American identity, affirming a model of love, resistance, and respectful association with others within a greater whole.

The act of formulating a new identity that would locate communities like "AmeRíca" and "nideaquínideallá" on a map involves a number of "walking bridges." One such "walking bridge" is that of the critical reader who is willing to engage in poems written in English, Spanish, and Spanglish, and who employs a dexterity of reading directionality—back and forth, diagonally, vertically, and horizontally. At the same time, this reader must pay attention to the ways in which Laviera ties orality, musicality, humor, and stereotypes to discussions of the creation of a more equitable and respectful society. In other words, similar to the approximating movements associated with the critical utopia, the movements and practices of Laviera's readers are both active and analytical. As I discuss below, confronted with stereotypes, neologisms, dramatic speech and parody, the reader's interpretive dominance is destabilized and s/he is spurred on to reflect and go "back and forth" over other examples of Laviera's poetry. In addition to underscoring a praxis of self-reflexivity and engaged analysis, the "walking bridges" in Laviera's poetry also highlight models of "branching out" through strategic "associations" with other colonized or minority cultures as well as the resistance to assimilation to a dominant core, as Flores has aptly suggested (1993: 185).[7] These models are outlined in the content of Laviera's individual poems ("AmeRícan," "boricua," and "asimilao"), as well as the scope of *AmeRícan*'s "Ethnic Tributes." The dominant core in Laviera's poetry is also linked to a critique of arrogance, (neo)colonialism, racism, snobbery, exclusion, and dominance of a variety of stripes. And just as the parameters of the critical utopia change and register an acknowledgement that there are "problems yet to be solved," the fact that Laviera includes poems such as "intellectual," "nuyorican," "spanish," and "english," in which he calls into question any airs of cultural, political, or linguistic superiority that one people or individual might claim over others, it would seem that Laviera also extends bridges to the "enemies" of AmeRíca. In other words, through the inclusion of these "enemies," Laviera's collection itself is an example of the movement of "branching out"; by not excluding the dominant core, positive associations with those who might currently marginalize AmeRíca's diverse citizenry are not precluded indefinitely.

Stereotypes and "Bad and Good Judgment"

Despite *AmeRícan*'s lack of the inclusion of an ultimate political "recipe" (as Marx stated) to arrive at a perfect society, this work strongly accentuates—in form and content—the need for "good" judgment and resistance in the face of stereotypes and what Laviera calls "bad intentions" in his poem "boricua." Recognizing this lack of a specific political paradigm of "macro" proportions, when viewing the whole of *AmeRícan* in its variety of spaces, languages, and referents, it is apparent that, unlike traditional socialist constructions that point to a time of final resolution, the concept of "good" judgment and resistance in this work are simultaneously instantaneous and never-ending. An on-going process that takes place in a multiplicity of ordinary places on a constant, day-to-day basis replaces the idea of an "end" with the need to act with "good" judgment and "resistance."

To understand the centrality of "good" judgment in Laviera's ideal society, it is necessary to turn to the second and third poems of this work, "intellectual" and "boricua." Together with the title poem and "asimilao," they represent two parts of a four-part *ars poetica* in *AmeRícan*. In the poem, "intellectual," we find a parody of academic snobbery and infallibility. It serves as an example of judgment guided by "bad intentions" and power:

so historically total
so minutely precise
so accurately detailed
so politically active
so grammatically arrogant
so academically prepared
so literally perfect
so ethnically snobbish
so aristocratically professional
so if you want to challenge me,
be prepared to lose the argument,
for I am too humanly infallible
about my researched assertions,
so take it or leave it,
the latter is your wisest choice,
do not arouse my anger,
i will reduce you to a
bibliographical ibidem,
demoting you to childhood,
in other words,
come out to kill,
and be dead
from the start. (1985: 15)

With this poem, Laviera's book sets the tone of *AmeRícan* with an unmistakably anti-intellectual stance. Like Nicanor Parra's anti-poetry that regularly assumes and parodies the voice of its subject to define by negation what his own poetry is not, in this poem Laviera takes on the voice of a particular subject to reject its place in this book. Judgment is a recurring and important theme in *AmeRícan*, and, as the second poem in this collection, "intellectual" indicates that judgment based on "bad intentions" and power is unacceptable in Laviera's vision of a new America.

My use of the term "bad intentions" in relation to judgment is based on the juxtaposition between "intellectual" and the poem that immediately follows it, "boricua," which proposes the ideal of creating community based on a judgment of "best intentions" toward others. In addition to providing this ideal of "good" judgment in the third poem, one of the general themes in

AmeRícan is the need to recognize a great diversity of voices in the American national identity—a theme that is underscored through the inclusion of a number of ethnic sketches in poems whose title identifies the ethnic origin of each group. In contrast to this theme of inclusion, the subject in Laviera's "intellectual" stands out in her/his distance and exclusion from others. This distance and superiority over others is established through the repetition of the sequence, "so," which is used as an adverb or adjective: "so historically total / so minutely precise / so accurately detailed...." Laviera is known for capturing the twists and intricacies of the speech of a variety of subjects. And, orality is of great importance in this poem. In English, the word, "so," and the suffix, "-ly," are not only used to highlight and add to the identity of its subject provided via the adjective, but when employed repeatedly and with a particular vocal inflection, they are often used in mockery.

The dark side of this linguistic parody begins at the end of first half of the poem where the culmination of the intellectual's "perfection" and "human infallibility" is highlighted via the incorporation another use of the word, "so." Previously this word signifies "to a certain degree," however, from this point forward, it means, "therefore": "so if you want to challenge me..., "so take it or leave it...," and "do not arouse my anger." In the first part of the poem the word, "so," relates to a self-judgment—a description by the intellectual of her/himself. In the second half, however, the word, "so," could best be related to the idea of "prejudging." The qualifications provided by the intellectual in the first part of the poem reveal her/his grounds for daring the absent interlocutor to establish an argument, and inevitably lose. Regardless of the interlocutor's argument, s/he will lose as s/he has already been prejudged by the intellectual who will "win" mercilessly. In fact, returning to the intellectual's claim of "human infallibility," the threats employed in the second part of the poem ("so not arouse my anger, / I will reduce you to a / bibliographical ibidem, / demoting you to childhood...") suggest that this intellectual's system of judgment is based on power and superiority. In this respect, as a poetic model of practice, Laviera's parody of intellectual superiority highlights its opposite—intellectual humility, judgment based on "good intentions," and respect toward others regardless of their academic pedigree.

The warning regarding infallibility is not limited to intellectuals, however, for, as we see in the third poem, "boricua," anyone with "prejudice" or "bad intentions" will be judged. It is significant that the centrality of "good" judgment is articulated in a poem that establishes Puerto Ricans as the model community of "love" and "love for respect." As Laviera states in "AmeRícan," and this is apparent in the number of "sketch" poems throughout, "Ricans" are the model community orchestrating this new paradigm for "America." They maintain this role because, as the poet states, they allow for "integration," "experimentation," and are generally a "humanistic" people that easily branch out and accept other peoples.[8] These "model" attributes are certainly present in "boricua," and the themes that come to represent them are "love" and "respect."

> we are a people
> who love to love
> we are loving
> lovers who love
> to love respect,
> the best intentions
> of friendship,
> and we judge from
> the moment on, no
> matter who you are,
> and, if we find
> sincere smiles,
> we can be friends,
> and, if we have a
> drink together,
> we can be brothers,
> on the spot, no
> matter who you are,
> and we have a lot
> of black and white
> and yellow and red
> people whom we
> befriend, we're
> ready to love
> with you, that's
> why we
> say, let there
> be no prejudice,

on race, color is
generally color-blind
with us, that's our
contribution, all
the colors are tied
to our one,
but we must fight
the bad intentions,
we must respect
each other's values... (1985: 16–7)

In this and other poems, the model community of racial love and respect—Puerto Ricans and Nuyoricans—is not passive; it loves and respects others, but actively judges and rejects bad intentions and stereotypes. Similar to "intellectual," the poetic subject provides an explanation of the basis upon which "we" make judgments. In "intellectual," the transition associated with the act of judging is the word "so;" in "boricua," this transition is expressed by the phrase "that's why we say." Unlike the former, in which the themes of superiority and exclusion are primary, "boricua" employs the ethic of inclusiveness to form the basis of judgment. In the previous poem, Laviera utilizes the word, "so," to parody the self-proclaimed superiority of the "intellectual," yet in "boricua," the repetition of the thematic words used to accentuate the identity of the poetic subject have a different effect. The word, "love" and its variants frame (identically) the poem at the beginning and the end. The Puerto Rican/Nuyorican community is a lover of all races and a lover of respect. Quite possibly a self-parody of the idea of the "Latin lover," this poem contains a certain cannibalistic quality. As I highlight in my discussion of "AmeRícan" in the final section of this essay, similar to the guiding concept of Brazilian Modernismo's seminal "Manifesto antropófago" ("Cannibal Manifesto") by Oswald de Andrade (1928), in "boricua," Laviera's model community takes on an imposed identity, which in this case is that of the "Latin lover." Upon claiming this identity, Puerto Ricans take it in and subvert it (or "spits out the malice" as Laviera states in "AmeRícan") to, finally, create something new. In the vein of "Manifesto antropófago," in "boricua" Laviera's model community of respect and love cannibalizes an imposed cultural identity to then actively select what is to be included or rejected. This active process of rejecting "bad intentions" and stereotypes while creating a new identity-based love and respect represents another poetic model of practice in *AmeRícan*.

As a critical utopia, however, Laviera's *AmeRícan* does not offer an overarching solution that will bring about a better America. In other words, while the title poem of the collection establishes an image of the ideal America as one of equality, humanity, and inclusiveness, different from traditional utopian constructs that often emphasize economic, political, and social initiatives or strict utopian binaries (as is exemplified in the polarized structure of "winning or losing" in the "intellectual"), there are no precise blueprints in creating a better America. Yet as we have seen in the previous two poems (two of the ars poetica of the collection), there are certain parameters that sustain Laviera's "walking bridges." Two distinct guidelines exist. One is the rejection of judgment based on "bad intentions," snobbery, and power, and the other is respect, love, and good intentions as exemplified in the model community, that of the Puerto Rican/Nuyorican. As "happy" as the latter may seem, however, the "Rican's" model guidelines are not passive. In the previous poem, for example, the boricua community "judges from the moment on." Nevertheless, in another, more aggressive work, "three-way warning poem," the poetic speaker creatively advises the audience agasinst stereotypes, typographically suggesting that those who choose to use them, will be cut.

1. sin nombre	2. Sin nombre the first
en	este
el	reo
fon	type
do	pu
del	er
nu	to
yo	rri
ri	que
can	ño
hay	sí
un	yes
pu	we
er	can
to	cut
rri	you
que	all
ño	in (1985: 49)

One key word goes unwritten in this poem, and it would seem that Laviera attempts to make this "walking bridge" lead directly back to the reader; if we, the readers, use stereotypes, we could be cut in two (1985: 49).

Form is significant in communicating Laviera's warning against prejudice in "three-way warning poem." Like many of the works in this collection, the poet is typographically inventive in the layout of this poem, which underscores the content of the poem itself. The implied reader must abandon learned systems of judgment when approaching the unknown ("sin nombre"); s/he will not understand the poem (i.e. the individual person, the "sin nombre") if s/he relies on preconceived notions of "knowing." This is a performance poem. If one reads from left to right, as is the norm in the Western world, the poem does not make sense—we do not understand. However, upon looking underneath the superficial and changing our manner of knowing, we read vertically and dig deeper. Nonetheless, even this act does not provide an immediate "key" to the poem. Upon reaching the word, "in," we are left with the unwritten interrogative, "in what?" At that point, we must step back and look at the layout of the poem, "two" columns. Yet, just when the implied reader may believe s/he has found the "key" to the puzzle, the situation of confronting the "sin nombre" repeats itself as s/he, once again, is back at the beginning of the poem. In other words, even when one has delved deeper to assign a name and individual identity on the unknown, this key does not unlock the identity of other "sin nombres." An important, yet often neglected or precarious, aspect of utopian projects is the place of the individual within the collective. Through this playful yet serious poem, Laviera stresses another model of practice—the ongoing need to move beyond stereotypes and recognize the individual behind the "sin nombre."

Interestingly, the distance between "we" and "you" and the poet's insistence on honoring the individual and her/his name continues to be a subject in Laviera's recent poem, "nideaquínideallá." In this work, "we" (Puerto Ricans, Nuyoricans, and Latinos) are constantly "misnamed": "We in all of us ustedes / siempre malnombreándonos" (2006a: 175). While the poem suggests that this "misnaming" is due to racism and a lack of care in accurately pronouncing Latina/o names, the poetic speaker allows himself the liberty to define his own name—it is "yet to be defined / evolucionario hybrid." His first name is "de aquí." "[D]e allá" is identified as one of his "last names" but later it is his "middle name." After a few updates and redefinitions, at the end of the poem the poetic speaker states that his "last new latest name" is "nideaquínideallá." Despite the evolutionary character of his name and the very unspecificity of place that it affirms—"neitherfromherenorfromthere"—he adamantly requests that we write this "name" correctly (with accents) and in Spanish but also "incorrectly" (without capital letters): "nideaquínideallá / escríbelo junto / sin letra mayúscula / gracias" (2006a: 175). Whether it be an "evolucionario" name as in "nideaquínideallá," a "sin nombre," or another persistent trace of culture and language that resists assimilation to assert its place within the dominant culture—an "AO," a capital "R," or a Spanish accent—, Laviera's poetry highlights the practice of respecting the individual and her/his name as well as the power of immigrant/migrant/minority communities to define change and continuity on their own terms.

"Ethnic Tributes"

The first section of *AmeRícan* is entitled "Ethnic Tributes," and the act of opening his book with poems such as "boricua," "arab," "black," "chinese," "jamaican," and "jewish" is certainly not coincidental. These tributes underscore, in a very performative manner, just how many "marginal" groups form part of and contribute to the identity of the United States. Whether by reproducing the "voices" of these groups as the speaking subjects ("I" or "We"), by constructing an image of them ("he," "she," or "they"), or by recreating and assuming the voice of these groups to speak about them ("he," "she," or "they), each page presents us with another group of Americans who have their own ethnic specificity. Nevertheless, vis-à-vis the poems, "intellectual" and "boricua," situated at the beginning of these tributes, we have received a warning against prejudice and any airs of infallibility. Like an extended "three-way warning poem," when gathered together—the warnings and the ethnic tributes—these poems seem to represent poetic models of practice as they suggest to the reader new ways of reading, judging, and acting; readers must think self-reflectively, going "across forth and across back / back across," judging their own prejudice and any facile interpretation of *AmeRícan*'s tributes.

In fact, *AmeRícan*'s poems constantly seem to attempt to destabilize the audience's temptation for interpretive dominance over the text and suggest the idea of an on-going and analytical process in defining a micro and macro national identity. This work's form, which relies heavily on dramatic speech with its tone, parody, and humor, attempts to spur the audience to actively go "back and forth"—or "backnforth" as we do in "nideaquínideallá"—over

Laviera's poems. One wonders, with curiosity and frustration, whether Laviera's ethnic tributes—to Chinese, Japanese, Arab, Jewish or African Americans, for example—are actually striving to unravel stereotypes harbored by his public or whether they are simply another reproduction of stereotypes themselves. Perhaps the most visual example of these ethnic tributes is the poem, "chinese."

>   all
>   those
>   fa
>   ces
>   hap
>   py
>   el
>   ders
>   trea
>   ted
>   with
>   res
>   pect
>   by
>   the
>   clan
>   won
>   der
>   ful
>   chi
>   nese
>   cul
>   ture
>   all
>   pay
>   ing
>   hom
>   age
>   to
>   the
>   wise (1985: 20)

Situated next to the title of the poem, the poem's layout, in the form of a diagonal line, reproduces the visual stereotype of "slanted" eyes. Furthermore, this layout renders the reading of the words in the poem to be abrupt and choppy. In other words, it is difficult to read the poem in a fluid manner without stops and pauses. One could argue that this may be another case in which Laviera tries to reproduce the speech patterns of the different peoples of America, which in "chinese" would be the speech of a non-native English speaking Chinese-American in New York. Looking beyond these features of the poem, however, we find a seemingly very respectful ethnic tribute to the Chinese. Their tribute—or rather "contribution"—to America is a communal respect for the elders and the wise. Nevertheless, after being destabilized by the layout of the poem, the reader may also question whether this statement too is a stereotype.[9] Both typographically as well as in the ways in which it seems to attempt to destabilize the reader, this poem is similar to "three-way warning poem." Both urge us to redefine our way of approaching stereotypes. When faced with the unknown ("sin nombre"), in the case of "three-way warning poem," Laviera seems to suggest that we go beyond and dig deeper—a lesson that is visually exemplified in the layout of the poem. In "chinese," we visually confront a stereotype that is represented on the page with a diagonal line only to later, perhaps, go beyond the visual to look at the elements of Chinese culture.

One poem that seems particularly problematic in terms of the question of stereotypes is "japanese (joke?)." "Three-way warning poem" indicates that anyone who uses stereotypes will be "cut in (two)." Nonetheless, it would seem that rather than deconstructing ethnic stereotypes this poem reproduces them. This anecdotal work describes the fictitious life of a Japanese-American who escaped to the mountains of Hawaii when his "mama-san" and "papa-san" were killed during the Japanese attack on Pearl Harbor. After forty years of living in seclusion, the Japanese-American comes down from the mountain in 1982:

> he arrived at sea-level
> he was prepared to die
> and, guess what, he saw
> the billboard toyota ads
> and he thought the japanese
> had won the war. (1985: 30)

Laviera associates Japanese culture with commercialism, arguably reproducing a stereotype prevalent in the 1980s that Japanese companies were taking over the United States. The paradoxical subtitle of the poem, "joke?," could be interpreted as a tactic on the part of the poet to compel his readers to think critically about the use and danger of ethnic jokes. However, the inclusion of the question mark that follows the word, "joke," can also be seen as a serious insinuation that, in fact, Laviera's association between commercialism and the Japanese and the economic power within the United States is "not a joke."

As noted above, one of the "walking bridges" that Laviera's poetry seems to highlight as key to constructing a new American identity is by "branching out" through what Juan Flores has described as strategic "associations" among other colonized or minority cultures (1993: 185). Laviera pays tribute to these colonized peoples throughout *AmeRícan* in poems such as "black," "cuban," "irish," "jamaican," "jewish," and "nuyorican." The African diaspora is registered numerous times, in "black," "cuban," and "jamaican," for example, recognizing a common historical thread and affirming a continuity of community despite distance and the particulars of their colonial history.

In *AmeRícan* we also find what the author has described in the poem, "english," and in an interview with William Luis (1992: 1028) as the "humanistic" quality of conquered peoples to branch out toward other peoples. However, in this interview, one of Laviera's remarks suggests that the idea of creating a work in which a diversity of peoples is represented does not originate in a "nuyorican" or Puerto Rican "humanism." The poet states, "In my poems everything is structured so that nadie me joda." Writing in three languages is a political strategy, he explains, through which the poet seeks to protect himself from criticism (Luis 1992: 1028). And, while the colonized and the marginalized maintain a predominant space in this collection, as we find in the examples of "spanish," "english," and "nuyorican," everyone—even the "colonizer"/ "metropolis"—is included. In other words, and as Juan Egea indicates, in this statement by Laviera we find an example of "defensive humanism."[10]

Branches and Leaves: Echoes of Walt Whitman

Although the comparison would require a much more in-depth analysis, it is worthy to note briefly that Laviera's "branching out" in his poetic construction of America is reminiscent of the utopian work of another New Yorker, Walt Whitman.[11] Like *AmeRícan*, Whitman's *Leaves of Grass* (1965) is epic in scope and celebrates the "common person," immigrants, and the diversity of peoples, voices, songs, and spaces of the United States. Albeit without the strong oral component captured by Laviera in his poetic sketches, as we find in "I hear America Singing," Whitman also pays tribute to the human voice and America's multiplicity of songs. In this poem Whitman perceives unity in difference: "I hear America singing, the varied carols I hear" (1965: 12–3). The theme of America as a nation defined by a unity as well as a diversity of geography, occupation, and race is also honored in the "branches" and "feuillage" (foliage) in "Our Old Feuillage" (or "American Feuillage"): "The seven millions of distinct families, and the same number of / dwellings—always these, and more, branching forth into / numberless branches, / Always the free range and diversity! always the continent of / Democracy!" (Whitman 1965: 171). Interestingly, the geographic vantage point from which Whitman observes and catalogues the peoples of America is New York ("Through Manahatta's streets I walking, these things gathering"), and, like Laviera, he strives to include "All characters, movements, growths—a few noticed, myriads unnoticed" (1965: 172).

As we find in Laviera's "Ethnic Tributes," Whitman's "Song of Myself" provides sketches of the lives of a variety of people in America—"Of every hue and caste am I, of every rank and religion, / A farmer, mechanic, artist, gentleman, sailor, quaker, / Prisoner, fancy-man, rowdy, lawyer, physician, priest" (1965: 45). Similar to Laviera, Whitman does not limit his portrait of America to the heroic and the mighty; he includes the "common" woman and man, "What is commonest, cheapest, nearest, easiest, is Me" (1965: 41). And while Whitman does not attempt to reproduce the oral qualities of the Americans included in his sketches, as with "Our Old Feuillage," his "I" claims to collect and articulate the voice of the oppressed:

> I play not marches for accepted victors only, I play marches for
>   conquer'd and slain persons. (1965: 46)
>
> ....
> Unscrew the locks from the doors!
> Unscrew the doors themselves from their jambs!

> Whoever degrades another degrades me
>
> ....
>
> I speak the pass-word primeval, I give the sign of democracy,
> By God! I will accept nothing which all cannot have their counterpart of on the same terms.
>
> Through me many long dumb voices,
> Voices of the interminable generations of prisoners and slaves,
> Voices of the diseas'd and despairing and of thieves and dwarfs ... (1965: 52)

In addition to memorializing these voices, Whitman recognizes the vitality of the diversity of sights, sounds, and people in the city (1965: 55–6). The spectrum of the people of the United States is celebrated, "I resist any thing better than my own diversity" (1965: 45). And, diversity is copresent with union, as it passes through "Me": "Do I contradict myself? / Very well then I contradict myself, (I am large, I contain multitudes.)" (1965: 88). Like Laviera's *AmeRícan* and, more specifically, the title poem "AmeRícan," Whitman's "Self" absorbs but does not devour diversity, "Absorbing all to myself..." (1965: 40) [...] "Regardless of others, ever regardful of others" (1965: 44). Similar to the "walking bridges" and indeterminacy we find in Laviera, "Song of Myself" "[does not] talk of the beginning or the end" but rather of the approximations to "perfection," "heaven," and "hell" in the "now" (1965: 30). And in "Our Old Feuillage" Whitman embraces a complex but unified American identity but admits not knowing how to name it: "O lands! All so dear to me—what you are, (whatever it is,) I / putting it at random in these songs, become a part of that, / whatever it is" (1965: 175). This expression of indeterminacy and not knowing the precise composition of America ("whatever" in Whitman) is also revealed in the title of Laviera's "nideaquínideallá." Proudly affirming his name ("neitherfromherenorfromthere") the poetic speaker explains that it is "impossible to blend / impossible to categorize / impossible to analyze" (1965: 175). Perhaps this indeterminacy of the exact contours of the identity of the United States is the most striking congruency between Laviera and Whitman.

Elusive "Enemies"

Before turning to the first word in the title of this section, my use of quotations for the word "enemies" warrants explanation. As noted above, the concept of the critical utopia and the metaphor of "walking bridges" both highlight an open-ended process of moving toward utopia. This concept of approximating the ideal is exemplified in the "back and forth" movements of Laviera's "walking bridges." It also acknowledges that there will be challenges that will need to be resolved along the way. Upon reading *AmeRícan*, it is clear that the "enemies" of Laviera's ideal society are not permanently codified as adversaries. They are, in this sense, "problems yet to be solved" and, at some point in time, these "enemies" may be allies. In other words, by rejecting the "us versus them" binary so central to utopian discourse, Laviera allows for possible associations with AmeRíca's current "enemies" in the future. While leaving open this possibility—this "walking bridge"—Laviera simultaneously incorporates the rhetoric of power of the dominant other to critique and redefine it to reflect the lived experiences of the those peoples living in "nowhere." As we will see in the following discussion of "spanish," "nuyorican," and "english," the conceptual and culturally dominant "enemies" of *AmeRícan* are key in Laviera's formation of a new American (U.S.) identity.

Turning now to the word "elusive" in literary works in which the nation or a political or economic system represents utopia, one finds a clear and identifiable target—an "enemy" country, people, or system that the utopian community rejects. Different from the binaries inherent to these paradigms, the "enemies" in AmeRícan are certainly less precise and are more conceptual and global in nature. Yet, while AmeRíca's "enemies" are elusive, they do reveal certain congruences. Similar to the global expanse of the colonized communities brought together in Laviera's AmerRíca, the "enemies" we find in *AmeRícan* share a common thread—they perceive themselves as superior for reasons of colonial heritage, economic power, or linguistic, cultural, or intellectual superiority. For instance, this critique of hegemony and arrogance is exemplified in the poem, "intellectual," through the portrayal of judgment based on "bad intentions" and an abuse of power and dominance. This colonized/colonizer dynamic is also registered in the poem, "spanish." The "enemy" in this poem is "arrogance," "pride," and a lack of solidarity with the colonized on the basis of a combination of colonial and linguistic superiority. Despite a lack of "maternal support," Spain's "language outlives [its] world power" and has become "major north and south american tongue" (1985: 33). Affirming the lived experience and contributions of the colonial "inferior," Laviera notes that the geographic expanse and longevity of Spanish is not due to any inherent quality of the language itself or to the Spanish people; it is rather due to the "humble" efforts of the colonized and the "folkloric flavorings of all your former colonies" and the "nativeness of the spanish / mixing with the indians and the blacks" that has "maintain[ed] your precious tongue." Reminiscent of phrases such as "do not arouse my anger" in "intellectual," the poem, "spanish," reproduces the rhetoric of power, which is specifically colonial in this case, in order to reveal the error of the "enemy" by stating, "we await your affirmation of what we have fought to preserve. [...] i'm your humble son" (1985: 33). In a very performative manner, Laviera presents its former colonial master with its own rhetoric of linguistic superiority, while at the same time highlighting a shared linguistic heritage. In this poetic model of practice, Laviera does not sever his relationship to the former colonial power, but rather "humbly" extends a "walking bridge" to Latin America's former colonial power to allow for possible relations in the future.

Laviera builds another "walking bridge" from an "inferior" community to the "superior" or dominant "mother country" in "nuyorican." In this poem, Laviera describes the lived experience of rejection and the feeling of being "nowhere" by a U.S. Puerto Rican who returns to his island homeland. In spite of the poetic speaker's expression of loyalty to Puerto Rican Spanish and his island heritage and although he indicates that poverty forced him to move away from the island, Puerto Rico rejects its "hijo de la migración:" "me desprecias, me miras mal, me atacas mi hablar." Yet, within this colonial situation, the native Puerto Rican condemns the Nuyorican for being too "American," while the former eats "mcdonalds en discotecas americanas." Despite Puerto Rico's hypocrisy and rejection of its migrant community, the Nuyorican can return to his own "Puerto Rico" in New York:

> [...] y no pude bailar la salsa en san juan, la que yo
> bailo en mis barrios llenos de todas tus costumbres,
> así que, si tú no me quieres, pues yo tengo
> un puerto rico sabrosísimo en que buscar refugio
> en nueva york, y en muchos otros callejones
> que honran tu presencia, preservando todos
> tus valores, así que, por favor, no me
> hagas sufrir, ¿sabes? (1985: 53)

Similar to "spanish" where the Latin American Spanish speaker preserves the former colonial tongue without its "maternal support," in this poem the "nuyorican" maintains the values and customs of the "mother country," despite the latter's rejection on the basis of cultural superiority. In "spanish," the colonized speaker merely requests Spain's "affirmation," and in "nuyorican," the migrant Puerto Rican asks that the island put an end to the suffering it inflicts on him. With this request, the migrant extends a "walking bridge" to his mother country. Like the critical utopia, which recognizes that there will be issues that will need to be addressed in the future, Laviera allows for future collaborations between the "inferior" and "superior" by following up this request with a question. Similar to the answer requested in "spanish" ("we await your affirmation"), by ending the poem with a query, "¿sabes?," Laviera invites an answer, and, thus, establishes the possibility for future dialogue. In both "spanish" and "nuyorican" this openness to respectful exchange or "branching out" in the future with those who might view themselves as "superior" represents another model of practice.

In both cases the theme and rhetoric of loyalty to an ungrateful master is part of Laviera's subversion of a master/slave dynamic in which the "slave" comes to assume a superior position in relation to the culturally dominant motherland. Nevertheless, even as these poems critique Spain and Puerto Rico for not accepting their culturally "inferior" Americans (South, Central and North), the role of the "enemy other" in *AmeRícan* is distinct from more utopian paradigms that draw strict lines between the "utopian" hero/community and the "dystopian" other/enemy. In fact, as noted above, I refer to the "enemy other" with quotation marks because, despite the collection's pronounced anti-colonial content, the poet does not further polarize the relationship between the "superior" and the "inferior" in a way that demonizes or permanently codifies the identity of the former further distancing it from the latter. Maintaining the theme of "branching out," these poems provide the "enemy" with "walking bridges"—an opportunity to redefine the relationship between the "core dominant culture" and the AmeRícan project of establishing associations between differences in a global community.

Juan Flores explains that Puerto Ricans interact with other groups in North America according to their spatial proximity and "congruent cultural experience" (1993: 191–2). Within the spectrum of strategic relationships in *AmeRícan*, on the basis of language and culture Spain and Puerto Rico are textualized as being in closer proximity to the Nuyorican. In other words, despite their lack of affirmation and acceptance of the Nuyorican, when one compares "spanish," "nuyorican," and another poem, "english," Spanish and Puerto Rican peoples are closer to the Nuyorican than the English. Moreover, it is because of these ties to their "motherlands" that the Nuyorican asks for acceptance. This aside, the poem "english" is similar to the previous two poems in the structure of power that it establishes between the metropolis and the colony. For example, and similar to the poems "intellectual," "spanish," and "nuyorican," in "english" we find a rhetoric of superiority/inferiority that has a certain master/slave or absolute monarchic twist:

your
forced
indulgences
our
backbones
constantly
searching
for-your-greatness ... (1985: 23)

Like the poem, "spanish," in "english" Laviera establishes a connection between language and colonial power. Different from "spanish" and "nuyorican," however, the cultural distance between the inferior "we" and its superior is more pronounced, and, in fact, is reminiscent of José Enrique Rodó's polarized vision between a cold and overly scientific Anglo world influence and a humanistic Hispanic colonial legacy in *Ariel* (1971 [1900]). In Laviera's poem, English (the global power as well as the language) is recognized in the world for its "growth," "definitions," "research," and "ambitions." Unlike "spanish" and "nuyorican," in this poem the poetic speaker (the colonized) expresses no cultural affinity to "english," and, in fact, is specific in naming the reason for this cultural distance; "english" "ex-creates" and "hates-love"—two qualities *AmeRícan* very explicitly associates with the model community: love and creating. Once again, appropriating and subverting the rhetoric of empire and cultural superiority, Laviera asserts that despite "english" ambition and growth, the "humanistic" growth of the world rests on the backbones of English speakers who are "forced" to speak the language of English-speaking (neo) colonial powers. In other words, just as the Spanish-speaking American preserves the Spanish language and as the Nuyorican preserves Puerto Rican culture—despite the loss of imperial power by the former and a pronounced case of colonial hypocrisy in the latter—in "english" the "backbones" (i.e. the person who is linguistically and economically distant from this kind of global expansion) seek to "re-define / ambitions / in-your-language / we / struggle / to / make / everyone / humanistically / proud / of / your / relationship / to / the / growth / of / the / world." Through negation, which in this case is articulated by the need to "re-define," Laviera indicates that economic growth and "ambition" are not the paths the English language should follow. As such, appropriating and "re-defining" the English language, the poet cannibalizes a language, which in this poem is expressly not his own (i.e., it is "your-language"), in order to (re) articulate "ambitions" and the relationship between (neo) colonial, English-speaking powers and the "growth of the world."

One common denominator between "spanish," "nuyorican," and "english," and the "re-definition" of a U.S. American identity is the movement of peoples either through immigration and/or colonialism. All of the peoples that make up the section of "ethnic tributes" are immigrant/migrant communities living in and making up a very diverse cultural and ethnic identity within the U.S. One of these (im)migrant groups in particular, the Nuyoricans—the model community that branches out to bring all other communities together—is linked via language and (neo)colonialism to Spain, English, the United States, and Puerto Rico. Furthermore, a recurring theme in all four of the previously mentioned poems is the power to define, recognize, and affirm (judge) on the basis of a dominant core culture. And while "intellectual" may at first seem unrelated to the topic of colonialism, as Ángel Rama, Mary Louise Pratt, David Spurr, and Martin Leinhard indicate, colonialism and writing are powerful associates in codifying identities and establishing dominant discourse.[12] In *AmeRícan*, Laviera incorporates these discourses of power to redefine them according to the lived experiences of the peoples of "nowhere"—those who contribute to the identity of the United States and the global community but whose contributions are left outside of the constructions of national and global identity in the name of assimilating to a preordained and codified core identity.

Throwing Out the "Melting Pot"
In two of the most famous poems of *AmeRícan*, the title poem and "asimilao," Laviera confronts the culturally dominant U.S. American identity by conceptually redefining the ethnic and cultural composition of the United States and does so by articulating this diverse composition on a linguistic level. In both poems, the act of redefining an American identity parallels

a call to recognize the ethnic and linguistic diversity within the United States—by the dominant core as well as by minority groups themselves. Accompanying this call for recognition is an affirmation of an on-going and real process of the creation of national identity that differs from assimilation, which in the United States has come to be known as the "melting pot."

The topic of assimilation is, of course, the topic of the poem, "asimilao."

> assimilated? qué assimilated,
> brother, yo soy asimilao,
> así mi la o sí es verdad
> tengo un lado asimilao.
> you see, they went deep.... Ass
> oh........they went deeper...SEE
> oh, oh,...they went deeper...ME
> but the sound LAO was too black
> for LATED, LAO could not be
> trans*lated*, assimilated,
> no, asimilao, melao,
> it became a black
> spanish word but
> we do have asimilados
> perfumados and by the
> last count even they
> were becoming asimilao
> how can it be analyzed
> as american? así que se
> chavaron
> trataron
> pero no
> pudieron
> con el AO
> de la palabra
> principal, dénles gracias a los prietos
> que cambiaron asimilado al popular asimilao. (1985: 54)

As he does in many poems in this collection, Laviera uses humor, tone, and language in "asimilao" to simultaneously highlight, linguistically deconstruct, and rearticulate a key issue in his redefinition of America—assimilation. The poem also provides another model of practice, that of questioning, analyzing, and seeing alternative but unrecognized realities that might run contrary to the status quo. In "asimilao" Laviera details the movements of "seeing" and recognizing an alternative process to assimilation. The poet's work to redefine this term is found between the title and the first word that is very importantly accompanied by a question mark. The distance between the words, "asimilao" and "assimilated" presents a conceptual gap that is further accentuated by the question mark; being asimilao is not the same as being assimilated, and the disparity between them requires us to question ("?") the application of the second to the first. This disparity of terms, vis-à-vis the use of the question mark and the poem's versatile use of both English and Spanish, indicates that the gap between these concepts is more than an issue of mistranslation. Once again, the theme of judgment comes into play in the space between these two words, as the second, the prescriptive norm, is rejected and put literally into question. The prescriptive norm is quickly corrected with humor, tone, and code-switching in the first and second lines as the subject writes/speaks against it in Spanish and English, communicating in a performative but real way that this norm does not register the reality of the speaker/writer. An affirmation (judgment) is presented, "assimilated." It is questioned with the query mark "?," and corrected to assert through the language and content of the poem to declare something else, "asimilao." While difficult to analyze and quantify in any concrete manner, attitude and tone are directly linked to the poem's process of questioning assimilation and the affirmation of "lo popular" as an alternative to it. Following the question mark and, as if to say, "are you kidding," the lines, "qué assimilated, / brother, yo soy asimilao," resemble an expository declaration after which the poetic speaker explains the reasons why the term, "assimilated," triggers his sarcastic reaction. Judgment, this time on the part of the speaker, comes into play as the "asimilao" provides a transition to the answer, "así" and, at the same time, spells out in Spanish phonemes this process of transculturation[13] ("así mi la o sí es verdad / tengo un lado asimilao") as if some of his interlocutors do not understand.

The poem has a debate-like structure—characterized by affirmation, questioning, correcting, and re-affirmation—and, fittingly, Laviera literally asks that his interlocutor judge once again the accuracy of the term, assimilation. Having already presented one variation on the word, assimilation, ("asimilao"), as well as literally spelling it out and, ("así mi la o"), the poetic speaker dramatizes the movement of "going deeper." Similar to the conceptual challenges (i.e., the interrogative presented via the distance between concept and form) and the typographic devices used in "three-way warning poem" and "chinese," "asimilao" proposes the movement of learning to read (people and their processes) in new ways. In "chinese," Laviera projects the movement of going beyond the title, the "slanted" layout, and the choppy speech of the poem to vertically and diagonally "go deeper" beyond appearance and prejudice. In "three-way warning poem" the poet suggests the action of reading vertically and cyclically to confront stereotypes. In "asimilao" Laviera details the movements of "seeing" and recognizing an alternative process to assimilation. As the poem progresses we "go deeper" and beyond the first word to encounter the truth ("verdad")

you see, they went deep.... Ass
oh........they went deeper...SEE
oh, oh,...they went deeper...ME [...] (1985: 54)

Reading "deeper" (vertically) we, the readers, are judged ("Ass") and challenged to see this different process: "Ass SEE ME." The first question mark has also prepared us for a problem ("oh," "oh, oh"); as we go deeper, the final phoneme that completes the so-called identity of the U.S. ("lated") does not fit: "but the sound LAO was too black / for LATED, LAO could not be / translated, assimilated."

Laviera establishes a connection between this alternative process to assimilation and the title of the book in asking, "how can it be analyzed / as american?" There is a clear reference to a structure of a scientific investigation (theory, investigation, and proof or disproof of the theory) and Laviera portrays a process of investigation—once again "going deeper"— that disproves the "rule": "chavaron / trataron / pero no pudieron." The element that is untranslatable, both in Spanish and English, is the piece that does not "melt"—the "AO." The concept and the very language of assimilation, according to this poem, does not reflect the reality of this poetic speaker as the poem "ends with a confident reference to the Black base of Puerto Rican popular culture" (Flores 1993: 194). The concepts of judgment and affirmation return in the final lines of the poem; the Puerto Rican judges and affirms his role in a process different from assimilation but also asks others (and I do not believe this petition is limited to Puerto Ricans although they are certainly important here) to recognize the contributions of Black Americans in constructing a new national identity.

As Laviera's 2006 poem "nideaquínideallá" illustrates, the persistent "AO" in "asimilao" has yet to disappear. In fact, the echo of this phoneme continues to resist codification and assimilation. The "I" in this recent poem "cannot be defined / cannot be categorized / cannot be pasteurizao / cannot be homogenizao" (Laviera 2006a: 173). Similar to "asimilao," when we read the second stanza of "nideaquínideallá" vertically, we find a repeated rejection of any preordained process of classification of one's identity—four times we read the word, "cannot." The impossibility of defining, melting or assimilating the poetic speaker's "name" is found in the penultimate stanza: "nideaquínideallá / impossible to blend / impossible to categorize / impossible to analyze / impossible to synthesize..." (2006a: 175). The poetic speaker's name has "yet to be defined," is "in between," and is difficult to place on a map. Literally "nideaquínideallá" is a name of origin (de) that negates two places (aquí and allá) that change according to one's location in space. It is precisely in this liminal space that the poetic speaker forges an identity in a creative "backnforth" movement and an "evolucionario" process of hybridization. Despite, or perhaps because of, the unspecificity and movement related to this space/name, the poetic speaker politely requests that we pronounce and write his name correctly, accents and all.

Together with "intellectual," "boricua," and "asimilao," the title poem constitutes the *ars poetica* of *AmeRícan*. Contrary to the example of exclusion, domination and "bad intentions" in "intellectual," "AmeRícan" endorses the inclusion of "all that is good" and the process of re-defining America from the lived popular experience of the marginalized. Of course, the far-reaching concept of constructing an ideal society on the inclusion of "all that is good" runs contrary to most examples of utopian discourse and provides another example of the openness of the critical utopia. Similar to the "walking bridges" extended to AmeRíca's "enemies" in "spanish," "nuyorican," and "english," the delineations Laviera draws between "us" and "them" are also more generalized to include "anything else compatible." Moreover, expanding upon the example of the Puerto Rican/Nuyorican community's "love" for and "best intentions" in branching out to others of all races in "boricua," "AmeRícan" confirms the role of the U.S. Puerto Rican/Nuyorican in re-defining America. In both poems the Nuyorican/Puerto Rican is the model community and the epicenter of social change:

> we gave birth to a new generation
> AmeRícan, it includes everything
> imaginable you-name-it-we-got-it
> society.
>
> we gave birth to a new generation,
> AmeRícan salutes all folklores,
> european, indian, black, spanish,
> and anything else compatible... (1985: 94)

Redefining the very word, "American," we find that the "Rican" orchestrates the formation of a new U.S. identity as the "Rican" is accentuated with a capital "R" and the accent on the "I."

In fact, as we find in "asimilao" and many other poems in this collection, the accented "í" and the capital "R" are just two illustrations of the ways in which "AmeRícan" provides an example of an alternative way of reading, conceptualizing, and defining U.S. identity. As with the critical utopia, readers of "AmeRícan" must think critically reaching beyond customary ways of reading and directionality itself. In terms of its visual appearance on the written page, the layout of the poem resembles that of a dictionary. Similar to the manner in which the Chicana writer and activist Gloria Anzaldúa (1999) highlights and repeats the title of her poem "To live on the Borderlands means you," to offer a variety of meanings of the border experience, Laviera sets apart the word, "AmeRícan," to offer a list of its multiple definitions. One of the definitions provided relates to inclusiveness, which is central to American re-definition and registered in a variety of manners throughout the poem. In this passage, for example, the idea of union among difference and plurality is accentuated by the hyphens that connect the words, "it includes everything / imaginable you-name-it-we-got-it / society." This union among difference is also underscored by the combination of the words, "all" and "anything else" between which we find a listing of different racial groups and ending with a colon to indicate that the expanse of "Rican" inclusiveness continues.

Following the colon we find a list of the many definitions of the word "AmeRícan." Through the repetition of the word "AmeRícan" and the definitions provided, the list itself underscores the process of self-affirmation and branching out, "blending and mixing" with other "compatible" communities in the United States. The word, "AmeRícan," is repeated twelve times and is spatially set apart yet aligned to Laviera's description of this new identity. Once again, the layout and language of the poem suggest a new way of "reading"—one may read vertically (the repetition of the word, "AmeRícan"), horizontally (linking the "Rican" American identity with its "compatible" others in the United States), find new meaning within individual words themselves ("AmeRícan"), and, at the same time, collect these readings into one. The "reading" movements highlight and parallel the trips the AmeRícan takes in her/his unending "walking bridges:"

>   AmeRícan,   across forth and across back
>   back across and forth back
>   forth across and back and forth
>   our trips are walking bridges! (1985: 94)

Walking on bridges that are often known for their instability—sometimes they are made of ropes, and thus, sway from side to side—the AmeRícan provides an example of reading the interactions of peoples within the United States by taking a traditional phrase that in itself implies an on-going process, "walking back and forth," and revising it by repositioning its "beginnings" and "ends" ("back" and "forth") and an adverb that implies the movement between them ("across").[14] Literally offering an alternative way of reading, Laviera's poem provides an example of a critical utopia in which its inhabitants go beyond (deeper, sideways, and between) simple preordained ways of understanding to repeatedly and critically approach the complexity of defining identity in the United States.

Although marginal groups are certainly not located in the "margins" of Laviera's poetry, another model of practice highlighted in this poem is that of examining "the whole page" of American identity to view and reevaluate the contribution of people who have previously been located "nowhere"—the blank space of the margin. True to the challenge posed by a generalized concept of a total and all-encompassing utopia and postmodern theory, Laviera situates the margin at the center while inscribing a new identity in which the center is not completely displaced, but rather included as one of many "American" parts of a greater whole. Moreover, by incorporating a discursive method also common in literary utopias and postmodern expression, Laviera appropriates and subverts aspects of past and present reality to define and articulate the parameters of a better society. As in Oswald de Andrade's "Manifesto Antropófago" (1928), the lexicon of Laviera's critique of domination and superiority points to cultural cannibalism:

> it all dissolved into itself, the attempt
> was truly made, the attempt was truly
> absorbed, digested, we spit out
> the poison, we spit out the malice,
> we stand, affirmative in action,
> to reproduce a broader answer to the
> marginality that gobbled us up abruptly! (1985: 94)

Similar to the attempt to prove the theory of assimilation in "asimilao" ("chavaron / trataron / pero no pudieron"), an attempt is "truly made" to go deeper and beyond a given and dominant identity to include other cultures (like the "AO"). After "absorbing and digesting" both the center and the margins, the "malice" is spit out to reveal that the "center" had previously only allowed for a limited answer to "marginality." Expanding upon the words, "all" and "anyone" and the hyphen and colon of greater inclusiveness, what is left over, after rejecting "the malice" are the previously marginalized voices and practices of the people who now claim their space "[blending and mixing] with all that is good." After spitting out the malice, we find "plena-rhythms in new york," "the soul gliding talk of gospel / boogie music," and "new words in spanglish tenements, / fast tongue moving street corner 'que / corta' talk" "abounding inside so many ethnic english / people..." (1985: 95). Laviera does not reject the "good" in culturally dominant cultures—he does not push aside "ethnic english people" to affirm their participation in a new national identity. While keeping these "good" parts, AmeRícan (both the book as a whole and the title poem) seeks a "broader answer to marginality" inscribing the voices and practices of others to reconfigure the identity and purpose of the United States. Of course, the act of self-affirmation in this collection goes beyond the theme of good and bad judgment and the use of simplified and limited terms associated with the dominant core of society to describe more complex processes of cultural interaction. Laviera's assertion of the need for self-definition and affirmation underscores the incorporation of the previously excluded or marginalized voices—rejecting bad and exclusionary judgment of others and limiting terms that "gobble up" the other "abruptly."

It is because of bad, exclusionary judgment and limiting "terms" that Laviera's act of self-affirmation is very closely bound to the need to redefine the language and terminology used to discuss cultural identity. Similar to his registering of an alternative to assimilation in "asimilao" to allow for the real but yet uninscribed black "AO," in "AmeRícan" Laviera redefines the language used to articulate the cultural composition of America and its ideological directions:

> AmeRícan, defining myself my own way any way many ways Am e Rícan, with the big R and the accent on the í!
>
> ....
>
> AmeRícan, defining the new america, humane america, admired america, loved america, harmonious america, the world in peace, our energies collectively invested to find other civilizations, to touch God, further and further, to dwell in the spirit of the divinity!
>
> AmeRícan, yes, for now, for i love this, my second land, and i dream to take the accent from the altercation, and be proud to call myself american, in the u.s. sense of the word, AmeRícan, America! (1985: 95)

Analogous to Laviera's efforts to "go deeper" and beyond a limited and dominant system of representation, words in his poetry undergo a democratizing process of redefinition and representation. Words are broken up to accent interlingual meanings or to expand the U.S. linguistic canon to include Spanish and Spanglish (Rauline and Laviera 1998: 157). Furthermore, in this and other collections of Laviera's poetry, capital letters are few in number. When they appear, as is the case of foregrounding, they stand out like the posters used by Brecht in "Mother Courage and Her Children" (1966) ["Mutter Courage und ihre Kinder"] to destabilize and produce new and critical ways of approaching the aesthetic on the part of the audience. In the process of "defining myself my own way," the "r" in "American" is capitalized to accentuate subjectivity within the greater whole.

Similar to this process, by reading both vertically and horizontally, "america" with a small "A" is accentuated as "new." Lacking its capital "A" and defined as "new" we recognize the signpost of a counterpoint literary utopia; the reality of the present in America is not "humane," "admired," "loved," "harmonious," "in peace" or collective. Yet, the space between the word, "AmeRícan," and the very explicit utopian effort to reach an ideal ("to touch God, further and further, / to dwell in the spirit of divinity!") is marked by a distance that still needs to be overcome—illustrated by the space between the word, "AmeRícan," and the collective endeavor of reaching a totality—the individual and the collective in reaching God. This distance is expressed in the last stanza of the poem in which Laviera states that an "accent" ("í") marks an "altercation." Calling upon the implied reader's expectations with another linguistic altercation, Laviera establishes the temporal and ideological path that will bridge this distance between the individual, nation and totality; redefining the abbreviation of the United States, Laviera notes that the altercation and its resolution will not occur until a more "little case" "us" is found in the U.S.[15] In other words, until the "Rican" can say s/he forms part of an "us" within the United States, s/he will not take away the accent that distinguishes the last two words of the poem, "AmeRícan, America!" An idea illustrated throughout the collection, the distance between these words is immense, as whole groups of people are marginalized in the space between. I would argue that it is because of the distance between "AmeRícan" and "America" that specificity (an accent and capital letter) marks the beginning of the book with its title, *AmeRícan*. Yet the last word in this poem and the collection itself is "America." Not coincidentally, this is the first time that this word is inscribed according to its traditional use; the "A" is capitalized, the "R" is not and the accent is not present. The word, "America," by itself is not the alpha and the omega. Totality, as very literally suggested in the second to last stanza of the collection ("to touch God, further and further, / to dwell in the spirit of divinity!") spans the gap between the individual subject, "I" (I'm a Rican), and the collective (u.s.). Unless the first (the individual) is recognized, the "omega" is incomplete.

According to Raúl Vidales, any utopian vision cannot be accepted as an attainable reality if it does not identify that which is possible (1991: 51). The many voices the listener and reader encounters in *AmeRícan* underscore the fact that the map of this ideal society is firmly situated in spaces that are familiar and easily recognizable—in streets, discotheques, and over the telephone—and that it is created by what Michel de Certeau calls the "practices of everyday life." And, as Flores argues, creativity and the quotidian are the locus of Nuyorican expression as it "responds to and articulates the creative experience of the people ... there is now a recognition that the life of poor people is legitimate and abundant source of cultural energy." Through "improvisation, communal participation and commentary on topical local events" (Flores 1993: 191), the voices in *AmeRícan* serve as models of practice in the formation of a critical utopia of "walking bridges." By including the spectrum of American voices and spaces in his works, Laviera offers a "broader answer" to the "marginality" of minority or colonized peoples and their position in "nowhere," the "border," or the "melting pot." And, through stereotypes, parody, orality, musicality, neologisms, code-switching, and typographic experimentation, Laviera's poems require the active participation and critical analysis on the part of his readers. In this sense, *AmeRícan* provides models of practice for approaching the creation of a new U.S. identity as readers must actively be engaged with considering preordained conceptions as well as alternative processes of what it means to be "American," in the "u.s." sense of the word. With our interpretive dominance destabilized, readers are spurred to go "back and forth" over Laviera's poems and to read and think in different ways—vertically, horizontally, diagonally and in multiple languages. In this essay I have highlighted this on-going process of analysis and self-reflection through the metaphor of the "walking bridge." With this metaphor I also suggest that Laviera's poems point to the act of "branching out" through "associations" and "strategic resistance," as Flores has noted, with other minority cultures or other colonized peoples. Reflective of my framing of Laviera's works within the concept of the critical utopia, to Flores' argument I add that Laviera does not preclude the possibility of "branching out" to the present "enemies" of AmeRíca. While firmly rejecting (neo) colonialism, racism, arrogance, exclusion, dominance, and snobbery, Laviera's poems extend "walking bridges" to these "enemies," thus allowing for the possibility of their becoming allies at a future point in time.

The etymological root of the word, "utopia," is both "good place" and "no place." The distance between a "good" place and "no" place often translates into a gap between theory and practice. Efforts to implement models of the ideal in the real frequently translate into a sublimation of racial, linguistic, or cultural specificity within or in the name of the greater whole. In an effort to establish unity of the larger community, the individual or any other who does not fit within this model is asked to sacrifice her/his specificity—either assimilate or step aside. *AmeRícan* counters this sublimation with poems that perform models of love, affirmation, and resistance. True to the political commitment of the Nuyorican Poets Café, the poetry in *AmeRícan* is a serious "contact sport" that in various ways seeks to push the listener and reader to actively confront these models and participate in the creation of a more "judicious" society. Focusing on the sensitivity of our ears and mouths, "the two most developed organs" (Luis 1992: 1024), these poems project the idea of listening, pronouncing, and analyzing words like "American" and "assimilation" in a different way.

Similar to the stubborn accent on the "Rican" part of "AmeRícan" and the "AO" in "asimilao," the accents in Laviera's recent poem "nideaquínideallá" demand that we (re)articulate models of affirmation, "strategic resistance," and associations to generate a "broader answer to marginality." Rejecting assimilation, Laviera's poetic models of practice underscore the need for critical thinking, "self-reflection," and branching out through "walking bridges" to other communities in an on-going process of approximating toward a complex but inclusive ideal. Whether through stubborn accents and diphthongs, parody, or the twists and turns of a "thousand voices," *AmeRícan*'s poems suggest that we "SEE" and "go deeper" in any effort to define an American identity and purpose.

ACKNOWLEDGEMENTS

I would like to acknowledge Stephanie Alvarez and William Luis for their dedication to publish this collection of essays on Laviera. I am grateful for the opportunity to participate in this important project and for the editorial support they have provided. Thanks also to Rubén Medina, who introduced me to Laviera's poetry and who helped me consolidate my ideas on the concept of utopia in Laviera's works.

NOTES

[1] See Nicholasa Mohr (1987) for a discussion of the history of "home" in Puerto Rican writers.

[2] I also discuss the connection between More's "utopia" and Nuyorican expression in DeGrave (2007). This present essay of Laviera's *AmeRícan* is adapted from my dissertation, DeGrave (2003).

[3] In *From Bomba to Hip-Hop: Puerto Rican Culture and Latino Identity*, Juan Flores notes that demographic changes in the United States "indicate that ... the term Nuyorican has become an anachronism." He adds that "Tato Laviera was one of the first to acknowledge the inappropriateness of the usage because of diasporic dispersion around the country, and proposed ... the alternative AmeRícan..." (2000: 186–7).

[4] As Juan Egea observes, the poem "political" seems to provide a somewhat unenthusiastic depiction of politics and community involvement:

i must get involved [...]

yet i take alternative roads,

to keep away from the involvement,

because community leadership,

leads to broken marriages,

leads to lack of trust [...] (1985: 79)

This depiction of politics can be approached in relation to the idea of critical utopias. Politics (or the state as indicated by Sargent) does not constitute the means through which Laviera projects his ideal society. Yet, in the end of the poem, the speaker articulates an alternative; he listens to the music and lyrics spoken within the community which, in turn, become "bullets" through which the speaker makes a "citizen's arrest."

[5] As is explained in more detail below, Flores (1993) discusses the topic of "self-affirmation and association," as well as "strategic resistance" among colonized peoples.

[6] While it is not within the scope of this analysis to examine the experience and the environment that Laviera's performance and reading of his poetry generate, another avenue of investigation of Laviera's poetry would be the possible ways in which the act of reading these poems creates what Benedict Anderson has described as an association

of a feeling of simultaneity, unisonance, and the "physical realization of the imagined community" of poetry and song (1996: 145). I thank Rubén Medina for bringing this aspect of Laviera's poetry to my attention.

7 In his introduction to Laviera's most recent collection, *Mixturao*, William Luis highlights a similar movement of what Flores has previously identified as a "branching out through strategic associations." As Luis explains, the repeated affirmation of the pronoun "we," now a "strong majority," is a "communal expression against the forces that produce and promote linguistic and political isolation" (2008a: xiv).

8 The idea of Puerto Ricans and Nuyoricans being a model community is also underscored by Laviera in an interview with William Luis: "We have a great ability for allowing integration, experimentation, and keeping a certain basic to ourselves without going through too many changes. In that way, the Puerto Rican persona is, I consider, an advanced person in society, in the humanistic category, in the social category, and in the political category, in terms of dealing with people, and in the spiritual category, in terms of accepting people. The Puerto Rican persona is very broad and he allows experimentation without a lot of psychological hang-ups. He is very broad natured and I think here's where our artistic totality lies; artistically we are very broad" (1992: 1028). Laviera further explains that "[t]he Puerto Rican consciousness has developed and I give that credit to my people; they've really branched out in a humanistic way which allows us to communicate" (1992: 1030).

9 Considering the overt rejection of stereotypes and bad intentions in poems like "boricua," however, the destabilizing formal techniques in *AmeRícan* seem to represent strategic cannibalizations of stereotypes whose purpose is to create the critical "good" judgment, similar to that of the "Ricans," in the potential citizens of an *AmeRícan* utopia.

10 I thank Juan Egea for indicating the importance of Laviera's comment from Luis' (1992) interview and for suggesting the pertinence of his concept of "defensive humanism" in *AmeRícan*.

11 The relationship between writing, hegemony, and identity is explored in Rama (1984), Pratt (1988), Spurr (1966), and Leinhard (1991).

12 The term "transculturation" was coined by Fernando Ortiz in *Cuban Counterpoint, Tobacco and Sugar* (1995 [1940]) to refer to "different phases of the process of transition from one culture to another ... [T]his does not consist merely in acquiring another culture, which is what the English word acculturation really implies, but the process also necessarily involves the loss or uprooting of a previous culture, which could be defined as a deculturation. In addition it carries the idea of the consequent creation of new cultural phenomena, which could be called neoculturation" (1995: 102–3).

14 I am grateful to Mark Evenson for pointing out the potentially unstable nature of walking bridges as this characteristic is key to my understanding of critical utopias in Laviera.

15 Rubén Medina kindly highlighted this reading to me.

123

The New Accent in American Poetry: Tato Laviera's "AmeRícan" in the Context of U.S. American Poetry

STEVEN P. SCHNEIDER

Much of the existing criticism on Tato Laviera's books of poems examines his work in the context of Puerto Rican or Nuyorican literature. This criticism tends to focus on the negotiation of biculturalism and linguistic play within his poetry and sees his code-switching as a resistance to the dominance of English. Véronique Rauline describes him as "a linguistic activist, because Tato Laviera does not only voice the linguistic confrontation, but the power of words as source of our imprisonment but also of our liberation" (Rauline and Laviera 1998: 162). Juan Flores, in his essay on Laviera and "Puerto Rican Language and Culture in the United States," observes that "rather than compensating for monolingual deficiency, code-switching often signals an expansion of communicative and expressive potential" (1993: 165). In a more recent essay, "¡¿Qué, Qué?!—Transculturation and Tato Laviera's Spanglish poetics," Stephanie Alvarez (2006) suggests that the blending of languages in Laviera's work contributes to his project of transculturation, whereby a new transcultural identity and culture can emerge. Unlike his predecessor René Marqués, author of the play *La carreta*, which dramatizes the longing for a return to the Island home, Alvarez points out that "Laviera sees the possibility of such a return to Puerto Rican culture not in the physical return to the island" (2006: 27). "Instead," she writes, "the poet calls for a new transculturation between the popular culture of the Island and that of New York. Laviera's "nuevo rumbón," or new transculturation, allows Nuyoricans to challenge the acculturating forces of Anglo society" (2006: 28).

In addition to this focus on language and identity in his work, much of the criticism also explores the influence upon Laviera of the island's rich Afro-Caribbean music and its oral literary tradition. For example, Susan M. Campbell in her article "Nuyroican Poetry, Tactics for Local

Resistance," notes that "Laviera's poetry reflects the thematic of Puerto Rican plena music through privileging the perspective of marginal people..." (2007: 117). Campbell also writes that "Laviera is recognized as the Nuyorican poet who most reaches toward Afro-Puerto Rican subjects and rhythms through his verse..." (2007: 127).

My review of several recent articles on Laviera's poetry reveals a glaring critical omission. None of the critics contextualize Laviera's work within a tradition of U.S. poetry, despite the fact that Laviera has lived most of his life in New York City and had published his work with Arte Público Press in Houston. Juan Flores, in his article "*La Carreta Made a U-Turn*: Puerto Rican Language and Culture in the United States" (1993), draws a distinction between Laviera and an older generation of writers from the Island like René Marqués, José Luis González, and Pedro Juan Soto, who "found hostility and estrangement in North American society" (1993: 172). He notes that Laviera's experience is different from many of his poetic island ancestors in that he moved to New York City at the age of 10 and spent only his boyhood years on the Island. For this reason and several others, this essay will argue that Laviera's work needs to be read within the larger context of U.S. poetry.

It is not my intention to contest the other claims for Laviera's work but rather to expand the critical conversation to include the American writers Walt Whitman, Langston Hughes, and Allen Ginsberg, all of whom Laviera has read and to whom his poetry can and should be connected. Rather than being uninformed and unconnected to this line of American poets, Laviera's work and especially his often cited poem "AmeRícan," the title poem of his third collection, can be better understood and richly interpreted within the context of these poets whose search for an expansive "American" identity are consistent with those of Laviera.

A good place to begin this line of comparison is with Whitman, the bard of democracy. While he has written extensively on his experience of America in longer poems like "Song of Myself" and "Crossing Brooklyn Ferry" and in numerous shorter lyrics like "For You O Democracy" and "The Prairie Grass Dividing," I want to take a look at one of his very short poems entitled "America," in part because its title is so very close to the title of Laviera's poem "AmeRícan." "America" first appeared in the New York Herald (11 February 1888) and then in the "Sands at Seventy" annex to *Leaves of Grass* in 1891–1892. The poem is just six lines:

Centre of equal daughters, equal sons,
All, all alike endear'd, grown, ungrown, young or old
Strong, ample, fair, enduring, capable, rich,
Perennial with the Earth, with Freedom, Law and Love,
A grand, sane, towering, seated Mother,
Chair'd in the adamant of Time. (1965: 511)

In this poem Whitman expresses his expansive and inclusive embrace of America, in which "all" are "all alike." The repetition of the word "all" in the second line is telling, with its emphasis upon everyone. This is preceded by the repetition of the word "equal" in the first line, where the emphasis is on equality. Much of the rest of the poem is made up of a series of adjectives to describe the citizens of Whitman's expansive vision of America: "endear'd," "young or old," "strong," "ample," "fair," "capable," "rich." Whitman's America then is a land in which people are not only equal—whether young or old, male or female—but also well endowed with such qualities as strength and capability. He addresses America as "Mother," a perennial and nurturing figure who embraces all. Larry Griffin, in his entry for the poem in *Walt Whitman: An Encyclopedia* notes that "Whitman's Mother provides readers with powerful associations, including the unlimited potential for revolutionary change in a feminine country where one enjoys the rights of 'life, liberty and the pursuit of happiness'"(Whitman 1998: 12).

In his poem "AmeRícan," Laviera also asserts an affirmative vision, tinged as it is by his own experience as a Nuyorican in New York. Laviera's vision of America, like Whitman's, is egalitarian but also places an accent on many ethnic subcultures blending into the larger banner of American identity. It is as if Laviera has seized upon the image of America as a "seated Mother / Chair'd in the adamant of Time" (Whitman 1965: 511) and embraced her as a mother divine who protects and sustains what Laviera calls in "AmeRícan" a "loved america" (1985: 95).

By the time Whitman had published his poem "America," he had witnessed the devastation of the Civil War and worked out his thoughts on democracy in *Democratic Vistas*, published in 1871. At the beginning of that essay, Whitman expands upon the phrase "e pluribus unum," which was found on the seal of the United States in 1776. In the first paragraph of *Democratic Vistas*, it sounds as if Whitman is addressing Laviera and future generations of émigrés to the United States:

As the greatest lessons of Nature through the universe are perhaps the lessons of variety and freedom, the same present the greatest lessons also in New World politics and progress. If a man were ask'd, for instance , the distinctive points contrasting European and American political and other life with the old Asiatic cultus, as lingering-bequeat'd yet in China and Turkey, he might find the amount of them in John Stuart Mill's profound essay on Liberty in the future, where he demands two main constituents, or sub-strata, for a truly grand nationality – 1st, a larger variety of character – and 2nd, full play for human nature to expand itself in numberless and even conflicting directions – (seems to be for general humanity much like the influences that make up, in their limitless field, that perennial health-action of the air we call the weather – an infinite number of currents and forces, and contributions, and temperatures, and cross purposes, whose ceaseless play of counterpart upon counterpart brings constant restoration and vitality . . .). (Whitman 1964: 361-2)

Whitman's embrace of Mill's concept of Liberty as the full play of human nature "in numberless and even conflicting directions" (Whitman 1964: 362), like the currents and forces of change in weather, makes ample room for poets like Tato Laviera who bring to this country their island heritage and linguistic play. While language purists would see Laviera's mixing or interpenetration of Spanish and English "as the tragic convergence of two non-standard vernaculars" (Flores 1993: 164), Whitman might see it as "the ceaseless play of counterpart upon counterpart," resulting in restoration and vitality.

One of the very first books of poetry Tato Laviera read after his family's arrival in New York City was Walt Whitman's *Leaves of Grass*. He recalls it being cast aside by a street vendor and picking up the book and feeling mesmerized by it. Laviera could not part with the book and held on to it for a very long time. It became in a way his "American Primer;" he learned new words from reading *Leaves of Grass*, American words, words that he hadn't encountered before. He was also influenced by the lack of capitalization in Whitman's poetry, something that would stick with Laviera when he composed his own poems (Schneider 2009).

American Primer (1987) was a small book compiled by Whitman's admirer and friend Horace Traubel. Traubel had edited Whitman's handwritten notes on the topic of language, wrote a foreword, and published the book in 1904. The volume contains a short foreword by Traubel that includes the famous quotation of Whitman calling *Leaves of Grass* "only a language experiment." *Leaves of Grass*, Whitman said, was

> an attempt to give the spirit, the body, the man, new words, new potentialities of speech – an American, a cosmopolitan (the best of America is the best cosmopolitanism) range of self-expression. The new
> world, the new times, the new peoples, the new vista, need a tongue according – yes, what is more, will have such a tongue – will not be satisfied until it is evolved. (Whitman 1987: viii-ix)

An alternative title for Whitman's notes on language, found on one slip of paper, is "The Primer of Words: For American Young Men and Women, For Literati, Orators, Teachers, Musicians, Judges, Presidents &c." (Whitman 1998: 16).

It is no wonder then that the young Tato Laviera found in Whitman's *Leaves of Grass* a primer to American speech. One could argue that perhaps the body of Laviera's poetry should be described as a "language experiment," mixing several dialects and linguistic registers. Although Whitman rejects in his *American Primer* "Spanish saints' names in the West and Southwest," preferring the Indian name for a place, he does "assert that the 'Real Dictionary' of American English, when it is written, will include all words—the bad as well as the good . . . . "And the 'Real Grammar' will be liberating rather than restrictive." (Whitman 1998: 16). Whitman understood that new developments in the sciences and in other spheres of life would produce new words.

The title poem of Laivera's third book, "AmeRícan," adds a new accent to American poetry. By capitalizing the R and adding an accent to the í, he posits a new way of seeing, pronouncing, and being American. It is a radical gesture, just the kind of neologism that Whitman— who came up with his own coinages like "camerado"—would appreciate. Ed Folsom, in his chapter on "Whitman and Dictionaries" in his book *Walt Whitman's Native Representations,* has discussed at length Whitman's interest in the competition during the nineteenth century between Daniel Webster's *An American Dictionary of the English Language* and the more conservative dictionary developed by Joseph Worcester, "more in line with British usage, dedicated to recording the heritage of the language instead of urging it to change" (1994: 15). Folsom observes that "though he owned editions of both dictionaries, Whitman of course was on Webster's side, looking for ways to tune English in an American key: 'The English language befriends the grand American expression . . . it is brawny enough and limber and full enough" (1994: 15). Later in this same chapter Folsom notes that "Whitman not only read dictionaries; he even toyed with the idea of writing one himself, keeping lists of words, noting odd pronunciations, singling out foreign words that should be added to the American language because they expressed things that no English words yet did" (1994: 16).

The innovative pronunciation and spelling of AmeRícan by Laviera is consistent with the kind of creative change in the language that Whitman himself would embrace. Moreover, it is responsive to the experience of Laviera, other Nuyoricans, and several other ethnic and racial minorities in that it straddles two cultures through its spelling and pronunciation. It looks familiar yet is different. AmeRícan sounds American but is not exactly so. Laviera's coinage speaks to the transcultural nature of his own experience and that of other Latinas/os. This is, in many ways, the subject of his work and the poem "AmeRícan."

Although not partitioned, the poem falls naturally into three sections. The first section is composed of three stanzas, each of which begins with the line "we gave birth to a new generation." Laviera himself is a member of this "new generation," so very unlike the "lost generation" in that "it includes everything / imaginable you-name-it-we got-it / society" (1985: 94). Laviera makes the kind of all inclusive gesture that Whitman makes when he writes "AmerRícan salutes all folklores, / european, indian, black, spanish, / and anything else compatible" (1995: 94).

In the second section of the poem, Laviera moves into a Whitmanesque catalog, reminiscent of the kind of listing Whitman engages in "Song of Myself." Each item in his catalog is introduced by the word AmeRícan, as if to suggest what follows is both an elaboration of the term and a creative definition of it. The first three images in Laviera's catalog invoke music: the composer Pedro Flores, Spanish *danzas*, gypsies, and *jíbaro* modern troubadours keeping the beat. His American / AmeRícan is, if anything at all, rhythmic and musical.

In the pivotal fourth stanza of this second section of the poem, Laviera describes the migratory nature of this "new generation," moving "across forth and across back / back across and forth back . . ." (1985: 94). Here he evokes their transitory nature, moving back and forth from one island— Puerto Rico— to another—Manhattan, one language to another, one culture to another. These lines echo Whitman's "Crossing Brooklyn Ferry," where he describes the hundreds on the ferry-boats that "cross, returning home." Whitman's poem is prophetic in that he envisions future generations who will see Brooklyn and Manhattan, "A hundred years hence, or ever so many hundred years hence, others will see them, / Will enjoy the sunset, the pouring-in of the flood-tide, the falling-back to the sea of the ebb-tide" (Whitman 1965: 160).

Laviera and other Latinas/os and ethnic minorities would come to see these very same islands one hundred years after Whitman composed "Crossing Brooklyn Ferry," originally titled "Sun-Down Poem." For them the challenge would be to not be "absorbed, digested." Laviera speaks for himself and others when he writes that "we spit out/ the poison, we spit out the malice, we stand, affirmative in action" (1985: 94). He boldly asserts a response to the "marginality" that threatened to gobble him and other ethnic and racialized minorities up, "walking plena-rhythms in new york, / strutting beautifully alert, alive . . . " (1985: 94). In the remaining stanzas of the second section of the poem, he continues to explore the richness of what it means to be AmeRícan, "defining myself my own way any way many / ways . . . we blend / and mix all that is good !" (1985: 95). Laviera's vision, like that of Whitman's, is celebratory, not pessimistic; integrating, not segregating.

Like Whitman, Laviera shares a palpable empathy for the American. In the third and concluding section of the poem, composed of two long stanzas, he once again invokes Whitman. Laviera is interested in discovering and "defining the new america, *humane america*," the "loved america" that dwells "in the spirit of divinity!" (1985: 95). Here one thinks of section five of "Song of Myself," in which Whitman embraces both the body (politic) and the soul. Whitman's revelation is declared when he writes: "And I know that the spirit of God is the brother of my own, / And that all the men ever born are also my brothers, and the women my sisters and lovers, / And that a kelson of the creation is love" (Whitman 1965: 33). Love is at the core of Laviera's vision of America, although he is realistic enough to know that Latinas/os and other ethnic minorities have not been universally loved or embraced by those who have come "across forth" to the United States long before him and who have had many generations to assimilate. Nevertheless, as he asserts in the final stanza of this signature poem, he longs to belong here, to make his second land his home.

> AmeRícan,   yes, for now, for I love this, my second
> land, and I dream to take the accent from
> the altercation, and to be proud to call
> myself american, in the u.s. sense of the word,
> AmeRícan, America! (1985: 95)

Laviera "dreams to take the accent from / the altercation" because to do so would signal an acceptance of himself and other Puerto Ricans, as well as Latino immigrants, as truly Americans. In the very last line he playfully undercuts this gesture by suggesting that the very accent itself has become part of our national heritage. This is certainly a radical notion, one that appears even more so today after the federal government has invested millions of dollars to build a Border Wall on its southern border with Mexico.

Langston Hughes is another American poet who Laviera sees as an important influence. Laviera remembers distinctly the first time in the early 1970s he heard Hughes's poetry being read out loud, in Spanish, on 126th Street in New York City. "I was so taken by his work that I went to the Tompkins Square Library right away to find more of his work. I then ordered some of his books and had them within two weeks. I saw Langston Hughes as an elegant figure who spoke for his own people yet touched a universal chord" (Schneider 2009). Hughes' many poems on the American Dream speak to the tragic consequences of segregation and discrimination. In "Refugee in America," "American Heartbreak," and "Democracy," Hughes laments the failure of the American dream to ring true for the African-American. Yet Hughes held out hope for social change, which he predicted in his poem "I, Too."

> I, too, sing America.
> I am the darker brother.
> They send me to eat in the kitchen
> When company comes,
> But I laugh,

And eat well,
And grow strong.

Tomorrow,
I'll be at the table
When company comes.
Nobody'll dare
Say to me,
"Eat in the kitchen,"
Then.
Besides,
They'll see how beautiful I am
And be ashamed –

I, too, am America. (1974: 275)

 The last four lines of this poem register the speaker's pride in his race and a rightful claim to American identity. The poem, spoken as a short dramatic monologue, calls to mind several of Laviera's own dramatic monologues, in which the speaker registers his or her point of view on the contemporary American scene. Laviera, like Hughes, his dark-sinned brother, is proud of his heritage. What is of special interest, however, is each poet's relationship to America. For Hughes, America is the land of the dream deferred, although the poet expresses an abiding hope that social justice will one day allow for Blacks to be fully integrated. For Laviera, writing a generation after Hughes, America is a place where his Afro-Caribbean, Nuyorican, hybridized identity and language are expressed and embraced: "AmeRícan, abounding inside so many ethnic english / people, and out of humanity, we blend / and mix all that is good!" (1985: 95). Like Langston Hughes, Laviera understands that "I, too, am America" (1974: 275).

 Both Hughes and Laviera are masters of the vernacular speech of their people and use the dramatic monologue effectively to register their concerns. In Hughes' famous poem "Mother to Son," a black woman speaks candidly to her son about the importance of persevering to overcome the obstacles and hardships of life.

> Well, son, I'll tell you:
> Life for me ain't been no crystal stair.
> ....
> But all the time
> I'se been a-climbin' on,
> And reachin' landin's,
> And turnin' corners,
> And sometimes goin' in the dark
> Where there ain't been no light. (1974: 187)

In this and other poems Hughes eschews literary language for the spoken language of the people, in this case, an African-American woman. He was especially interested in capturing the idiom of the common people. In his essay "The Negro Artist and the Racial Mountain," Hughes wrote about the courage to draw upon his experience as a black man in America and not to shy away from it. He draws a distinction between a self-styled, high-class Negro and the low-down common folks. It is the latter, he contends, who will provide the Negro artist with the material that could make him both original and enduring.

> But then there are the low-down folks, the so-called common element, and they are the majority — may the Lord be praised! The people who have their hip of gin on Saturday nights and are not too important to themselves or the community, or too well fed, or too learned to watch the lazy world go round. They live on Seventh Street in Washington or State Street in Chicago and they do not particularly care whether they are like white folks or anybody else. . . . They furnish a wealth of colorful, distinctive material for any artist because they still hold their own individuality in the face of American standardizations. And perhaps these common people will give to the world its truly great Negro artist, the one who is not afraid to be himself. (2004: 149)

Hughes' example of drawing upon the experience of "the so-called common element" provided Laviera with examples and the inspiration to people his poems with figures "not too learned to watch the lazy world go by" (2004: 149). Many of them are found as the speakers of his poems in the "Nuyoricans" section of his book *AmeRícan*. They may be tough-minded and found on street corners, like "esquina dude," or lonely and desperate for love and understanding, like the women speakers of the poems "mi'ja" and "brava." In each instance Laviera has discovered and given voice to characters that can "hold their own individuality in the face of American standardizations."

The speaker of the poem "esquina dude" knows that "nothing of / the past that is present is sacred." He integrates what he likes—Spanish and English in a range of registers that both challenges and startles the reader.

> i integrate what i like, i reject
> what i don't like, bro, nothing of
> the past that is present is sacred
> everything changes, bro, anything
> that remains the same is doomed to
> die, stubbornness must cover all my
> angles, bro, y te lo digo sincerely
> my judgement, bro, mi juicio, bro, bro
> bro, I tell you that life is based
> on the moment, el momento will
> catch up to you (1985: 58)

To survive on the street like "esquina dude," who is dealing in drugs, means to be alive to the opportunities and threats the present moment presents. His speech, with its repeated references to "bro" and its intermittent Spanish—"y te lo digo"—is in the spoken speech of the barrio in New York City, with which Laviera is intimately familiar. The speaker of the poem—"esquina dude"—seems to be addressing a client, to whom he speaks tenderly and harshly, consoling him while at the same time threatening him with violence. The undercurrent of meaning is that "business" deals must be honored or accounts may be settled in very unpleasant ways.

This message is driven home at the end of the poem, where the speaker makes the point that his message is clear and "can cut into any language." Laviera, of course, is punning on "cut" here, for throughout the poem the speaker makes reference to his knife—"yes, there are times when i open my blade / to cut, bro. . . . ." Fortunately, for the person being addressed in "esquina dude," all accounts have been paid.

> i know you play no games
> i'm glad you paid me, bro, porque
> cuentas claras conservan amistades
> you know exactly what I mean, gracias. (1985: 59)

"Clear accounts preserve friendships," ("cuentas claras conservan amistades"); that is a rule observed by both drug dealers and accountants. Laviera, slipping into English, then Spanish, and then Spanglish, attunes his ear to the people he knows best, those who struggle on the streets of the barrio to survive. In "esquina dude" he has used the dramatic monologue effectively to create a character who defiantly holds his "own individuality in the face of American standardizations."

The female speakers of "m'ija" and "brava" are also defiant. They speak to the loneliness and fear of their condition. Together they contribute to the series of poignant portraits Laviera presents in his work of Nuyoricans who struggle with and against their adverse circumstances.

In the beginning of the poem "mi'ja," the speaker is feeling depressed about not having anyone to celebrate her birthday. Suddenly, however, her mood changes when she receives a call from her *mamá* who calls to tell her she has cooked a "comidita" for her and baked her favorite "postre." The poem turns on this news, and after receiving a big "abrazo" from her *mamá* and blowing out the candles on her birthday cake, the speaker decides to celebrate by going out to buy a "sexy dress" and wearing it to a dance club where she plans "to boogie and dance so freely." The poem breaks into Spanish in the last five lines when the speaker recalls to a friend—"m'ija"—the fantastic time she had with a guy she met that night. "M'ija" is illustrative of the ways in which Laviera constructs a persona who reflects on a birthday she thinks nobody has remembered and suddenly changes to a happy occasion. It's not surprising that at the end of the poem the speaker resorts to her native Spanish to convey the lustful nature of her nightclub encounter and the fulfillment she demands for herself.

In "brava," the female speaker of the poem is angry, even defiant, about people telling her she must speak clearly in Spanish. It is the insistence upon this—"they kept on telling me"—that angers her. Caught between two cultures and two languages—she strikes back—linguistically, and asserts:

> I am puertorriqueña in
> english and there's nothing
> you can do but to accept
> it como yo soy sabrosa
> proud ask any streetcorner
> where pride is what you defend
> go ahead, ask me, on any street-
> corner that I am not puertorriqueña,
> come dímelo aquí en mi cara
> offend me. (1985: 63)

The speaker of "brava" is both courageous and defiant, proud of her hybridized identity, unwilling to compromise, swinging freely back in forth between her two languages. This is what makes her "sabrosa," literally "delicious," but also "tasty" and "pleasurable." She is not afraid to "bilingualize" her communication and will not be forced to compromise one identity for another. In this sense, the speaker of "brava" is reminiscent of Gloria Anzaldúa, who in the essays and poems in her book *Borderlands: La Frontera* (1999) embraces the transcultural identity and linguistic richness of living between borders, both physically and psychologically. The speaker of "brava" also shares a tough-mindedness and pride similar to the speaker of "esquina dude," in that she threatens physically and verbally anyone who tries to deny her identity as puertorriqueña.

These three dramatic monologues—"esquina dude," "m'ija" and "brava"—compose a sequence of realistic portrayals of life on the streets of the barrios in New York City. Laviera, like Langston Hughes before him, understands that the strength of his poetry comes from a willingness to embrace the authentic voice of the common people in his poetry. To give voice to the linguistic play and richness of his speakers rather than to homogenize their experience is a tactic Laviera shares with his predecessor Langston Hughes. Both Hughes and Laviera look for the authenticity of American experience in the "barrios" of New York City rather than on Park Avenue or Madison Avenue. Their "Americaness" as poets is linked by their willingness to engage and give voice to the poor and to people of color.

Like Walt Whitman and Langston Hughes, Tato Laviera also shares a very special connection with Allen Ginsberg. Laviera would see Ginsberg from time to time in New York City and hang out with him in Tompkins Square Park in the Alphabet City section of the East Village in Manhattan. He once heard Ginsberg give a reading of "Howl" (2004b) in the park and was struck by the Beat poet's passionate commitment to social justice. Laviera said he shares with Ginsberg a love of different languages, cultures, and a warm embrace of humanity. Laviera admired that "Ginsberg gave everyone his full love and attention" (Schneider 2009).

A starting place to compare the two poets' work is with Ginsberg's poem "America" and Laviera's poem "AmeRícan." Both poets make political statements and make use of Whitmanesque catalogues in their poems. Ginsberg's poem is a response to the political climate in the 1950s when the country was enmeshed in the Cold War. Ginsberg's "America" (2004a) combines political outrage, elements of satire and parody, as well as empathy for labor organizers, anti-Franco Spanish loyalists and Nicola Sacco and Bartolomeo Vanzetti. In some ways one could read Ginsberg's poem "America" in contrast to the more idealized and hopeful visions expressed by Whitman, Laviera, and Hughes in their respective poems "America," "AmeRícan," and "I Too Sing America." Ginsberg is responding to a particular time in American history when the nation was in the midst of a Cold War with Russia and the Beat poet parodies the fear and madness that gripped the country: "America it's them bad Russians. / Them Russians them Russians and them Chinamen. And them Russians. / The Russia wants to eat us alive. The Russia's power mad. She want to take our cars from our garages." (2004a: 649). Ginsberg assumes the voice of the angry and satirical prophet here, who makes fun of an America obsessed with the threat of Communism.

Nevertheless, all four poets—Whitman, Ginsberg, Laviera, and Hughes—share, according to Huck Gutman, a "commitment to celebrating simultaneously what Whitman called the "simple separate person" and the "en-masse"(Whitman 1998: 255). Each of these poets, in Laviera's words, "dream to take the accent from / the altercation," to live in a democracy where individuals contribute to and are accepted by the larger nation. All four poets use their poetry to overcome feelings of alienation and marginalization to talk back to America and reshape it through their poetic vision. It is in this sense that Laviera is truly an American poet.

Thirty years later, Laviera experiences a very different America in a very different time. Nevertheless, he must hear over his shoulder Ginsberg asking "America when will you be angelic?" (2004a: 647) and offers his own "angelic" vision, which "salutes all folklores, / european, indian, black, spanish, / and anything else compatible" (1985: 94). He celebrates, like Whitman, the people on the streets of Manhattan: "AmeRícan, walking plena-rhythms in new york, / strutting beautifully alert, alive, / many turning eyes wondering, / admiring!" (1985: 94–5). Ginsberg, in his poem, wants to love America but cannot, gripped as it is by the stranglehold of the military industrial complex. He muses, "America how can I write a holy litany in your silly mood?" (2004a: 648). Laviera has "spit out the malice" and turned his attention to "defining the new America, humane america" (1985: 95). Like Ginsberg though, he cannot fully embrace America—thus the accent and big R in his spelling of AmeRícan.

Both Laviera and Ginsberg express in their poetry a quest for personal identity and freedom in opposition to a consumer culture bent on assimilation and conformity. Moreover, each of them wrote poems intended to be declaimed, respectively, in the beat cafe of the 1950s and the Nuyorícan Poets Cafe of the 1980s. Laviera also shares with Ginsberg the sense that he is speaking for his generation. Ginsberg, of course, declared himself the spokesperson for the beat generation: "I saw the best minds of my generation destroyed by madness, starving hysterical naked" (2004b: 649). Laviera envisions himself speaking for a new generation of AmeRícans and declares at the beginning of the first three stanzas of his poem: "We gave birth to a new generation." He embraces his transcultural identity, the blending of languages and street musicians "beating jíbaro modern troubadours / crying guitars romantic continental / bolero love songs!"(1985: 94). One cannot help but think that Whitman, Hughes and Ginsberg would be pleased by the addition of the accent to "AmeRícan" and join Laviera in an embrace of the "lost America of love" (Ginsberg 2004c: 657).

Insular Interventions: Tato Laviera's Dialogic Dialogue with Luis Muñoz Marín and José Luis González

MARITZA STANCHICH

The tensions inherent in the canonicity of authors of the Puerto Rican diaspora in relation to literature in Puerto Rico have shifted significantly in the past decade or two, yet diasporic engagements with insular island literary figures and discourses still warrant a deeply comparative lens. The scholarship so far on Laviera's poetry has explicated well his profound artistic commitment to performance traditions in Puerto Rico, namely the so-called Negrista poetry of Luis Palés Matos, the declamation of Juan Boria, and the gamut of Puerto Rican musical genres. Laviera's virtuosic bilingual writing style, dizzying for its interlingual neologistic invention and resonances, has also been closely analyzed for embodying the very tensions of the fraught terrain of language politics in Puerto Rico, and between the island and the diaspora. Yet much of this analysis remains at the level of performance, not to suggest superficiality, but as fitting since Nuyorican poetics is considered in part a performance genre, and that Laviera's incredible ear for both linguistic practices and Afro-Caribbean performance traditions on the island and in the diaspora is in itself performative, live, and on paper. The social implications of these engagements also have been shown to be abundant.[1] While this multiplicity of performance can hardly be kept at bay in analyzing Laviera's poetic oeuvre, his scribal literary engagements with such major figures as the architect of Puerto Rico's Free Associated State status, Luis Muñoz Marín, as politician and poet, and the Marxist critic and political exile José Luis González, as intellectual and fiction writer, function to dialogically revise enduring insular distortions and misconceptions of literature of the Puerto Rican diaspora, and intervene in the very national discourses that in the past sought to define the diaspora from the perspective of the island. Laviera is hardly alone among writers of the diaspora in this respect, but his example is noteworthy in part because he has often been characterized as a Nuyorican writer. Indeed, in this way Laviera's work joins the ranks of authors who exceed that category, as diverse as Jesús Colón, Martín Espada, Aurora Levins Morales and Esmeralda Santiago, though all interrogate insular discourses in varying degrees and with distinct purposes.

The process of responding to and often contesting the island's intelligentsia discourses in Laviera's work has been widely explored in terms of the myriad ways Lavieras's first poetry collection *La Carreta Made a U-Turn* (1979) responds to the René Marqués play *La carreta* (1953) (Flores 1993: 168–81; Alvarez 2006; Waldron 2008), perhaps the most enshrined canonical text in Puerto Rico's educational system, and a bulwark of the *jíbaro* discourses of the era, which endure in today's popular lexicon, of the noble, humble, earth-bound, hard-working White peasant of the country's interior, most notably seen as the logo of the chief political party of the Muñoz era (Córdova 2005). In that same collection, and in all five poetry collections since, including the most recent *Mixturao* (2008a), Laviera engages, interrogates, contests and occasionally by turns reproduces and reconciles the discourses that promulgated the massive migration as crucial to the country's Operation Bootstrap industrialization project and then continued to define the diaspora on insular terms. That Laviera not only invokes but textually references two key figures as ideologically distinct, indeed contentious, as Muñoz Marín and González, suggests the degree to which the poet immersed himself in key canonical texts by both, an engagement sustained in various ways throughout Laviera's oeuvre. In so doing, Laviera grapples with the very legacy of the Muñoz era, documenting its collective memory as its descent begins after 1965, with perhaps greater relevance today during the dismantling and collapse of its most notable and enduring achievements. In the poems invoking González, Laviera stakes central, recurring thematic concerns and tropes seen throughout his oeuvre, such as linguistic patrimony and the poetic persona Papote.

Papote makes a major appearance in three of five of Laviera's poetry collections, perhaps most notably, as William Luis has noted (2009: 36), in the epic poem in *Enclave* (1981), titled "jesús papote" (1981: 12). The character culminates in a collective birth scream of a baby born to a drug-addicted mother, a repeated deep breathing unleashing a torrent of phrases echoing lines of diaspora concerns also found throughout Laviera's oeuvre (1981: 19), and the quiet aftermath, a meditation on the miracle of survival, endurance and life echoing John Donne (2001) and Edgar Allan Poe (2000) ("she got up to follow the bells the bells the bells," [1981: 21]). Here Papote is named Jesús Papote (though in lower case letters), lending both personal and biblical connotations to the name and this particular birth story (as Tato Laviera's full name is Jesús Abraham, with the story of Abraham also invoked in the poem [1981: 14]). The litany of chants here, "We, nosotros," repeated line by line and followed by lines such as "respectful of spanish-english forms / ...inside triangle of contradictions / ...nation-feeling-total-pride / ...hispanic hemispheric majority / ...latinos million bicultural humanists / ...folkloric mountain traditionalists / ... spanish tongue culture older than english / ...conceiving english newer visions / ...multi-ethnic black-brown-red in affirmations / ... (1981: 19–20), lend a sonic effect. It is amplified when read in tandem with Laviera's other collections, particularly those in which Papote also turns up echoing the line "triangle of contradictions," with the three words themselves simultaneously speaking to overarching themes, evoking trinities of cultural origins and practice, the Trans-Atlantic Slave trade, Spain/Puerto Rico/United States, Taino/European/African, Puerto Rican/Black/U.S Latino, Spanish/English/spanglish. These associations unpack all the diaspora/homeland/migrant baggage these imply.

The phrase echoes again the important poem "against muñoz pamphleteering," in the first section of *La Carreta Made a U-Turn*, called "Metropolis Dreams," which is said to pick up from where the play by René Marqués left off, but with a difference: Instead of the nativist return to rural Puerto Rico, the Papote persona ushering in the section "sat on a stoop" (1979: 14) and "decided to go nowhere" (Flores 1993: 170). The word "nowhere" as a metaphoric location is then repeatedly echoed in "against muñoz pamphleteering" several poems later. This poignant critique of the Muñoz legacy from the perspective of the diaspora, previously analyzed by Flores (1993), has recently been cited again by both Lawrence La Fountain-Stokes (2008) and Ramón E. Soto-Crespo (2009) as exemplary of Laviera's work and of Nuyorican subjectivity, though for distinct projects. The poem favors Laviera's scribal rather than performance style, repeatedly alluding to Muñoz Marín's perhaps most famous poem, "Panfleto" ("The Pamphlet," 2004 [1920]).

and i look into the dawn
inside the bread of land and liberty
to find a hollow sepulchre of words
words that i admired from my mother's eyes

words that i also embedded as my dreams.

now i awake to find that underneath
of your beautiful poetry pamphleteering
against the mob of stars took me nowhere
muñoz, took me nowhere muñoz, nowhere
where I see myself inside a triangle
of contradictions with no firm bridges
to make love to those stars.

inside my ghetto i learned to understand
your short range visions of where you led us,
across the oceans where i talk about myself
in foreign languages, across where i reach
to lament finding myself re-seasoning my
coffee beans.

your sense of
stars landed me in a
north temperate uprooted zone. (Laviera 1979: 18)

The resonance of phrases such as "mob of stars" and "re-seasoning my / coffee beans" as well as the reference to "dawn," "dreams," and "beautiful poetry pamphleteering" is unmistakable. Here is the young visionary voice of Muñoz Marín, of whom Laviera later wrote in a more conciliatory poem dedicated to him in *AmeRícan* (1985) "now i find traces of your bohemian days in the lower east side" (1985: 87):

He roto el arcoiris
contra mi corazõn,
como se rompe una espada inútil contra una rodilla.
He soplado las nubes de rosa y sangre
más allá de los últimos horizontes.
He ahogado mis sueños
para saciar los sueños que me duermen en las venas
de los hombres que sudaron y lloraron y rabiaron
para sazonar mi café...

El sueño que duerme en los pechos estrujados por la tisis
    (¡Un poco de aire, un poco de sol!);
el sueño que sueñan los estómagos estrangulados por el hambre
    (¡Un pedazo de pan, un pedazo de pan blanco!);
el sueño de los pies descalzos
    (¡Menos piedras en el camino, Señor, menos botellas rotas!);
el sueño de las nucas horizontales
    (¡Techumbre, hojas, yaguas: el sol es horrible!);
el sueño de los corazones pisoteados,
    (amor...Vida...Vida...Vida...!)

Yo soy el panfletista de Dios,
el agitador de Dios,
y voy con la turba de estrellas y hombres hambrientos
hacia la gran aurora...(Muñoz Marín 2004: 721)

[I have broken the rainbow
against my heart
as one breaks a useless sword against a knee.
I have blown the clouds of rose color and blood color
beyond the farthest horizons.
I have drowned my dreams
in order to glut the dreams that sleep for me in the veins
of men who sweated and wept and raged
to season my coffee...

The dream that sleeps in breasts stifled by tuberculosis
    (A little air, a little sunshine!);
the dream that dreams in stomachs strangled by hunger
    (A bit of bread, a bit of white bread!);
the dream of bare feet
    (Fewer stones on the road, Lord, fewer broken bottles!);
the dream of calloused hands
    (Moss...clean cambric...things smooth, soft, soothing!)
    (Love...Life...Life!...)

I am the pamphleteer of God,

God's agitator,
and I go with the mob of stars and hungry men
toward the great dawn...] (Muñoz Marín 1974: 199, trans. Barry Jay Luby)

While Laviera's work demonstrates a Spanish fluency unmatched by most Nuyorican poets, this English translation of Muñoz Marín's poem appears in *Borinquen*, a widely available pocket-sized anthology considered groundbreaking at the time, published by Knopf in 1974.

The mood of alienated exile in "against muñoz pamphleteering" is heightened by being written strategically completely in English, of the standard variety except for the refusal to capitalize, and referred to in the plural "where I talk about myself / in foreign languages" for New York's dizzying diversity, as well as for the full spectrum of African American, Caribbean and Latina/o English variants (Laviera's later often cited poem "nuyorican" is strategically written in only Spanish to challenge island misconceptions of the diaspora: "yo soy tu hijo, / de una migración / pecado forzado," *AmeRícan* [1985: 53]). In contrast to the impassioned musicality of many of Laviera's poems, the closing line's technical weather report sound of "north temperate uprooted zone" lands as flat as a gray New York sky. The stated opposition in the title "against muñoz pamphleteering" suggests an intervention in the protest vein of Nuyorican poetics, but without the percussive rhythms that marks so much of Laviera's and the collective performativity of many Nuyorican poets. The tone of this poem is of a deep sense of betrayal, especially when taken in the context of Laviera's overall body of work, which is so often marked by a celebration of, to use his neologism, AmeRícan affinity and fidelity to New York. Indeed, compared to the styles of the iconographic Nuyorican poets of his generation, the apocalyptic ironic surrealism of Pedro Pietri, the incorrigible cynicism of Miguel Piñero, the assertive attitude of Sandra María Esteves, Laviera's overall body of poetry by contrast comes off as relatively upbeat, putting solemn poems like this into relief even more.

Just as the collection picks up from where Marqués's *La carreta* left off, this poem begins from where Muñoz's "El Panfleto" prophetically trails off in ellipses "hacia la gran aurora...," with "and I looked into the dawn/ inside the bread of land and liberty," in an excavation of both Puerto Rican and U.S. national imaginaries, where the dreams repeatedly intoned throughout the second stanza of Muñoz's poem are imbricated with the powerful myth of the American dream, and in Laviera's poem "embedded as my dreams," here broken dreams in both contexts. Relayed as an individual, confessional meditation with collective implications, the "i" is brought into play with "my mother's eyes" and the "short range visions of where you led us."[2] The "hollow sepulchre of words" ..."admired from my mother's eyes"... "of your beautiful poetry pamphleteering" lends historical insights, because the mother here, like perhaps the majority of Puerto Ricans who left then, was likely a "Popular" (as the adherents of the political party Muñoz founded are called), entranced by Muñoz's poetic eloquence. The "pamphleteering" here and of the title refers not only to Muñoz's poem "Panfleto," of course, but also to one of the key propaganda instruments of mass outreach and communication used to build the Popular Democratic Party as the massive Muñoz era migration began, with radio broadcasts, stump speeches and pamphlets with such titles as "Catecismo del Pueblo" and slogans as "el que vende su voto vende sus hijos" along with the party's slogan "Pan, Tierra, Libertad" emblematically curved around the silhouette figure of the *jíbaro* in the rhetorical style common to Latin American and American populism of many ideological stripes. Demonstrating the constitutive relationship between literary, political and national canonical texts, both the poem "Panfleto" and the *panfletismo* of the epoch are deemed a "hollow sepulchre," from the perspective of the mass migration propelled in part by such rhetoric and consigned to inner-city urban poverty in New York. Such discourses are exposed as empty and declared dead, but nonetheless laid to rest with a sense of disillusioned sacredness.

Describing the era's main Popular Democratic Party slogan "bread of land and liberty" as "hollow," with Puerto Rican industrialization perhaps resonating with American and European modernity as T.S. Eliot grasped it, gathers more power from Laviera's previous poem in the collection. The latter invokes Muñoz's speeches, rather than poems or pamphlets, in "something I heard" (1979: 28), which suggests the same slogan as "empty," or as discourse to be manipulatively refilled according to political expediency— it is as if Laviera incorporated into his poem what Roland Barthes posited in *Mythologies* (1972 [1957]). Laviera's poem reads as follows:

on the streets of san juan
muñoz marín stands on top
of an empty milk box
and brings his land, liberty,

bread message to a people
robbed of their existence.
napoleón's father attentively
listened as muñoz said, "independence is just around the
corner."
napoleón's father took it
literally, he went around
the corner and found a donkey
tied up to a pole. (1979: 28)

Highlighting a broader betrayal here, not only is the phrase land, liberty and bread, with the word order changed as if it doesn't really matter, associated with the implied weak foundation of an empty milk crate (also suggesting hunger), but also with the broken promise of political independence. The poem's structure suggests the early formation of the Popular Democratic Party, during which Muñoz harnessed broader support with such pro-independence positions, before the purging of *independentistas* led to the creation of the Puerto Rican Independence Party. The hyphenation of the word "inde-/ pendence" in the second of four syllables suggests truncation, and moreover, is a poetic technique reminiscent of another famous poem of mock rhetoric by a politician sending soldiers off to war with empty platitudes, "next to of course god america i" (1926) by e.e. cummings: "why talk of beauty what could be more beaut-/ iful than these heroic happy dead" (1994: 31). Of course Laviera's refusal to punctuate is also reminiscent of cummings, and "something i heard" also seems to mock the notion of great leaders by bestowing the name napoleón (with the accented Spanish pronunciation echoing Ponce de León as well as lion) on a *jíbaro*, in playful mockery, or to valorize napoleón's father taking this literally as a superlative campesino heuristics.

Both poems levy sharp critiques at the chief architect of Operation Bootstrap, as Juan Flores has noted (1993: 173–4), for which the massive migration of unskilled agricultural workers and their families became a matter of orchestrated public policy (as did massive sterilization campaigns). Other poems directed at Muñoz and the Muñoz era offer different treatments, with "popular" in *AmeRícan* conveying the spent weariness reminiscent of painter Francisco Rodón's famous portrait of

Luis Muñoz Marín (1975): "your soul moves in listless/ circles turning like the old/ man carousel, turning like the/ old man carousel" (1985: 86). Also in *AmeRícan*, on the facing page, is a much more conciliatory tribute that excavates generational collective memory in "don luis muñoz marín," with its title of respect, and opening with Laviera's poetic mentor: "the poet jorge brandon, a sacred father-testament,/ praises your history, your expansion, your moving/ us into the center of the modern nineteenth century,/ where man is most advanced; as we left the motherland," and closing with "...and i tell you, thank you, for buying/ time, no matter what else is ever said, the elders/ believe in you and i believe in the elders" (1985: 87). This poem nonetheless illustrates that those who migrated were not only *populares* but the very *jíbaros* discursively marshaled to build consensus at that time, as Arcadio Díaz Quiñones so pointedly reminds:

> Una de las paradojas profundas de la historia puertorriqueña del siglo XX es que el Partido que forjó el mito del campesino "jíbaro," con los signos de sul cultura populista, créo vertiginosamente las condiciones para que los jíbaros reales emigraran en masa a los Estados Unidos, y acabó dándoles la espalda. (2000: 60)

> [One of the profound paradoxes of 20th Century Puerto Rican history is that the political party that forged the myth of the campesino "*jíbaro*" with the emblems of its culture as the basis of its populist politics, created accelerated conditions so that the real *jíbaros* would migrate en masse to the United States, and ended up turning its back on them.] (author's translation)

Indeed much literature of the Puerto Rican diaspora exposes the limits of such *jibarísta* discourse in ways that usefully challenge its coherence, especially around the constellation so implicit to nation-building as race and language. Throughout Laviera's body of poetry, such discourses are by turns celebrated as they are problematized, on occasion perhaps most importantly challenging the use of the *jíbaro* figure represented as white, as well as interrupting the racial harmonizing discourses orchestrated by such literary and sociological canonical works of the 1930s and '40s, namely Antonio Pedreira's *Insularismo* (1934), Luis Palés Matos' *Tuntún de pasa y grifería* (1937) and Tomás Blanco's *El prejuicio racial* (1942). Some authors of the diaspora implicitly and consistently challenge such configurations in their work, such as Aurora Levins Morales, who repeatedly represents jíbaros as females of color in her visionary history *Remedios: Stories of Earth and Iron from the History of Puertorriqueñas* (1998). Esmeralda Santiago's *When I Was Puerto Rican* (1993) documents the contradictory connotations of what it means to have been a *jíbara*, yet reifies and naturalizes such discourse while lamenting its rupturing effects. Laviera's representations of *jíbaros* by turns reproduce traditional tropes ("a música jíbara" [1979: 73]; "jíbaro" [1985: 44]) but more often racially revise this figure ("bomba, para siempre" [1981: 68]; "melao" [1989: 27]; "Tesis de Negreza" [2008a: 22]).

The racial and linguistic tensions inherent in the phrase "triangle of contradictions" elucidated earlier also resonates with the phrase "a three-way warning poem," first a subtitle to one of Laviera's key poems on race, and later the title of a poem dedicated to José Luis González. William Luis has already richly interrogated the Afro-Puerto Rican musical, poetic and spiritual references of the former, titled "el moreno puetorriqueño (a three-way warning poem)" from *La Carreta Made a U-Turn* (Luis 2009: 32–4), though I would add observations of the poem breaking with the racial harmonizing discourses of Tomás Blanco, who promoted Luis Palés Matos' then controversial poetry expressly for such purposes (Díaz Quiñones 1985). Structured in a sustained call and response pattern reminiscent of other musical and percussive Laviera poems, a disjuncture occurs in the flow of the performance between both sides, with the hyphenated word break technique seen above with "independence," here emphasizing embedded echoes of Tomás Blanco (to-/ masa, todos son blancos di-) while echoing the thematic refusal in the poem to accept or enact stereotypes while denouncing colonial clichés, a refusal to harmonize.

qué voy a ser yo como moreno puertorriqueñno. preguntar
¿dónde está mi igualdad?
viendo novellas sobre morenos esclavos, sin poder ver un moreno en la pantalla. la negra dorotea, el nené mingo, papá cortijo, la morenita to-masa, todos son blancos di-

ay baramba bamba
suma acaba
quimbombo de salsa
la rumba matamba
ñam ñam yo no soy
de la masucamba
papiri pata pata
loíza musaraña
bembón ay no canta

frazados, haciendo papeles sin
vida, haciéndose burla de mi
presencia. ... (1979: 46)

el cañonero es de acero
las puertas arrebatan

The subtitle of this poem reappears later in *AmeRícan* as the main title of a poem, "three-way warning poem" (1985: 49), dedicated to José Luis González and alluding to his perhaps most famous short story by extending its critique of racial and class marginalization to that era's intelligentsia neglect, distortion and exclusion of the diaspora in and from national discourses, especially surprising in the case of González, who dramatically challenged Eurocentric national discourses in the seminal *El país de cuatro pisos y otros ensayos* (1980), as Alvarez argues (2006: 41). The class implications are ironically suggested by the two-part poem labeled *"sin nombre"* and *"sin nombre the first"* (emphasis in the original), playing off the social importance accorded to surnames to denote privilege in a Latin American context in Puerto Rico in the first, and the roman numeral generational suffix in the Anglo American context in the second. The ambiguous anonymity of no name/sin nombre suggests collective circumstances as well as lacking the patriarchal lineage designed for the express purpose of inheriting monetary or property wealth, here nonexistent. The poem is relatively short and direct, deploying its critique of diasporic exclusion forcibly in striking visual verticality, with "en / el / fon / do / del / nu / yo / ri / can / hay / un / pu / er / to / rri / que / ño" revising the title of the story "En el fondo del caño hay un negrito" (González 1997b—originally published in 1950), while part two, "ste / reo / type / pu / er / to / rri / que / ño / sí / yes / we / can / cut / you / all / in," critiques stereotypes of the diaspora and advocates, at the moment of the affirming "sí / yes" switch to colloquial English, for inclusion to Puerto Rico's discursive national imaginary.

In Laviera's most recent poetry collection, *Mixturao* (2008a), he diplomatically challenges the history of linguistic exclusion of diaspora literature and linguistic prejudice against Puerto Ricans of the diaspora by island intelligentsia, in a poem dedicated to and critiquing González titled "Spanglish Carta," in allusion to another famous González story "La carta" (1997c—originally published in 1947). The poem, which also appeared in Puerto Rico's chief daily newspaper *El Nuevo Día* (May 6, 2007), opens rife with references to other famous González stories: "In the fondo of a new york city blackout / i read your stories time / and / time again dos negritos cucándome / mi búsqueda alla adentro" (2008a: 41). The aforementioned reference to "Al fondo del caño" is this time joined by "La noche que volvimos a ser gente" (González 1997—originally published in 1970), a later work by González that importantly not only takes place during a New York City blackout from the perspective of a character of the diaspora, but is narrated completely in vernacular speech, with the author embodying the non-standard Spanish rather than representing it as seen earlier in "La Carta," both sympathetically, the latter an especially humanizing portrait of vagrancy. Laviera's poem then makes highly specific references from the island's cultural history, the slum *el fanguito*, the tradition of *el baquiné* (a party for a baby's wake) reminiscent of Puerto Rico's most famous painting by Francisco Oller, and a reappearance of "papote sat on the stoop" as well as Muñoz's stars: "negroide mulatto of no stars / spanglish ebonic disparatero / physical expressions linguistically / crippled with no skies ahorcado / en el fondo fundillo del hoyo fango" (2008a: 42). While lamenting the pathologizing discourses that distort the persona's linguistic practices, the poetic performance defies them and proves them wrong, as seen in analyses of Laviera's often anthologized "my graduation speech" (Laviera 1979: 7; Flores 1993: 175; Alvarez 2006: 29–30).

The turning point in the poem occurs when Laviera defensively calls González to task for his perpetuation of these pathologizing discourses: "como novio en el altar I awaited / your latest pronouncements / to masticate your phrasings / even then siempre nos cucabas / criticisms of my non-linguistic nada," which alludes to a published interview with Díaz Quiñones (1976: 13–36) in which González rejects Hispanicism's linguistic nationalism, yet in the next breath reinscribes what came to be harmful elitist claims, as is also observed by Carlos Pábon (2002: 98). In response to an interview question on "the language problem" in Puerto Rico, González presents the local vernacular as "impoverished" rather than changed or enriched by English influence, blaming the middle and upper classes (Díaz Quiñones 1976: 24–5). The worst offenses González notes are not so much the use of English words as the translations of false cognates, such as the commonly heard "dar para atrás" for "give back" instead of "devolver" and what he calls the proliferation of obscene words in everyday usage (1976: 26–7). He also criticizes the widespread interchange of "r" and "l" pronunciations, lamenting not the so-called purity of the language but the lack of quality public education. Though he predicts and deflects charges of purism and elitism at several turns, he ultimately takes egregiously elitist positions, as is also observed by Pábon (2002: 98), invoking the "civilizing" discourse of hygiene, *"pensamiento correcto"* (correct thought), and what is now seen as Trotsky's hardline prescription for language and literary production. Advocating for "gente culta" (cultured people) to be "los custodios del patrimonio cultural de la nación" (the guardians of the nation's cultural patrimony), González states that: "En realidad, no habla bien quien no piensa bien, y, lo que es más importante, *no puede pensar bien quien no sabe hablar bien*" ("In reality, whoever doesn't think well, doesn't speak well, and, more importantly, whoever doesn't speak well cannot think well") (Díaz Quiñones 1976: 28—emphasis in original). González' lengthy response completely bypasses the Caribbean context, with its broad range of standard and non-standard language practices, and lambastes literary efforts documenting what he calls a "supuesto 'idioma puertorriqueño'" ("so-called 'Puerto Rican language'") as the laughing stock of the Spanish-speaking world (1976: 15). He warns against the "tribal" rather than "national" effect of a literature written in what he calls "un falso nacionalismo lingüistico" ("a false linguistic nationalism") (1976: 33).

Laviera's poem imparts the intellectual wounding caused by these remarks, especially coming from an otherwise intellectual and literary inspiration. The poem enacts a healing w/rite, ending in respectful tribute, in an ultimately grateful tone, the passage in itself acting as reconciliation, as well as an echo of Laviera's earlier poem dedicated to González: "But you inspired us into / penhood introspection / and we bestow upon you / an African chegüigó / Don José Luis González / reminding you that / en el fondo del nuyorican / definitivamente / hay un puertorriqueño" (2008a: 43). Once again refusing diaspora exclusion from national intelligentsia conceptions, the title of respect "Don" is nevertheless bestowed, though it was not in the dedication at the beginning of the poem.

Despite shifts in the relationships and the fluidity of travel practices between the island and diaspora Puerto Rican communities, such exclusions and distortions of the diaspora's linguistic practices as linked to their literary productions are still unfortunately common in Puerto Rico today. Hence Laviera's sustained dialogic dialogue with the writings of these late figures functions, in a Bakhtinian sense, to revise that situation. *El Nuevo Día* literary critic Carmen Dolores Hernández persists on this question, in her newspaper coverage and in her latest book of interviews *A viva voz: entrevistas a escritores puertorriqueños* (2007), a companion to her earlier book of interviews with diasporic authors, and which includes a jacket blurb by Laviera. In it she asks nearly every interviewee about their attitudes toward literature of the diaspora, and some answers, namely by the otherwise accomplished authors Hjalmar Flax and Javier Ávila, were shocking for their misconceptions, prejudices and ignorance on the subject. The most erudite response, however, came from poet José Luis Vega, former Dean of Humanities at the University of Puerto Rico, Río Piedras campus, and recently presiding over the Academia Puertorriqueña de la Lengua Española:

> Creo que Puerto Rico es un país desdoblado que, respondiendo a esa realidad, ha producido una literatura desdoblada, con una parte de ese doblez aquí y otra allá. Y no se trata de catagorizar, de decir si es o no puertorriqueña esa literatura que se escribe allá: desde la que se escribe en español riguroso hasta la que escribe en ingles y todas las variantes intermedias. Está ahí, es un fenómeno que existe. Lo que debemos hacer es fijarnos en las cimas. (2007: 302)

> [I think Puerto Rico is a doubled country that, responding to that reality, has produced a doubled literature, with one side of this doubling here and the other there. And this doesn't try to categorize, to say if the literature written there is or is not Puerto Rican, ranging from what is written rigorously in Spanish to what is written in English and all the variations in between. It is there; it is an existing phenomenon. What we should do is practice the exegesis it calls for.] (author's translation)

Toward that end, Laviera's profound literary engagements with two major figures such as Muñoz Marín and González produce a dialogic dialogue that acts as a cultural remittance, to invoke Flores' recent theory on the contributions of return migrants from the diaspora to the island (2009), one that addresses the canonicity of Puerto Rico's literary, linguistic, and political discourses to challenge its historical conceptions of the Muñoz era diaspora towards a more profound and more mutual reconciliation.

NOTES

[1] Discourses that directly correlate master standard language practices and ideas are also discussed by Negrón-Muntaner (1997: 269–70) and Mignolo (2000: 263–6).

[2] "Short range" echoes later in Laviera's oeuvre, with "short range citizens" in a poem thematically similar but in full musical performance mode, titled "migración" and featuring another persona, Calavera, also "sentado en los stoops," the Spanish word for skull here suggesting Laviera's contemporary urban Thinker-cum-poet in Auguste Rodin's Dantesque sense of the image (1988: 37–8).

155

—III—
CREATIVE ACTS OF HEALING

157

Acts of Resistance: Creativity, Coalition, and Consciousness in *King of Cans*

JACQUELINE LAZÚ

For more than thirty years, Nuyorican poet/playwright Abraham "Tato" Laviera (1950-2013) built the tools of a literary system. With a characteristic appreciation for unidealized, hidden beauty, agony, humor and creativity, Laviera has helped define Nuyorican aesthetics. Affected by a variety of intersecting cultural and historical legacies, Nuyorican aesthetics are not defined by a didactic, prescriptive agenda despite having to respond for decades to the judgments of American and Puerto Rican canons. It is characterized by its fluidity and adaptability. In fact, it summons the "back and forth" (Mercer 2005) dialectic that is a byproduct of the dialogue between artworks, traditions and canons. In its evolution it has worked to reconcile relationships within the spaces in which it recreates itself. One distinctive space for negotiating these possibilities has been inner cities, where migrants initially formed their networks. In one of his last dramatic works, *King of Cans* (2008b), Laviera highlights another layer of this literary system: the process of imagining and projecting communities in an effort to reterritorialize identities by creating frameworks for collective action.

King of Cans premiered in 2001 at the Red Carpet Theatre in El Barrio, revealing one of the most complex symbolic systems to date for Laviera. In this musical epic Laviera presents a very likely yet fantastical society based on a group of homeless people organized around the business of picking cans. The empowerment of this marginalized community through a planned course of social mobility injects doses of reality into the chimerical drama. *King of Cans* is, simultaneously, a historical tribute to the Nuyorican school of literature and through its historiography a discourse on social order and political economies. It is a detailed epic of more than eighty pages, two acts and seven original songs. Laviera developed the play while working with gifted and talented inner-city youth at Talent Unlimited, a non-profit organization in El Barrio. During this time, Laviera became enthralled with an image that is familiar to neighborhood residents: homeless men and women pushing along shopping carts packed with trash bags of cans. Equally intriguing was the business plan that developed as these workers mapped the neighborhoods, collected, and sold the cans. They made steady profits at the recycling center at 111th Street and Park—to the frustration of local officials who had their eye on rising real estate prices and eliminating the presence of this homeless culture (Lazú 2008).

Like the public, glass-walled lives of the homeless in the United States, the audience witnessing Laviera's play can see everything that the characters do. There is no privacy or shelter from public scrutiny. We do not know how or where the story began. In fact, we are forced to interpret only the present lives of the characters. Somehow, however, we begin to believe, along with the main character, Latero, in the potential success of their entrepreneurship even while working with the most unlikely variables. The energetic main character is leading a group of homeless people in the business venture that involves picking cans for selling and recycling in exchange for cash. The multilayered structure of the business, however, is unique. Latero insists on dealing only in penny denominations. He inspires a work ethic and solidarity among his *workers* despite their evident skepticism. Latero's workers are individuals that share the stigmas and labels that constitute the reality of homelessness in U.S. cities. On the other hand, they also have remarkable characteristics and an agency that is rarely given attention in conventional modes of social order and common narratives about the homeless. As the story develops, they experience mutiny, love, deception, death, and success among their ranks. Without reverting to romantic images of the streets or idealizations of blight, Laviera reveals some of the internal and external forces that shape the experiences of poverty and homelessness. In fact, we never see any another space beyond the society of the can-pickers. We never see dominant society or The Powers That Be, although the consequences of its existence are an undeniable presence in the drama. These details are consistent with Nuyorican aesthetics, particularly in the tendency to present individuals and their communities revealing paradoxes and intersectionalities in ways that are both nuanced and hyperbolized.

Nuyorican Transformative Aesthetics
Nuyorican expressive culture has made a distinctive contribution to US and Latin American cultural life and has revealed the principles, techniques and practices of a unique aesthetic culture. Laviera himself, representative

of the early generation of Nuyorican writers, recognized that Nuyorican is a style and school of writing (Hernández 1997: 80). Partially located in the broad stratum of Brechtian realism, Laviera's theater, as Nuyorican theater does, often blurs the traditional boundaries between aesthetics and politics and fuses didactic realism with traditional theater traditions. But realism in the Nuyorican drama is often paradoxical, an illusory figuration of an esoteric reality. Nuyorican aesthetics cultivate cultural awareness, and unravel it from the enigma of nationalism for the Diasporic subject. In the theatre, individuals and communities are rematerialized with their historical legacies and the effects of the institutionalized inequalities that shape their subjectivity, while still projecting familiarity, aspiration and potentiality.

In *King of Cans*, a sensationalized world under the subways of New York offers a concise and discursive space for the transformation of society. The play opens up with an allusion to a theater production. Laviera intends for the audience to understand that this is a play and the very first words in the script are: "Method acting. On stage. Final Call" (Laviera 2001: 1). The "scene" that follows is a dress rehearsal of sorts where the characters appear to be channeling Stanislavski and method acting. Yet this drama is far more suggestive of a Brechtian epic or the Theater of the Oppressed. While the audience is not necessarily a participatory audience, it is immediately invited into active engagement with the drama as drama, establishing clear limits to realism in the play. Furthermore, the play can also be understood within the traditions of agitprop theater, even as it proceeds as a musical theater piece—a genre that Laviera increasingly explored in his dramaturgy. His interpretation of reality as a performance is filtered through genres that test the limitations and plasticity of realism and challenge conventional discourses on poverty and the inner city.

Music has been an integral source of thematic and structural inspiration to Laviera and other Nuyorican writers. In fact, Laviera's first book of poetry, the neo-canonical *La Carreta Made a U-Turn* (1979), is divided into three separate sections, the first "Metropolis Dreams" is certainly an ode to the city with poems like "subway song" and "the last song of Neruda." The other two sections directly reference their musicality in the titles "Loisada Streets: Latinas Sing" and "El Arrabal: Nuevo Rumbón." These include poems that reference the various genres that would continue to inspire Laviera's repertoire like "a sensitive bolero in transformation," "the congas mujer," "tumbao," "the salsa of Bethesda fountain," "summer congas," "la música jíbara," and "el sonero mayor," among others. In *King of Cans*, there are choruses, musical breaks, and full choreographies. Interestingly, the songs in *King of Cans* can offer more story than the dialogue itself. While the musicality of the play establishes some aesthetic distance from realism reinforcing Brechtian technique (Brecht 1992: 138), the drama, like Laviera's poetry, functions as allegory. The actual "play" opens with what he calls a "performance poem/song," which introduces the names of the characters (Laviera 2001) and conjures Nuyorican poetry.

While there are definite references to cultural legacies, the community in Laviera's *King of Cans* is not an identifiable ethnic community. In fact, none of the characters is ascribed an ethnic or racial identity, but the play is imbued with cultural signification. Most of the characters reflect a trajectory that William Luis (2008a) has traced as evolving in the poetic works of Laviera; he sees the trajectory as culminating in the title of Laviera's *Mixturao* (2008a). Poems like "español," "bilingue," "nideaquinideallá," and "mixturao" "[represent] a communal expression against the forces that produce and promote linguistic and political isolation." Language for Puerto Ricans has long been used as a metaphor of cultural identity. The bilingualism of Nuyoricans has just as persistently been seen as a cultural deficit. The perceived peculiarities of "Nuyoricans" including language, as well as the class and racial politics that once betrayed their association with the United States, and therefore against Puerto Rico, became points of departure for the articulation of an identity politic. And so, Laviera's potentially generic characters become Nuyorican through their language choices, their calques and their *gufeo*[1]:

YOUR HIGHNESS:
What's his problem BUELAQUERA, o bellaquera, that's bilingual for horny, yes you're right. Six months without a woman and four years in the play, how do I know? I listen to him over the phone...

CAST:
Metete Viagra brother...

YOUR HIGHNESS:
He's sick, you know enfermito. He has a bilingual condition.

SUBWAY MISS CAN:
What condition?
YOUR HIGHNESS:
Medical. QUINOSAYLAYPAIRAY.

SUBWAY MISS CAN:
QUININOSAYLA what language is that?

YOUR HIGHNESS:
En español, la manguera está agotá, o la longaniza está floja.
In spanglish lack of plátano or soft morcilla and in English
Quinosayle para. (2001: 3–4)

This ludicrous word play of Your Highness is a display of her irreverent personality and of Laviera's characters' predisposition to *el gufeo*. She is Latero's most devoted disciple and appears to love him, but she resents his commitment to Subway Miss Can and despises what she perceives as her lack of dedication to him and the cause. This is enough for her to make him a direct target of, at times, harsh teasing and criticism. The exchange is also a more serious allusion to the physical toll of substance abuse and addiction that we see in nearly every character. Above all, the word play represents the cultural and linguistic particularities of the Nuyorican experience. As in the title of one of the opening poems of *Mixturao*, "nideaquinideallá" Laviera's characters firmly situate themselves in the multiplicity of their hybrid linguistic identity (Luis 2008a).

These various linguistic features are fused in the dramatic narrative with other elements that speak for Nuyorican aesthetics. Space, is another feature reassembled in the Nuyorican theatrical text world. It is a space that is significant to both the self (writer) and the community (audience). For the earliest writers of the diaspora, reterritorialization was a process that was significantly dependent upon the image of an idealized island paradise from which the migrants had been displaced. Then the complex streets of New York and especially the Lower East Side of Manhattan were the common location for the articulation of Nuyorican identity. But the very concept of space has been dispersed in the Nuyorican text. The inspiration now lies in whatever community Puerto Ricans live. And while the creativity and self-awareness of individuals in these spaces is paramount, there is often, simultaneously, a stimulus for solidarity within and between people affected by the politics of alienation in dominant cultures. Indeed, the articulation of subjectivity in the Nuyorican text, reflects a decolonial, transformative aesthetic frequently rooted in the solidarity of collective action.

Social Stratification and Alternative Economies

In *King of Cans*, transformative action is exemplified by the political, social, and financial goals of a group of people facing difficult social, economic, and physical obstacles. They strive to organize around what they consider to be their livelihood and possible outlet for the cycle of dependency and invisibility in their lives as homeless people. Latero insists that they organize, perhaps unionize, and expand their can-picking business. Dealing exclusively in penny denominations, they intend to create an alternative economic structure that will uplift them on their own terms while using standard models of free enterprise that they have re-signified. Latero sings:

> At collecting cans during fifth avenue parade
> We have read in some guide to success that
> In order to get rich to make it big
> We have to sacrifice ourselves by digging
> Deeper and deeper into the extra
> Can margin of profit
> We're on our way up the
> Opportunistic ladder of success
> Ladder of success in ten years
> We will quit welfare to become
> Legitimate businessmen
> I will soon become a latero executive
> With corporate conglomerate intents
> SO GOD BLESS AMERICA. (2001: 5)

The workers recognize how they are defined and treated by the general society and throughout the play are skeptical of Latero's optimistic plan. Subway Miss Can, while committed mostly because of personal feelings for Latero, who saved her from a life of violence and prostitution, is particularly cynical. But she is also as quietly hopeful as the others who nevertheless continue to trust Latero's plans and allow him to save the pennies that they make in the daytime and nighttime operation.

> SUBWAY MISS CAN:
> Sure, you're working in an empty lot
> run by St. Church that you don't even
> own. You are employing people who for
> the rest of society, they don't even exist.
> You are associating with people who are winos,
> Crazy, degenerate, sick, who live by the moment,
> And you're trying to build a career with
> Them by establishing a can business selling
> Operation, how marginal can you get? (2001: 17)

In this scene, as in others, Subway Miss Can vents her frustration at Latero directly but will just as vehemently defend him and his plan in his absence. Her frustration is also a voice of reason recognizing the cycles of dependency that can disenable the homeless in US cities. At the same time, the workers also recognize their social capital as an organized force. They sing:

> A whole day's work
> One hundred cans
> Six hours
> Forty blocks
>
> A dollar an hour
> Self-employed
> Who will believe
> We're not homeless bums...
>
> We are legalized by law
> the bottle cap law
> the state of New York
> We work against pollution
> for the environmental cause
> re-cycling. (2001: 7)

By the second act of the play, Latero's dream to expand the business beyond picking cans starts to take shape as the scene opens with the sight of a new sign in the lot that reads: "Latas Inc. We buy cans. Mailboxes. General services. Check cashing." In inner city, poor, and working class iconography, they now offer the services of a neighborhood currency exchange and have also become retail purchasers of cans. This is an ironic and humorous signifier as currency exchanges often represent alternative banking and indirect systems of financial services for urban communities. For Latero's group, it is advancement in their social and economic status. Still dealing in pennies, they talk about the future possibility of dealing in nickels.

The choice to deal in pennies is especially peculiar and resounding. Off all U.S. currency, there is no higher contested monetary unit than the penny. For many critics, the penny is a useless denomination. Inflation has devalued the penny to a degree that many argue it should no longer be minted and some even go as far as to suggest that its circulation be ceased. Economists Thomas J. Sargent and Françoise R. Velde (2002) explain that small change is one of the classic problems of monetary history. The fact that coins were commodity money, that is, they were worth their weight in the metal they were minted from, made production very expensive. This would lead to shortages, which resulted in inflation and the depreciation of the change. The solution was the creation of fiat money in the 19th century—money not literally equal to the proclaimed worth (Sargent and Velde 2002: 5). The US penny has suffered the same fate. Initially minted in copper, the demand for the metal during World War II for weaponry led to it being made from zinc, thus the silver penny during that era. It was then continued in the cheaper metal with a thin coating of copper overlay. The government acknowledges that the penny (as well as the nickel) cost more than its worth to produce. Critics further argue that the attachment that Americans have to the penny is emotional, as they tend to hoard and collect pennies more than they actually exchange them.[2]

This argument, however, exposes the polemic of an unequal economic structure and the social stratification that results from it. It is the impetus for Latero's alternative economic model. To one level of society—the privileged, the penny represents something dispensable, worthless, and even void of the symbolism of "good luck" it once possessed. The reality for the poor, however, is that collecting change, especially the neglected penny, can add up to numbers that few imagine possible until they go to exchange them. The key, however, lies in the patience to collect and exchange them, like the can-pickers, who collect the cans and then exchange them. A single penny and a single can will not be worth much on its own but in mass may represent a viable income. The same philosophy could apply to the entire concept of collectivity. If they collect enough cans, enough pennies, enough workers, enough activists, enough voters, enough support, their lives could be transformed. Latero responds to Your Highness's frustration to dealing in pennies:

YOUR HIGHNESS:
A mere 25 dollars for all that work.
That's gross. All we net is 5 measly dollars.

LATERO:
500 pennies gross. 100 pennies net. Our
currencies is pennies. Plus, our business
has grown 1000 per cent. We now can facilitate
5000 cans a night. (2001: 14)

Already relegated to an economic subculture, the idea for Latero may be not only the unobvious value of patiently collecting a large number of pennies but also the psychological impact of dealing with more actual units. Latero's business venture exposes the monetary value of pennies and cans, by rescuing, reassigning, and re-signifying their symbolic value for those who accept it. It is an opportunity for the poor and the homeless to collect wealth that others reject simply because of perception.

Laviera's *King of Cans* accords cultural capital to the strategies of survival of the city's homeless population. Actor Efraín Nazario, who played "Latero" in the premiere performance, recalls Laviera's director assignment to his actors (Lazú 2008). He encouraged them to speak to and research the lifestyle of the neighborhood's homeless and their approach to this trade. Nazario spoke with one individual who regularly collected over $200 of cans a week. His system was based on a careful mapping of the residents and businesses that would regularly sort their trash, as well as knowledge of those residents who did not sort it. But Nazario also recalls the correlation that became evident to him during his method research—an association between homelessness, mental illness, and drug addiction. This too becomes a focal point of Laviera's characterizations.

Epistemology of Homelessness and
The Symbolism of the Nuyorican Poet

As *King of Cans* progresses, it is clear that there is mutiny in the ranks of Lateros Inc. There is a corrupt cop and an informant among them who eventually trick and kill their intellectual leader, The Brain. The traitors are able to poison him primarily because of his drug addiction. The spiritual leader Reverend Sidewalk, who delivers a powerful eulogy toward the beginning of the second act, pulls the group together. The loss of The Brain is significant because he is the realistic strategist to Latero's idealism. Before his death, he writes a proposal to expand the goals of Latas Inc. into party politics and local governance and ultimately inspires Latero to run for local office. His loss inspires personal as well as business reforms for Lateros Inc. As a result of The Brain's death, Reverend Sidewalk decides to address his own addiction to alcohol. During most of the play, the Reverend carries a tank on his back that he constantly drinks from, visibly displaying the weight of his addiction.

In fact, addiction appears as a principal social and cultural obstacle to the otherwise brilliant strategizing of this group. It is a fissure through which the enemy infiltrates and the greatest threat to the loyalty of group members. Even the leader of the group is defined in terms of his addictions, "Latero drinks beer after beer as he writes incessantly" (2001: 12). Alongside the problem of dependency is the impact of the laws and practices affecting the homeless, people with mental disorders, as well as the people who live, work, and/or interact with them on a daily basis. In effect, all of society is impacted by these issues and yet communities of color and the poor face the greatest challenges as they continue to manage the superstructure with fewer options. Addiction, crime, public health crises, ignorance and discrimination further exacerbate the predicament of the homeless. Communities have been systematically charged with finding solutions when the government opts out. In New York and other major cities, studies have found that many homeless people suffer from alcoholism, drug addiction, mental illness, or some combination of the three, often complicated by serious medical problems. The era known to researchers as "deinstitutionalization" (from the 1950s to the present) was a complex rethinking of issues related to mental disorders impacted on the one hand by advancements in the field of psychiatry and public awareness inspired by the Civil Rights movement. On the other hand, paired with economic recessions, it led to the wholesale discharge of patients onto city streets and an unprecedented increase in homelessness with no significant increase in support services (Marvasti 2003: 9–19). In *King of Cans* the characters speak to the impact of deinstitutionalization just prior to deciding that they will campaign and elect Latero to run for a local political office. In unison they sing:

SONG:
...You are also to blame for this
the crimes, the drugs, infectious disease
You led the sick from state to streets
skyscrapers rise communities at risk
Please just don't walk on by
take action fight oppression...

But Laviera is not simply pointing a textual finger at an external population. In fact, the story is made even more complex as we realize that there is a personal symbolic system in the play. The characters represent a historical allegory to the Nuyorican school itself. The publicized personal struggles of the movement's artists was concretized in the 2001 Miramax biopic, *Piñero*, based on the life and art of Nuyorican poet/playwright, and co-founder of the Nuyorican Poet's Cafe, Miguel Piñero. Laviera pays tribute to Piñero and other Nuyorican poets in *King of Cans* as the characters in the play conjure the brilliant but troubled group of writers. Through this allusion, he also identifies and demystifies the conditions of the homeless by taking them momentarily out of the realm of the invisible and repositioning them among esteemed and mythologized figures. For example, The Brain serves as a representation of Piñero. This is evident on one level by those who recognize the shrouded prodigy of the artist interspersed with the struggle of drug addiction that was highlighted in the movie. Laviera makes it most obvious, however, when he is poisoned, lured by the belief that he is being offered drugs. Like Piñero, The Brain makes a special request to his friends. His dying wish in the second act evokes Piñero's living will in the famous "A Lower East Side Poem" in which he requested:

Just once before I die
I want to climb up on a

tenement sky
to dream my lungs out till
I cry
then scatter my ashes thru
the Lower East Side. (Piñero 1985)

Similarly, The Brain asks Latero to cremate his body and then "Spread my ashes throughout this lot." Like the anti-hero mythologized in *Piñero*, The Brain, although void of the recognition and thus compassion of society, is temporarily resignified as an enabled subject who is a victim of circumstance but also an agent of his destiny.

Latero's final eulogy as delivered by Reverend Sidewalk summons Piñero's eulogy by the poet/playwright Pedro Pietri and exposes the connection between Reverend Sidewalk and the Pietri. The moment is also featured in the movie Piñero, and represents one of the many things that Reverend Sidewalk and Pedro Pietri have in common. Pietri, also a founding member of the Nuyorican Poet's Café and the Nuyorican movement, devoted his artistic career to negotiating theatre as a tool of public discourse and resistance. Eternally engaged to community activism through his art, he was not only a prolific writer in poetry, theater, and performance art for more mainstream audiences but also among avant-garde and experimental publications and venues. He engaged music and popular culture in performances like *Mambo Montage* produced in 1987 with Adal Maldonado featuring the music of and starring Tito Puente. That same year he was ordained by the Ministry of Salvation and eventually inaugurated his Church of the Mother of Tomatoes; a roving performing ministry that preached to the "poetry-deprived," advocating for AIDS education and condom use offering a comedic and experimental platform for his work with prison inmates and the mentally ill. While Laviera's *King of Cans* was developed a few years prior to the Reverend Pedro Pietri's death from stomach cancer in March 2004, the play also captures Pietri's long-term struggle with alcoholism and "self-medication"—habits often attributed to the loss of his first daughter and the consequences of post traumatic stress disorder from his service in the Vietnam War (Center for Puerto Rican Studies nd: 11–2). Despite Pietri's prolific career, his condition often translated to a personal and financial struggle for him, and was certainly reflected in the character of Reverend Sidewalk. He was a spiritual leader and inspiration for the group, while struggling to resolve his own personal challenges. The words of Reverend Sidewalk throughout the play are both biographical and prophetic:

> REVEREND SIDEWALK:
> My stomach and my liver,
> My intestines and my vessels,
> Have changed from blood to wine,
> I need a gallon a day,
> A gallon a day,
> Where can I go for help? (Laviera 2001: 9)

Both Reverend Sidewalk and The Brain bring their unique capacities to the group in their path toward transformation—above and beyond their own serious personal challenges.

Lastly, the enigmatic character of Latero is in many ways correlated with the author himself. He is the main source of energy for the group and executor of the business venture. He organizes and directs and with great confidence appoints himself leader on several occasions. The description of Laviera by Carmen Dolores Hernández in *Puerto Rican Voices in English: Interviews with Writers* does justice to the personality of the legendary writer, which he appears to reflect on through Latero:

> Tato Laviera seems to bring the gregarious, carefree sprit of Santurce wherever he goes. Ebullient, assertive, talkative, he is never at a loss for words—or for rhythm. The transitions from prose to poetry, from English to Spanish, from factual conversation to an inspired recitation are made in an instant.... His poetry has acquired the sensibility, however, of the man who, having entered into a different reality, has had to suffer from unexpected prejudice and discrimination. Wiser, but not necessarily sadder, Tato Laviera has fought back with the most enduring weapon of all. His poetry is a documentation of injustices, of painful dualities, of uncertainties; it is also a testimony of the strength of the Puerto Ricans in New York who have defended their distinctness. (1997: 5)

In Latero we find the wit and humor of Laviera's poetic voice as well as the relentless drive for creativity and social change. There is no stronger example than the characterization of Latero as an incessant writer. Laviera is arguably the most prolific of the Nuyorican poets, having published multiple anthologies of his works, plays, lectures, songs, and performances. Like Latero, Laviera created much of his work in collaboration and partnerships with communities. Among his last works for the theater is a four-part theatrical history of the Puerto Rican community in Chicago developed with youth of the Paseo Boricua community. Perhaps one of the most significant and powerful analogies between the life and vision of Latero and Laviera is the application of this art and social resistance despite the greatest odds. Like his fellow artists, Laviera struggled with illness and personal obstacles. In the last decade of his life, Laviera managed the effects of diabetes and insulin dependency that left him legally blind, and many times struggling for his livelihood. For a brief period in 2010, Laviera was left homeless after an emergency brain surgery. Community members organized to help secure housing for the beloved artist. His artistic response to these challenges was to transform the very process of writing.

Like Latero, who is seen writing a proposal and a speech, organizing and running for office while continuing to manage the business, Laviera's work is skillfully multilayered. Latero says at the very beginning that Subway Miss Cans "...is our eyes and ears." And, in effect, throughout the play, Latero does not seem to ever really "see" the opposition and the conspiracy against him. The community and his friends act as lens for him. All the while he uses his voice and his writing for resistance. At the very end of the play Latero is arrested, and only then does he realize that Narco Cop and The Champ were traitors using his business to run a drug ring. Fortunately, Subway Miss Can, Your Highness, and Reverend Sidewalk had been collecting evidence and are able to free him at the end. By then, they have also been able to raise the small penny fortune needed to nominate Latero and win a public office position at the "County Committee of Election District number seven of Assembly number eight." Like Latero, Laviera worked collaboratively with the community members at nearly every stage of writing and development. The blindness of his later years did not disable him in his role as storyteller, as he often worked with collaborators who transcribed his art. In effect, it amplified his creative approach and thematic commitment to the history of Puerto Rican in the United States. As William Luis states, "Laviera smells, sees, listens, tastes, and touches all that surrounds him. But Laviera does not have to use all of his senses to understand and chronicle the various rhythms of his society..." (2008b: 1).

Aligned with post-structuralist critiques of community, Laviera's work does not shroud the oppressive effects that communities themselves can have on individuals, especially those placed outside of the dominant social group, as are the homeless, the disabled, the poor and critically underserved. Marion Young adds that, the idea of community can "[validate and reinforce] the fear and aversion some social groups exhibit towards others" (1990: 235). Laviera presents the liberating potential of diversity and the anonymity that the city offers as a challenge to the normative ideal of communities. There is no other visible community in the play to judge Latero and his colleagues. In this utopic space of the urban underground, where the homeless can organize without the judgment, likely reactions and possible repercussions from dominant groups, the questions change. As James DeFillippis and Peter North suggest, the questions are not: Are there communities? (Yes) Or, can they act collectively? (Yes) Rather: When do they emerge? How are collectively organized, community-based agents constructed? How do they act and with what success? (2004: 77). The society of *King of Cans* is utopic for the safety of its anonymity and ultimately the success of the play in proving the emancipatory potential of the city and grassroots organizing. But at the same time, the infiltration from within by characters like The Champ and Narco Cop reveal Laviera, the realist, inserting a Marxian critique of the schism between class and community in urban politics. Latero asserts in his final speech that homelessness is "an endless situation with no remedy in sight... a telling legacy we are all passing on" (2008b: 79).

Laviera's narrative identity and aesthetic projections express the *epistemic disobedience*[3] that has been an instrument of the Nuyoricans' decolonial praxis from its inception. Along with the multiple artistic approaches they take to making resistance perceivable, and the intersecting cultural and linguistic interactions expressed through their writing, the Nuyoricans have been engaged in the political and economic environment. During the post-war growth phase in New York City that brought many of them and their parents to the U.S. mainland, dynamics of race and class were manifested in several important ways, accounting for the drastic, contentious infusion of African Americans and Puerto Ricans into the city's economy. Andrés Torres explains that they could not fully share the benefits of growth. The subsequent long-term decline— which spelled serious difficulties for many New Yorkers—occasioned a steady fall in living standards for most native minorities (1995: 24). The Nuyoricans' view of these societal conditions, laid out by their aesthetics, effectively introduced new ways of reading the processes of cultural development.

Conclusion

In *King of Cans*, Laviera documents his place in the collaboration and aesthetic legacy of Nuyoricans. Early Nuyorican expressive culture, including Laviera's work, was characterized by examinations of the physical and social troubles of the community. While Puerto Ricans communities remain among the poorest and most underserved in the United States, they have also vehemently resisted the cultural and economic oppression that has succeeded modern colonialism. In some cases, this translates to collective forms of resistance that lie outside of the structures and social relations of bureaucracy and the formal economy. For example, the work of Dale Nelson (1996) reveals that while Puerto Ricans in New York in this generation were less likely to vote, they were more active in protesting and more likely to join community organizations than other groups. In fact, their attitudes toward voting were attributed to the politically alienating experience and lack of desire to participate in a system that offered few rewards or incentives (Nelson 1996). In the Nuyoricans' narrative identity, this has translated into an evolving praxis. At times, this is transmitted through rudimentary theatricality, humor that toys with conventions, transgressions, violence and stereotypes. Other times it reflects complex metanarrative, poetic lyricism, polyphonic textures, entrepreneurship, and political engagement. By all accounts, it challenges the orthodoxies of a universal aesthetic criteria.

In *The King of Cans*, the development of the homeless community rests on creative approaches to working within the semi-permeable boundaries and immediacy of their environment. The reality of their marginalized status calls for a plan within the capitalist, market-based exchange; the economic structure that essentially sustains the social and cultural inequalities. And yet, as Kobena Mercer has described, this reality is also reflective of the distinctive experiences of the Diaspora. They are able to grasp the contradictions that capitalist globalization produces as "an unintended consequence of its intrinsic need to find new markets" (2005: 145).

In *The King of Cans*, the imagined community is a coalition of homeless people living in a seemingly utopic space with little to no contact with the hegemonic structures that created and/or sustained their social and economic circumstances. Led by the assertive, relentless, and idealist vision of the *King of Cans*—Latero—a coalition is formed. The coalition is not ideal. Each individual brings in unique circumstances that cross paths at their shared struggles with poverty and addiction. They also bring to the new community a vision of solidarity that leverages their individual capacities: Subway Miss Can's eyes and ears, The Brain's strategizing, Your Highness's confidence and organizational skills, Reverend Sidewalk's spiritual and ethical guidance, and, of course, Latero's energy and idealism. In the end, there are victories. They win the elections, and their business seems to become viable; victories suggesting that they may just escape what they once believed was their unavoidable destiny: systemic poverty and dependency.

Laviera's pioneering vision continues in the form of a unique decolonial aesthetic. His narrative identity is reflected in the intersecting motion of language and cultural practices. Most importantly, his work represents a social agency that resists categorical approaches to identity, and reveals the ontological dimensions in the writings of the Diaspora. One of the primary elements that emerged from the Nuyorican philosophy of *El gran florecimiento* was the cultivation and expression of a distinct "Nuyorican" culture. Artists grappled to understand and communicate what was "Nuyoricanness." Laviera and other Nuyoricans emphasize identity as embedded in overlapping networks of associations that constantly transform through time and place. Moreover, the work raises important questions about the value structures connected with comfort, beauty, worth and its relationship to art, particularly the theater. Laviera and his cohort were at the vanguard of artists with a subversive tendency to insert new meanings and practices that challenge the status of their art form in relation to dominant social values.

NOTES

[1] Similar to the Puerto Rican cultural practice of "vacilón" and "relajo," the word "gufeo" refers to the idea of having fun by making fun, teasing, joking, riddling, and "goofing" around.

[2] See Margolick (2007) for a brief popular history of the cent.

[3] Walter Mignolo proposes "epistemic disobedience" as one of a series of tools with which to dismantle the impositions of Eurocentric roots of knowledge, constituted from Western universalisms. In Estéticas Decoloniales. International Conference. Estéticas Decoloniales: Sentir - Pensar- Hacer. Abya Laya / La GranComarca.Facultad de Artes - ASAB de la Universidad Distrital Francisco José de Caldas. Bogotá. Colombia. 6-10 Nov. 2010. Available from http://www.youtube.com/watch?v=mqtqtRj5vDA&feature=related [Accessed 25 July 2011].

Azucarao: Tato Laviera and the Poetics of Health Promotion

GLENN MARTÍNEZ

Over the past twenty years, type 2 diabetes has emerged as a leading chronic illness that disproportionately affects Latinas/os in the United States. Mexican Americans and Puerto Ricans have prevalence rates of diabetes nearly two times higher than non-Latinas/os (National Diabetes Education Program 2008). Diabetes is a group of diseases related to the body's inability to properly use insulin in transporting broken down sugars and starches from the blood into cells (American Diabetes Association n.d.). The build-up of glucose in the blood can lead to numerous complications, including kidney failure, blindness, and limb loss. The prevalence of diabetes is inordinately high among Latinas/os in the United States, and the complications of diabetes also disproportionately affect the Latina/o population. According to the Office of Minority Health, Latinas/os are 1.5 times more likely than non-Latinas/os to begin treatment for end-stage renal disease. Similarly, Latinas/os are 1.6 times more likely than non-Latinos to die of complications related to diabetes (Office of Minority Health n.d.).

For Tato Laviera, the diabetes epidemic was more than just a statistic. For Laviera, diabetes was a reality with which he lived every day. Laviera was diagnosed with diabetes in 1984. He became legally blind and suffered from kidney failure due to complications from the disease. Diabetes led to Tato Laviera's untimely death in 2013. As the nation's foremost Latina/o poetic voice and as one of the most socially committed artists in recent memory, Laviera is more than just a victim of the disease. Over the years, he became a leading activist in the fight against diabetes, a selfless promoter of diabetes awareness, and a powerful voice to combat the detrimental effects of *el azúcar* (sugar).

In 2006, Tato Laviera developed a unique health promotion event called the "Diabetic Sugar Slam" to address the diabetes epidemic and to raise awareness about the importance of controlling sugar content. The Sugar Slam, according to Laviera, is a community event designed to tell the story of the threat of sugar in music, poetry, and open verse. In the same year that the concept was developed, the American Diabetes

Association awarded Laviera its Trailblazer Award in recognition of the poet's efforts in promoting awareness about diabetes among Latina/o communities in New York.

This essay sheds light on the poetics of Tato's health promotion efforts by showing how his own personal coping with disease and disability and his evolving poetic voice coalesce to produce a powerful source of knowledge in the fight against the ever-increasing prevalence of type 2 diabetes in Latina/o communities. I was fortunate to sit down with Laviera to talk about his disease and disability (Martínez 2008). In this conversation, Laviera discussed his own personal coming to terms with diabetes and how the disease shaped his outlook on life and modulated his own poetic voice. In an effort to understand the unique qualities and the singular impact of Laviera's health promotion efforts, I will draw from this conversation and from Tato's published poetry to piece together the poetics of health promotion. In doing so, I hope to bring to light a valuable, though highly personal, facet of the poet's voice, which will aid in the interpretation and appreciation of his work.

Tato Laviera's newest collection of poetry, *Mixturao* (2008a), more than any other reflects the varied and experience-inflected evolution of the poetic voice. Language and bilingualism are the most salient and recurrent themes in Laviera's entire corpus of poetry. However, underneath language and bilingualism always lurks an expression of the self that is more profound than language itself, indeed that goes beyond language, subdues it, and shows its inherent limitations. This play on the theme of bilingualism can be seen vividly in a cross-section of the poet's most widely read poems.

In Laviera's first collection of poems, *La Carreta Made a U-Turn* (1979), "my graduation speech" stands out as an emblem of the bilingualism theme. Bilingual through and through, the poem begins and ends with the internal struggle of the bilingual self. "i think in spanish / i write in english" (1979: 7) is the internal duality that opens the poem. The poem ends with a self-recognition, a graduation of sorts, in which the poet recognizes that his speech—in Spanish, in English, in "spanenglish"—is "to matao." Laviera's graduation in the poem is a commencement into the world of biculturalism and bilingualism, into the development of a legitimate space for a poet and a wordsmith who can freely and unashamedly declare "ay virgin, yo no sé hablar" (Alvarez 2006).

In his 1988 collection, *Mainstream Ethics,* Laviera once again embraces the theme of bilingualism. In the poem "conciencia," the poetic voice that had graduated into self-acceptance speaks once again. But rather than speak for itself, it now speaks for others. The ever-present "i" of "my graduation speech" would seem to be enduring the labor pains that will give birth to a renewed sense of "nosotros." "a ver si," the poet asks,

un nosotros
un nosotros verdadero
un nosotros poderoso
un nosotros lleno
un nosostros amoroso
a ver si
 un nosostros humano
alzamos las voces. (1988: 50)

The bilingual and bicultural voice that emerged in "my graduation speech" now begs for a chorus of voices, a chorus that will at once embrace the unique inflections of the bilingual voice and speak out for those who remain silent. The poem culminates in the statement "la lengua es / la ametralladora / de la libertad" (1988: 51). In this poem, the poet unites the acceptance of a bilingual voice with a realization of the power of voice to mark injustice and to incite social change.

The title poem of Laviera's latest collection, *Mixturao,* reflects what I believe to be the culmination of this evolving theme of bilingualism. The poem is dedicated to "English only" and addresses English itself as the agent of its own privilege. The poet positions English together with its recurrent slogan, "speak only English or die" (2008a: 29) against a fully fledged, fully harmonic chorus of voices. The "i" of "my graduation speech" and the emerging "nosotros" of "conciencia" now become an affirmative and emphatic "we-who" - "we who engage ... we-who integrate ... we-who create ... we-who are at peace" (2008a: 29–30). As noted by William Luis, the use of the first person plural pronoun in this poem is articulated with all the force of an invincible majority (2008a: xiv). The power of the constellations of voices funneled into the poet's single voice embodies the power of *la lengua* suggested in "conciencia." The cutting and crucial nature of language thus crystallizes when the poet speaks not only for himself and not only with his conscience, but when he speaks for and from the majority. The centrality of language in Laviera's poetics is incontestable. The achievement of a majority bilingual and bicultural voice that allows him to contest the privileged monolingual and monocultural demands of the dominant society and that permits him to demand that society understand before obtaining the privilege of uttering the word "mixturao" is, without a doubt, the crown jewel of Tato's poetics.

The poetic trajectory that chronicles the maturation process of Laviera's voice is intimately tied to the body. For Laviera, language is not only an external force that brings people together culminating in an invincible majority, it also permeates internally into the flesh of the speaker. In the poem "Word," from the collection *Mixturao*, Laviera makes the relationship between language and the body clear. "Poetry was meant to be heard / Poetry was meant to be read" (2008a: 3) the opening lines of the poem proclaim. As the poet describes these functions of poetry, he continuously draws on bodily images and processes. Poetic subjectivity, for example, is intimately bound to bodily organs as seen in the poet's fusion of the "I" and the "eye": "silent reading internality between eye-of-I." Subjective experience, furthermore, is likened to bodily experiences such as "absorption," "orgasm," and "touching":

"Poetry was meant to be read"
Silent reading internality
Between **eye**-of-**I**
Involved in total
Self-**absorption**
Capturing intellect
Treasures pleasures
Orgasmic intonations
Dignified silence
Intimately **touching**
At innermost (2008a: 3—author's emphasis)

On the oral plane, Laviera is no less insistent on the embodiment of poetic experience. In the third stanza, the poet once again links poetic signification and musicality to body parts, that is, "timpani," and bodily experience, for example, "muscling."

"Poetry was meant to be heard"
Spoken word
Oral transmission
Listener exposed to
Vocabularies
Ear's timpani
Exploration vowels
Consonants physically
Muscling personal
Voices integrated
Stimulated tonalities (author's emphasis)

The integration of poetic and bodily experience is often overlooked in Laviera's poetics as it has been overlooked in Chicana feminist literature (Bost 2010). Bodily imagery has consistently been inserted into the interstices of language and identity in Laviera's poetic oeuvre. Let us recall that as far back as "my graduation speech," Laviera described acculturation in physical-biological terms, "tengo las **venas** aculturadas" (1979: 7). This physical-biological condition of acculturated veins can be linked to the poet's characterization of his language as "matao." The bodily imagery is also present in *Mainstream Ethics* (1988). In the poem "conciencia" the poet seeks to expand linguistic emancipation by shifting from the poetic "i" to the "nosotros." The "nosotros" that the poet refers to is not just a chorus of voices; rather it is also a gathering of bodies, of "mil pellejos" (1988: 50). The bodies that make up the "nosotros" are also bodies subject to injury and to scaring. "hasta aquí llegan **las llagas** de la búsqueda," the poet states triumphantly as he goes on to define the fullness of "nosotros." "Nosotros" must, therefore, overcome injury and find ways to heal the body. Language becomes precisely this vehicle needed for healing.

un nosotros humano
alzamos las voces
constantemente
al ritmo de insistencia
resistencia
un nosotros crítico
que abre la boca

que no se estanca
un nosotros que declara (1988: 51)

In "conciencia" we therefore see that the association of "venas aculturadas" and "matao" language can be inverted to the point where human, collective, critical, and empowered voices become associated with bodily healing. In "Mixturao," finally, the biological function of language culminates in the form of a defense mechanism, a kind of anti-body that wards off and defeats bodily threats. This is evident in the repeating refrain "Speak only English or die" that appears a total of five times throughout the poem (2008a: 29–30). The refrain is defeated each time, and the threat of death is shunned. The poem ends with the following stanza:

so enter our multi-lingual
frontiers become a sharing
partner maybe then I might
allow you the privilege
to call me a tremendous
continental "MIXTURAO." (2008a: 30)

The mixturao "multilingual frontiers" thus become a source of vitality and healing.

Laviera's poetic trajectory was inscribed not only in his poetic work but also in his life. As a victim of the debilitating effects of diabetes, he courageously took it upon himself to engage in a unique and highly personalized style of health promotion. I find it interesting that Laviera's driving preoccupation with language and its intimate connections to the body should also emerge as the central locus of his health promotion effort. The evolution from the "i" to the "we" in Laviera's poetic compositions is also evident in his health promotion work. Underscoring Arthur Frank's idea that "seriously ill people are wounded not just in body but in voice" (1995), Laviera's health promotion effort seeks to engage the embodied voice of diabetics. From this voice it arrives at knowledge and awareness that will put a stop to the persistent trek of diabetes across generations of Latinas/os (Chabram-Dernersesian and de la Torre 2008).

In my interview (Martínez 2008), Laviera painfully recounted his own coming to terms with the disability engendered by diabetes. I remember asking him specifically about the issue of knowledge and whether he felt that a lack of knowledge and awareness led to his own downward spiral in managing diabetes. I was surprised by his response. He said that rather than lack of knowledge, his own problems emerged more from a denial of knowledge. He remembered how physicians who surrounded him would encourage him to be careful and to pay more attention to his health. "Vivía al despacho de la botella, no del licor pero de la cerveza, y nunca le hice caso a todas esas cosas. Un descuido, un descuido total" (Martínez 2008: 1). When I asked about the onset of his vision impairment, the theme of denial emerged once again. "I started seeing a small circle in my left eye. The stupidity of my denial and my lack of health value in my life led me to be in the passion of the illusion. Creí que eso se podía limpiar con algo." Laviera, however, describes a turning point in his coming to terms with disability.

> But I didn't pay attention to it. I just kept on walking the streets in the dark like nothing. Until on July 4th, under the fireworks in the skies of New York, I kept looking at it *y ya se me fue*. I remember walking to the Metropolitan Hospital and some kids were celebrating in the street, I could hear them ... and I asked them for assistance and they didn't want to assist me... And that's the moment that I woke up from this illusion but it was already too late. But then, when I found out I had kidney failure, I woke up and that day I became an activist. Right there, you know. (Martínez 2008: 1–2)

Laviera describes his awakening as one of self-discovery. The loss of vision and the news that his kidneys no longer functioned brought him to a realization of the precarious state of his own health. He laments that his discovery came too late for himself; however, he describes how too late for him can be just in time for others. I asked Laviera if he felt angry with himself for letting his health deteriorate to the point of vision impairment and kidney failure. "I really think that I have reconstructed the anger," he responded, "to have created a whole new life for myself" (2008: 2). The idea of reconstructing anger is key to Laviera's health promotion effort and his acceptance of himself as a mouthpiece for diabetes awareness. Rather than focus on his own disappointment and disability, Laviera has preferred to use his disability and his experience as a way to bring about greater awareness of the disease. "I have channeled my energies towards positivity," he added.

Laviera chooses to be positive even in the face of his debilitating condition. So, from the inner struggle of coming to terms with his own illness, Laviera "graduates" into a conscious desire to help others who share his lot.

Laviera's graduation led him to consider how health information is communicated and disseminated in the Latina/o community. He recalled his efforts combing through the available literature on diabetes and his realization of the lack of clear health communication. He summarized his findings as follows:

> The thought that people spend thousands of hours writing these manuals and then they've got to give it to someone who can edit it into a pamphlet that nobody reads because they're not people friendly. It's just there because you need to look good, not because you need to funnel this information to someone who's actually going to read it. The print is too small. The language is too technical. The information presented doesn't apply. (Martínez 2008: 3)

After noting these problems, Laviera described how he tried to field test some of these pamphlets. "So, I started collecting all of these pamphlets and taking them to the community for people to read." His field tests confirmed his initial impression: "It was just information that was not culturally sensitive, not easy to read. It was too much language." In bringing this information into the community and scanning the reaction, Laviera discovered a collective voice within the community. He discovered that health information was encoded not in technical language, complex figures, and pristine pie charts, but rather that it was encoded in stories.

> Everybody had a diabetes story. And those stories are actively in the community. Active, you know, like radiation. They are alive. It's like you could touch it. Like an electric cable. You could just go into the community and touch anybody and see that there is a story there. And I found that people were really traumatized in their own pride, traumatized by telling these experiences. Experiences about their uncles, their aunts, their *abuelitas*. And I started seeing that the younger people were talking about the elders. It was rampant and I decided to create music and art out of it. (Martínez 2008: 3)

Figure 1. *Publicity for the Diabetic Sugar Slam.*

The discovery of diabetes stories became an inroad for Laviera to infuse health information into the community. The knowledge and information embedded in these stories connected Laviera to the community through his own diabetes story. The discovery of these stories effectively served to merge the poet's own "i" experience into a broader "nosotros" experience. The story of diabetes in Latina/o communities is no longer a statistic but rather has become a collage of integrated and inextricable experiences that bind a community together through the resources provided by language. The realization of the centrality of diabetes stories, the prominence of the embodied voice in the community, thus becomes the focal point of Laviera's

Figure 2. *Family Promoting the Diabetic Sugar Slam.*

health promotion effort. By recognizing these stories and creating artistic channels for them to be heard, "la lengua" becomes "la ametralladora de la libertad." Through language, through free and creative expression, Laviera sets out to encourage a liberation from the weighty chains of diabetes in the community. It is, in the end, "la conciencia" that pushes the poet toward the community and that merges his voice with that of the community.

The acceptance of his own disability and the discovery of a unified community voice led Laviera to create the Diabetic Sugar Slam. The Sugar Slam is a performance art contest in which participants are asked to provide a three-minute testimony using rap, poetry, song, or storytelling about the dangers of sugar contents or how diabetes has affected a family member, a friend or society in general. The contest brings together community members from different backgrounds and different age groups using different methods and techniques of creative expression.

The unifying theme of sugar and its debilitating effects through diabetes, furthermore, ties the disparate voices together in a bond of (comm)unity that draws on an inner determination to defeat a highly debilitating disease. By bringing together community voices and by teasing out a very human instinct toward survival and well-being, Laviera creates a unique conduit through which to infuse health information into the community. As contestants developed their entries for the Diabetic Sugar Slam, Laviera described how he would work with them not only to hone their creative voices but also to mold their stories to accurate and appropriate health information. In pulling together the voices of the community, Laviera created a majority voice that would channel his own anger and the anger of the community into a positive force that infused health information into the community on its own terms, in its own voice and for its own purposes. The poetics of Laviera's health promotion thus consists of a process of "disinvention" of technical and scientific language and a linguistic reconstitution that embeds knowledge in experience, and puts knowledge at the service of action (Makoni and Pennycook 2005). Traditional health promotion, in Laviera'a view, places action at the service of knowledge. In order to acquire knowledge about health conditions it was necessary to invest considerable effort in deciphering the technical details presented in brochures, pamphlets, and other conduits of health information. The Diabetic Sugar Slam turns this on its head by foregrounding the combination of experience and creative expression and through this concoction arriving at usable and reliable health information. It is a "mixturación" that, just as in his poem "Mixturao", drives its participants to a sense of pride, autonomy and self-efficacy, that is, a view of themselves as able to effectively confront and manage the challenge of diabetes (McAlister, Perry and Parcel 2008: 171).

Like his entire poetic corpus, Tato Laviera's health promotion effort is embedded in and draws its strength from the community. Like his poetic corpus, his health promotion efforts also become directed towards the liberation and affirmation of the community from which it springs. In this study, I have uncovered how the poetics of Tato Laviera's health promotion activities aligned with his own principles of poetic creation. At the same time, I have shown how his unique approach to health promotion lifted up a majority community voice that resisted passivity in confronting the diabetes epidemic and that reclaimed health knowledge on its own terms and in its own uniquely modulated voice. I hope that this facet of Tato's work becomes a rich and meaningful part of his enduring legacy.

Barrio, Body, Beat: Tato Laviera and the Holistic Rhythm of *Mestizaje*

ISRAEL REYES

Tato Laviera poses an important question in his poetry: how can the poet critique and celebrate Puerto Rican culture and the diasporic experience, act as satirist and singer of odes to the Nuyorican community, and serve as historian, troubadour and healer through writing and orality? Laviera takes a holistic approach in his role as a poet because he speaks and writes about Nuyorican life from its most intimate spaces as well as from a critical distance. His poetry engages other members of his Nuyorican community in direct dialogue, while addressing a wider, more global audience and readership. His holistic approach also imagines the real bodies of his community as well as the community as a body. For Laviera, poetry and music act as *purgas* (purges) of social ills brought on by discrimination and poverty as well as *remedios* (cures) for self-inflicted wounds such as drug addiction and sexual exploitation. His poems shift focus from the individual to the community, from the community to the world, and from particularity to universality. Laviera's poetry combines barrio, body and beat in order to promote the spiritual and material health of the Puerto Rican community, while acknowledging and addressing the cross-cultural exchanges and *mestizaje* that are part of the diasporic experience.

The term "holistic" is most often associated with alternative, "New Age" medicines, although "holistic" and "holism" appear as concepts in a variety of disciplinary studies such as anthropology (Parkin and Ulijaszek 2007), philosophy and the philosophy of science (Fodor and Lepore 1992; Caruana 2000), and cultural studies (Craige 1992). In the areas of complementary and alternative medicine (CAM), James C. Whorton describes in his essay "From Cultism to CAM: Alternative Medicine in the Twentieth Century" (2004) how notions like holism in CAM developed in the United States as a rejection of the "rigid distinction between mind and body that [...] had turned medicine onto a path of denying any influence of the psyche upon the material body" (2004: 300). Alternatives to modern "allopathic" medicine have been practiced in the United States since the turn of the last century, but the popularity of CAM increased dramatically alongside the cultural and social movements of the 1960s and '70s, when "holism" began to function as a generalized term for almost any form of CAM. Whorton notes that, by the 1970s, "holism was medicine that repudiated Cartesian dualism to embrace an understanding of human beings as organisms whose mental, emotional, and spiritual powers were fully integrated with, and affected the functioning of, their bodies" (2004: 300). By the late 1970s and early 1980s, the concept of treating the "whole person" had gained enough respectability among mainstream modern medical practitioners that they formed the American Holistic Medical Association, and in 1991 the National Institutes of Health established the Office of Alternative Medicine to evaluate the efficacy of alternative therapies (Whorton 2004: 302–3).

As Judith Fadlon argues in *Negotiating the Holistic Turn: The Domestication of Alternative Medicine* (2005) the gradual increase in acceptance of holistic medicine has occurred in tandem with a steady process of "domestication," (that is, when foreign and marginal cultures have gained more prominence in the mainstream as part of a general pattern of cultural plurality) (2005: 20–3).[1] Fadlon describes the process of domestication not as one of subduing or overpowering difference, but one in which the sentiment of being a "stranger at home" in the context of a postmodern, globalized society has generated a sense of "alienation and loneliness" (2005: 24). The turn to holistic approaches in medicine reflects a "nostalgic quest for community and for 'things as they used to be'" (2005: 24). Similarly, the holistic approach to the poetic articulation of a diasporic identity that one finds in the work of Tato Laviera imagines the body as a site of negotiation between marginality and a reaffirmation of Puerto Rican cultural traditions and systems of spiritual belief. In the case of Laviera's poetry, this negotiation takes the forms of code-switching between English and Spanish, free-verse rhythms that echo Afro-Caribbean musical traditions, and a thematic celebration of cultural and racial *mestizaje*.

Additionally, with his celebration of cultural pluralism, his rejection of the dualistic separation between mind and body, and his invocation of Afro-Caribbean traditions of spirituality, Tato Laviera performs a holistic poetry in which language and rhythm promote individual and collective health within the Nuyorican community. Many of Laviera's poems articulate the heterogeneous *mestizaje* that informs and shapes Puerto Rican, Nuyorican and even "AmeRícan" identities. Laviera works with a Nuyorican aesthetic that challenges the rigid parameters of the binary thinking characteristic of Western, North American culture. Through bilingual (or "interlingual") poetics, multivocality, and themes of political protest, the linguistic mobility of Laviera's poems reflect the cultural contradictions, racial mixings, and political struggles that characterize the Nuyorican diasporic experience, which is part of the larger Puerto Rican national family and similarly heterogeneous history of *mestizaje* in the Americas. Yet some of these same poems also conceive of a holistic relation between the geographic spaces of intercultural mixing, the pleasures and pains of the *mestiza/o* body, and the Afro-Caribbean rhythms that suffuse Nuyorican poetics. On the one hand, Tato Laviera's Nuyorican aesthetic articulates the linguistic, cultural and racial multiplicity of the diasporic experience, while on the other hand these poems conceptualize a communal and cosmogonic uniformity of the human spirit.

Laviera's poetic style reflects the speech of the Nuyorican community, which mixes to varying degrees Spanish and English in everyday discourse. The most commonly used term that describes this linguistic practice is "bilingualism," but Bruce-Novoa (1990) has developed the term "interlingualism" to refer to the kind of literary Spanglish that appears in Laviera's work. For Bruce-Novoa:

> Interlingualism is a linguistic practice highly sensitive to the context of speech acts, able to shift add-mixtures of languages according to situational needs or the effects desired. This practice rejects the supposed need to maintain English and Spanish separate in exclusive codes, but rather sees them as reservoirs of primary material to be molded together as needed, naturally, in the manner of common speech. (1990: 50)

Laviera's interlingual poetry makes use of language textually and performatively rather than "receiving" it as an unalterable system that privileges linguistic authenticity. Therefore, while Laviera writes about bilingual subjects who inhabit a culturally heterogeneous enclave, he uses interlingual poetics to articulate his holistic vision of the diasporic imaginary. Nuyorican poets like Laviera encode the migration of Puerto Rican culture in their interlingual poetry as a way to resist stasis and remain culturally mobile in their urban U.S. context. They also imagine an intercultural space where an imaginary island—a source for their cultural, racial, and ethical selves—emerges from the "concrete jungle" of the barrio. Laviera's poetry creates a viable mode of expressing a *mestizo* Puerto Rican consciousness by moving between Spanish and English, thus sustaining a dialogue with the island while confronting the harsh reality of the urban context.

Tato Laviera's poetry takes poetic license with the dual linguistic registers of the Nuyorican dialect to resist cultural assimilation but also to contest discourses of cultural authenticity. In the poem "my graduation speech" from Laviera's first published collection, *La Carreta Made a U-turn* (1979), Laviera ostensibly laments his inability to speak correctly in either Spanish or English. The poem begins by stating "i think in spanish / i write in english," which, according to Juan Flores, "illustrates that the apparent contradiction between thought and language [...] can be and is controverted in the course of actual conceptualization and verbalization" (1993: 175–6). The poem reproduces the Spanglish of the Puerto Rican community in New York, and the title, written in all lower case, suggests that the speaker's education is incomplete:

> tengo las venas aculturadas
> escribo en spanglish
> abraham in español
> abraham in english
> tato in spanish
> "taro" in english
> tonto in both languages (1979: 7)

This interlingual poem employs some of the code-switching characteristic of bilingual speakers, which Guadalupe Valdés Fallis defines as "an alternating of languages within a sentence or phrase" (1976: 879). These alterations should not be considered interference, for although the bilingual subject may not be aware of the switches from one linguistic code to another, "important social information concerning interpersonal relationships, group membership, values, relative status, power, and prestige, can be conveyed by a change in language" (1976: 879). While Laviera's poem employs interlingual poetics to convey the diasporic subject's self-perceptions of marginality, inadequacy and disenfranchisement, Stephanie Alvarez argues that this poem and the Spanglish in which it articulates the diasporic experience "reveal the survival skills and creativity of the Nuyoricans who, surrounded by such despair and poverty, are able to not just survive, but also create, among other things, an entirely new language of their own. That language, Spanglish, the result of the Nuyoricans' resistance to hegemonic acculturating forces, proves that transculturation can be a resistance strategy" (2006: 30).

Yet Laviera's code switching also expresses an embrace of otherness, of the other that resides in the self. In an interview with Pablo Martínez Diente, Laviera states: "El lenguaje en inglés tiene unas tonalidades que el lenguaje español no tiene, y el lenguaje en español tiene unos sentimientos que el lenguaje inglés no tiene, y entonces combinándolos los dos a veces me salen unos capullos de alegría, un amor más amplio que los dos idiomas separados, aunque se llama code switching [sic]" (2006: 158). It is this amor that Laviera represents holísticamente as a coming together of bodies, minds and spirits that promotes the health of the Nuyorican community. The speaker in Laviera's interlingual poem "graduation speech" perceives his cultural and linguistic confusion at a corporeal level, where he has "las venas aculturadas." His veins are acculturated and his interlingual writing—"escribo en spanglish"—reflects the embodiment of Nuyorican cultural hybridity. As the text moves from Spanish to English, the reader becomes aware of the irony that even though the speaker thinks he is a "tonto" in both languages, he is able to communicate with a community of bilingual speakers like himself, while the monolingual reader remains on the periphery of this poetic exchange and can only partially access the intimate knowledge that is being shared. The interlingual poetics then become a form of empowerment and cultural affirmation, which sends a conditional invitation to monolingual readers to consider the ethics of intercultural engagement.[2]

This theme appears repeatedly in Laviera's poetry, which not only imagines a holistic union between language, culture, spirit and the body, but also attempts to heal the communal body through a celebration of Nuyorican rhythm and music. In another poem from *La Carreta Made a U-turn*, "the nuevo rumbón," Laviera reproduces the percussive rhythm of conga drums in order to purge the Nuyorican body of the deleterious effects of heroin addiction and cultural alienation:

    congas   congas   congas
    congas   congas   congas

desperate hands need a fix from
the healthy skin of the congas
congas the biggest threat to heroin
congas make junkies hands healthier

las venas se curan ligero
con las congas conguito congas
congueros salsa de guarapo
melao azucarero (1979: 53)

This poem uses repetition as well as the characteristic Spanglish to invoke the healing properties of Afro-Caribbean music, which reconnects the addict's body to a spiritual tradition—"the voodoo curse / of the conga madness" (1979: 53). The music also functions as way for the Nuyorican community to cohere around a common purpose: "the congas clean the gasses / in the air, the congas burn out / everything not natural to our people" (1979: 53). In *Creole Religions of the Caribbean: An Introduction from Vodou and Santería to Obeah and Espiritismo* (2003), Marguerite Fernández Olmos and Lizbeth Paravisini-Gebert argue that music plays a fundamental role in the way Afro-Caribbean religions strengthen the bonds between community members as well as unite the material and spiritual worlds: "Consecrated drums and the polyrhythmic percussion they produce, along with clapping, the spoken or sung word in repeated chants and dance [...] produce an altered focus of consciousness that beckons the supernatural entities and communicates between worlds" (2003: 11). It is this holistic quality in Laviera's poem that bridges the divide between languages, cultures and bodies as a kind of *sanación*, or healing, both for the addict and for the Nuyorican subject alienated from his or her cultural heritage.

In addition to the Afro-Caribbean religious traditions that he integrates in his poetry, Laviera also turns to the Christian notions of salvation and redemption in his holistic approach to purging the societal illnesses and personal addictions from the bodies and spirits of his Nuyorican community. In "jesús papote," from the 1981 collection *Enclave*, Laviera rewrites the Christmas miracle as a ghetto Nativity scene, in which a junkie prostitute mother gives birth to the eponymous child in a tenement basement:

> she loved heroin slow motion ejaculations
> exploding nervous system open-preyed flesh human
> body not feeling dry winter air christmas eve
> noche buena 12 o'clock tranquility night of peace
> no mangers night of hope heroin reaching embryo
> about-to-be-born little child silent night feeding
> tubes struggling to survive being born to die (1981: 13)

This long, narrative poem portrays the degradation of the woman's body by drugs and by the men with whom she has sex in order to obtain the heroin she craves. The heroin acts as an erotic defilement of the sacred body of the mother and the innocent body of the unborn child. As the poem emphasizes the sensorial thrill the junkie receives from the drug, it also depicts the sacrilege that heroin commits against the sanctity of life through the Christmas allegory.

The narrative structure of the poem begins *in medias res*, with the unnamed mother finding refuge in a tenement basement after scoring a fix. It then moves on to the first-person perspective of the unborn child, who offers up his prayer while in the womb: i am jesús papote I have no last name so call / me jesús papote" (1981: 13). This yet-to-be embodied voice recounts through analepsis (flashback) how his mother attempted to escape her drug addiction by returning to the healing climate of Puerto Rico: "quietly sunset lowering her thighs cooled refreshed / stimulated sauna touches moon-lit beauty mark smiled" (1981: 16). The unborn child pleads with his mother not to return to New York, yet when she does return to find employment she also succumbs to her addiction. The urges arise from the unborn child himself: "[...] i was restless i was acting up i had relapsed / i was choking I needed it she said no she said no" (1981: 17). The mother finally does surrender her will to the addiction; she returns to the streets to prostitute herself to score the money she needs for her heroin fix.

This struggle reveals how the harsh urban reality alienates the mother from the Puerto Rican culture that nourishes both the body and spirit. The unborn child becomes an enemy from within for the mother who battles against addiction, and she, in turn, defiles and destroys her own body and destines her child to a stillborn fate. While the mother lies doped and unconscious, jesús papote fights to emerge in the world, yet his voice goes unheard as he announces his stillbirth: "why do i have to eulogize myself / nobody is listening i am invisible" (1981: 19). He must call upon the larger spirit of his community and "of all the faiths and of all the beliefs" (1981: 20) in order to bless his own emergence:

> with the silent love of all my
> people, with the final resolution
> of our nationhood, i am asking
> for my blessings BENDICION
> BEN ... DI ... CI ... ON (1981: 21)

It is only at this point that the mother regains consciousness and takes her newborn child to a church where the bells of a Christmas midnight mass call to her. As with the congas in "the new rumbón," the bells in "jesús papote" are a rhythmic sound that calls to the isolated and desperate Nuyorican subject who searches for a spiritual and physical healing in the presence of community. In a final act of redemption, the mother offers up jesús papote "to the people miracle cherubims flautists" for a divine benediction (1981: 21). The poem's allegorical rewriting of the Nativity integrates Christian faith into the Nuyorican imaginary and solidifies a holistic union between the individual, the people, and a divine cosmos.

Despite this call for a holistic communal healing, Laviera also recognizes the possibility that his poetic texts can create a distance between himself as a poet and the community from and to which he speaks. In "para ti, mundo bravo" from *La Carreta Made a U-turn*, Laviera acknowledges his role as a "historian / who took your actions / and jotted them on paper" (1979: 13). The lives of the people among whom he has lived and observed provide him with poetic inspiration, but he emphasizes that his poetry is not meant to exploit the experiences of this community:

> in the final analysis
> i know that the person
> in this society most
> likely to suffer ...
>
>   is you, out there
>   sometimes living the
>   life of a wandering nomad
>   to taste the breadcrumbs
>   of survival ... (1979: 13)

By setting the stanzas off from one another, the poem reproduces visually the intersubjective distance that Laviera recognizes as part of the poetic process. As the reader's eye moves from one side of the page to the other, s/he confronts a moment of self-recognition as well—"is you, out there"; the reader, too, participates in the poetic act so s/he must also acknowledge the separation that allows the poet to represent the Nuyorican experience. The moment of separation is a creative moment, but Laviera does not wish to create conflict between himself and his poetic community, even when he holds a critical mirror up to the poverty, drug use and violence that plague the Nuyorican urban enclave.

Laviera shows that the interlingual representation of the common language of the Nuyorican enclave from which he speaks and to which he addresses his poetic voice can act as a way to confront the divisions that fragment the larger Puerto Rican community. This commitment to articulate a collective voice while recognizing the individual struggles of various mainland urban and island experiences, as well as acknowledging the critical role of the poet, artist, and historian, resonates with the Nuyorican aesthetic of the poet as a public artist, or "troubadour," as Miguel Algarín describes in his introduction to *Nuyorican Poetry: An Anthology of Words and Feelings*:

> The poet sees his function as a troubadour. He tells the tale of the streets to the streets. The people listen. They cry, they laugh, they dance as the troubadour opens up and tunes his voice and moves his pitch and rhythm to the high tension of "bomba" truth. Proclamations of hurt, of anger and hatred. Whirls of high-pitched singing. The voice of the street poet must amplify itself. The poet pierces the crowd with cataracts of clear, clean, precise, concrete words about the liquid, shifting latino reality around him. (1975: 11)

In this way, Laviera establishes a bond with the Puerto Rican community in New York by integrating the poet's craft into the collective identity and experience of those Nuyoricans he represents in his work.

While many of Laviera's poems celebrate the language and culture of his community, other poems employ the critical distance of satire to depict Nuyoricans' faults and foibles. In *Enclave* (1981), Laviera offers a critique of sanctimoniousness and hypocrisy in the poem "juana bochisme." The poem depicts a caricature of the gossiping neighbor who wags her tongue at all the sexual indiscretions and peccadillos of her neighbors:

> y la victoria ascensor, me dijo manny parque
> que lo oyó de tito esquina que lo habían llamado de puerto rico,
> te lo juro, lo que pasa en nueva york inmediatamente lo saben en manatí,
> se me perdió el hilo . . .sí, ajá, es así (1981: 27)

Unlike his Spanglish poems, Laviera uses Spanish exclusively here in order to replicate more faithfully the kind of gossip mongering that older and younger generations of Puerto Ricans will immediately recognize. Yet the poem offers gentle mockery, since "juana bochisme" could be anyone's mother, aunt, cousin, or friend. Puerto Ricans of all stripes laugh at the caricature because it reflects the guilty pleasure we take in neighborhood gossip, even as we recognize its divisiveness and hypocrisy; there is a little bit of "juana bochisme" in all of us. Laviera emphasizes the urban reality that often pits neighbor against neighbor by using words associated with city life for the last names of the people in juana's bochinche litany: "victoria ascensor," "manny parque," and "tito esquina." This focus on the city and the social relations between community members situates the poem within the larger theme of *Enclave*, whose title is a Spanglish pun that combines the English "enclave" (an enclosed geographical territory) and the Spanish "en clave" (in key, in the key of, or in the sense of). The title encompasses the location, music and meaning that are part of the Nuyorican urban experience. The musicality of Nuyorican gossip reverberates throughout the Barrio, from the elevator (ascensor) to the park (parque) to the street corner (esquina). The gossip also travels back to Puerto Rico, transmitting the *bochinche*'s sounds and rhythms to the extended Puerto Rican national family. By making this satirical critique from within the collective imaginary of the Nuyorican community, "juana bochisme" holistically unites critical distance with shared intimacy, corrective laughter with pleasurable familiarity, and barrio knowledge with island kinship.

Laviera draws from this intimate knowledge to reach outward to a broader sense of what it means to live in a multicultural, cosmopolitan world. His poem "AmeRícan" (1985), from the collection of the same name, epitomizes what Juan Flores calls the moment in Nuyorican culture of "branching-out, the selective connection to and interaction with the surrounding North American society" (1993: 191).[3] As in the title of his collection *Enclave*, Laviera employs a Spanglish pun with his neologism "AmeRícan" that fuses the Anglo American national space with a Hispanic/Latino self-affirmation. The orthographic play on the word "American" represents a textual and oral strategy for "defining myself my own way any way many / ways Am e Rícan, with the big R and the / accent on the í!" (1985: 95). With this poem, Laviera resituates the Nuyorican enclave outside a space of cultural balkanization by celebrating the geographical and identitarian mobility of the diasporic Puerto Rican nation:

>   AmeRícan,   across forth and across back
>   back across and forth back
>   forth across and back and forth
>   our trips are walking bridges! (1985: 94)

The term AmeRícan also embraces a much larger diasporic community of Puerto Ricans who have created their own porous enclaves in other U.S. cities such as Philadelphia, Chicago and Boston. Laviera's holistic approach to culture and identity constantly shifts so that any hierarchical notion of authenticity gives way to a more inclusive and egalitarian sense of belonging. Betty Jean Craige, in *Laying the Ladder Down: The Emergence of Cultural Holism*, argues that a dualist model of culture pits individuals and groups against one another and places them on a hierarchical "ladder" of privilege and dominance, while "in the holistic model such domination is understood to imperil the whole system, since the health of a society depends upon the health of the interdependent individuals composing it" (1992: 36). Likewise, in "AmeRícan," Laviera describes how the process of *mestizaje*, in which the diasporic Puerto Rican nation "absorbed, digested" those cultural elements with which it has come into contact, has also "spit out the poison," "spit out the malice," "to reproduce a broader answer to the / marginality that gobbled us up abruptly!" (1985: 94). Once again, Laviera employs a corporeal metaphor here to represent the unbreakable bond between the body and the spirit as the Puerto Rican community seeks to promote its own health and survival in the larger, often hostile world. In his interview with Martínez Diente, Laviera describes how his poetry belongs to a broader audience and reaches out to embrace universal themes: "You don't write only for yourself, once you put it on paper it does not belong to you. Many people can pick it up and treat it in many forms, so I am very respectful of the form that I put in print" (2006: 152).

Laviera continues to experiment with poetic interlingualism and explore the theme of cultural heterogeneity in his most recent poems. In "nideaquínideallá" (2006a), Laviera rearticulates the geographic, linguistic, and identitarian mobility that characterizes the diasporic Puerto Rican imaginary. As he did in "graduation speech," Laviera describes the mutability of his name and how shifting from English to Spanish destabilizes meaning and notions of cultural authenticity:

> my first name is de aquí
> my last name is de allá
> my last name is nideaquínideallá
> yet to be defined
> evolucionario hybrid (2006a: 173)

While "graduation speech" highlighted the irony of the bilingual speaker as a "tonto" who can communicate in two languages, "nideaquínideallá" draws from the destabilization of a linguistic border to project outward toward a wider space of communicative and identitarian possibilities. The interlingual text moves between languages to show how the Nuyorican subject is a constantly evolving "hybrid," one who confronts the marginal space created by the diasporic experience in order to defy the restrictive orders of linguistic purity and cultural authenticity. Yet this hybridity is not limited to the confines of an ethnic enclave for Laviera, for he sees the interlingual strategies of his poetic discourse as a means of "[...] fermenting / secretive universal / garabatopandegato pan / continental yearnings" (2006a: 175). The ludic tongue-twister of "garabatopandegato," which combines the word garabato (scribble) with the colloquialism pan de gato (a mixed-up mess, literally a cat turd), articulates the cultural and linguistic mixtures that form part of the diasporic imaginary. The "pan" in that neologism is then echoed in "pan / continental," a play on the more familiar term "Pan-American." These hemispheric "yearnings" stretch across a wide swath of geographies and cultures, and they are articulated in the hybrid poetic rhythms that give sonority to a rewritten American Dream. Laviera makes it clear that orality and textuality function together in this affirmation of a universal *mestizaje*: "nideaquínideallá / escríbelo junto / sin letra mayúscula / gracias" (2006a: 175). As the poet verbalizes his new name—a name that emphasizes the diasporic experience of displacement—he asks that it be written down as a testament of pride to a hemispheric audience. No longer the "tonto," the bilingual Nuyorican subject calls out to the world from his space of marginality, and it is this voice—Laviera's voice—that embraces difference even as it affirms identity.

This dual register of simultaneous universalism and particularity reveals the holistic approach that Laviera employs to both celebrate and scrutinize the complex and ever shifting Nuyorican imaginary. His poetry also unifies the mind and body through rhythms that are perceived viscerally and in the blood. The interlingual texts he writes and performs reshape the cultural landscape of marginality, which counteracts the rigidity of atomistic systems. As Betty Jean Craige writes in *Laying the Ladder Down*, "The lesson of cultural holism is that our health—as individuals, as a society, as a species—depends upon our keeping the whole in mind. We cannot exploit, or neglect, any particular set of individuals and expect our global human community to thrive" (1992: 116). When Tato Laviera takes such a holistic approach to the poetry that articulates the diasporic experience of the Nuyorican subject, he not only promotes the health of his own enclave but that of the wider world around it, because to isolate one from the other would perpetuate the hierarchical separatism that maintains the status quo and debilitates both individuals and the larger community. When Laviera writes in "nideaquínideallá" that "backnforth here soy de aquí / cannot be defined / cannot be categorized / cannot be pasteurizao / cannot be homogenizao" (2006a: 173), he combines barrio, body, and beat to resist the powerful temptations to establish dominance through discourses of cultural purity. Such discourses have the deleterious effects of isolationism, self-loathing and antipathy toward one's neighbors. Laviera's poetry reconnects the Nuyorican subject to his or her cultural heritage while reaching out to a world of difference, thus taking a holistic turn toward healing divisiveness and inequality. As one of the many poetic voices of the Puerto Rican diaspora, through barrio, body and beat Tato Laviera epitomizes the troubadour who makes his home in mobility and who always travels with his home in the rhythm of his Nuyorican heart.

NOTES

[1] Fadlon's ethnographic study focuses on holistic medicine in Israel, but she draws many comparisons between Israel and the United States, particularly in terms of holism's connection to cultural pluralism. It should also be noted that the social movements that have promoted alternative medicine range from the far left, New Age philosophies to Christian fundamentalist anti-vaccination campaigns. See Schneirov and Geczik (2004).

[2] Sommer (1999) identifies bilingual textual strategies as one way that minority writers articulate a "rhetoric of particularism," which scrutinizes the discourses of critical mastery that often politicize multicultural readings and pedagogies.

[3] Also see Edrik López's (2005) essay which analyzes a number of texts, including poems by Laviera, according to the four moments in Nuyorican consciousness outlined by Flores. López focuses on "the troping of space, the way corresponding representations from various texts inform readers of the manifestation of a discursive community" (2005: 206).

203

La palabra, conciencia y voz: Tato Laviera and the Cosecha Voices Project at The University of Texas—Pan American

STEPHANIE ALVAREZ and JOSÉ LUIS MARTÍNEZ

> *Word. Syllable. Letter.*
> *Universe. Expression. Sound.*
> *That is all there is. That is all a word contains.*
> *To control them, and to own them and to cherish hem.*
> *That's what we are looking for.*
> (Laviera in Sandoval 2009)

In The Beginning: José Luis' Story

The Spring of 2007 marked the first of many visits from Jesús Abraham "Tato" Laviera to The University of Texas–Pan American (UTPA) in Edinburg, Texas, just minutes from the U.S. Mexico border. He was invited to participate in UTPA's Festival of International Books and Arts (FESTIBA). Laviera conducted a poetry reading, poet/critic talk with Prof. Stephanie Alvarez, and a writing workshop, all in the same day. His poetry captivated UTPA students, faculty, staff, and community members in a very special way. "*La lengua es la ametralladora de la libertad*" (language is the machine gun of liberty). Laviera's energy filled the room in a manner that was quite different from the accustomed way of doing business in the Río Grande Valley. "*Papote, sat on a stoop.*" Everyone knew he was not from the Valley, he was "different," he wore a dashiki, he wore a *plenero* style hat, but he spoke Spanish, he spoke English, and he spoke Spanglish—in many ways just like many in el Mágico Valle del Río Grande/The Magical Rio Grande Valley. "*Tengo las venas aculturadas.*" Laviera spoke prophetically, he spoke with grace, and he did so in a way that resonated with a community that understands the issues and themes of struggle, justice, *lengua* and *cultura*.

It was an honor to meet such a distinguished poet, but it was an even greater pleasure to meet such a kind and generous human being. Therefore, when Laviera mentioned that he was interested in visiting Mexico for the first time, the decision to drive him was an easy one. Although Laviera was a bit incredulous about how close we actually were to the U.S. Mexico border, after a twenty-minute drive we arrived at the edge of the U.S. side of the Progreso International Bridge. We decided to walk across the bridge to Las Flores, Nuevo Progreso as this oftentimes reduces the long wait times on the return.

While walking the bridge, exactly half way along the bridge fence there is a plaque that demarcates the line of separation between the United States and Mexico. When we reached this mark, Laviera asked to stop for a minute to take in the moment. The image and idea of Laviera on the Progreso International Bridge with one foot in the United States and the other in Mexico was a powerful moment that neither of us will ever forget. Laviera did not say much about that experience, only that it would one day be the inspiration of a future work.[1] We continued on our way until reaching the other side/*el otro lado* and were welcomed by a bustling Las Flores street on a cool March evening.

Having made it across, we quickly found a place to achieve one of our primary objectives for the evening, some Progreso style *lonches*, a taco of sorts made with small fried *bolillo* bread instead of tortillas. Once seated at plastic table on the sidewalk next to a large makeshift travelling food cart, Laviera asked for a detailed description of the area. Las Flores is a small tourist town where one can find everything from pharmacies, dentists, doctors, liquor stores, *tortillerías*, and so much more along five city blocks. Cars drive up and down the busy two-way street with music blaring from storefront speakers, and young children sing and play small accordions in the hopes of receiving a tip. The sounds of people selling *aguacates* (without the seed, as this cannot be transported across the border), hammocks, roasted almonds, Chiclets, and other items filled the atmosphere. Despite the unusually cool weather, it was a very busy evening in Las Flores. In many ways, this might be different than a busy evening in the Lower East Side, but maybe not?

On our drive back across the border, Laviera inquired about my experience growing up in The Río Grande Valley. I explained how my vantage point was that of an undocumented immigrant that arrived in

South Texas at that age of four. How I began to migrate from Texas to work in the fields of Illinois, Montana, Minnesota but, primarily Michigan at the age of seven, and how I had worked until the very same day that I went off to college. I described the work we did, how we were paid, life in the migrant labor camps, and how the little money we earned in the summer had to last us the entire winter in Texas. I explained that my seven brothers and I completed high school and achieved a college degree. We usually left school early and came back late, depending on the crop cycle that particular year. We worked on weekends and after school when work was available to help our parents make ends meet. I clarified that we grew up in South Texas in a home in a colonia with no telephone, indoor plumbing, or bathroom until I was in middle school, and that many migrant families in the Rio Grande Valley continue to live this way. I also shared some of my experiences of how Mexicans were treated in Michigan and other states.

The visit wrapped up very pleasantly and Laviera returned to New York. As Director for The College Assistance Migrant Program (CAMP) at the UTPA campus, I extended an opened invitation to Laviera. The CAMP Project is funded by the National Office of Migrant Education and is intended to serve as a very intense support system for migrant farm worker students as they transition from high school to post-secondary education. During their first year of college, students are provided individual tutoring, life skills seminars, modest financial stipends, and some receive housing scholarships. The UTPA CAMP Project services an incoming group of seventy migrant farm worker students every year. As CAMP Director, I realized that despite our strong support system, we were not bringing out the enormous potential that these students had nor were we using their lived experiences to help fuel their academic pursuits. The vast majority of our migrant students are the first generation in their family to pursue a post-secondary education—or graduate from high school for that matter. Therefore, it was difficult for them to have a reference of what life would be like as a college undergraduate. Thus, the staff looked for ways to feed the student's self-motivation to succeed academically. We tried anonymous surveys, group meetings, and mentoring sessions. Still, we felt that we could be doing more; we just were not sure what or how.

Therefore, when I informed the CAMP staff that Laviera was interested in working with migrant farm worker students in some form or fashion, they were naturally interested. After multiple discussions, the idea of

Figure 1. Nuestra Voz, Nuestra Lucha *by María Lourdes Alvarez was created as one of her testimonios for Cosecha Voices and has been adopted by the student organization as their symbol.*

creating an academic Spanish course for credit revolving entirely around migrant students, documenting their lived experiences, emerged. With the support of Academic Services and working through our office in Student Support Services, the course took form with the efforts of the Chair of the Department of Modern Languages, Prof. Glenn Martínez, and Prof. Stephanie Alvarez. Prof. Martínez suggested an Advanced Composition course, and with the approval of the Dean, the class was offered in the Fall 2007. The Advanced Composition course entailed writing about the migrant farmworker experience in Spanish. It was a rare occasion in which the institution acknowledged and gave credit to students for the knowledge they possessed while still assisting in the further development of their education (Delgado Bernal 2002: 117). We were not certain what would come from the course but our selfish hopes were that Laviera, through his course contributions, could help students understand the tremendous importance of their work—and that of their families—to the well being of our nation. We believed that if students could come to that understanding the importance of their stories, there would be no telling how far their new *conciencia* could take them.

Dancing Horses, Mariachis, and Rosarios
Needless to say, Laviera had an impact on the Valley, and the Valley also had a profound impact on Laviera. Laviera, a dedicated observer of enclaves, marveled at the rich culture of the Valley and in particular of *familia*. He stressed over and over again that back home, *familia* is not as strong and united. He constantly reminded the students that where he is from, children are largely raised in homes without a father. He expressed the fact that it was a gift our students should treasure. In fact, migrant farmworker families are very united. The entire family depends on each other to work and provide for the family. As Daniel Rothenberg notes, "The family provides an organizing principle for daily life, a much needed sense of stability and order" (1998: 276).

Laviera was exposed to the experiences, traditions and cultural realities of the migrant farm worker families living in the *colonias* of South Texas. He did so, not only through the Cosecha Voices students' stories, but also by participating in various family events. On one occasion, Laviera's visit coincided with José Luis' mother's *rosario* in honor of El Niño Dios (baby Jesus). In this common tradition, many families put the baby Jesus to sleep on Christmas Eve and awaken him on Candle Mass, February 2nd, with a rosary on both days in his honor. In addition to prayers, candles and singing, oftentimes, families will have food, *danzantes* (*matachines*), *bolos* (goodie bags) for the children, and even fireworks. This was an emotional and spiritual experience for Laviera. He asked many questions as he absorbed the scene through sound, taste, and feeling.

On another occasion, Laviera's visit coincided with the birthday celebration of Mr. Gabino Martínez, a patriarch of the very large Martínez family, who was celebrating his 89th birthday in Donna, Texas.[2] The patriarch was the father of nine children, had 45 grandchildren, 52 great grandchildren, and two great-great grandchildren. The celebration took place outdoors at the residence of one of Mr. Martínez's daughters, who shares a large piece of property with her sister. The party started with the entrance of the mariachis. Two dancing horses had been hired for this occasion. Throughout the celebration Laviera savored endless provisions of *mole*, tortillas, *arroz, frijoles, asado,* and drinks. He repeated frequently as he ate, "Está bueno el condenado." In the background, music came from the band led by Mr. Martínez's son and grandson. Laviera insisted on meeting the Martínez patriarch, and thanking him for inviting him to be a part of the celebration. Often times, later, he still marveled at the event saying he had never seen anything like that in the United States.

Letting Go.
Migrant farmwork is literally consuming Chicanas/os. Even those who eat the fruits and vegetables picked and packed by them are in essence consuming Chicana/o migrants. Consider the title of one of the most important works in Chicana/o literature to see the inference of consumption, Tomás Rivera's *...y no se lo tragó la tierra*. This novel tells the story of a young boy who literally refuses to be consumed, in this case by the earth that opens up to swallow him. Nevertheless, the novel much like Laviera's own writing portrays the numerous means in which the characters resist consumption on many levels, including education. Migrant farmworkers such as Rivera, who make it to the university are those who have fought and survived consumption. Nevertheless, once at the university, these students continue to fight being swallowed up. For as Angela Valenzuela reveals "schooling is a subtractive process. It divests these youth of important social and cultural resources, leaving them progressively vulnerable to academic failure" (1999: 3). She contends that "rather than centering students' learning around a moral ethic of caring that nurtures and values relationships, schools pursue a narrow, instrumentalist logic.... Thus, teachers tend to be more concerned first with non-personal content, and only secondarily, if at all, with their subjective realities" (1999: 22).

Cosecha Voices is a critical pedagogical intervention that through performance, *testimonio,* and voice carves an academic space that centers the migrant students' experiences and subjective realities in the hopes that these students may empower themselves to resist consumption. Cosecha Voices intentionally taps into, rather than subtract, the students' vast funds of knowledge by means of the *testimonio* (Moll, Amanti, Neff and Gonzalez 1992). During his trip to Progreso, Mexico, with José Luis, Laviera imagined a hand beneath the dirt holding on to the roots of a fruit and another reaching above with a pencil in the hand. This image of the triumph of *conciencia y voz* over consumption (subtraction) symbolizes in many ways the guiding principles of the Cosecha Voices class and is captured by the painting of María Lourdes Álvarez, a student of the Spring 2009 course.

To achieve the objectives set forth for the class the educators[3] collectively understood that we could not rely on their formal academic training. Instead professors, students, and administrators all relied on their "cultural intuition" which Dolores Delgado Bernal explains "extends one's personal experience to include collective experience and community memory and points to the importance of participants' engaging in the analysis of data" (1998: 563). While Delgado Bernal refers to the research process, it applies to the pedagogical praxis of Cosecha Voices. For if students are acknowledged as holders and creators of knowledge and educators rely on performance and *testimonio* as pedagogy we, both students and professors, are collectively producing and analyzing "data" that would lead to the articulation and sharing of knowledge. At times professors struggled to not fall into the trap of "is this academic enough?" However, as Alvarez reminds us we must create strategic interventions within Spanish programs to empower Latina and Latino students and validate their self-worth (2013: 139). Therefore, we relied on our "cultural intuition" to trust Laviera. Laviera's insistence fueled our participation and allowed us to "let go" and rely on his years of experience and own cultural intuition to reverse the detrimental practices of subtractive schooling.

El primer día de clase
On the first day of class with Laviera, August 2007, students were excited and nervous. They did not know who Laviera was except that he was a famous poet and this, in part, drew many of them. Prof. Edna Ochoa, creative writer and scholar of Mexican and Chicana/o literature, was the instructor of this first course. Prof. Alvarez coordinated the project and attended the first class and all bi-weekly workshops with Laviera in Fall 2007. She would go on to co-teach the course with Laviera in Spring 2009 and Fall 2009. On the first day, Prof. Alvarez provided a borrowed

video camera. Although she barely knew how to operate it, she felt that this was a historic moment that needed to be documented. Silvia Solis, Prof. Ochoa's graduate student, had an interest in film ethnography, attended the class and filmed all of Laviera's classes for two semesters.[4] Everyone was curious, including Camp Director, José Luis, who attended many of Laviera's classes and wanted to see what would happen. All of the professional participants, after all, had witnessed his performance and writing workshop in the Spring of 2007 and were eager to see how the students would respond.

Laviera led the students in two exercises in an effort to have the importance of voice resonate. "La voz" and "owning the word and the mic" would become the central tenants of Laviera's classes. Laviera chanted and students repeated in rhythmic fashion:

Cada palabra es un universo.
Cada sílaba es una expresión.
Cada letra es un sonido sin fin.

With the lessons learned from José Luis's stories, Laviera envisioned a class in which students documented their migrant experiences from the time they prepared to leave their home in the Río Grande Valley to the time they returned. He wanted to document what he called the thirteen stages of the migrant farmworker experience, which Laviera likes to compare to the thirteen Stations of the Cross. The stages include; la noche antes, el viaje, la llegada, el hogar, la cosecha, la escuela, la salud, el día de pago, juegos/fiestas, la familia, la comida, la lucha y el regreso.[5]

Each semester began with an analysis of "la noche antes." Laviera asked students to close their eyes and imagine the night before. What did they see, what did they smell, and what did they hear? He encouraged them to think of the details. Laviera asked them to write a sentence, just one. Students from the Spring 2009 class recounted;

"Al poner las maletas en la troca, mi mamá le echa agua bendita a la troca para que no nos vaya a pasar nada malo en el camino."[6] (Norma)

"La aroma a cloro y Fabuloso por los paseos de la casa me hacían la despedida más real."[7] (Joanna)

"Tengo una ansia que me come, porque sé que el viaje va a ser muy largo, así me lo han dicho, y también porque las personas con los que me voy a ir no los conozco."[8] (Héctor)

Students took turns reading out loud their sentence. Laviera constantly interrupted them shouting "Freeze" and reminded them of the chant "Cada palabra es un universo. Cada síííííílaba es una ex-pre-sión. Cada *le-tra* es un sonido sin fin." Students would read and re-read their sentences aloud. Sometimes, they read to continue practicing the act of reading aloud. Other times, Laviera was so amazed by their words, worlds, and experiences that he simply wanted it repeated so he could relive the moment. The focus at all time was as much on content as it was on the performance of the word(s)/world(s). In order to emphasize the performance of the word, Laviera interjected another pedagogical technique. He chanted repeatedly and the students joined in;

> You gotta say it correctly,
> dance the word out,
> daaaaance it (clap, clap),
> daaaaance it (clap, clap),
> put form (with hands make the shape of curves from top to bottom) to it.

Joanna, when thinking back to that first class, recalls:

> First day of class it was crazy that we got to write right away. He made it easy to come out of the shell and just write down our thoughts. It didn't matter if it didn't make sense as long as we wrote them out, something was to come out of our own writing that would inspire us to keep writing without fear of what could be said or how we said it. I honestly wasn't convinced that he would get me to write down my story, and so I was wrong by the end of the course. I was truly amazed with what I wrote and was able to share with my family and friends (Zuñiga 2013).

Nuyorican in the Valley: "Sir, ¿por qué grita el señor?; Tejiendo Lazos
Once the course was underway, the educators realized that there might be some bridges that needed to be built to blend the Nuyorican with a room full of Chicana/o migrant farmworker college students. Following the very

first session, a student pulled José Luis aside and asked, "sir, ¿por qué grita el señor?" To many migrant farmworkers, who typically hear screaming from insensitive growers or crew leaders, the raising of one's voice is often interpreted as a sign of disrespect. Anna recalls the first day of class and says, "Tato was another type of person, the type that I had never met. I remember thinking, who is this crazy man yelling in class. The room is not that big, and I am pretty sure we could all hear him if he talked normal" (Muñoz 2013). The notion of an insensitive instructor could not be further from the truth of what Laviera brought to the classroom. Still, it was going to take some work to bridge the two worlds. José Luis shared with Laviera an experience where a grower and his crew leader were yelling at him and his brothers demanding that they work faster. He explained how his father had proceeded to tell the boys to get in their pick-up truck. His father then proceeded to tell the crew leader in a very firm voice, that if he, as their father, did not scream at his children demanding that they work harder, he was not going to stand around and allow someone else to do so either. There were definitely some cultural practices that would require some better understanding on the part of both Laviera and the students. The students were from rural Mexican or Mexican American communities, often shy, and more soft-spoken than this Nuyorican from a large metropolis. Both were right and Laviera was working on limited contact hours with the students and was pressing forward with them at a fierce pace, but after the talk, the fierce pace became a little more gentle, a little.

The educators also realized that getting students to open up about their migrant farmworker experiences was going to take a great deal of skill and work. We recalled that on the very first day of class, one student in particular could not get past her first two sentences before breaking down into tears. In fact, she excused herself from the room two times because of her emotional state and was unable to read in front of the group on those two occasions. The guilty culprit was the writing prompt of "la llegada;" what the students found when they arrived at their destination. The same student later confessed that she had never been so disappointed in her life than the time her family arrived in Iowa and seeing their home for the first time, after her family had been promised so much more from a trusted family friend. Irasema in her *testimonio* tells; "Llegando al lugar, el paraíso no fue cómo nosotros esperábamos." Students shared similar stories. Ayme writes of her arrival; "La tarde que llegamos a un campo de trailas del estado de Indiana lágrimas rodaron. Nos habían mentido, los apartamentos que el contratista nos había describido se convertían en trailas viejas, destruídas y en pésimas condiciones. ¿Cómo pudo Don Sebastián decirnos que íbamos a vivir en un lindo lugar, que no habría problema, que todo iba a estar bien cuando él bien sabía que no era verdad."[10]

As the course unfolded and students understood where Laviera was coming from, who he was, and the impact he was having, not only on their writing but on them as persons, their impressions of Laviera began to change. Furthermore, through the work Laviera had done in getting students to refine their personal *testimonios*, students began to see the awesome contributions that they and their families have made on the well being of this country; in more ways than we can count. Norma recalls, "When meeting him I got intimidated, because he would talk really loud, and I would get scared. As the semester went by I got used to his screaming and loudness, I realized that was his personality and his way of being" (Pérez 2013). Belinda, remembers, "...I had been warned about "Tato." They told me he was cool but scary sometimes because he would scream at them. So, my first day, I was scared. When I first saw him, I noticed that he could not see very well and thought that I would just not speak, and he would not notice me and wouldn't scream at me. Ohhh but he did, he was aware of EVERYTHING. I believed he first screamed when he asked us to introduce ourselves. He would say that we had to own our name. To speak Sssss P. E. A. K kkkk." However, Belinda soon lost her fear and now attributes his "loudness" to pedagogy. "The times he screamed was not because he was getting mad at us, it was so we could speak louder and make our voice heard (which was the whole point of the class. Bringing that hidden voice of our migrant experience out)" (López 2013). Anna finds similar meaning in Laviera's yelling; "Now that I think back to our classes, I like to imagine that Tato would yell because he wanted to wake us up from this life of silence and blindness to the injustices our families and ourselves had endured" (Muñoz 2013).

Performance as Pedagogy

We all understood the need for the students to find and own the voice of those experiences as a means of empowerment and liberation, just as Marcos Pizarro, in his book, *Chicanas and Chicanos in School: Racial Profiling, Identity Battles, and Empowerment* (2005) points out. Pizarro argues, "Many Chicana/o students are socialized by the schools into a voicelessness that is often difficult for them to acknowledge. Educational empowerment for Chicanas/os begins with helping these students claim their voice and recognize their own insights on their lives and schooling" (2005: 259). Laviera purposefully utilizes performance in the classroom as a means of resisting educational consumption. The classroom became a counter space where the possibility for empowerment was fomented through the conjoining of the aesthetic and political to account for and give an account of the multiple narratives of being part of a migrant farmworker family. The performances were enhanced with the assistance of Prof. Edna Ochoa. As an actress, playwright, and director, she often incorporated her own dramatic exercises into the class. Performance, one of the students' favorite in-class activities, allows students to literally voice their experiences. bell hooks reminds us, "trained in the philosophical context of Western metaphysical dualism, many of us have accepted the notion that there is a split between the body and the mind. Believing this, individuals enter the classroom to teach as though only the mind is present, and not the body" (1994: 191). Laviera and Prof. Ochoa understood clearly the need to connect both body and mind to create knowledge not only through the writing of *testimonios*, but also through the performance and the witnessing of the dramatic acts by the students and professors. In considering the role of drama in the course, Cosecha Voices student, Palmira, observes the "usage of drama in the class helped us to connect further than the educational purpose. It helped us as students to bond in similar experiences we had lived.... It lets the students feel they are not in a classroom where they are set to sit and just listen to the professor like in a typical classroom" (Cepeda 2013).

To facilitate the performance, Laviera divided the students into families. The students would choose their family names and assume the roles of different members of the immediate and/or extended family as well as other community members. Laviera prompted students with one of the thirteen stages noted previously. At times, Laviera had specific questions for the students to address. On occasions he prompted them with a theme, for example, a conflict at school, a romance at a party, a problem on the road. Students were given very little time, usually between five and ten minutes to create a skit. The students, almost always nervous or giggling, exchanged ideas. Laviera constantly put pressure on them, reminded them of the time, shouted at them, and provided them with ideas. While they interact, Laviera sits nearby and listens intensely. Due to his blindness, he relies almost exclusively on his hearing and tries to feel the movements and savors every word. Often times, Laviera gets annoyed at other students talking and screams "Me voy a agallar." Students were unfamiliar with the word and would mouth "agallar?"[11] Nevertheless, they got the gist. The skits the students spontaneously developed and performed varied between funny, heartbreaking, serious, thoughtful, truly astounding, and at times all of these at once.

In Fall 2009, the student workshop on "la escuela" developed a number of memorable in-class skits. Three, in particular, stand out; each was performed in class during Fall 2009. Students worked in groups of two or more for approximately ten minutes to compose a skit related to "school en *el norte*." The skits are performed without a script. The following are transcriptions of the recording of the students' in-class performances. They reveal that school personnel rarely value the lives of Chicanas and Chicanos and farmworkers. In fact, the skits expose that school culture is downright hostile.

Skit 1, Scene 1

María 1: Me voy a voltear para que no me moleste.[12] (*She turns around*).
Tom: (*He approaches the girl*) What's up María? (*He knocks down her notebooks*).
María: (*She bends down and picks up her books*) Tom, ¿qué quieres? What do you want?
Tom: I see you guys have infested our school this season again. (*Talking to the girl while she gets up*)
María: Why do you say that? Why do you always have to be so mean?
Tom: Because you are always here and come... (*She interrupts him*).
María: Whatever Tom, leave me alone. (*She turns around and ignores him*).
Tom: You know what I'm talking about.
María: Tom, shut up. Seriously, I'm not going to put up with you.
Tom: I'm not going to say a lie, just because I have money to buy food. Now I'm going to buy some pizza. (*He starts to walk away*).
María: Whatever Tom, do whatever you want.
Tom: I'm just saying that...
Scene ends.

Skit 1, Scene 2
María: (*Speaks to herself*) Entre mí, a veces pienso ¿por qué siempre viene y me molesta? Mejor, voy a tomar mi comida.[13]
Lunch Lady: (*The student playing Tom is now the lunch lady*) What would you like to get little girl? (*He crosses his arms*). (*Class starts to laugh*).
María1: What do you have to serve?
Lunch Lady: Umm... Food. (*Class laughs*).
María: Yes, I know its food but what do you have? Do you have any tacos? Something?
Lunch Lady: What are tacos? (*Class laughs*).
María: Forget it. Just forget it. Do you have anything with salsa?
Lunch Lady: Is that music? (*Class Laughs*).
María 1: Umm... Yeah. No, just forget it. I'll just take the ham... (*She points with her finger*).
Lunch Lady: Umm... That's a hot pocket. (*Class laughs*).
María: Ok, I'll take the hot pocket.
Scene ends.

Skit 1, Scene 3[14]
María 1: (*Directing to Laviera*) Me estoy sentando en la mesa para actuar.
María sits down in a chair pretending it's a table. Meanwhile her friend approaches and sits down next to her.
Carlos: (*The student playing Tom and the lunch lady is now Carlos*) ¿Cómo estás, María?
María: Hola Carlos, ¿cómo estás?
Carlos: Bien. Nada más que Tom siempre me anda molestando.
María: A mí también, nunca me deja en paz. Maldito Carlos, I mean Tom.
Carlos: (*He starts moving his hands, making signs*) Antier él y sus primos me pegaron atrás en el jungle gym.
María: Te lo hubieras... (*She takes a deep breath*) ... nada olvídalo. (*Class laughs*).
Carlos: (*He starts moving his hands*) Es que yo estoy muy chiquito, y me falta mucha comida. Me faltan muchas fuerzas.
María: Y a mí ganas no me sobran.

Carlos: ¿Y cuándo llegaste?
María: Hace dos semanas
Carlos: ¿Dos semanas?
María: Sí.
Carlos: A penas tengo una semana, yo...
María: De veras. (*She acts surprised*) ¿Y tienes history con Mr. Ethridge?
Carlos: No. (*He shakes his head*) A mí me tocó con Ms. Carlson.
María: Bueno, este ... ¿tiene hora de receso él?
Carlos: Sí. (*Shaking his head*)
María: Ok, si quieres nos juntamos allí para no estar solos.
Carlos: Ok.
María: Ok.
Scene Ends.

Skit 2[15]
Female Student 2: (*Yelling from across the room as she encounters a friend*) Hey, Rosita! (*Se saludan with joy, as they high five each other. Give a hug and a kiss on the cheek. Then bounce their hips with one another. Both are wearing backpacks*). Espérame. (*The class starts to laugh*) N'ombre, espérate ¿dónde estabas tú?
Rosita: Hijo'su. (*She puts her hands on her face*) ¿Oyiste lo que pasó en el gym?
Female Student 2: ¿En el dónde?
Rosita: (*Makings signs with her hands*) En el gimnasio.
Female Student 2: Ahh, en el gimnasio.
Rosita: Sí.
Female Student 2: N'ombre, yo estaba en primera fila, Rosita. ¿No sabes lo que pasó? (*Class laughs*)
Rosita: (*She gets excited.*) ¿Qué pasó?
Female Student 2: ¿Pos tú dónde andabas?
Rosita: Estaba en el baño.
Female Student 2: Ahh.
Rosita: (*She starts moving her hands and puts them in her face*) Es que en el lonche me comí unos Doritos, pero hijo'su.
Female Student 2: (*Pointing at the other student back and forth*) Fueron los jalapeños que le echaste, yo te vi. Le pusiste bastantes.

Rosita: (*Moving her hands up*) ¿Pero qué pasó? Dime.
Female Student 2: (*She puts her hands on the other students shoulder then starts moving them as she starts talking*) Ah, sí. Bueno, deja y te cuento. N'hombre Rosita, fue una masacre. No sabes, cuerpos tirados, dientes volaron y sangre por todos lados. Fue como en *Al rojo vivo*, estuvo esa pelea. (*Class laughs*)
Rosita: Ayy.
Female Student 2: Sí, fue entre Billy y Kevin y Juan y Nachito.
Rosita: (*Moving her hands*) Ay pobre Nacho, lo vi en la enfermera. ...en la enfermería.
Female Student 2: N'ombre, eran los dos todos sangrientos y todo. ¿Sabes qué pasó? Mira déjame y te cuento. (*Class laughs*) Es que estaban Juan y Nachito, estaban jugando y luego vino Kevin y Billy. (*Moving her hands as if throwing a ball*) Y luego Billy que agarra la pelota y se la avienta a Nachito y le dice, you Mexican go back to your contri (*Class starts laughing*).
Rosita: Nooo...
Female Student 2: Y así le hizo y se agarraron y tú sabes que Juanito son unos de ésos que no se dejan, y agarró a Billy y n'ombre, le dio unas... tú sabes. Fue horrible, Rosita, horrible.
Rosita: (*Asking curiously*) ¿Y quién ganó? ¿Quién ganó?
Female Student 2: Ayy pues no sé. A todos se los llevaron. ¿No viste a los... ¿cómo se llaman? (*Making signs with her hands like guns*) ¿A esos que tienen las guns y todo? (*Student from the class shouts out and says los guardias*).
Female Student 2: Los guardias. Y vinieron los guardias, y se llevaron a todos.
Rosita: Hijo de su...
Female Student 2. ¿Oyes, oyes a dónde vas tú?
Rosita: Ya pa'l bos. (*She points with her hand*).
Female Student 2: ¡El bos! (She *moves her hands and jumps*) Ya vámonos. (*They turn and start running*).
End of scene.

Skit 3
Teacher: Now, I'm going to take roll. (*She grabs her notebook and starts to take roll*) John Smith.

John Smith (*performed by female student*): Here
Teacher: Mary Shart...
Mary: Here.
Teacher: Maa.. (*She takes a long pause*)... Mau... Rea Cor ... tadeo
María: Umm... It's María.
Teacher: Ohh... ok. What kind of name is that? (*Class sighs oooooh*).
María: What do you mean?
Teacher: It's because it sounds too Mexican.
María: It's Mexican, actually.
Teacher: Oh, ok. Now that I'm done taking role, I'm going to assign seats. (*She looks at the list*) You, Maurea...
María: (*She interrupts*) María, por favor.
Teacher: Can you go sit (*she looks at the room*) like in the last row, (*Pointing to the seat*) in the corner. (*Class laughs*).
María: But, why?
Teacher: I don't know, it's because you're Mexican. You Mexicans don't belong here. (*Class sighs ooooooh*).
María 4: You're being racist. You know that?
End of scene.

Skit 3, Scene 2
Karen starts giving instructions and tells Laviera, ok we're in the cafeteria. While I'm in line.
Scene starts.
María: Umm, ay se mira bien fea esa comida. No sé, no quiero de eso. Hasta se mira que hay una mosca, ¿verdad?[16]
Karen: Sí, ay no sé ¿qué es eso?[17]
White Female Student (*played by a Chicana*): (*Pretending to talk with a friend while sitting down in lunch*) Look at her. (*She points with her finger*) What's her name? Is it something like María or something like that? She is always talking in Spanish. I don't understand. She just doesn't get it, that we are not in Panama, we are in this U.S. María: (*Turns her head and she is talking to her friend while covering her mouth*) Oyes, ¿cómo que Miss White nos estaba mirando muy feo?[18]
Friend: No sé.[19]
María: Sí, ya sé. No sé, se me hace como que nos quiere decir algo.[20]
White Female Student: Someone has to say something. We just can't

let people run around talking their language when they know they're in America. (*She stands up from her seat and starts walking towards María and her friend*) Excuse me, umm. What's your name?
Karen: Karen
Anglo Female Student: Karen?
Karen: Yes.
Anglo Female Student: Ok, well I was looking and I noticed that you were talking in Panamanian or I don't know, whatever it is.
María: (*She interrupts*) Spanish.
White Female Student: Or wherever you are from. I don't know if you noticed, but we're in America. In America, we all speak English. So, I just want to let you know that. So, next time you can just practice it a little.
María: (*Talking to Laviera*) Oh this is in my head, en mi pensamiento. (*She starts thinking to her self*) Cómo le quisiera decir algo pero después con qué cara le digo a mi mamá que me expulsaron.[21]

The performance of the experiences proved to be of great importance in the classroom. For the migrant farmworker performance is perhaps even more profound as the same bodies subjected to the physical wear and tear of farmwork now become the very sites for healing and empowerment. Essentially, we all engaged in performing or enacting what Cherrie Moraga calls "theory in the flesh." Moraga explains that "a theory in the flesh means one where the physical realities of our lives-our skin color, the land or concrete we grew up on, our sexual longings-all fuse to create a politic born out of necessity. Here, we attempt to bridge the contradictions in our experience" (1981: 23). Laviera created a space where the flesh was enacted to relive and reveal their experiences, bridge the contradictions, convert them into letters, syllables, sounds, words and voice.

Therefore, the utilization of performance in the classroom can be viewed as an oppositional pedagogical praxis that creates a space that leads students to desarrollar their own voice, their own *testimonios*. After all, the performances were the in-class activity that would lead to students writing their *testimonios* at home. It may seem too simple; dramatic interpretation of lived experiences. However, joining together performance and performativity in the classroom creates a decolonizing space for these students to come to terms with their lived experiences, which they embodied. As Annabel states, "through drama he taught me how to heal wounds" (Salamaca 2013).

Coming to terms with their experiences and healing potentially empowers them to the degree that it could possibly emancipate them from future consumption. As they see themselves reflected in their own performances or the performances of their peers, students begin to recognize how their own multiple performances throughout the years have allowed them to resist consumption. They come to realize their own resiliency and agency as subaltern subjects through past, present, and future performances. Their performances in our classroom are attempts to understand past performances and shed the need for future performance. Anna reveals:

> I loved the drama part of class. That gave me the confidence to speak, yell, and act about topics that I had never considered important. In my opinion, the use of drama let us see exactly what had been silenced for so many years. I was seeing how my experiences were similar to those of others that had migrated to other parts of the country. I remember watching the acts and thinking about how similar injustices had happened to my aunt, mom, and even to myself. . . . As we all know, we do not see it until we see it right in front of us and that is exactly what drama did to all of us. (Muñoz 2013)

Drama also helped to create a feeling of community in the course. Erika observes:

> Drama was the key to the class; it was what made it different from the rest. It helped me become engaged in class and be closer to my classmates. We were all a big family! I felt that role-playing gave us a better understanding that even though we all migrated to different states and live in different circumstances, we all had a lot of things in common. When preparing the sketches it wasn't hard to know what to do because we all were the same and presenting in class at first I was nervous, but the more I did it the more I felt comfortable. It showed us a lot of things that I learned about my classmates and even my own experience as a migrant! (Salamaca 2013)

Erika and Anna see drama as key to (re)witnessing their own experiences and those of others in their family and creating a sense of *familia*. Roberto confirms this and states, "the use of drama also helped fortify the friendships within the course. As we were separated into families, we had to take on certain positions within these families. Not only would these interactions take place within the class, but they would also be used in a sense of familiarity to one's peers outside the classroom. No longer would one be a single student, but knew that each had peers to rely on" (Reyna 2013). Therefore, drama was important because it revealed those experiences embodied in the flesh of one student, but also because watching those performances revealed collective experiences that proved critical to writing the *testimonios* and creating digital *testimonios*.

Testimonio and Voice

The use of *testimonio* was intentional. We did not want to facilitate a process that would lead students to write simply autobiographical pieces. The *testimonio*, unike the autobiography, "entails a first person oral written account, drawing on experiential, self-conscious, narrative practice to articulate an urgent voicing of something to which bears witness (Blackmer Reyes and Curry Rodríguez 2012: 525). Moreover, as Delgado Bernal, Burciaga and Flores Carmona observe, central to a pedagogy of *testimonio* is the goal of intervention (2012: 368). Cosecha Voices, as noted earlier, was developed as an intervention to create a space in which students could find their own voice to possibly lead them to self-empowerment and greater self-determination. Laviera envisioned an intervention that like the *testimonio* "disrupts silence, invites connection, and entices collectivity (Delgado Bernal, Burciaga and Flores Carmona 2012: 370). Moreover, the *testimonio*, while personal, is "not meant to be hidden, made intimate, nor kept secret" (Blackmer Reyes and Curry Rodríguez 2012: 525). For these reasons, students routinely were asked to read their *testimonios* aloud in class and were required to present them in public.

At the end of the semester, Laviera insisted on a formal presentation of the *testimonios* organized for the community and parents. Invitations were created and given to students to invite their parents and family members. The public presentation of their written and digital *testimonios*, especially at the end of the semester, proved powerful and moving. They were particularly important because they publicly validated the experiences and languages of the students and their families in an academic space, something often not possible. Parents, at times, came to the university to receive instructions on financial aid or how to assist their children so they could succeed academically. However, never before had these parents witnessed the public acknowledgement of the importance of their work. It should also be noted that almost all students acknowledged their parents in their written *testimonios*. Often times, when those acknowledgements were read aloud, students broke down into tears. Palmira ends her *testimonio* declaring "Estoy muy agradecida con Dios por haberme dado estos padres maravillosos. Siendo migrante me ha enseñado a valorar todo lo que tengo y lo que soy ahora" (Cepeda nd). Palmira's family did not attend the public presentation. However, many months later and, after having presented her *testimonio* at several venues, she texted Alvarez and Solis that she read her *testimonio* to her mom and both cried.

After the end of the class, students have gone on to present their *tesimonios* all over the country. In fact, they formed the "Cosecha Voices Student Organization" in Fall 2008, in order to travel and participate in conferences and invited readings. As of 2013, the students have presented at over ten conferences and been invited speakers at over ten universities and cultural centers. These include the Nuyorican Poet's Café, Taller Boricua, University of California-Irvine, Michigan State University, and Kalamazoo College, to name a few. The first, and one of the most memorable presentations, was when Cosecha Voices presented the keynote at the National C.A.M.P. conference in San Juan, Puerto Rico, in October 2008. This moment was special since it was a homecoming of sorts for Laviera. *El Nuevo Día* published a two-page spread featuring Laviera "Con su *Mixturao* en la Isla." The keynote proved memorable and the students' *testimonios* brought some three hundred plus audience members to their feet with a standing ovation. The response solidified for the students the need to continue sharing their *testimonios*. They collaborated with Prof. Stephanie Alvarez and Orquidea Morales to publish some of their *testimonios* online through the Cosecha Voices Website and YouTube channel, with the ultimate goal to publish a book of their *testimonios*. The students recognized the need to share their *testimonios* and for other migrants to engage in the writing of their *testimonios*. The students would get the opportunity to do both by participating in workshops for migrant middle school students.

Middle Schools

José Luis revealed to Laviera that some of the most vulnerable of migrant farmworker children are those enrolled in middle school. After all, at age twelve children can legally work in the fields. However, often the children are much younger and in some rare cases, children can be as young as ten and still legally work in the fields. Laviera then decided to reach out to the middle schools. In Spring 2009, Cosecha Voices, in collaboration with Region One Educational Service Center and UTPA, held its first middle school writing workshop as part of FESTIBA: Festival of International Books and Art. José Luis Martínez was now a Migrant College Access Specialist with Region One, serving the 24,000 migrant farmworker students of the Río Grande Valley. He organized the event with Prof. Alvarez and worked with various school districts to bring over one hundred middle school migrant students to campus. Cosecha Voices students served as mentors to the middle school migrant students during the workshop. On four different occasions between 2009 and 2012, Cosecha Voices has brought approximately 400 total migrant middle school students from over 20 different schools to UTPA to participate in a day-long writing workshop lead by Laviera, facilitated by Cosecha Voices students, and organized by Stephanie Alvarez and José Luis Martínez. They have also held workshops on three occasions at school sites, impacting an additional 200 students.

During the campus workshop, the middle school migrant students take a Cosecha Voices student led campus tour and a Cosecha Voices college class. The first question asked is how many have ever written about being a migrant? The answer has always been zero. The middle school students listen to Laviera recite poetry and guide them through the story-telling process based on the same themes discussed in the college class. The workshops usually address "la noche antes de la partida,"[22] the "trip hacia el norte,"[23] and an experience in schools up north. The students are told that they may speak or write in any languages they wish: Spanglish/Tex-Mex, Spanish, English. They are encouraged to write using the vocabulary of their lived experiences. The middle school students work with Cosecha Voices students, teacher(s) or counselor(s) from their school, seated at tables in groups of eight to ten. The young students are often unsure of what to do, what to write until the Cosecha Voices students start sharing with them their stories. Soon, the fear is lost, students are talking, sharing, and writing until Laviera asks for students from each table to take the microphone and share a line from their story. A couple of students will come forward and with prodding more come forward. By the end of the six-hour workshop, the students are flocking to the microphone. Cosecha Voices students serve as real life examples that it is possible for migrants to go to college. In the 2011 workshop evaluations, all of the teachers and counselors responded positively, and without prompting noted the importance of telling and sharing the middle school students' stories. The teachers and counselors noted the value of middle school migrant students interacting with college migrant students.

The middle school students were elated, as were their teachers and counselors. In the 2009 workshop, of the 61 anonymous student evaluations, only two displayed dissatisfaction with the program: "I didn't like it because I don't like to write" and "I didn't like it." The others, however, reveal their contentment. One student wrote in the evaluation "I feel happy I expressed my migrant experience. I never told anyone about that." Another student states, "I think its cool, nobody ever asks me those questions." More comments include; "I felt happy because I finally, I get out my shyness out and for the first time I talk about my life." Other students explain what it felt like to share their experiences and listen to the experiences of others just like them, migrants. "I felt so I don't know like I could tell everyone what I do and not be afraid," "I felt realization of this whole world hit me. Though it was interesting to tell about myself, I got to experience what everyone else has gone through." In the end, the process of emancipation through the reclaiming of their voice had begun for many and was expressed through their *orgullo*;[24] "I felt so proud and good." "I feel that we let out how we feel about people who treat us like we're nothing." "Happy because I am proud to be a migrant." The process reveals what many believe, that affirming a student's identity, culture, language, and experiences will give them the confidence to succeed. Two students express this new found confidence in their evaluations and exclaim, "I didn't think I could write like I did before, now I think writing is cool," "I didn't believe I could write before either or make a poem; but I'm glad these people inspired us to write." The notion of voice and being heard was not lost amongst these children. As two students observed "I felt good telling people about when I moved. It's good to know that my voice is being heard." "It felt good because writing about them took a huge load off my back and now more people will know of the stories."

Despite the consistent reflection by the students about how the workshop made them feel good, the writing process was not easy and students often had to confront many disagreeable or upsetting experiences. Nevertheless, it was necessary to help students eventually come to terms with their experiences and celebrate them. "While writing about my migrant experience I felt really bad remembering all the things I went through, but then I remember it was worth it." One student interviewed by the local paper summed it all up and told the reporter, "It's like they actually care about us" (Berghom 2009: 8B). The student's response, which reveals surprise at the "caring," reveals that in fact "rather than centering students' learning around a moral ethic of caring that nurtures and values relationships, schools pursue a narrow instrumentalist logic" (Valenzuela 1999: 22). The middle school students' responses, therefore, reveal what is possible when the students' lives are centered in the educational environment and an ethic of caring fuels the pedagogy. For these students, Cosecha Voices does what has rarely been done in an educational setting for migrants—valuing their lived experiences—and the end result for one student is "I felt a feeling that I've never felt before. The feeling of happiness."

Laviera's Commitment.
In conclusion, it is important to affirm Laviera's indispensible role in Cosecha Voices. If it were not for Laviera, there would be no Cosecha Voices. At the same time, it is vital that readers understand Laviera's commitment to Cosecha Voices. Nothing reveals his commitment more than what he went through to be with us. A typical visit to the Valley from the time he left his home in New York to his arrival at the McAllen International Airport in McAllen, Texas, and back reveals his *compromiso*.[25] Laviera awakened in the very early hours of dawn to get to the airport (often times just after receiving dialysis), proceed to the ticket counter, check his luggage, go through security, board the plane, work through a layover in Houston or Dallas, and get back on a second plane. He did all of this on his own, unaccompanied by any assistant, with only the assistance of kind personnel at the various airports and airplanes.

He stayed at the Best Western in Edinburg alone. Some may underestimate the *valor*[26] it takes for him to find his way to the restroom, dress himself, and find his way through the hotel room to answer the door using only his ears and hands to guide him to the door. He would ask us to knock and knock until he reached the door. He became great friends with one of the cleaning ladies at the hotel, Lupita, who would bring him coffee and breakfast in the morning and assist him in many other ways. José Luis was the one who most often helped Laviera in the evenings and would place towels all along the bathroom floor to help guide him to the shower and he always asked to put his toiletries in the sink so he could find them and avoid knocking them on to the floor. As if this *sacrificio* was not enough, Laviera usually had to undergo at least one dialysis treatment during each of his visits to the Valley; and on occasion he would deliver a workshop or board the plane only hours after the procedure. He would take a taxi to dialysis in Edinburg because he did not want anyone waking up at 4:00 a.m. to take him to the medical center. However, someone from Cosecha Voices, usually José Luis or Stephanie, always picked him up after dialysis. It was often those moments of picking Laviera up from dialysis and finding him in the large room filled with dozens and dozens of people having their blood cleaned, that cemented for us a deep understanding of his incredible commitment. There are probably very few people who understand the size of Laviera's sacrifice for Cosecha Voices. Laviera never made a big deal of his sacrifices. It was part of his every day life. Still, all of us who have benefited from all of his sacrifices would be remiss if we did not honor them.

We recall December 2009. Laviera came to campus to hold what would be his last Cosecha Voices class and perform and host what would be the second of three "Edinburgo Poet's Café" performances. After the first semester of the Cosecha Voices class, José Luis left the CAMP program, and CAMP never funded the class again. However, with the help of Prof. Emmy Pérez and the support of her Chair, Prof. Pamela Anderson Mejías, the English MFA program brought Laviera as a Visiting Poet in Residence for two semesters, Spring 2009 and Fall 2009. He worked with the MFA students, co-taught with Pérez and founded with her the Edinburgo Poet's Café. He also taught Cosecha Voices for free during those two semesters. It should be noted that Laviera was paid very little for all of his work. That evening in December 2009, something seemed wrong. Laviera was not himself. Nevertheless, he performed and the Edinburgo Poet's Café, which included readings by Cosecha Voices and English MFA students, went off without a hitch. Soon, we would learn that the incident that led to him needing emergency brain surgery in December 2009 and resulted in his subsequent homelessness occurred either just prior to his departure to the Valley or during that trip. Even after this tragic episode, Laviera healed and we all wished to continue the class, but no one would fund it. Students desperately tried to raise money so the class may be offered again to other migrant students through the sale of Hot Cheetos and cheese, workshops, and even car shows. The class never resumed. Laviera, however, did return to do several middle school workshops. In March 2013, Laviera was to revisit the Valley and conduct another middle school workshop with the Cosecha Voices students in Robstown, Texas, home of the Cotton Pickers. Unfortunately, Laviera was not able to join us as he fell ill and was confined to the hospital once again, this time for over nine months, until his death on November 1, 2013. Despite his hospitalization and death, his spirit lives on as students and professors continue to honor his memory and work through their own discussions, pedagogical practices, and daily acts.

In the End: Impact
This article began with a statement Laviera made in an interview (Sandoval 2009) for a news story. He stated, "Word. Syllable. Letter. Universe. Expression. Sound. That is all there is. That is all a word contains. To control them, and to own them and to cherish them." These were Laviera's objectives for Cosecha Voices. The fulfillment of those objectives were to come about through the students' exploration of their own migrant farmworker experiences by writing their *testimonios*, creating digital *testimonios*, the performance of those *testimonios*, and the archiving of them online (www.utpa.edu/cosechavoices). The students' *testimonios* emerged through critical reflection of one's own experiences and of others in the class by means of performance in the classroom. The word would be the path to *conciencia*, with the hope that it would lead to the affirmation and celebration of experiences once silenced, and that such affirmation would allow for self-empowerment. Paulo Freire wrote of such a process. In fact, Freire observed that, "There is no true word that is not at the same time praxis. Thus, to speak a true word is to transform the world" (1993: 87).

Laviera led students on a journey to speak a true word. Those true words and their articulation were as Paulo Freire writes "...a serious and profound effort at *conscientização*—by means of which the people, through a true praxis, leave behind the status of *objects* to assume the status of historical *Subjects*—is necessary" (1993: 160). Critical to this process is that "...by making it possible for people to enter the historical process as responsible Subjects, *conscientização* enrolls them in the search for self-affirmation..." (1993: 36).

Students in an anonymous survey taken four to eighteen months after enrolling in the class reveal their transformation into historical "Subjects" and self-affirmation. One student said, "Cosecha Voices brought back the shine in me that the careless people dulled away after not believing in me." Another stated "Cosecha Voices has motivated me to stand up for what I believe in and for others as well." A third student reflected, "The best part of Cosecha Voices is being able to relate my story to others and being able to talk about my migrant life without any shame about it."

Some four to six years later, when asked about the impact of the class and Laviera specifically, the answers reveal the long-term impact. Anna believes that "his classes gave me the confidence to speak up in future courses" (Muñoz 2013). For Joanna the "greatest impact was to believe in myself and my writing struggles we had to overcome or what language I would write my words in, because no matter how small the sentence or how I wrote it down it could have an impact with the reader" (Zuñiga 2013). Annabel says, "He inspired me to be myself and to feel proud of my farm-working back ground. Something I had no opinion, talking about farm work was only spoken with family or other students who knew what a migrant was and what they did. Tato and Cosecha Voices politicized me and made me aware of my own situation. I was not supposed to be there... Tato, Stephanie, my parents (and their job/lifestyle) and Cosecha Voices were one of those factors that gave me the strength to not give up and graduate from college. They gave me a sense of purpose and belonging in a place where I thought and felt I did not belong." Moreover, for her "Cosecha Voices and Tato validated our lived experiences and helped us develop our confidence, self-esteem and leadership" (Salamaca 2013). Roberto clearly articulates his own *conciencia* and self-affirmation. Roberto reveals, "My perspective changed by knowing the importance that it is to know where one comes from, where in the past I only wanted to forget and assimilate. The pride that came with this new way of thinking has brought me to where I stand today" (Reyna 2013).

As a freshman Juan enrolled in the class, and in an interview with a UTPA reporter stated "I feel more confident about myself now that I'm in this class. It has helped me move on and learn to overcome anything" (Sandoval 2009). However, it is perhaps Belinda's end of the class *testimonio* that best encapsulates the connection between *palabra, conciencia* and *voz* that Laviera tried to develop through his participation in Cosecha Voices:

> Quisiera que con mi voz de mi experiencia, los demás se dieran cuenta del esfuerzo que uno tiene que hacer para poder sobrevivir. Mi lucha ha sido informar e intentar de enseñar lo duro que la vida puede ser cuando uno es migrante, enseñar que un migrante no tiene la vida tan fácil como aquel que ni siquiera sabe lo que es un azadón o cómo se trabaja en la cosecha. Con mi voz quiero hacer aquéllos que no entienden, que el migrante vale mucho, y no sólo vale por el ser humano que es sino también por lo que hace. El migrante trae comida a la mesa de millones de personas en el mundo y aún así es discriminado que por ser cochino o mexicano. La lucha no es sólo de uno, es de muchos de nosotros que hemos trabajado en la cosecha intentando ganarse la vida con el sudor de su frente. Juntos podemos unir nuestras voces y hacer que la gente nos mire de otro modo, que nos aprecien y nos valoren (López 2009).[27]

Belinda's words are reminicent of the poet's own philosophy. A philosophy reflected in his own poetry. In his poem "conciencia" Tato's pedagogical theory and practice emerge:

> ...comiendo el mango agrio de ilusiones
> la cáscara podrida carcajada del progreso
> hasta aquí llegan las llagas de la búsqueda
> a ver si cerramos los ojos
> tan siquiera un momento
> a ver si
>   un nosotros
>   un nosotros verdadero
>   un nosotros poderoso
>   un nosotros lleno
>   un nosotros amoroso
> a ver si
> un nosotros humano
> alzamos las voces

constantemente
al ritmo de insistencia
resistencia
un nosotros crítico
que abre la boca
que no se estanca
un nosotros que declara
somos el mar de nuestro destino
somos la lengua de nuestras acciones
no tememos al miedo
sabemos que el sin hablar nos oprime
que caiga lo que caiga como caiga
cuando caiga que caiga donde caiga
el silencio nos mata aquí
inundémonos con la mirada fijada
con la pelea externa
pónganse ciegos
no oigan la soledad
háganse soldados de su destino
sin parar
...
la lengua es
la ametralladora
de la libertad
háganlo para el futuro
de nuestros hijos
oigan no se achanten
ganaremos. (1988: 50–1)

Laviera's "conciencia," like his pedagogical practices, reveals the need to fill in the gaps of silence through collective action and voice. Key to that collectivity, though, is "la lengua." For Laviera, it is the *lengua* that is the key to liberation. Lengua that flesh from which syllables, letters, universes, expressions, and sounds converge to form *la palabra*. The *palabra* emerges from *concienia* and then is voiced. At UTPA those palabras resulted in a harvest of voices, voices of the harvest: Cosecha Voices.

NOTES

[1] Laviera wrote the play *La media* about a Mexican woman who lived in the United States, but struggled to define her identity as a Chicana. Edna Ochoa performed the play twice in New York in Spring 2008 and Summer 2011. A reading of the play also took place in Spring 2008 in Edinburg, Texas.

[2] Gabino Martínez and Laviera would later pass away in the same week; October 28, 2013 and November 1, 2013.

[3] "Educators" refers to José Luis Martínez, Laviera, Prof. Alvarez and Prof. Ochoa.

[4] Silvia Solis (2009) would go on to write her master's thesis on Cosecha Voices to fulfill the requirements for a Master's of Art in Interdisciplinary Studies.

[5] The night before, the trip, the arrival, the home, the harvest, school, health, pay day, games/parties, family, food, the struggle, the return.

[6] As the suitcases were put in the pick-up truck, my mom puts holy water on the truck so that nothing bad will happen to us along the road.

[7] The aroma of Clorox and Fabuloso throughout the halls of the home made the goodbye more real.

[8] I have anxiety that eats away at me, because I know that the trip will be very long, that's what they have told me, and because I do not know the people with whom I will go with.

[9] Arriving at the place, paradise was not as we had expected.

[10] The afternoon that we arrived at the trailer camp in the state of Indiana, tears rolled. They had lied to us, the apartments that the contractor described to us became old trailers, destroyed and in awful condition. How could Don Sebastián tell us we'd live in a beautiful place, that there would be no problems, that everything would be fine when he knew very well that it was not true.

[11] Another word for *enojar* or to get angry.

[12] I'm going to turn around so he doesn't bother me.

[13] To myself, at times I think why does he always come and bother me? It's better that I take my food.

[14] Scene 3 Translation

María 1: (*Directing to Laviera*) I am sitting down at the table to start acting.

María sits down in a chair pretending it's a table. Meanwhile her friend approaches and sits down next to her.

Carlos: How are you María?

María: Hi Carlos, how are you?

Carlos: Good. It's just that Tom is always bothering me.

María: Me too, he never leaves me alone. Damn Carlos. I mean Tom.

Carlos: (*He starts moving his hands, making signs.*) The day before yesterday he and his cousins hit me behind the jungle gym

María: You should have .... (*She takes a deep breath*) ... nothing, never mind.

Carlos: (*He starts moving his hands.*) It's just that I am too small, I need to eat more. I am not strong.

María: And for me, the desire is overwhelming.

Carlos: And when did you arrive?

María: It's been two weeks.

Carlos: Two weeks?

María: Yes.

Carlos: I barley have been here a week, I...

María: Really? Do you have history with Mr. Ethridge?

Carlos: No. (*He shakes his head.*) I got Ms. Carlson.

María: Well, um ... do you have recess with her?

Carlos: Yes. (*Shaking his head.*)

María: Ok, if you want we can meet there so that we are not alone.

Carlos: Ok.

María: Ok.

Scene Ends.

Skit 2

Female Student 2: (*Yelling from across the room as she encounters a friend*) Hey, Rosita! (*The greet each other with joy, as they high five each other. Give a hug and a kiss on the cheek. Then bounce their hips with one another. Both are wearing backpacks*). Wait for me! (*The class starts to laugh.*) Man, wait, where were you?

Rosita: Oh my.... (*She puts her hands on her face*). Did you hear what happened in the gym?

Female Student 2: Where?

Rosita: (*Makings signs with her hands*) In the gymnasium.

Female Student 2: Ohh, in the gymnasium.

Rosita: Yes.

Female Student 2: Man, I was in the front row, Rosita. You don't know what happened. (*Class laughs*).

Rosita: (*She gets excited.*) What happened?

Female Student 2: Well, where were you?

Rosita: I was in the bathroom.

Female Student 2: Ohh.

Rosita: (*She starts moving her hands and puts them in her face*) It's just that at lunch I ate some Doritos, but man!

Female Student 2: (*Pointing at the other student back and forth*) It was the jalapeños that you put on them, I saw you. You put a lot.

Rosita: (*Moving her hands up*) But, what happened? Tell me.

Female Student 2: (*She puts her hands on the other students shoulder then starts moving them as she starts talking*) Oh, yeah. Well, let me tell you. Man, Rosita, it was a massacre. You have no idea, bodies thrown, teeth flew and blood all over the place. That fight was like *Al Rojo Vivo* [Spanish-language TV news show] on fire. (*Class laughs*).

Rosita: Oooh.

Female Student 2: Yes, it was between Billy and Kevin and Juan and Nachito.

Rosita: (*Moving her hands*) Oh poor Nacho, I saw him at the nurse ... in the nurse's office.

Female Student 2: Man, they both were bloody and all. You know what happened? Look, let me tell you. (*Class laughs*) It's that Juan and Nachito were, were playing and then came Kevin and Billy. (*Moving her hands as if throwing a ball*) And later, Billy grabs the ball and throws it at Nachito and tells him, you Mexican go back to your country. (*Class starts laughing*).

Rosita: Nooo...

Female Student 2: And that's how he did it and they started fighting and you know that Juanito is one of those that doesn't back down and he grabbed Billy and man, he gave him some ... you know. It was horrible, Rosita, horrible.

Rosita: (*Asking curiously*) And who won? Who won?

Female Student 2: Well, I don't know. They took all of them. You didn't see the ... what do you call them? (*Making signs with her hands like guns*) Those that have guns and all. (*Student from the class shouts out and says los security guards*).

Female Student 2: The security guards. And the security guards arrived and took everyone.

Rosita: Son of a ...

Female Student 2. Hey, hey where are you going?

Rosita: To the bus, already. (*She points with her hand*).

Female Student 2: The bus! (*She moves her hands and jumps*) Let's go already. (*They turn and start running*).

End of scene.

[16] María: Uhh, oh that food looks really bad. I don't know, I don't want any of that. It even looks like there is a fly, right?

[17] Karen: Yes, oh I don't know, what is that?

[18] Hey, it's like Miss White was giving us a nasty look, right?

[19] Friend: I don't know.

[20] María: Yes, I already know. I don't know, it's like she wants to tell us something.

[21] Oh this is in my head, in my thoughts. (*She starts thinking to her self*) How I would like to say something but, then how can I look at my mother and tell her that they expelled me?

[22] The night before the departure.

[23] The trip up north.

[24] Pride.

[25] Commitment.

[26] Courage.

[27] I wish that with my voice of experience, others would realize the effort that one must make in order to survive. My struggle has been to inform and try to teach how difficult life can be when you are a migrant, show that a migrant does not have it as easy as those who don't even know what a hoe is or what it is to work in the fields. With my voice, I want those who don't understand, that a migrant is worth a lot, and she/he is not worth something just because he is human but also because of what he does. A migrant brings food to the table of millions of people in the world y even so she/he is discriminated for being dirty or Mexican. The struggle is not just of one person, it is of many of us that have worked in the fields trying to earn a living with the sweat of our brow. Together we can unite our voices and make it so that people see us differently, so they appreciate and value us.

— IV —
AFRO-LATINIDADES

Speaking Black Latino/a/ness: Race, Performance, and Poetry in Tato Laviera, Willie Perdomo, and Josefina Báez

LAWRENCE LA FOUNTAIN-STOKES

New York-based, U.S. Latino/a spoken-word/performance poets of Afro-Hispanic Caribbean descent such as Tato Laviera, Willie Perdomo, and Josefina Báez offer, in their works, a complex view of the specificities of their racial and ethnic identities in a broader (urban, transnational) social context. Laviera, a key member of the 1970s Nuyorican poets' movement, reconceptualizes the meaning of Africa (as a geographic referent) and black diasporic Caribbean culture in his poetry. Willie Perdomo, a younger poet who takes up the Nuyorican aesthetic project through the lens of contemporary African-American hip-hop culture, also makes links to the high Black American canon (especially to Langston Hughes [2002]). In her performances, Josefina Báez filters Dominican culture through American soul and jazz (Billie Holiday and the Isley Brothers) as well as through classical Hindu dance and philosophy, and creates Dominican York poetry closely linked to earlier Nuyorican poetics. These three performance poets are highly visible and well recognized exponents of poetic traditions centered on orality but restructured according to their insertion in other discursive cultural models, such as poetry of resistance, youth culture, and postmodern dance/performance art. All three highlight a New York City experience in rich transnational, multiethnic, and multiracial dimensions. Their creative work is extremely revealing of the complexities of race, gender, and ethnicity within contemporary American culture.

Preludio: Wherein the Poetic Truth? The Streets in Afro-Latino Rhythms
The genealogy of spoken word in the United States is diverse, with twists and turns that go through native and African American storytelling, religious preaching, political oratory, expressive musical culture, the Harlem Renaissance, and the poetry of the (predominantly white) Beat

generation poets, who hearken back to powerful public voices such as that of Walt Whitman infused with jazz. These generative moments coexist and become intermingled with Puerto Rican, Cuban, and Dominican traditions brought by urban, seaside, and countryside peasant immigrants to the United States since the late nineteenth century. In the case of the Puerto Rican Diaspora, these include poetic forms such as the *décima*, call-and-response Afro-Diasporic musical forms such as the *bomba* and *plena* (or spoken newspaper), and other practices that install community sentiment: "el jibarito" Rafael Hernández's nostalgia in "Lamento borincano" or Canario's *plenas*, on the one hand (see Glasser 1995); Julia de Burgos's tortured lyrical and patriotic feminist affirmations, on the other; and Luis Palés Matos and Fortunato Vizcarrondo's Afro-Puerto Rican verses caught somewhere in between. In the case of the Dominican Republic, we can think of *merengue, bachata, amargue*, the cadences of the festival tradition of *Gagá*, a creolized version of the Haitian *Rara*, and of the poetry of Pedro Mir and Manuel del Cabral, among other cultural forms brought by mass migration since 1965. In the Cuban one, we can think of music such as rumba, mambo, and *son* and the poetic tradition of Nicolás Guillén, of a migration that originates in the nineteenth century but intensifies after 1959. These disparate strands come together in New York City in the 1970s among the predominantly Puerto Rican working class community and result in what is now known as Nuyorican poetry, a movement developed and institutionalized by individuals such as Miguel Piñero and Miguel Algarín at spaces such as the Nuyorican Poets Café in Loisaida (the Lower East Side of Manhattan), and that continues to this day (see Noel 2008, 2011).

Unfortunately, the Puerto Rican (and more broadly, insular Hispanic Caribbean) contribution to the development of spoken word in the United States is not fully acknowledged in some recountings of its history. An example: Marc Smith and Mark Eleveld's anthology, *The Spoken Word Revolution* (2003), a major text, makes no explicit mention of any of the key Nuyorican poets or of the Nuyorican production of the 1970s; the Nuyorican Poets Cafe is only addressed by Bob Holman, after his intervention and transformation in the late 1980s, giving the impression that there was no real Café before he arrived. (In fact, Holman's association with the Café was quite controversial, as Algarín has discussed in more recent interviews and Ed Morales notes in *Living in Spanglish*.) The foundational role of the

Nuyorican is thus made invisible, its history silenced: the Puerto Rican specificity of spoken word thrown back in the closet. But as Fortunato Vizcarrondo would say, "¿Y tu agüela, a'onde ejtá?" Why are Puerto Rican or Nuyorican/Hispanic Caribbean poetic antecedents hidden in the kitchen? In fact, they demand to be brought out and shown the light, to be spoken *Aloud*, as in the 1994 anthology of the same name edited by Miguel Algarín and Holman himself, a collection of *"Voices from the Nuyorican Poets Café,"* including an entire section of "Founding Poems," by the likes of Pedro Pietri, Sandra María Esteves, Tato Laviera, and Jorge Brandon.[1]

What are these foundations? Algarín and Piñero's *Nuyorican Poetry: An Anthology of Puerto Rican Words and Feelings*, published in 1975, just one year after the establishment of the Nuyorican Poets Cafe in Loisaida, gives us some clues. Algarín's introduction to this volume, entitled "Nuyorican Language," serves as a manifesto and description; in fact, Algarín can be called the "high theoretician" of the Nuyorican beat. I wish to highlight three key aspects of his elucidation: the streets as compositional theme and location of performance; the poet as troubadour or oral bard; and the centrality of Afro-Diasporic music and culture. These elements coalesce into what I would call "the bomba poetics of the Afro-Nuyorican trovador,"[2] one whose craft is precisely centered around orality. Algarín proclaims:

> The poet blazes a path of fire for the self. He juggles with words . . . He carries the tension of the streets in his mind and he knows how to execute his mind in action . . . The poet juggles with every street corner east of First Avenue and south of Fourteenth Street ending at the Brooklyn Bridge . . . poetry is on the street burning it up with its vision of the times to be . . .

> The poet sees his vision as a troubadour. He tells the tale of the streets to the streets. The people listen. They cry, they laugh, they dance as the troubadour opens up and tunes his voice and moves his pitch and rhythm to the high tension of bomba truth . . . The voice of the street poet must amplify itself. The poet pierces the crowd with cataracts of clear, clean, precise, concrete words about the liquid, shifting Latino reality around him.

Ismael Rivera is "el sonero major" (sic) ... The troubadour among troubadours is the man who sings the live sweat pulse of a people ... Ismael is Nuyorican rhythmic communication. Stripped, Ismael is the clean, unspoiled voice of Puerto Ricans both in New York City and the island of Puerto Rico. (1975: 10–1)

These passages are rich in geographic specificity, marking a shared and continuous cartography of community: from Loisaida extending across the ocean back to Puerto Rico. Music (salsa) is portrayed as intimately related to poetry. Unfortunately, the aesthetics are strongly gendered masculine, a characterization that women have had to vigorously struggle against for decades. In fact, the inclusion of female poets such as the Dominican-Puerto Rican Sandra María Esteves also serves to amplify the "insular" scope, to include other Caribbean islands besides Puerto Rico; Tato Laviera's poem "the africa in pedro morejón" (Laviera 1979) will serve as a reminder of the centrality of Cuba.

The reference to the medieval courtly tradition of troubadours is striking: the notion that the ghetto-inspired Hispanic Caribbean poets of New York maintain or reproduce this pre-modern technology in what would soon be a post-modern environment. In his introduction to *Aloud*, Algarín describes even further how the tradition of the rural Puerto Rican *trovador* becomes reconfigured in the Nuyorican Diaspora, leading to the modern-day poetry slams.[3] And this craft, transmitted from Old Europe through the Caribbean and brought to the metropolis, is intrinsically linked to Africa and its *griots*,[4] to the rhythm of *bomba*, to Maelo's voice and performances, in an open proclamation of the centrality of the African roots of Puerto Rican (and Hispanic Caribbean) culture, ones that have been greatly contested and, in turn, reaffirmed (in the case of Puerto Rico) by individuals such as Luis Palés Matos (1995 [1937]), Tomás Blanco (1985 [1948]), José Luis González (1980), Isabelo Zenón Cruz (1975), Luis Rafael Sánchez (1997), and Mayra Santos-Febres (1991, 1996, 2005);[5] in Cuba, by Nicolás Guillén, Georgina Herrera, and Nancy Morejón; and in the Dominican Republic by Blas Jiménez, Norberto James, and Silvio Torres Saillant. The Hispanified *Provençal* troubadour's odes of courtly love to lovely maidens become popular refrains in their rural Puerto Rican "middle passage" and are profoundly transformed into English, Spanish, and Spanglish poems of denunciation of oppression and of unbounded love for a marginalized space and community in New York.

In his essay "Nuyorican Aesthetics" (1987), Algarín will further draw attention to orality ("the expression of the self orally"); the need to master "one language or both to a degree that makes it possible to be accurate about one's present condition: psychic, economic, or historical" (1987: 163); the way linguistic variation affects poetry, given the differences between the stress system in English and the syllabic system in Spanish, and the way Nuyorican verse combines both; and the psychic importance of community performance as therapy: as he states, "transformations before the public eye are a very important way of psychic cure." In *Aloud*, Algarín will show how these linguistic elements which originate as a culturally-specific form take free reign and are even incorporated into the work of African American poets such as Tracie Morris who, in a full embrace of Afro-Diasporic trans-linguistic commonality, proclaims: "Morenita, morenita men have named you . . . / Not Latina. Morenita. / Negrita chiquitita / de Estados Unidos" (1994: 102).

Uno: Tato Laviera and Pedro Morejón Dream of Africa

In his essay "Qué Assimilated, Brother, yo soy asimilao: The Structuring of Puerto Rican Identity in the U.S." (1993), Juan Flores proposes four definitive moments in the awakening of Nuyorican cultural consciousness. According to Flores, after an initial denunciation of urban poverty and abandon, Nuyorican poets turn to Puerto Rico, but particularly to the African and indigenous roots of island culture. The eventual disenchantment with the island (or at least with its official, white-washed dominant sector) brings with it a renewed interest in New York, "an awakened cultural consciousness" (1993: 190) as well as "an awakened national consciousness, or consciousness of nationality" (1993: 191) and an identification with Afro-Caribbean traditions. Finally, there occurs a branching out: a selective connection to and interaction with the surrounding North American society, including a "growing-together" (1993: 192) towards groups in closest proximity, such as African Americans and members of the Caribbean Diaspora.[6] In this as in other essays, Flores grounds his analyses on the work of Tato Laviera, finding a particularly rich exemplification of these trends in this poet's development in his first four books: *La Carreta Made a U-Turn* (1979), *Enclave* (1981), *AmeRícan* (1985), and *Mainstream Ethics* (1989).

The characteristic hybridity of Nuyorican poetry and its multiple gaze towards the city and the island of origin becomes apparent from a brief glance at the cover of Laviera's first collection, *La Carreta Made a U-Turn*, something Francisco Cabanillas has also observed (2004: 899). The cover photograph by Dominique portrays an urban cityscape, that of a partially-blocked (or barricaded) snow-covered street with a large "DETOUR" sign; next to it sits a supermarket shopping cart with a conga, a guitar, a *pava*, and a paper shopping bag with a wooden souvenir machete sticking out. Here, the three-part progression of René Marqués's 1953 play *La carreta* [*The Oxcart*] from countryside, to urban slums of San Juan, and finally to the Bronx becomes that of "Metropolis Dreams," "Loisaida Streets: Latinas Sing," and "El Arrabal: Nuevo Rumbón." In his rewriting, Laviera begins with the city, goes on to talk about women's experiences, and then concludes with a celebration of Black culture, Africa, and music, in a sequence that goes from more English to a full embrace of Spanish. And instead of going back to Puerto Rico, as in Marqués's play, Laviera metaphorically goes back to Africa, spiritually and linguistically (as in the turn to Yoruba in "felipe luciano, i miss you in africa").

What is this "nuevo rumbón" (new rumba)? It is one of hope and celebration, a triumph over desperation. In the first poem of the section, congas are central: synecdoches for music, an anaphora by its repetition, almost onomatopoeic in their cadences, concrete poetry in their placement of six repeated words in three columns on the page. These congas appear as a threat to drugs, better than drugs as they become purifying filters. Afro-Caribbean music, which stems from the sugar-cane plantation, recalls the history of slavery and the continued oppression in the American ghetto, bringing warmth in winter both for Latinas/os and African Americans, serving as a cure. The poem jumps from this multilingual term (congas) to stanzas in English and Spanish, alternating as the poem proceeds. At the end, the poetic voice insistently repeats "chévere, rumbones, me afectó / me afectó, me afectó, me afectó / chévere [] rumbones [ ] me afectó" (1979: 54), as the words in the last verse jump across the page with marked spaces in between.

Another poem, "the africa in pedro morejón," presents an Afro-Cuban dreamscape, a Diasporic Cuban celebration of African synchretism in Caribbean music and life, as told to the Nuyorican poet by the "high priest Pedro . . . / in front of an abandoned building" (1979: 58). In this poem, Cuban mambo and *guaguancó*, Dominican and Haitian *merengue*, and Puerto Rican *guaracha* and *plena* all come together in synchrony. Source and origin are confused in Morejón's mind, Cuba seen as Africa and vice versa: "sometimes I think that cuba is africa, / or that i am in cuba and africa at the / same time, sometimes I think africa / is all of us in music / musically rooted way way back / before any other language" (1979: 57). The poetic voice struggles with the real, present-day Africa, which is modernized, as opposed to fantasy depictions of it as timeless. His dream leads to an Afro-centric celebration and validation of Africa as a site of origin of advanced thought, and also to a meditation about racial prejudice in the Americas, the hereditary logic of the one-drop of blood (that is to say, the rule of hypodescent), and a play on the strange ideology of dilution and "mejoramiento de la raza": while white will never make black, black can eventually make white. Here, Spanish becomes a language that facilitates the transmission of secrets, of opinions that could lead to violent repression.

Finally, in "savorings, from piñones to loíza" we have food, music, and celebration of Puerto Rico, through a specific geography of black culture in the northern coast, different from that of Luis Palés Matos, which was centered on the south (from Guayama to Ponce).[7] Food becomes life, a source of bodily sustenance, but also a geographic map of African heritage and persistence in the so-called New World. Music ["tru cu tú [ ] tru cu tú / tru cu tú [ ] tru cu tú / tu [ ] tu [ ] tu," (1979: 59)] with a disappearing echo in the distance, becomes a memory of idealized landscapes of the mind.

Laviera's poems celebrate a heritage of blackness and reinterpret it through diverse means and cultural forms. Just as in Palés Matos, the map of the Caribbean is reconstituted as one of the Diaspora, linking across the Atlantic, joining modern day Africa with its dispersed populations, something the Spanish critic Antonia Domínguez Miguela (2003) has explored at length in an essay on this subject. Laviera addresses Palés Matos's contribution and identity in other poems, such as "chorna" (in *AmeRícan*) and "homenaje a don luis palés matos" (in *Enclave*), where he challenges his so-called whiteness; he also pays homage to other key Black poetic figures such as the famous *declamador* Juan Boria in a poem by his name ("juan boria," also in *Enclave*). In fact, in an interview with Carmen Dolores Hernández (1997), Laviera describes in detail the specificity of his life experience as a Black Puerto Rican man, and the profound link to masters such as Palés Matos and Boria.

Dos: Willie Perdomo's Black Boricua Angst

—Hey, Willie. What are you, man? Boricua? Moreno? Que? Are you Black? Puerto Rican?
—I am.
—No, silly. You know what I mean: What are you?
—I am you. You are me. We the same. Can't you feel our veins drinking the same blood? (1996: 19)

Willie Perdomo is, of his generation, the poet who has most poignantly addressed the inner turmoil of self-identity, of being labeled and expected to comply with externally-determined cultural norms, with what Michael Omi and Howard Winant (1994) describe as "racialization," the mostly involuntary (but culturally- and historically-specific) process by which an individual is assigned a racial classification (in this case, in the United States).[8] In his poem "Nigger-Reecan Blues," Perdomo's poetic persona ("Willie") autobiographically rearticulates this sensibility and crisis, that of being Black and Puerto Rican, one experienced decades earlier by Piri Thomas and described in *Down These Mean Streets*. It is no surprise that the poem is dedicated to Thomas in *Aloud* (1994: 111–2), although the dedication does not appear in Perdomo's first anthology, *Where a Nickel Costs a Dime* (1996), a book named after a verse by Langston Hughes, a figure about whom the poet has also written a children's book (2002). Most jarringly, "Nigger-Reecan Blues" is about people's refutations, their refusal to recognize that "Willie" can be, in fact is, Puerto Rican.

As the anthro-political linguist Ana Celia Zentella (1997) has shown in her analysis of El Barrio (or Spanish Harlem) entitled *Growing Up Bilingual*, Black Puerto Ricans (in New York and elsewhere) are often pulled by demands to identify as African Americans. These usually come from the outside: from African Americans themselves and from whites who refuse to recognize the existence of a heterogeneous Black (Latina/o) population. But as Perdomo shows, this phenomenon also operates within the Puerto Rican community itself. "Nigger-Reecan Blues" is precisely a chronicle or depiction of numerous encounters by the poetic subject in which his identity is questioned at times, how he is told he is not a Puerto Rican, and assumed or declared to be African American, on the basis of his phenotype or physiognomy, by a whole chorus of voices: some anonymous, others clearly identified (la madam blankita, the taxi driver, the newspaper, his professor, his compai Davi). The orality in the poem is two-fold: one, because it is a poem composed in dialogue or rather a community cacophony, of voices shouting at Willie, and Willie talking back; another, because it is a spoken-word poem, meant to be recited and heard out loud.

The poetic speaker's insistence in his ontological unity as a self-contained human, multifold and diverse, is flattened, challenged, and denied, by those who want to classify him into rigid, mutually-exclusive categories. In the poem, "black" stands for African American, while "africano" becomes a sign of Afro-Diasporic Puerto Rican identity, one that is fully embraced in other texts, such as in "Writing About What You Know," a poetic essay included in Perdomo's more recent book *Smoking Lovely* (2003), in which the poetic persona "Papo" thinks of "conga, Santería ritual, black-on-black crime, Cheo Feliciano singing 'El ratón,' the violent *El Vocero* headlines, and finally decides to use his block" as ways to describe his "style" (2003: 65).

"Nigger-Reecan Blues" operates between affirmation ("Yo soy boricua! Yo soy africano!") and refutation ("I ain't black!"). This refutation or insistence in difference comes close to or can be confused with denial, although it really has much more to do with the workings of race in the Caribbean, where a light-skinned person like Perdomo in fact would usually not be identified as black, but rather mulato or trigueño, an intermediate racial category that oscillates between black and white according to the particular social context. The subtleties or dynamics of this system of classification are eclipsed in the United States by the dominant views, and the poetic speaker is thus at a loss. (In fact, it is suggested that Puerto Ricans themselves set apart their own racial typology and begin to ascribe to the dominant U.S. model.) Towards the end of the poem, the poetic voice accepts that his struggle is somewhat futile, particularly given the common situation of oppression that "spics" and "niggers" share alike. At the core of the poem is a hermeneutical question and struggle: who controls the meaning, the right of interpretation, over who one is? At the end, the poet adopts a pragmatic approach, seeking to overcome his impasse:

I'm a spic! I'm a nigger!
Spic! Spic! Just like a nigger!
Neglected, rejected, oppressed and dispossessed,
From banana boats to tenements

Street gangs to regiments
Spic, spic, spic. I ain't no different than a nigger! (1996: 20–1)

These lines suggest that, at least for the poetic speaker, the most efficacious form of resistance is to acknowledge the power of discriminatory labels and outside constraints, and protest the system of oppression which marks both identities (that of Puerto Rican and black) as inferior. It is white racism, after all, which holds different people of color down, even when black and Puerto Ricans themselves may participate in maintaining these categories in place.

Tres: Josefina Báez Looks East, and Finds the Familiarity of Otherness
The poetry and performance of Josefina Báez, particularly her one-woman show *Dominicanish* (performed with live musical accompaniment, initially a saxophonist and more recently a trumpet player) represents an interesting twist. With this approach she proposes "Dominicanish" as an invented tongue, a cultural shorthand, a new creation, what we could call a variant of Nuyorican, particularly one that privileges Afro-diasporic Dominican expression in New York and redefines Dominican culture to include Haitian elements, and North American Black pride, and the experience of ESL (English as a Second Language), of being a monolingual immigrant that has to learn and adapt linguistically and culturally *a la fuerza*.[9] This hybrid language and experimental cultural practice is presented as a variant of Dominicanyork identity (as defined by Luis Guarnizo and others), an identity Báez embraces, one which differs radically in terms of race and phonetics from the polished prose of Julia Álvarez's (nearly white) García girls (that is to say, the protagonists of Álvarez's best known debut novel, *How the García Girls Lost Their Accents*), who, in fact, became distanced from Spanish en route to become more fully assimilated Americans. Báez's work differs from Álvarez's (and from Laviera's and Perdomo's) in its stylistic modality: the performer fully incorporates dance, movement, and music to her presentation; she also offers a more dissonant narrative of black Latina/o identity and culture.

What Báez does share with these authors is a directness that comes from speaking from personal experience. This autobiographical component is strongly mediated by a postmodern sensibility that seeks to deconstruct the notion of transparency and thus incorporates various types of additional materials, movements, and sounds that can serve to disorient or rather, to re-Orient spectators or readers with a mixture of South Asian, Caribbean, African American, and U.S. Latina/o elements. The artist engages in a free flow of associations that lead her to link apparently disparate or only tangentially (obliquely) relevant materials. What brings all of them together is her strong stage presence, and the strength of her dominant themes: race, music, language, urban space, interpersonal relations, all mediated through an immigrant "structure of feeling" (as elaborated by José Esteban Muñoz in *Disidentifications*, following Raymond Williams). Observe the following passage:

> Aquí los discos traen un cancionero.
> Discos del alma con afro. Con afro black is
> beautiful. Black is a color. Black is my color.
> **My cat is black.**
> But first of all baseball has been very very
> very good to me
> Repeat after me   repeat after you
> (Báez 2000: 26—emphasis in the original).

As these verses show, music and the 1960s U.S. "Black is Beautiful" socio-cultural movement (particularly as it is manifested through popular culture and the arts) facilitate a process of racial awareness and pride that was not readily available to the immigrant poetic speaker from Spanish-language Dominican sources. This process is linked by contiguity and concatenation to primary language acquisition or ESL (the elementary statement "Black is a color" and later "My cat is black," reminiscent of early language teaching), self-awareness and the rise of consciousness ("Black is my color"), the financial remuneration of sports as a tool of social ascent and immigrant success ("baseball has been very very / very good to me"), and finally, to rote pedagogical practices ("Repeat after me") with a twist ("repeat after you"), a gesture understood to give the student learners (and by extension, audience members, spectators, or readers) more active agency in the process of cultural reception of her work. Báez's pedagogical enactment is different from the scene of miseducation described by Laviera in one of his best known poems, "my graduation speech," where the poetic speaker laments (in what can be read as a painful or ironic tone) his lack of linguistic knowledge of standard English and Spanish, leaving him speaking everything "matao" [incorrectly, "broken," or literally "dead"] (1979: 17). In fact, Báez's poetic speaker will claim to have full mastery of English, to such an extent that other students make fun of her for her "corny vocabulary," a knowledge that brings her close to being a "bilingual nerd" (2000: 32), and which ultimately leads her to Brandeis High School in New York City (which is affiliated to Brandeis University in Massachusetts), "Writing phrases and sentences in perfect syntax / Filled and full of sensual images" (2000: 33).

Báez's resignification of race and of blackness in particular occurs in a specific socio-cultural context, that of island and diasporic Dominican prejudice against the black race, a prejudice that was legally institutionalized during the period of Rafael Leónidas Trujillo's dictatorship and maintained under the so-called "democratic" authoritarian regime of Joaquín Balaguer, but which already was well entrenched in dominant intellectual circles in the nineteenth century (for example, in the absolute omission of mentions of blackness in Manuel de Jesús Galván's foundational novel *Enriquillo*, 1879–1882), as Lorgia García-Peña (2008a) has explored. For complex (and not so complex, racist) historical reasons, in the Dominican Republic, blackness is associated first and foremost with Haitianness, a rather convenient (and oppressive) mental strategy that allowed individuals (or forced them, under the rule of law) to literally "white-wash" the legacy of slavery in the island (and their own personal and familiar histories), and somehow pretend that there were or are no black people of Dominican extraction; thus everyone was officially classified by the government as either indio (indigenous Taíno) or blanco (white, i.e., European). While Báez does not explicitly address this repressive historical and governmental legacy, her work serves as a broader socio-cultural corrective.

In *Dominicanish*, Báez proposes that music serves as an educational/pedagogical tool, and plays with literal translation to convey or recapture the depth of meaning that is lost as terms become commonplace. This is the case of her translation in the above passage of "soul" as *alma*: it is clear that she is referring to soul music, that is to say, an African-American secular musical tradition which nevertheless claimed some link to spiritual, religious practices. The translation of "soul" as *alma* achieves a denaturalization of the term; the image we are left with in Spanish ("discos del alma con afro") is literally that of records that contain a soul (metaphysical entity) with an afro (a large head of curly/nappy hair); records of the soul, that are dear to the soul, to the innermost dimension of who one is.

In the above-quoted stanza, everything (racial empowerment, music, language acquisition) is humorously (or tragically) subsumed under the mantra insistently repeated throughout the performance: "But first of all baseball has been very very / very good to me" (2000: 26). This phrase, repeated three times and later rephrased at the end of the performance ("I have been very good to baseball too," [2000: 49]), serves as a reminder of dominant conceptions of Latinos in the United States as baseball players/athletes and of the "factory," "plantation" or "greenhouse" notion of the Dominican Republic as a site where raw "talent" can be signed and developed by professional teams for very low costs (see Burgos 2007). In fact, this phrase has a complex history, that alludes to Sammy Sosa's difficulties with the English language in the 1990s but actually originated in the 1950s with the American sport press' relentless harassment of black Cuban and other black Latino players such as Minnie Minoso (Saturnino Orestes Armas Miñoso Arrieta), the first black Latino player to ever play for a Major League white team (the Chicago White Sox).[10] As Jules M. Rothstein comments,

> Minnie Minoso, a Cuban immigrant who began playing baseball on sugar plantations, became fodder for parody and derision when he said, "Baseball has been very, very good to me." Minoso's heartfelt remarks—both the content and the accent—have been mocked time and again. Minoso came from poverty to fame and financial security while playing a game that gave him pleasure. As the first dark-skinned Hispanic in the major leagues, he understood the nature of gratitude, whereas those who mocked him showed that they knew little of struggle, and even less of thankfulness. (1998: online)

The phrase became particularly disseminated as a result of a television skit in three early seasons of NBC's *SNL* [*Saturday Night Live*] (1978–1980) where Garrett Morris played the fictional baseball player Chico Escuela, described as "a player for the New York Mets who provides sports commentaries on Weekend Update" (*SNL* n.d.). The portrayal of Escuela (a name chosen, one imagines, ironically, to mock or make fun of the character's apparent lack of "schooling") is marked by racism and insinuations of illegality and ignorance. For example, in one sketch with Jane Curtin and Bill Murray, initially aired on December 8, 1979, it is insinuated that Chico is the father of an illegitimate child with a 19-year old Florida resident called Anita Dark (once again, a name suggesting mockery, as in "Anita [=I need a] Dark [man]"). Chico is introduced by Jane (whose name he mispronounces "Hane") as he goes on to state:

> Thank you, Hane. Basebal bin berra berra good to me. Anita Dark bin berra berra good to me... but Chico can't talk about it. In sports, Charles White won the... how do you say... Heisman Trophy. Now, look at this run. Charles White is the best football player. He runs with authority. Chico run from authority... but I can't talk about it. (*SNL* 1979)

Most remarkable or shocking of all is to think that an African-American actor (Garrett Morris) would lend himself to such a debased portrayal of a Black Latino character. The so-called "phonetic" transcription of Chico's speech is particularly virulent, although it could also (purposely? humorously?) be seen as alluding to baseball player Yogi Berra. In the highly racialized context of the sketch, the fact that he describes a man with the surname "White" as "the best" also serves to rub salt in the wound.

Interestingly enough, even if some dominant U.S. television representations of Black Latinos are negative, other television programs served as positive representations or as sources of role models for Josefina Báez. This is the case of the musical variety and dance show *Soul Train* where her idols, the Isley Brothers performed:

> Last Saturday my teachers sang in Soul Train
> Now I don't care how my mouth look   I like
> what I'm saying
> Boy   girls love you   she does   she doesn't
> **A   mor   And   More** (2000: 28—emphasis in the original)

Identification with these Black American performers facilitates the physical linguistic adjustment that allows the poetic speaker access to the English language as a complement to (and not substitution for) Spanish. Language and race are mediated through love, an affect or emotion that can surpass the difficulties and pains of migrant experience (something also suggested by Chela Sandoval, in broader terms, in her *Methodology of the Oppressed*).

For Báez, Dominicanish is a way of putting the mouth, resisted by a person reticent of vocal gymnastics, of engaging in *gimnástica bucal, o sea, de la boca*; it is a way of speaking acquired by watching performances of the Isley Brothers on *Soul Train* ("No, no, no, Samantha/ Ronald is the cutest and then Marvin," (2000: 34)—emphasis in the original) but also by walking through the streets of Washington Heights and Harlem and imbibing of the multiple stimuli all around, including the same "Julio and Marisol" AIDS prevention cartoons (2000: 38-9) that Perdomo mentions in his "Letter to Pedro Avilés" (1996: 68).[11] Báez, thus, can be seen as a Black Dominican Baudelaire, a contemporary Walter Benjamin or Michel de Certeau of the northern Manhattan experience, a female Dominicanyork *flâneur*.

Báez's linguistic, performative experimentation comes closer to the verbal acrobatics, word plays and language games of performers like Guillermo Gómez-Peña who have also taken up issues of Spanglish and postmodernity, but differs in her conscious incorporation of jazz music in her performances (especially the saxophone and/or trumpet), and in the Afro-Caribbean specificity. Báez's particularity resides in the triangular configuration of influences and geographies that she maps: Nueva York, La Romana, and India, source of the Kuchipudi dances, jetis, and Shiva Shambos that characterize her movement on stage, or the Vedic and Hindu philosophy and epic poems that she quotes; South Asian traditions integrated into a Dominican Afro-American discourse that privileges above all the soul music of the Isley Brothers, Billie Holiday, Ella Fitzgerald, and Earth, Wind, and Fire, but also Dominican rhythms ("Pacheco tumbao añejo / Pacheco flauta [ ] Pacheco su nuevo tumbao [ ] el / maestro [ ] el artista [ ] Tremendo Cache," [2000: 42]). The route to this cornucopia of culture is precisely the route of migration, the path from Spanish to English and beyond: to Dominicanish, to the "om" of inner meditation and the "is" of existential being, that of a distinctly black Dominican woman in America who speaks like a Nuyorican and combs her hair like an African American:

Me chulié en el hall
Metí mano en el rufo
Craqueo chicle como Shamequa Brown
Hablo como Boricua
y me peino como Morena. (2000: 43—emphasis in the original)

As these verses show, being a Black Dominican in New York (for Báez) means coming in contact with (and sharing life experiences with) African

Americans, Puerto Ricans, and Afro-Diasporic people in general; having life defined by commonalities and cultural borrowings and exchange.

Conclusion

The poetry and performances of Laviera, Perdomo, and Báez serve to highlight, celebrate, discuss, and lament the experiences of being a Latino/a of Black heritage in the United States. In the case of Laviera and Báez, this is done mostly as a cause for celebration and cultural validation, tying in black forms from the Caribbean. (In this sense, it is useful to note the closeness in age of the two poets, the fact that both were born in the Caribbean, and that both are dark-skinned.) In the case of Perdomo (who is younger, was born in the United States, and who is light-skinned), the imposition of the category of blackness as intrinsic or the dominant marker of his identity causes initial resistance and anger, but is overcome as part of an anti-racist project of cultural solidarity and empowerment. All three poets emphasize their strong affinity for music; Báez and Perdomo's strong connection with African American culture (soul music and jazz in the case of Báez, jazz and Langston Hughes in the case of Perdomo [2002]) shows the richness of Afro-Diasporic continuities and the appeal of U.S. culture to Hispanic Caribbean immigrants, something the Puerto Rican bibliophile Arthur (Arturo) Schomburg and the Puerto Rican labor organizer and journalist Jesús Colón had observed in early twentieth century New York. The work of Laviera, Perdomo, and Báez, as well as that of other writers such as Piri Thomas and Marta Moreno Vega, reminds us of the richness of Black Latino/a culture, and the many struggles that lay ahead in order to obtain full cultural recognition and to overcome multiple forms of racism and oppression.

NOTES

[1] This section includes poems by Miguel Algarín, Richard August, Jorge Brandon, Américo Casiano, Jr., Lucky Cienfuegos, Víctor Hernández Cruz, Sandra María Esteves, Lois Griffith, Tato Laviera, Pedro Pietri, Miguel Piñero, Bimbo Rivas, Ntozake Shange, and Piri Thomas.

[2] According to *Webster's Third New International Dictionary*, "(1) one of a class of lyric poets and poet-musicians often of knightly rank flourishing from the 11th to the end of the 13th century chiefly in Provence, the south of France and the north of Italy and cultivating a lyric poetry intricate in meter and rhyme and usu. of a romantic amatory strain [*Meriam Webster Online*: "whose major theme was courtly love"]—compare TROUVère. (2) a strolling

minstrel; also: anyone who in music, verse, or rhetorical prose promotes some cause."

3 "The modern Slam is the creation of Marc Smith, who continues his weekly bare-knuckles events at the Green Mill in Chicago. The idea for the Slam grows out of ancient traditions of competitive and/or linked rhymes between orators—from the Greek mythological tale of Apollo and Marsyas to the African griots, from the Sanjurokuninsen, or imaginary poetry team competitions, of tenth-century Japanese court poet Fujiwara no Kinto to the African-American 'dozens.' It is a tradition that still exists very actively on the island of Puerto Rico, where El Trovador improvises in the plaza, spontaneously pulling into the verse the life of the folks in the small town, the tragedies that have occurred in their families, the gossip that surrounds their private lives, and the celebratory passages that talk about births, deaths, weddings, and baptisms. All of this is compacted into ten-syllable lines with end rhymes. El Trovador moves from town to town in the outskirts of big cities of the island and is received grandly by the townsfolk, who look forward to regaling him with laughter and drinks when he is entertaining, and/or criticizing and insulting him when he is either too rigid or too drunk to deliver the goods. This tradition of El Trovador coming to perform to the audience for their approval or being punished by their disapproval is totally alive at the Nuyorican Poets Café" (Algarín 1994: 16).

4 According to *Merriam-Webster Online Dictionary*, "gri·ot: Pronunciation: 'grE-"O. Function: noun. Etymology: French. Date: 1906. : any of a class of musician-entertainers of western Africa whose performances include tribal histories and genealogies."

5 Also see Ramos Rosado (1999). For a historical perspective, see Sued Badillo and López Cantos (1986).

6 Flores borrows the term "growing-together" from J.M. Blaut.

7 See Girón de Segura (1968) where she states: "Si pensamos por un momento en nuestra topografía, notaremos que Puerto Rico tiene dos zonas donde impera la raza negra. En el norte, Cangrejos (Santurce) – Loíza – Carolina. En el sur, San Antón – Salinas – Patillas – Guayama – Arroyo. Los negros en el norte bailaban bomba en los palmares de Loíza y Cangrejos. En el sur, la bomba se bailaba (y todavía se baila) en San Antón y los 'brujos' los duchos en el arte de la brujería, del maleficio y del 'ventenconmigo' se concentraron en Guayama" (1968: xxvii).

8 See Noel (2008, 2011) for extensive discussion of Willie Perdomo's life and work.

9 On the subject of black culture in the Dominican Republic, see: Andújar Persinal (1997), Franco (1998), Chapman (2002). For detailed analysis of Báez, see García-Peña (2008a, 2008b), Méndez (2012), Rivera-Servera (2000, 2002).

10 My appreciation to my former student William (Bill) Trenary, who was the first to inform me about Minnie Minoso and Chico Escuela.

11 For more information on the Isley Brothers, see see https://www.facebook.com/isleybrothers/. [Accessed February 14, 2014].

"Kalahari" or the Afro-Caribbean Connection: Tato Laviera and Luis Palés Matos

ANTONIA DOMÍNGUEZ MIGUELA

The history of colonization in Puerto Rico has influenced its development as a nation between two cultures and languages and the relationships that have been established with other Caribbean countries and the United States. Puerto Rico, after all, has always been considered a bridge nation between the Caribbean and the North American colossus. The development of national identity in Puerto Rico has implied a series of contradictions, which are reflected in its national literature. Many critics have pointed out that Puerto Rican literature is split between two shores: Puerto Rican literature written by Island authors and Puerto Rican literature written in the United States. Puerto Rican literature on the Island has been characterized by a number of recurrent themes concerning the definition of cultural and national identity as a way to solve the contradiction of being a Caribbean nation that is still a U.S. territory yet culturally and linguistically different. This fact has always been an obstacle to the consolidation of the bonds with other Caribbean countries like Cuba, for example.

However, after the migration of more than half of the population of Puerto Rico to the United States, Puerto Rican national and cultural identity underwent important transformations on the mainland. The concentration of migrants from different Latin American and especially Caribbean countries on American soil has facilitated the development of a sense of community and brotherhood among Caribbean people in the United States. Furthermore, the contact between Caribbean and American traditions found a way of expression in unique cultural products like salsa but also in an emerging U.S. Caribbean literature.

Unfortunately, U.S. Puerto Rican literature has been ignored for a long time on the Island, mainly because of their use of English and the particular themes concerning life in the northern barrios. It was a literature at first identified as Nuyorican but which has recently spread all over the United States. In the last two decades, the consolidation and recognition of U.S. Puerto Rican authors by the academy has been translated into a growing interest on this literature and the connections with the Island and the Caribbean literary tradition. These bicultural authors show a clear influence from two cultural and literary traditions that needs to be explored.

This essay is an attempt to briefly describe the strong literary connections between the Island and the mainland through the work of two distant Puerto Rican poets: Luis Palés Matos and Tato Laviera. Both of them share many concerns regarding national and cultural identity; themes like race and popular culture, among others, gain special prominence in their poetry but what is especially remarkable is the common use of a poetic language that pays homage to the Afro-Caribbean component of a transcultural people. Because of the time that separates them, it is obvious that Luis Palés Matos is an important literary source for Tato Laviera, who recovers Palés Matos's poetic message and language and makes it valuable for present times. Nuyorican poets like Tato Laviera who began writing in the seventies and eighties needed to find a literary language suitable for their distinctive experience and identity as a displaced people. After encountering racism in the United States because of their skin color and language, many also turned back to the Island to understand their racial and cultural identity.

Laviera, in fact, to some degree turns back to Palés Matos. Luis Palés Matos (admired and criticized by many) is the figure of the poet in search of his own voice. When he finally finds it, his poetry becomes music, color, rhythm and vitality. His poetic collection *Tuntún de pasa y grifería* (1995 [1937])[1] is a masterpiece where he established what was later on defined as *poesía negrista*.[2] In his poetry, there is a conscious attempt to suggest a new poetic language in which the Black heritage is present as an example of still to be exploited sources that can express the Caribbean's distinctiveness. In his poetry we find a clear process of literary *mestizaje*, which lets him depart from the standard Spanish that was dominant in mainstream poetic productions and embark in the wonderful project of turning local and Black speech into a poetic language. Palés Matos recovers and pays homage to the African component of the Puerto Rican people and restores the African-Caribbean cultural tradition as a valuable source of artistic expression of the Caribbean soul. He also departs from traditional modernist poetry toward what has also been defined as *antipoetry*.[3] We can easily understand why Palés Matos was so strongly criticized by the cultural elite due to the general belief that national identity resides in the history of the great families that can trace back their origins to Spanish conquistadors. However, this is undermined by the inclusion of the Mulatta/o as representative of Puerto Rico and subsequently of the Caribbean. In some way, pure lineage, which in Palés Matos's times was encouraged and celebrated as symbol of a romantic concept of the nation, is equally proved unstable and considered a mere illusion. This reaffirmation of racial identity and the celebration of black roots is something that we will find again in the work of Tato Laviera.

Tuntún de pasa y grifería is an aesthetic exercise in which the poet tries to suggest the possibility of a new poetic expression using a language of his own where there are not only European and native "ingredients," but also Afro-Caribbean ones that help to create a new Puerto Rican poetry based on the Spanish language but with a distinctive African "flavor." At the same time, this renovation of the poetic language suggests the need to emphasize the qualities from each of the races that meet in this fantastic amalgam that is the Caribbean. These are times of oppression and crisis of identity in the Caribbean but especially in Puerto Rico since the establishment of the American power prevents the normal evolution of an White emergent creole elite, obsessed with pure lineage and with staying attached to the land of their supposedly Spanish ancestors. The lower classes, though highly aware of racial classification in Puerto Rico, also need to look for strength inside themselves, in their multiracial heritage.

Palés Matos's creation of a new poetic language is achieved by means of exploiting the musical and productive resources of the Spanish language in order to make it sound distinctively Afro-Caribbean. To find their "own distinctive voice" he includes an area-specific vocabulary, exploitation of the productive resources of the language (such as in the formation of new words) and renovation of the set of elements and images used to describe and represent the Caribbean experience. It is obvious that there is a significant Spanish ingredient in the Caribbean, but in Palés Matos's poetry we find that it is not only Hispanic, but also African. Palés Matos attempts to create a new poetic language in which all influences meet to describe the unique Caribbean identity, as the product of mixtures. His interest in experimenting with the language possibilities suggests his earlier concerns about poetry. Like most avant-garde artists, he tries to find a new language by including some components that have been missing. This becomes an attempt to break with the academic and intellectual poetry that was trapped in a terrain of universalistic Hispanism. His poetry tries to present what the Caribbean multiracial situation can contribute in the search for its own voice.

There has been some criticism[4] on his use of Blacks limited to a fantasizing world of savages, primitivism, sensuality, and voodoo. It is much more perceptive to "read" those poems trying to find what makes them "Caribbean" taking the Afro-Caribbean theme as an example of the possibilities that are waiting to be explored. It seems to me that the ideal image of the Negro is for Palés Matos an image of the vitality and resources that are still to be discovered inside the people of the Caribbean. With his poetry he is suggesting the richness of influences that meet in these people, and he tries to bring to the surface all the qualities hidden inside of them that they need to acknowledge. A starting point for this process consists of a recovery of the most outstanding qualities inherent to the "race." His own fascination for his African heritage makes him take the Black race as an example because it is one of the races underacknowledged until that moment.

Pales Matos could as easily have chosen the indigenous but he finds in the African element the vitality and purity that is of greater help to achieve his goal. This becomes an example of racial pride by emphasizing those aspects that make the Black population so distinct and superior to the White: their vitality, their rhythm, their courage, their strength against adverse circumstances, even their eroticism. However, we have to be careful when interpreting the function of his poetry so that we don't confuse it (as some critics have done in my opinion) with an attempt to define the Caribbean only by means of Black aesthetics, exaggerating the African component in the Caribbean. His poetry represents a new strength coming from one of the many ingredients present in the Caribbean because in the African he finds what he was looking for: vitality, strength, courage to fight and speak for oneself, liveliness. For the first time, the criollo stops being the main character of a national literature, and the myth of the rural *jíbaro* shows a clear decline to an already disappearing image of the model White Puerto Rican, descendant of Spanish culture.

For Palés Matos the African component is seen as an open door to vitality in the combination of Indigenous and Spanish elements, and it is represented in the literary figure of the Mulatto as Arcadio Díaz Quiñones points out: "la mulata es, pues, la heroína del drama, síntesis del pueblo y de la tierra a la que pertenece" (1982: 90). The mulatta, then, can be seen as an image for the Island. Vitality is within her, but she just has to use it as Palés Matos is suggesting in "Mulata Antilla": "Eres inmensidad libre y sin límites / eres amor sin trabas y sin prisas; / en tu vientre conjugan mis dos razas / sus vitales potencias expansivas." The same idea is repeated in other poems such as "Plena del Menéalo":

> Mientras bailes no hay quien pueda
> cambiarte el alma y la sal.
> Ni agapitos por aquí,
> ni místeres por allá.
> Dale a la popa, mulata
> proyecta en la eternidad
> ese tumbo de caderas
> que es ráfaga de huracán,
> y menéalo, menéalo,
> de aquí payá, de ayá pacá
> menéalo, menéalo,
> de aquí payá, de ayá pacá
> menéalo, menéalo.
> ¡Para que rabie el Tío Sam! (1995: 159)

The figure of the mulatta serves the poet to address the issue of colonialism and the complex relationship between Puerto Rico and the United States. The cultural difference is clear. Puerto Rico may be American soil, but Puerto Rican culture is alive through the mulatta and represents the distinctiveness of Puerto Rican racial and cultural history. Palés Matos is important in establishing the fact that Africa cannot be ignored as an important element in the Caribbean and in the Américas.

Among the main techniques used by Palés Matos to introduce Africa in his poetry and create this new poetic language we find the introduction of a new vocabulary apparently (or at least in some primary stages along history) alien to the Spanish language. We have to distinguish two main lexical sources: native and local words and African words. The addition of local vocabulary has as its main function to speak about the islands in their own language, and doing so becomes an attempt to give predominance to the local over the ever-present burden of the Caribbean's Hispanism. We can find a great number of these words; some of them are "bochinche," "funche," "mandrugo," "mariyanda," "chango," "burundanga," "cocolos," "fufú," "ñeque," "melao," "malanga," "ñañigo," "caratos," "quimbombo," "calalú," "foete," "gandinga," "bembe," "prángana," "guanabana," "mamey." Most of these words make reference to particular objects and places in the Caribbean (among others fruits and dances). Though most of the time they are of Caribbean origin, in some instances it is difficult to say if they are of Indian or African origin, due in part to the early arrival of black populations to the island.

These words usually appear in Palés Matos's verses together with another group of words that make reference to people, places, and objects from Africa such as "calabó," "cocorocó," "gongos," "tembandumba," "baquiné," "adombe ganga monde," "Ecué," "Changó," " Ogun Badagri," "balele," "candombe," and "carabalí." The African element is, therefore, emphasized at the same level as the native one. It is especially significant how both lexicons are mixed within the poems suggesting this multicultural feature of the Caribbean: "Sombra blanca en el baquiné / tiene changó, tiene vodú. / Cuando pasa por el bembé / daña el quimbombó, daña el calalú" ["Lamento"] (1995: 122). At the same time the previous quotation would be almost incomprehensible for an ordinary Spaniard (like me) and this tells us much about Palés Matos's intention: he is "defamiliarizing" the Spanish language, creating a new literary language where the common Caribbean people can recognize themselves. This is a recurrent technique in postcolonial literatures, including Latin American literature. This is a means by which a new discourse is created, and, as Homi Bhabha points out, it is "a discourse at the crossroads of what is known and permissible and that which though known must be kept concealed; a discourse uttered between the lines and as such both against the rules and within them" (1994: 89).[5]

Palés Matos tries to africanize the Spanish literary language in many ways. He explores any resource to make his poems sound African. One of the most important of these resources is rhythm. He tries to imitate African rhythms and its special syncopated rhythm by distributing stresses along the sentence in such a way that they remind us of drumbeats. For example, in this stanza we can see how the last acute stresses combine with the previous ones to set a constant pattern which reminds us of beats that set the rhythm of the song: "Calabó y bambú / Bambú y Calabó / Es el sol de hierro que arde en Tombuctú / Es la danza negra de Fernando Poó / El alma africana que vibrando está / en el ritmo gordo del mariyanda" ["Danza Negra"]

(1995: 117). In the last sentence the stress pattern is quite consistent in the combination of stressed and unstressed syllables suggesting that repetition and at the same time alternation of stress: UUU / UUU / UUUUUU / UUUUUU / UUUUUU / UUUUUU.

It is also worth noticing the consistent use of acute accents at the end of every line, which helps us set a regularity within the apparently irregular syncopated rhythm. Besides, the insistence in the use of plosives and nasals also helps to set the rhythm. The combination and repetition of plosives imitates the drumbeats, while the nasals give the poem that musical quality so typical of African songs together with the predominant use of the vowels "u," "o," and "e," the two latter usually stressed: "Por la encendida calle antillana / va Tembandumba de la Quimbamba / Rumba, macumba, candombe, bámbula/ entre dos filas de negras caras. / Ante ella un congo gongo y maraca / ritma una conga bomba que bamba" ["Majestad Negra"] (1995: 127).

The use of these special rhythmic patterns functions as a breaking off with the regular patterns common in the canon of Hispanic literature. Therefore, we can say that the introduction of these apparently irregular rhythmic patterns of African origin suggests the possibility of renovation and new ways of expression in poetry that can give a more accurate sense of the Caribbean experience. This does not mean that the only way to renovation is in a movement back to Africa, but it encourages the awareness of exploitation of the different heritages and gives an original voice to Caribbean poetry. The message is that originality is possible even though this poetry is based on an imposed language—Spanish—to which this heritage is almost completely alien.

The use of onomatopoeias[6] and *jintanjáforas*[7] also suggests the possibilities of the creation of new poetic expressions by the new formation of acoustic effects inside the language. Some of these onomatopoeias are "tucutú," "tocco-tó," "prupruprú," "cro-cro-cró," ("Danza negra") "ñamñam," "co-co-quí," "Cúcurucu," "coquí, cocó, cucú, cacá" and "tumcutum." The *jintanjáfora* is another way to create words with a powerful musical component so that they can be passed off as real words. This may be especially the case with these apparently African nouns: "Mussumba, Tombuctú, Farafanga" ("Pueblo Negro"), "Manasa, Cumbalo, Bilongo," "Sosola, Babiro, Bombassa/ Yombofré, Bulón o Babissa ("Candombe"). It is also interesting to notice how word derivation can also help the poet to give that message of innovation, the creation of a new poetic language by inventing new words either coming from nowhere or derived from another word. Here are some examples: ñáñigo "ñañiguear" (verb), "culipandear" (verb), "Kalahari," and "obsede." We should not forget that his poetry is full of new and striking images that once again suggest the necessity for an innovative way to describe and speak about the Caribbean. Therefore, we can find extensive, amazing combinations of adjectives and nouns: "Humean, rojas de calor, las piedras," "luz rabiosa" ("Pueblo Negro"), "mermelada de oraciones" ("Ñáñigo al Cielo"), "hedionda luz amarilla," "luna podrida" ("Candombe"), "sol de hierro," and "ritmo gordo" ("Danza Negra").

All these features are part of the attempt at renovation that Palés Matos is suggesting in *Tuntún de pasa y griferia*. He uses this work as a personal artistic manifesto and a pan-Caribbean hymn.[8] Palés Matos's poetry is undoubtedly that breeze of fresh air that Caribbean poetry needed to speak with its own voice. His poetry is that new literary language born of the daily life but with a new flavor, a new musicality. The best image of this creation is embodied in the poem "Kalahari," in which the poet comes across a new word that stands for that part of himself and of the whole Caribbean that was hidden inside of him:

No sé por qué mi pensamiento a la deriva
fondeó en una bahía de claros cocoteros,
con monos, centenares de monos que trenzaban
una desordenada cadena de cabriolas.

¿Por qué ahora la palabra Kalahari?

Ha surgido de pronto, inexplicablemente...
¡Kalahari! ¡Kalahari! ¡Kalahari!
¿De dónde habrá surgido esta palabra
escondida como un insecto en mi memoria;
picada como una mariposa disecada
en la caja de coleópteros de mi memoria,
y ahora viva, insistiendo, revoloteando ciega
contra la luz ofuscadora del recuerdo?
¡Kalahari! ¡Kalahari! ¡Kalahari! (1978: 129)

Palés Matos is a pioneer within the *Negrista* movement, in his vision of the Mulatto Caribbean and in his recognition of a Caribbean cultural synthesis. This is especially important for a Puerto Rican poet since at that time a new nationalist ideal was starting to emerge. The pan-African consciousness displayed by Palés Matos and other intellectuals was helping to develop, as Antonio Benítez Rojo concludes, a new form of nationalism, one that considered Blacks, Whites, and Mulattos equally important within the collective space of the nation (1998: 360).[9] He feels the need for a new and more "authentic" poetic vocabulary to deal with this new description of the nation in literature. He belongs to a time and a social and cultural context that includes the demise of authority of older paradigms, which gives way to new perspectives on Puerto Rican identity.

Palés Matos has influenced the work of many Puerto Rican and Caribbean writers, and his influence is present not only in the work of island authors such as José Luis González, Luis Rafael Sánchez, Ana Lydia Vega, Rosario Ferré, and Edgardo Rodríguez Juliá, among others, but also many outstanding Puerto Rican authors in the United States such as Tato Laviera. Palés Matos' use of the figure of the Negro in his poetry illuminates the most forgotten and invisible aspects of the Caribbean soul whose African beats and rhythm penetrate in this way in the literature of Puerto Rico, the Caribbean, and North America. His great achievement is to redefine Puerto Rican national identity throughout its Afro-Caribbean character. His *negrismo* is an admirable attempt at rediscovering that marginalized history of Puerto Rico and the Caribbean, which can be traced back to Africa and which contributes to Caribbean syncretism. His work represents a more sincere alternative to official history, which silences the voices of people of color and therefore leaves aside one of the most important and distinctive constituents of the Caribbean.

The influence of the Afro-Antillean poetry of Luis Palés Matos, however, goes beyond the borders of the island. When asked about the influences that may have inclined him to be a writer Tato Laviera responds: "When I was 6, I studied under Juan Boria... He recited "Canción festiva para ser llorada," Luis Palés Matos's greatest poem. I think that was very important for me. Years later I wrote a poem, "don luis palés matos"... It's all in "black" language. It took me two years to write it. I wanted it to be the finest black poem in the history of Puerto Rico" (Hernández 1997: 79). Contemporary Puerto Rican authors in the United States like Tato Laviera are also deeply concerned about writing a similar history of the "other" Caribbean in the U.S. north and pay homage in their works to this vision of Caribbean unity and to the figure of the mulatta/o as the symbol of the defining synthesis of the Puerto Rican and subsequently of the whole Caribbean. Among some Nuyorican poets and especially in Tato Laviera's poetry, we frequently find a conscious attempt to rescue the rhythms of the mulatta/o as representative of a racially mixed people with a Caribbean heritage. He does not only look for his Puerto Rican roots solely in the *jíbaro* or in the national Creole elite but also and especially in the popular culture of the island, placing special emphasis on the African-based *bomba* and the *plena*. They are the precious inheritance of his ancestors who struggled to resist colonial oppression on the island in the same way Puerto Rican migrants fight against injustice and misery in the United States.

When comparing the social and political context of the work of both poets, we can also find some interesting parallels: whereas Palés Matos was addressing the African heritage to appeal for a multiple but unifying racial conception of the Caribbean, Tato Laviera tries to do something very similar with African and Caribbean elements for the Latino and Puerto Rican communities in the United States, where racial tensions and discrimination further complicate the development and assertion of a new identity after migration. Laviera, as Luis Palés Matos had done before, finds in the African component a new source of vitality and creativity, the possibility for something new that fully makes justice to the history of his people.[10] This process of recovery of a cultural and racial past is something very common among Puerto Rican writers (and also other ethnic writers) in the United States who go back to Puerto Rican cultural heritage in order to understand themselves and be able to describe the new Puerto Rican/Nuyorican identity. In this process the indigenous and African heritage gain relevance as Juan Flores perceptively points out:

> The racism encountered in the U.S. impels the Nuyorican even
> more resolutely toward the Taíno and Afro-Caribbean background,
> which constitutes the major thematic reference point and expressive
> resource in Puerto Rican culture in the U.S. It is the colonized within
> the colony whom the Nuyoricans identify as their real forebears in the
> national tradition, a continuity which is readily evident in much of the
> music, poetry and art, and in many aspects of daily life. (1993: 189)

For Tato Laviera the recognition of a Puerto Rican heritage also implies a critical revision of this national heritage from the perspective and experience of migration. After migration Puerto Ricans have to face a different racial classification in the United States. Many Puerto Ricans suffer a severe shock once they realize they are now simply Black for Americans, even though they were never so fully aware of skin color back on the island. This idea is masterfully exposed in the poem "negrito" from the collection *AmeRícan* describing the first words the poet hear on U.S. soil:

su tía le agarró
la mano y le dijo,
"no te juntes con
los molletos, negrito".
el negrito
se miró sus manos
y le dijo,
"pero titi, pero titi,
así no es puerto rico."
....
nueva york lo saludó,
y le dijo,
"confusión." (1985: 41)

His aunt is clearly trying to avoid the fact that his nephew is associated with a racial group that has suffered greater racial and social discrimination in the United States than on the island. At the same time, the new situation makes the young Tato to be aware of the implications of racial classification and identification: he knows that he is as black as other African-Americans, but there are different perceptions of race between the U.S. and Puerto Rico. Thus, his aunt wants to emphasize his belonging to a cultural identity as Puerto Rican rather than a racial one because she knows what being black means in the U.S. The experience of discrimination because of their skin color leads Laviera and other Nuyoricans to become very critical with the "official" version of the national culture and national identity in both places. Laviera realizes it is necessary to consider all versions of it by recovering the oral culture of the popular working classes.

Because Spanish is the popular language used at home and with friends and relatives, it needs to be introduced in any literary expression about Puerto Ricans in the United States as a symbol of their island culture and a symbol of survival. The presence of Spanish is everywhere in Laviera's transcultural work: poems written entirely in Spanish, scattered Spanish words in a poem written mainly in English and finally poems written in Spanglish. Bilingual poetry and Spanish are already present in Laviera's first poetry collection, *La Carreta Made a U-Turn* (1979) which is a clear response to a hallmark in the national literature about the Puerto Rican migration, *La carreta* (1991 [1953]) by René Marqués. This play deals with migration from the island, and it portrays the hardships Puerto Ricans face in New York and their return to the island. Marqués describes the experience of migration as a process of cultural loss and individual degradation, but Laviera opposes this vision in his work, where the "oxcart" does not come back to the island but stays in New York,[11] implying that Puerto Rico is not the necessary final destination for the salvation of the migrant. Puerto Rico is the geographical and metaphorical place where they can find and understand the historical roots of migration and the problem of a national definition that had been previously imposed by the elite to which René Marques belonged.

Although *La Carreta Made a U-Turn* does denounce the miserable situation of Puerto Ricans in El Barrio, the book is not filled with anger; on the contrary, and most especially in its third section "el nuevo rumbón," it becomes a return to the roots of his Afro-Caribbean heritage that is incorporated in the urban setting of El Barrio. In Laviera's search, Luis Palés Matos' poetry becomes the Latin American literary equivalent of what he tries to do in the present and in a very different time and context. A transcultural process takes place, by which the African elements and a new language are necessarily introduced in the literature of the "new Puerto Ricans" in the context of the northern barrios. Laviera's collection seems at times contradictory as it represents the reaffirmation of the migrant who is in the United States to stay and also the coming back to the cultural and racial roots. As Juan Flores remarks, "One of the many ironies about *La Carreta Made a U-Turn* is that it is indeed, a return to Puerto Rico" (1993: 171). While this return is more spiritual rather than physical, *La Carreta Made a U-Turn* can be considered Laviera's most "Caribbean" collection and a first step in his own development as a Nuyorican poet.[12]

Tato Laviera, like many other Latino/a authors, writes a literature of survival and cultural resistance through his "tropicalizing" poetry. He needs to address the situation of mainland Puerto Ricans from a Nuyorican perspective, revisioning Puerto Rican national identity and challenging official attempts at cultural assimilation. The influence of Latin American culture and history is underestimated or misinterpreted by mainstream ideology and its assimilationist assumptions. Migration and life in the U.S. has changed Puerto Ricans and transformed them into something different. Yet they are still full of possibilities, and still Puerto Rican. They are a people with a Caribbean heritage that integrates African, indigenous, Spanish, and other European elements. In Tato Laviera's poetry non-European elements are especially relevant as symbols of cultural and ethnic revival and resistance,[13] and, as in Palés Matos' poetry, they also prove to be powerful tools for innovation and artistic creativity not only in literature but also in music and all arts.

It is at this point where tropicalization becomes central since it functions as a strategy of resistance to acculturation and as a statement of racial affirmation at the same time. Originally coined by Puerto Rican poet Víctor Hernández Cruz in his book *Tropicalization* (1976),[14] the term is used to define a set of cultural and literary techniques that seek "to imbue a particular space, geography, group, or nation with a set of traits, images and values" (Aparicio and Chávez-Silverman 1997: 8). Tropicalization works within Laviera's poetry in two clear ways: on a formal level, through the oral tradition, Afro-Caribbean vocabulary and symbols introduce African elements from the cultural and racial heritage of Puerto Rico and the Caribbean and through bilingual poetry and the introduction of Spanglish as a new literary language. Laviera's poetry is full of imagery, vocabulary, and rhythm related to Africa, whose presence permeates the cadences of oral speech and street jargon.

Tato Laviera's work stands out as an example of a poetry coming from the daily "vital rhythm" Palés Matos used to talk about, but Laviera puts a special emphasis on Afro-caribbean music and oral tradition. The oral quality of the colloquial language penetrates his poetry, thus letting the reader "hear" street language. Tato Laviera's poetry collections *La Carreta Made a U-Turn* and *Enclave* are more strongly connected to the poet's insistence on establishing an Afro-Caribbean connection recovering the rhythm and tradition of Puerto Rican popular culture strongly grounded in an African tradition. For Laviera this connection is primordial because it shows the power of Afro-Caribbean roots and rhythm in the development of Puerto Rican identity in the United States. The oral tradition is extremely useful and a great artistic resource for Laviera, just as it was for Palés Matos, because the non-European cultural heritage he wants to recover belongs to the realm of oral culture. The oral tradition is the channel through which the creativity of common people has been transmitted from one generation to another. African slaves managed to maintain some of their original culture through the transmission of chants, songs, and folktales, which talked about the African element in the new world.

Afro-Caribbean music permeates many of his poems, whose rhythm is created out of repetitions and the use of African rhythms together with pauses that emphasize the thematic and formal variations. The presence of these rhythms can be clearly observed in most of Laviera's poetry collections, which include musical poems that recover the sounds and rhythm already present in the poetry of Luis Palés Matos. Music, as a fundamental element of oral popular culture of Puerto Rican life in the United States and the island, sets the rhythm within the poem and penetrates the literary production in the mainland, becoming a symbol of survival and the poetic soul of a people. As Félix Cortés, Angel Falcón, and Juan Flores comment: "Music served as a cohesive cultural force among the migrants, being a recognized form around which Puerto Ricans gathered in homes, hometown clubs and social events. The traditional rhythms became a tool of cultural survival, a carrier of national identity and unity against the opposing conditions" (1976: 126). Laviera is aware of the need to recognize the colonizer's language in literature, just as Palés Matos did in his poetry. Paying homage to the master, Tato Laviera acknowledges Palés Matos' role in the creation of a new poetic language that "Africanized" literary Spanish to describe the "other" Puerto Rico: "orgullos cadereando acentos al español/ conspiración engrasando ritmos pleneros/ a la lengua española pa ponerle sabor" (1981: 66). Drums and congas are relevant tropicalizing elements whose beats permeate most of Laviera's lines, as we can see in poems like "el moreno puertorriqueño (a three-way warning poem)," which reminds us of some of Palés Matos poems like "Danza negra," "Ñam-ñam," "Lamento," or "Majestad negra":

Qué voy a ser yo como moreno
puertorriqueño. preguntar
¿dónde está mi igualdad?
viendo novelas de morenos
esclavos, sin poder ver un
moreno en la pantalla. La

ay baramba bamba
suma acaba
quimbombo de salsa
la rumba matamba
ñam ñam yo no soy
de la masucamba

.....

Ñam ñam yo no soy
De la masucamba
Ñam ñam yo no soy
de la masucamba. (1979: 46)

Laviera is clearly rescuing the technique and sounds of the poetic language that Palés Matos used to give voice to the Afro-Caribbean presence in Puerto Rico. In New York, the Puerto Ricans' voice is similarly recovered through Laviera's celebration of Puerto Rican popular culture. Whereas Palés Matos addressed the figure of dark-skinned Puerto Ricans as the most creative elements in the Caribbean, Laviera appeals to the relevance of mainland Puerto Ricans as a people with a rich Afro-Caribbean heritage that is going to transform the American space. Palés Matos introduced African sounds and rhythms to transform "official" literary Spanish, and in a similar way Laviera attempts to tropicalize American literature through the recovery of Puerto Rican oral popular culture and the use of Spanglish as a literary language.

The oral quality of Laviera's poems in the last section of *La Carreta Made a U-Turn*, where Spanish predominates, also constitutes an element of cultural rediscovery. Even though this last section is supposed to be about Puerto Ricans who stay in New York (instead of coming back to the island as in René Marqués' *La carreta*), it is at the same time a group of poems dedicated to Puerto Rican cultural heritage as it survives in the "tropicalized" space of New York. The content elements for this tropicalization are many: congas and the *rumbón* ("the new rumbón"), Puerto Rican food and smells ("savorings, from piñones to loíza"), Puerto Rican's dark-skinned color reflections ("el Moreno puertorriqueño—a three-way warning poem"), summer warmth ("summer wait"), *tumbao*'s rhythm ("tumbao [for eddie conde"]), *congueros* ("summer congas," "orchard beach y la virgin del Carmen"), salsa ("the salsa of Bethesda fountain"), *bombas* ("canción para un parrandero"), *décimas* ("la música jíbara"), orality ("doña cisa y su anafre"), *santería* ("santa bárbara"), *plena* dancing ("coreografía"), and the memory of poet and activist Felipe Luciano ("felipe luciano I miss you in africa"), of Cuban Pedro Morejón ("the africa in pedro morejón"), of Ismael Rivera ("el sonero mayor"), and of Jorge Brandon ("declamación").

All these elements are from Puerto Rico or from Puerto Rican culture in the United States, and they all carry a strong connection to the African heritage for Puerto Ricans who are now in the United Sates, thus proving the importance of cultural resistance and affirmation in the new context. Laviera is trying to acknowledge the importance of them in Puerto Rican identity in the United States as opposed to what René Marqués was trying to suggest in *La carreta*. Nuyoricans do not intend to come back to the island or to a previous version of Puertoricanness but they will stay in the mainland fighting acculturation through the survival of these cultural references—Puerto Rican identity is now a much more complex issue, requiring a revision and reaffirmation of a cultural and racial past. The revision is as important as it was for the African element in Luis Palés Matos's attempt to redefine the Afro-Caribbean qualities of Puerto Rico.

Most of these poems are predominately written in Spanish, a language that is present in all Laviera's poetry collections, reminding the reader that Spanish is alive for the bicultural self. As Frances Aparicio comments, the words in Spanish "function as 'conjuros,' as ways of bringing back an original, primordial reality—Puerto Ricanness" (1998: 149). Spanish taken from daily conversations and from family contexts have strong psychological implications for the migrant. For instance, the oral tradition is kept alive through the practice of story-telling, which has been transmitted especially by women. The poem "ay bendito" from the collection *AmeRícan* (1985) is a clear example of orality, street language, and popular culture becoming poetic language in the words of typical Puerto Rican or Nuyorican gossip. Words from a common conversation among women in the street are enough to transcend the paper, recover the language and feelings from the people, and offer the reader the real sounds of oral Spanish:

> ¡ay, madre!
> ¡ay, Dios mío!
> ¡ay, Dios santo!
> ¡me da una pena!
> Ay, sí la vida es así, oiga.

Pero, ¿qué se puede hacer?
Nada, ¿verdad?
Fíjese, oiga, fíjese.
Oiga, fíjese. (1981: 45)

This poem brings center stage one of the bases of popular culture and a precious oral heritage for Puerto Ricans. The emotions and world visions of a people are reflected in this type of street community language. In the section "values" and "nuyoricans" of *Enclave* (1981), Tato Laviera takes us again to the street sounds and rhythms, focusing on an oral tradition that consolidates the idea of community as a site of resistance and relief. Some poems are oral portraits of Puerto Rican characters like "ay, bendito," "pai," "pana," "criollo story," "craqueao," "esquina dude," "enchulá," and "m'ija": "i've been dying to call you m'ija / to tell you that last night i was / celebrating nothing, nothing to do/ no money, no dress, nobody, m'ija, / un tremendo down, life is hard, even / on my birthday, eso te ha pasao a tí / también, verdad" (1985: 62). The importance of oral speech culminates in the concluding title poem "AmeRícan," which presents a substitute for "Nuyorican." "AmeRícan" plays with the spelling of the controversial word 'American' (in contrast to the Spanish/hemispheric word "americano") and the pronunciation of "I'm a Rican" in colloquial language. The typography is unusual: capital "A" for 'I' and capital "R" to emphasize the Spanish pronunciation of the letter "r" followed by the "í" with the accent make sure the effect of the mixture of languages as a symbol for Puerto Rican identity, blending the Afro-Caribbean heritage with the U.S. experience: "AmeRícan, defining myself my own way any way many / ways Am e Rícan, with the big R and the / accent on the í!" (1985: 95). These word games and tropicalizing techniques, which attempt to attract the reader's attention towards the multiple influences of a transcultural community, such Puerto Ricans in the United States, parallel Luis Palés Matos' use of defamiliarizing terms and phonetic spellings of African words in his poetry. They are both creating a poetic language whereby Puerto Ricans can recognize themselves and their complex, empowering heritage.

Laviera's indebtedness to Palés Matos is fairly explicit in some of his poems in *La Carreta Made a U-Turn* (1979), whose oral quality and rhythm resemble that evoked in Palés Mato's poetry. However, the rhythm is now talking about a different place far from the Caribbean. This space is influenced and produces new rhythms but is still impregnated by the ancestral rhythm, as we can observe in poems like "the new rumbón," "orchard beach y la virgen del carmen," "el sonero mayor," or "tumbao":

> tucutú pacutú   tucutú pacutú
> tucutú pacutú   tucutú pacutú
> ....
> pito que pita
> yuca que llama
> salsa que emprende
> llanto que llora
> última llamada sin fuego
> tumba que le tamba
> tumba que la bamba baja
> que pacheco se inspira
> que ismael la canta
> oh! y el baquiné
> ....
> and the park those ghetto parks
> the living-room-kitchen
> of many desperate souls
> tumbao movements
> street gutted salsa (1979: 49)

The Afro-Caribbean rhythm is expressed through repetitions, pauses, and recurrent rhythmic patterns in much the same way Palés Matos did. These rhythms are still present in the new space, but the recovery of an African heritage is not uncritical. The African roots have evolved in the new land and have merged with other racial and cultural elements, but the roots are everywhere:

> yes. we preserved what was originally african,
> or have we expanded it? i wonder if we have
> committed the sin of blending? but I also hear
> that AFRICANS love electric guitars clearly mis-
> understanding they are the root. (1979: 43)

Though somehow transformed, the African elements remain and combine with other elements as important factors in the new creation of a transcultural identity or a "tremendous continental 'MIXTURAO,'" as Laviera explains in his most recent collection (2008a: 29).

Afro-Caribbean rhythm and Black urban speech intonation are underlying elements in Spanish and English. Oral tradition and oral speech from mulattas/ os and "morenos/as" become central in the formation of the poetic voice. It is the voice of the common people transmitted through the pan-Antillean rhythm that we found in Palés Matos's poetry, which now becomes a powerful bond that extends over the Caribbean to embrace a whole race. The tropics are coming to the U.S. and are here to stay. Africa and the Caribbean is everywhere, taking many forms, constantly changing and evolving as the times change as well. Salsa is just one of the great products of the evolution and contact of different Afro-Caribbean rhythms in the new world. As a product of transculturation the salsa exemplifies how the African heritage permeates the present experience of Puerto Ricans through their music and rhythms: "the internal feelings we release / when we dance salsa / is the song of manu dibango / screaming africa" (1979: 53-4). Salsa is a symbol for the new Puerto Ricans in the United States and for the multiple racial heritage that Laviera wants to celebrate and acknowledge—hence salsa becomes a celebration of blackness, in any language and in clear connection to ancient rhythms.

The relevance of music and Puerto Rican oral tradition as a way to reaffirm the African heritage in Laviera's poetry is further consolidated in *Enclave*. The title itself already becomes a play in words meaning Puerto Rico or the New York enclave of Puerto Ricans but also meaning the musical term "en clave" (clef). Musical forms like the *bomba* and the *plena* set the form and content of many poems like "olga pecho," "juana bochisme," "tito madera smith," "unemployment line," "juan boria,"[15] and "bomba, para siempre." This last poem, "bomba, para siempre" closes the collection with the recurrent connection between the music and Afro-Caribbean roots:

> bomba: bring in jazz, and meringue, blend africa:
> bomba: puerto rican history for always, national pride
> ....
> un negrito melodía he came along

improvising bomba drums on dancer's feet,
choral songs, sonero heat, snapping hands,
sweat at ease, melodía sang,
he sang like this:

se queda allí, se queda allí, se queda allí, es mi raíz
....

métele encima el jazz, el rock o fox trot inglesa,
la bomba se va debajo, ay virgen no hay quien la mueva. (1979: 68–9)

The *bomba* is a symbol for Puerto Rican culture, which stays alive and resists cultural and linguistic acculturation. The roots stay there underlying the linguistic surface as the poem starts in English but soon switches to Spanish. Laviera emphasizes the role of music as a way of cultural resistance and celebration of an African core, which remains after transculturation. As Stephanie Alvarez points out, "Laviera evidently indicates the importance of music before the word on the basis that Africans who came to the Caribbean were from many different areas of Africa and didn't speak the same language, and so their primary form of communication became music" (2006: 37). Just as Laviera is creating a transcultural product where the African roots surface, the African population did something similar, which Palés Matos celebrated for the first time in his poetry. In "Hacia una poesía antillana" (Palés Matos 1978) his comments on the Africans' power to resist acculturation surprisingly echo the concept of transculturation, exemplified in Laviera's poetry.[16] This recovery and transformation of the African heritage in his poetic language is similar to Palés Matos' attempts, and it becomes another transcultural production which creates a Caribbean connection between Latinos and African Americans. It is important to add "that through transculturation one can fight and heal the wounds from acculturaling forces" (Alvarez 2006: 39).

The role of language in the tropicalization process is actually another strong connection with Palés Matos since he was the first to introduce the sounds and rhythms of African people in "White" Spanish poetry. He is clearly feeling inspired by Palés Matos's use of poetic language to celebrate an African heritage that has been previously ignored—Palés Matos was the first poet not only to mention but also to celebrate the African heritage of the island. Laviera shares with other Latino/a and Puerto Rican writers like Ed Vega, Ernesto Quiñonez, and Judith Ortiz Cofer, among others, the conscious use and manipulation of language in their works. As Luis Palés Matos had done before with African words in a different historical and cultural context, Tato Laviera defamiliarizes the literary language using both Spanish and English interchangeably, but especially using Spanglish as a challenging new literary language that best represents the Caribbean experience in the United States. A recurrent and already traditional technique to defamiliarize the English language is the use of foreign words and phrases that appear in the English text and that may become disturbing factors when their use renders the reading. Laviera himself warns the reader in the poem "barrio (forenglishonly)": "el ingles / se deforma / con el / calor de / tu cultura" (1988: 4).

When Laviera writes poems in English, it is not Standard English but a "re-territorialized" English or a new variety coming from a particular people with a Caribbean heritage. Standard English is manipulated so that it becomes impregnated by a cultural and linguistic Afro-Hispanic substratum. What at first sight may look like lack of linguistic competence is, in fact, creative and innovative experimentation with literary language. As Frances Aparicio points out, tropicalizations provide "new possibilities for metaphors, imagery, syntax, and rhythms that the Spanish subtext provide U.S. literary English" (Aparicio and Chávez-Silverman 1997: 203). The rhythm from Puerto Rican and Caribbean music permeates the literary language, thereby becoming the real artistic language on a higher level than Spanish or English: "sometimes i think africa / is all of us in music, / musically rooted way way back / before any other language" ["the africa in pedro morejón"] (1979: 43). It doesn't matter if he writes in English or Spanish; the rhythm and the beat are there at the core.

Laviera's poetry is written in English, Spanish, in both languages, and in Spanglish because for the poet none of them can be enough on its own. He never forgets to pay tribute to both Spanish and English because they represent two important cultural traditions and they are also symbols of the political history of Puerto Ricans. The community of Puerto Ricans on North American soil speaks both Spanish and English but also Spanglish, and even though some may consider it a linguistic aberration, Spanglish is the language of the people on the street. It is another way of expression for the community and is equally valid as a literary language. Already in the poem "my graduation speech" from *La Carreta Made a U-Turn,* Laviera brings attention to the language conflict within the Puerto Rican migrant community:

> i think in spanish
> i write in english
> ....
> tengo las venas aculturadas
> escribo en spanglish
> ....
> english or spanish
> spanish or english
> spanenglish
> now, dig this:
>
> hablo lo inglés matao
> hablo lo español matao
> no sé leer ninguno bien
>
> so it is, spanglish to matao
> what i digo
>   ¡ay, virgen, yo no sé hablar! (1979: 7)

This poem introduces the reader into the linguistic diversity within the collection as a clear representation of the Puerto Rican community. Laviera directly confronts the issue of language as a problem affecting Puerto Ricans everywhere and also creating a distance and a tension between Puerto Ricans from the island and on the mainland as it is described in the poem "brava" in *AmeRícan* (1981). The poetic voice is a Mulatta proud of being Puerto Rican, multicultural and multilingual:

> tú sabes que yo soy that
> i am puertorriqueña in
> english and there's nothing
> you can do but to accept
> it como yo soy sabrosa
> ....
> go ahead, ask me, on any street-

corner that I am not puertorriqueña,
come dímelo aquí en mi cara
offend me, atrévete, a menos
que tu no quieras que yo te meta
un tremendo bochinche de soplamoco
pezcozá that's gonna hurt you
in either language. (1981: 63)

These poems present a situation that seems to be very difficult for Puerto Ricans in New York. They seem to be lost with no languages, but at the same time the very language used in the poem suggests that this very "disparate" language is the most appropriate one. This new language resembles that "Kalahari" found in Palés Matos: a new poetic language that more accurately represents the experience of a forgotten part of a people. These lines from *Enclave* express the relationship between the people and language "la vida es un inglés frío / un español no preciso / un spanglish disparatero" ["abandoned buildings"] (1981: 33). It is a language of a people that is not Puerto Rican as before and not American either, but a hybrid product coming from the Caribbean and mixing with the many cultures within North America.[17]

Tato Laviera's poetry is a fantastic amalgamation of Afro-Caribbean, European, and United States elements. His poetry speaks about and for the people in a new literary language, which comes from the people and at the same time is a connection to the ancestors. Like the word "Kalahari" for Palés Matos, it was "escondida como un insecto en mi memoria ... y ahora viva, insistiendo, revoloteando" (1978: 129). The African word, with its sounds and rhythm evoking ancient times, comes back to the present and becomes a rich ingredient in Laviera's poetry. It pays homage to Palés Matos's contribution to a celebration of the African component in Puerto Rican identity. But the rich *mestizaje*, whose ideology Palés Matos understood as "*antillanismo*," has evolved to a further developed concept of Afro-Caribbean identity in the United States. The African heritage present in the Puerto Rican community stays alive through the poetry of both authors as a sign of the richness and complexity of Puerto Rican racial and cultural identity. It becomes a connection full of possibilities while it challenges the historical and geographical distance between the extended Puerto Rican communities of the Island and the mainland.

NOTES

[1] Songs about Blacks and Mulattos.

[2] Mónica Mansour in her work *La poesía negrista* traces its origin to Luis Palés Matos's poetry: "La poesía negrista como movimiento literario fue inaugurada hacia 1926 por el puertorriqueño Luis Palés Matos y fue enriquecida por las aportaciones capitales de Nicolás Guillén, Emilio Ballagas, Regino Pedroso, Manuel del Cabral y sus seguidores" (1973: 9).

[3] See Julio Marzán's (1995) perceptive analysis of Palés Matos's work as *antipoetry*. Marzán states: "*poesía negra* must be understood in a broader context of the century, playing its part in literature as jazz had patently done in dance and music—and literature. In that dynamic, spontaneous jazz poems were also an antimatter that removes the white mask from an inherently mixed culture. Similarly, in an island that until the late 1950s excluded from public air waves the musical legacy from Africa—*plena, guaracha—poesía antillana* was to Palés a countercultural expression, an antipoetry" (1995: 517).

[4] Paul A. Davis states that Palés Matos "was content with his stereotyped images, abounding in vacuous exoticism" (1979: 78), whereas Nicolas Guillén used to focus on the "real" black man.

[5] Similarly, Gilles Deleuze and Felix Guattari, in their analysis of minor literatures in Europe, argue that the first feature of this type of literature is the deterritorialization of the dominant language by a minority group whose language has been dismissed. Deleuze uses the example of Kafka, a Jewish writer in Prague, and describes his way to deterritorialize the German language: "One way is to artificially enrich this German, to swell it up through all the resources of symbolism, of onerism, of esoteric sense, of a hidden signifier.... Since the language is arid, make it vibrate with a new intensity. Oppose a purely intensive usage of language to all symbolic or even significant or simply signifying usages of it" (1986: 19).

[6] Onomatopoeias were the central elements in "Diepalism," a movement named after the surnames of its creators, Luis Palés Matos and Juan de Diego Padró, who proposed a new onomatopoeic poetic language.

[7] As David Colón defines it, "*Jitanjáfora* is a term for the use of onomatopoeia in Spanish Afro-Caribbean poetry... to invoke an aesthetically Africanist sensibility into the poetic expression. ¡Mayombe-bombe-mayombé! Is sound poetry; although it is a visual presentation, it is of a phonetically induced sign. ¡Mayombe-bombe-mayombé! Does not look like African language, but to the *negristas*, it surely sounds like it" (2001: 277).

[8] It may be quite illuminating to listen to what Palés Matos himself declared about his ideas about aesthetic renovation and its implications on a more social and political level:

> El poeta tomará asunto para su arte de su propio ambiente, de la baraja de intereses y pasiones que le rodea, del ritmo vital en que se desenvuelve su pueblo, y estilizándolo a

golpes de gracia, de ironía y selección, le quitará pesadez y cotidianismo, que es como romper las estrechas fronteras regionales e intentar fortuna en espacios mas dilatados de universalidad, sin que se quiebre por ello la raíz viva que le sostiene adherido a su tradición y a su pueblo. (quoted in Díaz Quiñones 1982: 93).

[9] "En las Antillas hispánicas, donde una minoría negra era objeto de discriminación, la conciencia africanista sirvió para organizar una nueva forma de nacionalismo—sobre todo en Cuba—que buscaba colocar a blancos, negros y mulatos por igual dentro del espacio colectivo de la nación" (Benítez Rojo 1998: 390).

[10] Many critics have already pointed out the influence of Afro-American poetry of the sixties: "There are many elements characteristic of much new Puerto Rican poetry which were clearly drawn from the Afro-American poetry of the period of 'Black Power' and the democratic, nationalist organization in the Black community. Such elements include the militant tone of anger and struggle, the declamatory and musical quality of the presentation, the street imagery of Black youth and culture . . . " (Cortes, Falcón and Flores 1976:144). However, we want to emphasize the influence that comes directly from the Caribbean *poesía negrista* inaugurated by Luis Palés Matos as it has been somehow underestimated by the American academia.

[11] In an interview Tato Laviera confirms his intention when writing *La Carreta Made a U-Turn*: "In *La Carreta Made a U-Turn* I bastardized the most sacred Puerto Rican book... Yo también tengo tres secciones. He began in *la montaña* and continues in San Juan, and then goes to the metropolis. I began in *la montaña* and instead of ending in the Island, I make a U-Turn and go to *el arrabal*, into the streets of Loisaida" (Luis 1992: 1028).

[12] In later works such as *Enclave* (1981), *AmeRícan* (1985), and *Mainstream Ethics* (1988), Laviera develops what Frances A. Aparicio defines as "an ontology of America," and "proposes a reconceptualization of the term America" starting from "a new pan-Latino identity," (1993: 29) and finally embracing many other ethnic groups.

[13] For further inquiry into this topic see Alvarez (2006).

[14] For Victor Hernández Cruz, the tropicalization process allows him to transform the poetic language into something strange for the Anglo reader as it is defamiliarized by the images and signifieds from a Latin American culture. The linguistic pun and the intrusion of objects and images alien to the American landscape allows the creation of a defamiliarized world within the Barrio and the urban space, which is consequently transformed and permeated by Puerto Rican rhythms, traces, and values.

[15] For Tato Laviera it is important to recognize the influence of people like Juan Boria, Felipe Luciano, Jorge Brandon, or Pedro Morejón. For instance, Juan Boria was a great influence as transmitter of a "negrista" poetry by Luis Palés Matos or Nicolas Guillén.

[16] "El nuevo medio puede resultar hostil a la cultura dominante y favorable, por el

contrario, a la dominada. O pueden los hombres de esta última, por sutiles tácticas de su subconsciente colectivo o simplemente para subsistir, adoptar el tren de las formas y representaciones de la primera e infiltrar paulatinamente en dichas formas su propio espíritu modificándolas con tan corrosiva eficacia que den pábulo al nacimiento de una actitud cultural nueva. Ese es a mi juicio, el caso de las Antillas" (Palés Matos 1978: 239).

[17] As Miguel Algarín states in what can be considered the "*Nuyorican* Manifesto," their poetry emerges from a new language that embraces the Caribbean and North America represented in the two languages that form their heritage: "The conflicts are many. Languages are struggling to possess us; English wants to own us completely; Spanish wants to own us completely. We have mixed them both" (1981: 90).

–V–
TESTIMONIO

Tato in His Own Words— A Collaborative Testimonio

TATO LAVIERA and STEPHANIE ALVAREZ

Introduction

Tato Laviera often proclaimed that very few of his poems were autobiographical. But many who knew him well disputed that claim. Nevertheless, as a poet and playwright, Laviera in many ways could be considered a *testimionalista* in the Latin American sense of the literary genre. After all, he loved what he calls "characters." His poems and plays were often based on real-life "characters" of his many communities. "*Testimonio* has been critical in movements for liberation in Latin America, offering an artistic form and methodology to create politicized understandings of identity and community" (The Latina Feminist Group 2001: 3). While the *testimonio* is a genre in its own right, from his first poem Laviera was aware of documenting the world that unfolded before him. The first words of Laviera's first poem, "para ti, mundo bravo," of his first collection of published poetry, *La Carreta Made a U-Turn*, states: "in the final analysis / i am nothing but a historian / who took your actions / and jotted them on paper" (1979: 13). Since Laviera's own poetry provided a *testimonio* of Nuyorican life, it is only fitting that we share his own testimony. After all, as Delgado Bernal, Burciaga, and Carmona remind us "As a process, *testimoniar* (to give testimony) is the act of recovering... One's *testimonio* reveals an epistemology of truths and how one has come to understand them. *Testimonio* bridges or serves to connect generations of displaced and disenfranchised communities across time" (2012: 364–5).

Testimonio is also allowing the subject to speak. The collaborative *testimonio* presented here was constructed through an arduous process. Alvarez collected all of Laviera's published interviews: Luis (1992), Hernández (1997), Martínez Diente (2006), Ochoa (2009), and Alvarez, Luis and Ochoa (2010). However, all of the questions were deleted so that the reader could hear Tato speak in his own voice. When there were instances in which the same experience or information appeared in more than one interview, the interview in which it was first published was used. Alvarez wove the interviews together to create a cohesive and coherent narrative that traces Laviera's life as well as his artistic influences, development, and theories. In addition, Laviera reviewed the *testimonio*, provided feedback, filled in gaps, and corrected errors.

Alvarez uses the term "collaborative *testimonio*" a term coined by Aída Hurtado,[1] to refer to the work of various individuals. To begin with there are the questions of the interviewers, Laviera's own telling of his experiences and ideas, and Alvarez own intervention and consultation with the poet. As Hurtado (2014) explains, in these cases where the *testimonialista*'s articulations are combined with the skills, experiences, and views of the *testimonialista*'s work "I'm not sure that '*testimonio*' alone is viable. Simultaneously, you need a "researcher," or perhaps more accurately a "collaborator" to manage, organize, conceptualize, and carry out the project at all levels." Hurtado asserts that "through the process of doing this, you are also 'testifying' because your own experience is in the mix of creating the new product—hence the name 'collaborative testimonio'." Using such a term allows us to address issues of authorship regarding *testimonios* in which a question persist: "although the pre-selected witnesses appear to speak in the first-person, who is actually in control of their words? Who is the author?" (Volex 1997).

While Laviera was charismatic and not known to be shy by any means, he was very private about personal matters. With his impending illness, we felt it was important to allow Laviera to speak in his own words. The task of publishing the *testimonio* became even more urgent with his death. In many ways, the purpose of this collaborative *testimonio* is "telling to live" as articulated by the Latina Feminist Group (2001). The collaborative testimonio was (re)constructed to allow Tato's life experiences to live in his own words. Finally, we should remember "fundamentally, however, the objective of *testimonio* includes the knowledge that reflection and speaking lead, eventually, to liberation" (Blackmer Reyes and Curry Rodríguez 2012: 527). I clearly remember when William Luis, Edna Ochoa and I interviewed Laviera in Reinosa, México, on the other side of the US border. At the conclusion of our interview Laviera emphatically states: "*ya, me despojé*." We are grateful to have a record of his *despojos* and we now present them to the greater public.

NOTES

[1] Hurtado has been developing the concept of "collaborative testiomonios" over the last couple of years while working on two projects; re-interviewing respondents from her book *Voicing Chicana Feminisms: Young Women Speak Out on Sexuality and Identity*. (2003), and a project where she is constructing the history of Chicanas/os that attended the University of Michigan from the 1970s to the 1980s.

I. Early Years.

I was born in Santurce, Puerto Rico. I'm a true Cangrejero. I was born in 1950, in the midst of the boot and the strap during the springtime of the Commonwealth. I was born during the era of Rafael Cortijo y su combo and Ismael Rivera who used to work for my father. My house was in the heart of Santurce, at Bella Vista Street, number 329. Father Junquera, from Sacred Heart parish, baptized me. My mother was very religious. I had to go to Mass at 6:00 A.M. every Sunday. My father, Pablo Laviera, was a contractor. He helped build the first Tartak furniture store near Stop 24. He also worked out on the island. In Cayey, he worked on the first public housing constructed in that town. This was 1954. Later, he also helped in the construction of University Garden's urbanization. I remember I used to write up his payroll when I was 4 years old.

My sister is Ruth Sánchez. She's considered a great beautician. She used to do Celia Cruz's hair. She is a true matriarch, the strength of the family. She's like a tree in the center of my family, and I am the strongest branch. My first thoughts are of sounds, music, and words associated with a place I used to go to every Sunday called Piñones. I was born during the era of Rafael Cortijo y su combo and Ismael Rivera. I used to write jingles, especially around Christmas. I went to school when I was 2 years old. My mother put me in a private school. So when I went to public school, I got skipped from the first to the third grade. When I was young, I always won prizes for good behavior, for religion class, and for interest in my studies. But then afterwards I became corrupted. After public school I went to Padre Berrio's where I completed the third grade. In the fourth grade, I went to Cantera, Padre Celestiano in San Juan Bosco, a very well-known school in Puerto Rico. At San Juan Bosco there were attendance cards, and I was put in charge of them. But the students who didn't come to school bribed me. They gave me fruit, gum, bananas, whatever. I was an altar boy from the time I was six, a very good altar boy, and then my family left for New York City in 1960.

We came on July 2, 1960, when I was 9 years old. My mother told me, when I was still Jesus Laviera Sánchez, "*Negrito, vamos para el aeropuerto*" because my sister was eight or nine months pregnant. She was the girlfriend of the leader of a very important gang, Las Calaveras, from Castro Viñas Street. So my mother left without telling my father. He did not know she was pregnant. My mother wanted my sister to give birth in New York City, away from my father's anger. My niece was born

27 days afterward. I didn't know I was coming. When I came here, I didn't know what New York was. The Lavieras never migrated. Only two women came because of different reasons. My father's side of the family had come from rich blacks who migrated to Puerto Rico from Maracaibo, Venezuela. They settled in Canóvanas, which they preferred to Loíza because there were too many poor blacks in Loíza. And when I left my house, I didn't know I was coming to the United States.

I was on the plane and I had vivid images, which I included in the poem called "negrito," in *AmeRícan* [1985]. Once on the plane, I thought the U.S. was all white, and I was scared I'd be the only Black person going there. I was totally terrified when the plane was landing. And in my poem called "negrito," I say:

> el negrito
> vino a Nueva York
> Vio Milagros
> en sus ojos
> su tía le pidió
> un abrazo y le dijo,
> "no te juntes con
> los prietos, negrito" (1985: 41)

My uncle used to work in the airport, so my family came to meet me by the plane. When I came down from the plane, I saw these Black people and I felt good. But my tía política grabbed my hand and said: "No te juntes con los prietos, negrito." It was the first thing that I was told and here I'm thinking that there weren't going to be any Black people around. I responded: "Pero Titi." And she said: "No te juntes con los moyetos, negrito." "Pero Titi." "Si los cocolos te molestan, corre y si te agarran, baila." That was my first welcome to New York. Nueva York me saludó y me dijo "confusión." My family proceeded to take me to the Williamsburgh [Brooklyn] area, which is all Black, and so my whole image changed; I didn't know what was going on. First I thought everyone was all white and then my tía me dice eso and proceeded to take me to an all Black area. I was totally shocked. Plus, I didn't know I was coming here and after six years my life was totally transformed.

Becoming a Poet

Empecé como poeta cuando era joven porque me encantaba cambiar la lírica de las canciones. No me gustaba la letra y yo quería imponerle mis propios detalles pero fueron con unos autores de música de Puerto Rico, como Rafael Hernández, Pedro Flores y Silvia Rexach porque me encantaba esa letra puertorriqueña de llantillo de jíbaro; y también yo crecí dentro de los ritmos pleneros caribeños de la bomba y la plena puertorriqueña que viene del español pero tiene el negro al fondo de los ritmos. Todas las navidades hacían lo que se llama parrandas navideñas que iban de casa a casa con música y a mí me encantaba eso. Cuando me transferí a Estados Unidos, ese ambiente cultural se mantuvo. La familia mía vivía en estos vecindarios donde había poetas de la isla de Puerto Rico que hablaban totalmente en español y a mí me encantaba ese sonido del declamador. La poesía de ellos es lo que se llama oral poetry, pero los fundadores fueron esos declamadores puertorriqueños y boricuas que hablaban exclusivamente en español y tenían eso de que hacían las mejores poesías de Latinoamérica y ellos eran los que propagaban esa difusión lingüística. Eso existía en el pueblo donde nosotros vivíamos. Y de ese llanto, pues de declamación de pararnos en la esquina y declamar en español, es lo que yo cogí de ese estímulo de poder escribir mis letras.

I remember when I was four or five years old that my brother and my sister went to una demostración en el Hotel Normandie en Puerto Rico, en San Juan, porque había un grupo que se llamaba Cortijo y su Combo que eran negros, y fueron el grupo más popular que ha dado la isla de Puerto Rico en términos de música de su tiempo, y como eran negros no los dejaban entrar a tocar en los hoteles en San Juan, la capital, y yo me recuerdo escaparme de los cinco baños de la casa mía que eran a dos millas y me perdí buscando a mis hermanos y hermanas, y esa paliza que me dieron... Me dieron cuarto palizas por todos los lados y una vieja que me vio me dijo, "¿ves?, por estar detrás de la contra bomba que te gusta negrito" y me dieron por todos lados. Por entonces yo me metía a un sitio que se llamaba Piñones, el sitio donde se cayó el avión de Roberto Clemente y quedó un area que en ese tiempo no tenía carreteras y tenía muchas tienditas que freían alcapurrias y ahí yo me iba a escuchar ese ritmo, y también me gustaban las canciones populares de muchos compositors, que estaban "muy calientes" como decimos nosotros, y esa cosa del ritmo con el lenguaje de canciones me inspiraban a mí a re-escribir las canciones que no me gustaban, y de chiquito las ponía mi ritmo y empecé escribiendo lo que ahora se dice jingles, y me recuerdo que las Navidades yo siempre tenía uno y me inventaba unos ritmos populares como unos coros, y después it was made longer.

If I wouldn't have come to the States, I would have been the governor of Puerto Rico. There's no doubt in my mind about that. When I first came to this country and went to school, my teacher was a nun who had left the order but was still teaching there. When I was in fifth grade, I told her my name was Jesús Laviera Sánchez. And she said I couldn't be Jesús because I was black, and I didn't know any English. From then on, they omitted my name, Jesús. I immediately became Abraham. So in May of 1960 I was Jesús Laviera Sánchez, and in September, three months afterward, when I started classes here, I was Abraham Laviera. That affected me a lot. That's when I decided to be a writer, to go back to my name. When I became a writer, I said, "I don't want to be either Jesús or Abraham"; I used my nickname, Tato, the name my brother Pablo gave me. That's what made me a writer, that moment when they took away my name, Jesús. As a Nuyorican, Puerto Rican, Boricua poet, I needed to write the greatest English poem as a challenge. So I did it: the poem that defines me is "Jesús Papote."

The first poem I wrote was "even then he knew," of *La Carreta Made a U-Turn* [1979]. An incredible thing happened. I was sick y estaba con la curandera, Pura, me estaba haciendo una limpieza and there was a building they were fixing across the street from where I was living, on 7th street. I was very ill that day y vi por la ventana un negrito sentado descalzo en un edificio abandonado. And this kid, I called him Papote, was sitting on the steps of the building at 1 o'clock when I came out; he was sitting there at 3 o'clock when I came out again. I looked out the window at 5 o'clock and he was there; él estaba descalzo. I looked at him and then me cogió pena. I said: "Mira, espera allí." I went to get him a sandwich and a soda. I came down the stairs, and when I went out he was gone. He was there for five hours. So I went and sat on the stairs and wrote my poem about that kid en la bolsita en dónde estaba el sandwich. And this great Puerto Rican painter, que ahora es dueño de una montaña, came by. I read him the poem and inspired him so much that he came back with a painting three hours later. It was right there that "papote sat on the stoop... and he decided to go no where." Entonces, yo subí, se lo enseñé a la curandera y ella me dijo que eso era un espíritu que había venido y que yo no podía ver ese espíritu más porque mira lo que es la suerte, después ella fue abajo y me trajo uno de esos libros de record donde uno pone accounting y me lo regaló y me dijo llénalo. Y ahí fue que ese poema se volvió en una pintura, que la señora me dio el libro y ese poema que se llamaba "even then he knew", y ahí fue donde empezó mi carrera como poeta. That was the calling. It was a concrete calling and there it emerged. This happened in July, 1965.

Después llené muchos cuadernos y escribía. Yo enseñaba, y tenía mi propio programa de enseñar a los muchachos. Después de la escuela venían a mí y yo les enseñaba a escribir su tarea de homework y así les enseñaba a todos. Los tenía en un programa comunitario y a los dieciséis años fui director de una escuela que se llamaba Universidad de la Calle y tenía programa de coger a los muchachos a terminar el GED o sea el equivalente de la escuela superior y tenía una clase de college prep. Aquéllos que ya habían pasado el equivalente que querían ir al colegio yo tenía un programa de transición y era en una universidad que se llamaba Rutgers, en New Jersey. Se estaba graduando la primera clase de estudiantes de una universidad que se llamaba Livingston College que surgió de los riots de Newark en New Jersey. Entonces, la Universidad de Rutgers decidió crear un colegio para ayudar a estos muchachos de Newark para ir a la escuela porque se estaban graduando de los cuatro años y no sabían escribir. No encontraban a nadie que podía ayudar a estos muchachos y me escogieron a mí, era estudiante de primer año del colegio y de momento yo soy maestro de basic writing, recursos básicos de escribir, en el Departamento de Inglés de Livingston College. Para mi comunidad eso fue una hazaña, eso fue lo más grande de la comunidad. Yo recién entraba en el colegio y ya estaba enseñando en la universidad, en el Departamento de Inglés.

II. The poem, the poet, and the critic

One of the most important components of my poems is the title. I live for the title. I am a title poet. The words of the title are the ultimate essence, and the background of my writing is to bring the title to its most total development. So, the religious allows me to concentrate on the titles. The titles are occasioned and have all kinds of innate, internal, and spiritual bodies. They have some kind of goodness or badness, they have a total experience to them. The religious and the discipline of dealing with the title bring out the social and the political. The religious gives me the discipline to get into the background of the poem and the essence of the title.

There is the occasional poet in me, and I think he has to do with the Puerto Rican feeling of Spiritualism. You see an object, and it represents thought, spirituality, physical presence, and history. Through Spiritualism, the person in front of me is always present in history. Through vibrations, I can define that person at any given moment. What has been called the "real maravilloso," the clash of African religions, Caribbean rhythmic patterns, and the footing of bomba and plena, and the religious framework of Catholicism, have allowed me to look into the soul of characters. Fifty percent of my poetry, of my recitals, are for the black constituency of the United States for three reasons: they are very interested in my sense of Caribbean blackness, and of urban blackness, and they are interested in the rhythmic quality of my poetry. Whether or not you like it, if you're a Caribbean writer, in the United States you don't write in white verse, you write in black verse. You write with the attitudes of blacks which are very important to the Puerto Rican community. I define blackness in my poem "the salsa of bethesda fountain" from *La Carreta Made a U-Turn*.

The beauty of our New York is also a prominent influence and is a fact that I have mentioned several times, and which can be found in an event of mine. Some time ago a friend of mine and I went about to locate every single community that was from the Caribbean, in New York. There is a quarter or enclave and then I went to look at all the Latin American countries that were represented in New York, and we found them in Queens. I found all the Caribbean countries, I found all the Latin American countries, with their little enclaves, the retention of their home values and in that there is a representation of the world. However, when they bombed Manhattan, it was the first time the United States had received the bomb. It had been bombed in Hawaii, but not in the mainland and when Manhattan was bombed I knew I loved Manhattan as an island as much as I love Puerto Rico. And because of those things, I love Manhattan more than I love Puerto Rico. The limitations are that I am limited in my experiences of adapting other languages in their native form and I don't think I've gotten enough rhythms, I tried to catch them but it's not that it is easy to experience them, and I like that impossibility.

Poetry does not belong to you, once it is written. I respect a bad review as much as I respect a good review because somebody spent time on it, and on who I am. I thank anybody who writes about the poem. I fall in love right away with the critic, and there are very little number of people that take the time to take your words and analyze them. That to me is ultimate respect. Any kind of criticism is a good fuel. Hay poemas que yo escribo exclusivamente para los críticos. Son los críticos que me traen chavo. It's the critics, you know, mira existe un movimiento, ¿right? So, you know, you always have to be ready. Hay gente que estudia tu trabajo o están buscando cómo escribir el trabajo de ellos y lo que necesitan son líneas, you know. I know that. You know, so éste es un poema que yo lo escribí para críticos porque hay muchas posibilidades ahí que empieza en la casa, en la sala, en el cuarto, en la cocina, abajo, en la sociedad, en la esquina, en el classroom, en la computer, ¿right? Y alguien puede escribir encima de eso muy chévere, tú sabes. Estoy haciendo transiciones de dedos, tú sabes, que cada línea es un dedo. So, yo sé que la gente escribe encima de eso, igual que como escribe encima de una canción. You know, hay people all they need is a poem, or you know or the resource or the reference and they read books.

Influences

I have personal definitions for how I'm stimulated by others. I call them "schools." Some of our poets use very muscular verbs. Others are spiritual, satiric, and comic. Our poets have that crude raw power of politics at the elementary level, and some have the Afro-American rooted lyrics, the rap quality. I have a lot of respect for poets. If you give me a poem I can teach it to you. I teach the poem, not the poet. You give me the poem of a poet and I'll break it down for you. I will do an experiment so you really get to learn it and be enthusiastic, but my contribution in that area is to be able to define the poem of the poet rather than the poet.

Bueno, de Cuba fue Nicolás Guillén, de Perú fue Nicomedes Santa Cruz, de méxico-americanos me conmovió mucho la poesía de Alurista y me encantó muchísimo el trabajo de Rolando Hinojosa y su descripción de acá del Valle. Siempre mencionó que yo tenía que venir a visitar y estar un momento acá en esta parte de Texas. En el oeste me influyó mucho el trabajo del chicano José Montoya de Sacramento, California. De México no tuve mucha conexión a menos que no fuesen los cantautores. Estudié mucho de México los cantautores, había una genialidad en ellos. Siempre consideré la lírica como la mejor poesía popular, pero a veces hay una lírica que realmente toca pueblos. Y el romanticismo mexicano ha sido muy importante aunque mucha gente cree que es popular, pero ha sido una embajada de conexión a otros pueblos. Considero el canto mexicano como una embajada lírica estudiada y fermentada y copiada, expresada. Y es la autoridad, es la autoridad.

When I was 6, I studied under Juan Boria. He was asked by the Salesian Fathers, who ran the San Juan Bosco School, to give a Saturday workshop for the students. He recited "Canción festiva para ser llorada," Luis Palés Matos's greatest poem. I think that was very important for me. Years later I wrote a poem, "homenaje a don luis palés matos." It's in my book titled *Enclave* [1981]. It is all in "black" language. It took me two years to write it. I wanted it to be the finest black poem in the history of Puerto Rico. Juan Boria read it for my personal pleasure on a beautiful night in Lincoln Center. I also remember that my uncle, Felipe del Valle, took me to meet Luis Palés Matos who used to go to tertulias in 1958 at a club in Stop 17. I was afraid because my uncle told me that Palés Matos was a seven-foot black giant, taller than the giant of Carolina and with a huge bemba. But he was a gentle man who hailed from Guayama, a town in the south of the island.

Cuando conocí a un gran poeta puertorriqueño que se llamaba Jorge Brandon poeta, pintor y dibujante, que era inventor del coco que habla, yo tengo su voz, y por él conocí las 100 mejores poesías que él había editado en el idioma español, y por él aprendí carisma, cadencia y persecución de palabras. Aprendí la tonalidad de aprender y memorizar la prosa, porque la poesía was meant to be read and was meant to be heard, que ésos eran los dos temas poéticos y aprendí a meterme a la historización de declamación, y en esos tiempos no se llamaba performance. El poema hay que respetarlo para declamarlo, entonces yo me encuentro en la urbe americana dentro del inglés, y estando con este bohemio viejo que me estaba enseñando todas esas ténicas en español y de un momento a otro se formó todo para yo escribir mi primer poema.

Bilingually, we [Algarín, Pietri, Sandra María Esteves] are able to have universal friendships. We're all old friends. Algarín's poetry is muscular vision; Pietri's is a linguistic celebration; Sandra María Esteves's is spiritual essence. And one of our great teachers was a "declamador" whose name was Jorge Brandon. He was a great historical figure. He's the tie that binds us to Puerto Rico. I love the name of Nuyorican because of two things. It's a style of writing. I always say that I'm Nuyorican, even though I was born in Puerto Rico, because of my style of writing. Many island writers gave definitions during the fifties, but the one that stuck, that spelling, is due to Algarín and Piñero. And it's not only a style but a school of writing too.

No tengo vinculación poética con la cultura mexicana, sino más bien como una vinculación lingüística, porque al fondo del poema es donde está la cultura natural que surge de la expresión. Entonces, después que uno tiene las expresiones, uno puede buscar el ritmo y la rima y la superficie de la palabra; en ese código existe mi conexión total con la cultura mexicana. Simplemente porque los mexicanos siempre fueron los productores y los que se adueñaban del medio de todo el país latino. Eran los más avanzados, los más conectados con el estado, lo mismo con las películas o las comedias, con el desarrollo novelístico de la televisión y algunas veces también, con la radio. No te imponían cultura pero eran exponentes, importadores y exportadores, de su cultura. Su temática musical era tan avanzada y tan querida que muchas de sus canciones fueron inmediatamente incubadas en el portafolio de la mente de otras naciones. Y a la misma vez sus personajes eran los personajes más populares de mi país, de Cuba, de Panamá. Eran los personajes mexicanos, que por la cultura de ellos, nosotros nos identificábamos. Jorge Negrete, Cantinflas, Pedro Infante... Aunque teníamos nuestra propia cultura puertorriqueña, nuestros propios ritmos, la que se imponía más y la más exportada era la raíz mexicana. Yo me crié con los que yo les digo "Las tandas corridas y dos más". Una vez me quedé dormido en un cine viendo cuatro películas mexicanas que las dieron una por una y yo me quedé, jovencito, perdido, y me estaban buscando y me encontraron viendo una película, dormido con una película de Jorge Negrete. Y mi mamá me dio un pellizcazo que todavía lo siento, te lo juro. Y los códigos de los dichos, del machismo, se integraban también por imágenes de "El Gallito", las pistolas, el caballo, y todo el mundo quería expresarse al sentido de esos romances y de ese canto a la mujer. Y ese machismo y el vaquerismo de pistolas tenían todos los símbolos machistas pero a la misma vez tenían unos símbolos humanos y unas historias de amor. Y también desarrollaron unas imágenes feministas desde el cine. Y toda esa cultura se penetraba en el hondo de nuestros seres, you know... so aunque yo era puertorriqueño yo tenía el mexicano siempre, como... era como un... ahm.... Bueno, tú prendes la televisión y la programación es mexicana, pero también había unos códigos super impuestos en nuestra mente, y siempre aunque decíamos "¡Ay, yo no soy mexicano, yo no soy!", siempre en gestos queríamos ser mexicanos. No fue hasta que vine aquí a la frontera y empecé a ver la otra cosa del mexicanismo. Era que el americano no pudo penetrar más en México, se metió a otro nivel, pero no pudo. O si cruzó el puente del Río Grande de una manera se trajo de regreso un país revolucionario y peleador por su tierra. Los mexicanos compitieron contra los americanos y sus pistolas y su imperialismo. Los pararon y crearon una visión, la primera visión latinoamericana, y de todo eso se está haciendo un subconsciente, que yo en los últimos diez años empecé a verlo: la grandeza de su hazaña.

Mi vinculación con América Latina empieza en Cuba. Los ritmos cubanos y la Revolución Cubana nos empezó abrir nuestra mente hacia los países latinoamericanos. Nosotros aquí teníamos un buen conocimiento de la música. Por ejemplo, Carlos Gardel me enseñó que un hombre, un momento y un ritmo pueden ampliar la música a otras culturas. Era como un virus. Se infiltró por todos lados. Cómo una figura puede impulsar la música de su país y poner el tango en el mapa del mundo. De la cumbia, nos gustaba el ritmo, pero no entendíamos la grandeza hasta que nos dimos cuenta que se había adaptado a la música de otros países, que era un ritmo mayor. Se había ampliado a muchos países, y se había metido en la música de otros países. Por ejemplo, hay una cumbia colombiana, una mexicana o, acá en Texas, hay cumbia tex-mex. Había una grandeza en ese ritmo. Y el merengue, aunque ahora es el baile número uno, nos ayudó a empezar a responder a la temática latinoamericana porque Puerto Rico siempre tuvo un sistema académico avanzado y había mucho deseo por la escritura y la literatura, especialmente la poesía. Y acá en los Estados Unidos, Puerto Rico empezó a meterse en la cultura de la música popular, que ha tenido un sentido de temas más revolucionarios, pues empezó a integrar una conciencia revolucionaria, porque el pueblo de Puerto Rico siempre ha tenido una ala independentista muy fuerte que, aunque no peleó armada, siempre tenía un vistazo de conciencia que no dejó y no ha dejado que Puerto Rico sea un estado de los Estados Unidos, por lengua y por cultura. A Puerto Rico le encanta desarrollar esos temas del español y no aceptar el inglés totalmente. Nos vimos ya en un estado bilingüe. Y acá en los Estados Unidos hubo un nacimiento grande de revolución y antipatía americana y de acoger a Latinoamérica. Y la literatura que los latinoamericanos desarrollaron explotó por todos lados. La segunda cosa más importante fueron los libros latinoamericanos que inmediatamente se traducían a veinte, treinta, cuarenta lenguajes, y esa literatura de ese pueblo fue separándose mundialmente y ahí fue donde yo empecé a conectarme con los quehaceres de los pueblos latinoamericanos.

III. My Poetry

To create a book of poetry, to me, is a political jumble. It's not how come I wrote the poems. They have to be first of all political, because I have to sell the books. Who wants to print achievement? I mean, for me to have printed four books in ten years, it is a remarkable achievement. The poet in me is at the minimalist edge of society. In order to contain that minimalist in me, I have had to become sharp in many respects. I have not been criticized linguistically; and politically I have never misspoken. Based on the four books, I have remained politically correct. I have heard that for every 3000 poets, only one gets published.

The only way that I could have published my books, and reprinted so many times, is to have some kind of connection. The spiritual force guides my poetic persona. When you call yourself a poet, you define yourself as someone who doesn't appear in the growth of the GNP of U.S. society. Before, the poets of God were heralded, but now we are unheralded. But if you give me a moment, I will read my poetry.

It's not the best poetry because I know what the best poetry is, but it's very well connected, well grounded, you know, it hits the nerves of my people in general. It comes as close as any other books in reaching the general population at different levels of my people. So, yo tengo una intención, un derecho de integrarme a las actitudes y diversidades de mi pueblo y tratar de dedicarle en diferentes niveles con diferentes personajes y diferentes momentos a mi pueblo. Tengo una conexión, no es un derecho, es un compromiso con esa historia, y en una lectura aunque no te guste todo, tú puedes ver que he hecho un intento, eso de intento es bien en general, pero hay muchos momentos específicos que ayudan, como uno nunca sabe cuando tú tienes un hit, tú puedes tener ocho canciones y solamente de una sale un hit. Yo nunca sé cuál poema la gente escoge, yo nunca sabía que "my graduation speech" [Laviera 1979] iba a ser un hit tan grande como ha sido, you know. A mí no me gusta mucho ese poema pero ese fue el hit, ahí fue donde salió en la revista de *Centro de Estudios Puertorriqueños* y nuestros amigos, Juan Flores, John Attinasi y Pedro Pedraza cogieron *La Carreta Made a U-Turn* para hacer un estudio general y ahí fue donde surgió un movimiento literario en las escuelas y fue con *La Carreta Made a U-Turn*. La definición es de Juan Flores y ahí surgió un movimiento, you know, y salió. Fueron los críticos que ampliaron, you know, el compromiso del libro. So, desde ese momento cuando escribo, escribo con los críticos en mente. Yo sé que algunos poemas ellos los van a usar como off shoots o como records. Y a veces uno, you know, a veces se encuentra una luz, ¿right? You know so surgen luces y estrellas, entonces uno empieza a "combinar lingüísticas en proporciones humanas."

I only have eight autographical poems; I don't like to talk about myself. I have two in my book *AmeRícan* [1985]. One is titled "negrito" and reflects my experience when I came to New York in a Trans Caribbean flight with a plane that had six motors. The first thing I heard from my aunt when I came into this country was no te juntes con los prietos, negrito. She used to live in a mixed neighborhood in the Lower East Side. She didn't want conflict. Up until then I thought the United States was all white because of the snow. The other poem was about something that happened to me as a child. My father was a Nationalist and hid arms in coffins and buried them. When I was 4, I found one of the coffins while playing in the yard. I wrote it down twenty years later in the poem "boyhood" [Laviera 1985]. Despite that I am not the aggressive type of poet, I stood in my community working, and being in politics, and doing my poetry, negotiating the system, not revolting against the system. There is a language that is subtle in my work that means exile and revolt. However, there is sternness in me about making definitions that is clearly different from the national mood. It's like defining our own society inside the society, spinning it out, meant to create a new mood, not only for myself but for others around me. It is an exile because it does not accept the norm of the society definitions of me... I try to challenge them by rewarding them. It takes along time for people to get used to them ... there is a deep humanity. Also the exile is to retain what could and make sure that it is recorded, the monologues, the nuances, especially for women.

I can't say which are my favorites, but I can tell you the poems that always impose themselves on my reading. I wrote a poem for my nephew "just before the kiss" [Laviera 1981]. That's a fine poem, you know, it has the canela, it has the cinnamon, it has all the colors, it has the love, it has Spanish and English and it's a love poem and people love it. People love it y cada vez que repito ése me sale el companion poem que es "standards." Esos dos siempre se han impuesto en mis lecturas. Yo nunca sé lo que voy a leer. Por ejemplo, yo fui a Connecticut ahora, a Hartford, y el director nacional me llamó y me dijo, "no te puedo pagar mucho, pero quiero que vengas y leas este, este y este poema, ¿alright? Y yo, I'm good at that, I do what you tell me, because that's what I'm there for right? Pero cuando llegué allí era un movimiento criollo boricua, era como un jíbaro, you know. Era de Puerto Rico y el mayor de Hartford is a Puerto Rican, there's the capital, y era un criollo español y allí no era para Nuyoricans, eso no era para spanglish, eso era para poemas criollos, ¿you know? "Bacalaitos", "sky people", you know, poemas that make you remember the island of Puerto Rico and its rich culture, yo lo cambié inmediatamente. I didn't do any of what he told me, you know, porque no cabía ahí, you know. So, pero los poemas esos, "just before the kiss" y "standards" se imponen siempre, no importa. "No te voy a leer hoy, no te voy a leer hoy. Sacúdete, salte, vete, shh." Se me meten, esos dos. Son los más que se me meten. De mis favoritos, te puedo decir uno. Me encanta "intellecutal" porque me encanta el negrito porque yo tengo nomás que veinte poemas que son autobiographical. Y ese "intellectual" [Laviera 1985], fue cuando me sacaron del high school para enseñar en Rutgers in the English Department y el Senate no me quería en el English Department, y tuvieron una reunión para sacarme después que me dieron el puesto. It was a big deal in that community that I came out of high school to teach at the English Department at Rutgers y cuando cogí la guagua para ir para allá, yo escribí ese poema en la guagua y cuando fui para allá al Senate eso fue lo que dije y me fui. Y la semana siguiente vine a enseñar, so ese poema is a speech of defiance. So ese se puede decirse que sí está bien cómodo en el oro de mi historia, ése fue un gran momento para mí. ¿Me entiendes? English Department, y un negrito from high school. Y, and I was good at teaching. Yo tenía una escuela y yo siempre he enseñado en la escuela. So, I love that poem, it's very important. Y "negrito" porque fue lo primero que me pasó a mí cuando vine a este país. Y eso lo tuve que escribir en español, no pude escribir eso en inglés. Y lo escribí veinte años después, pero ése fue un momento muy importante. Mi tía, yo bajando del avión, y ahí me cogió así y me dijo "no te juntes con los prietos, negrito." That was the first word that I ever heard in this country. "No te juntes con los moyetos, negrito." I never forgot that.

IV. The poems and collections

La Carreta Made a U-Turn began as a play, based on René Marqués' *La carreta*, as with *AmeRícan* and with my version ya metiéndome en la sucrusal americana y definirla a ella misma. Este libro tiene un poema de los diez grupos étnicos más populados de Nueva York. No hay distinción, hay un deber. Whether I like it or not I live in this society, I am inside the American society, I am not inside the Puerto Rican society, and I have to sobrevivir aquí. Yo no puedo odiar a todo el mundo, yo tengo que buscar la manera de representarme distintivamente pero a la misma vez defender a la otra gente con quien estoy. Entonces, el cuarto libro es *Mainstream Ethics* [1988]. Si yo estoy metido en la mainstream de los Estados Unidos, puedo hablar de éticas y puedo hablar de la Statue of Liberty, puedo hablar de guerrilla, puedo hablar de ya estoy libre, entonces la quinta function que es la *Mixturao* [2008], que tuve que salirme de los Estados Unidos para redefinir or indefinirme con lo que está pasando, latinoamericano, con una versión un poquito más amplia, con unas formas hemisféricas dentro de personajes que viven aquí y es la quinta etapa, eso me ha cogido como 10 años. Pero eso fue porque en los 90 yo me pasé escribiendo obras de teatro al tiempo que mis libros de poesía se estaban reprinted, estaban viviendo. Recibía muchas reseñas y master's theses and doctoral theses, el lenguaje se quedó vivo, *La Carreta Made a U-Turn* fue el primer libro que produjo la empresa de Arte Público Press, y después de eso surgió un estudio grandísimo, del Center de Estudios Puertorriqueños, publicando una revista y ahí vino el dinero. Arte Público Press is the largest Hispanic press in the United States, the oldest, tiene ya casi 300 libros, pero empezó con el libro mío, le di una fundación, eso me ha gustado porque la empresa no murió tras los primeros 2 ejemplares. *La Carreta Made a U-Turn* históricamente es un vanguard del movimiento literario en los Estados Unidos, esto me gustó, que el trabajo produjo otros trabajos, a rewarding knowledge, a nice ego... Egos are important, for my own revolution, my own porfundidad de ser.

La Carreta Made a U-Turn

I hold a couple of records. I like that, you know. In *La Carreta Made a U-Turn* I bastardized the most sacred Puerto Rican book, the best play, René Marqués's *La carreta*. First of all, I used his structure. I'm a Marquesian and Marqués defines my poetic structure-he always has. Yo también tengo tres secciones. He began in la montaña and continues in San Juan, and then goes to the metropolis. I began in la metrópolis and instead of ending in the Island, I make a U-turn and go to el arrabal, into the streets of Loisaida. If Doña Gabriela went back to Puerto Rico, in *La Carreta Made a U-Turn*, my characters go back to New York. My book becomes an extension of his; it's a fourth act to his play. In my first section, which is written mainly in English, I include references to Muñoz Marín. In the second, I include all women. I believe that politically I have to write about women. Of all the poems I have written, forty-one of them have characters which are exclusively women. Yo estoy solito all afuera with that. And good characters, characters of women that I respect and that women use. I had to make sure that I have women that speak in my poetry by themselves and have a very feminine structure. There is also a Black structure. *La Carreta made a U-Turn* was to proceed deeper into New York, but I ended it in Spanish because politically, if I didn't end it in Spanish, being in the U.S., then I would have been in trouble. So how could *La Carreta make a U-Turn* and proceed into the U.S. and not end in Spanish? I make a historical decision to the effect that Doña Gabriela did not go back. The Doña Gabrielas of Puerto Rico stayed here, and they established themselves in all American towns. Even though u-turn means they stayed in the United States, the book had to finish in Spanish.

"angelito's eulogy in anger" [Laviera 1979] is a bilingual poem. Its structure is determined by the use of English of the left column and of Spanish on the right column. I wrote it in front of my cousin's coffin. I had a conflict, because the poem came out in Spanish and English at the same time. I wanted to talk to the parents but also to the community, to America. It was a challenge. The anger came because I couldn't say everything in Spanish or everything in English. I recited it aloud that night. I didn't want anybody to go without understanding it. I didn't want people to say, "It's nice, but I didn't understand it in the other language." So I made a decision that the moment was a bilingual moment. Neither Spanish nor English was sufficient for the opportunity. And as a colloquial poet, neither Spanish nor English was sufficient for the situation in which I found myself.

Enclave

As a Nuyorican, Puerto Rican, Boricua poet, I needed to write the greatest English poem as a challenge. So I did it: the poem that defines me is "jesús papote." It is totally in English, and it marks my conquering of the verbiage of the English dictionary. "jesús papote" is very structured. First of all, it's a nine month cycle; there are no commas, so its all conceived in the breath of the woman's push to give birth; it happens on Christmas Eve, which is supposed to be the most serene night in the Christian calendar. Our time is defined by Christ's birth. We live in the image of Christ's death and in Christian time. To take the moment of his birth, to put the trauma of death inside the month of his birth is the very structure I use to tell history. I think the Catholic in me provoked the universality in the poem. Each piece or part had to do with looking into a character and understanding its good and bad points. There is a lot of religious symbolism in it. The fact is that I end en la misma misa del gallo, at 12:00, Midnight Mass. The Jesús Papote legacy was to be in church with God; it was almost like saying Christ has to come many more times. The old Christ has to incarnate himself, the new Christ has to give us a new image of what the world is about, because the Bible, as much as we try to interpret it, does not give us the moment in time that we live under. Christ was someone who was crucified and killed and resurrected. My Jesús Papote had to be crucified by society in the womb, so that in his birth, at least when he comes out, the voice would be heard. I was looking for a voice and he gave me a voice that I wish my people would listen to for once. In order for him to have qualified to be the voice, he had to go through an enormous struggle, so when he said that word, "Bendición," it was pure. His resurrection was coming into the world. He came as a hero who could at last speak to my people on something which I didn't find in anybody else. My Puerto Rican people do not have a hero—I couldn't find one. So, having crucified him in the womb and at the point of his birth (or at the moment of his death), my people would say let's listen to this character. I was looking for an epic character who my nation would hear, because my nation doesn't listen to characters. I think I succeeded in making him an epic figure, and that was my goal. He had to go through all those things so that everyone in my community could just lean back and hear this guy say "Bendición" and live. I guess his womb was his crucifixion and his birth was his resurrection.

AmeRícan
I once wrote a poem titled "Nuyorican" that expresses the feelings of many Puerto Ricans who return and feel rejected. It is very hard, after they have suffered for being Puerto Rican. That's what I say in that poem, but every verse ends with the question ¿sabes? (you know?) that softens the accusation. I have no problem. Everybody receives me well. I introduced Juan Boria to New York audiences. I wrote about him, that's why I have no problems in Puerto Rico; I'm very connected. El movimiento puertorriqueño izquierdista estaba pasando por una transición, y es que ya ellos no están anti-Nuyorican como veinticinco años atrás, cuando muchos de ellos no lo querían aceptar y Miguel Piñero y Miguel Algarín le dieron final resting place to the problem

que estuvo cien años en desarrollo entre Nuyorican y Puerto Rican. Hubo muchas transiciones con la palabra y finalmente ellos dos le dieron el final resting place to the definition, ya Nuyorican está aceptado.

I never know which is going to be a hit. "my graduation speech" fue un surprise hit. Otros son los five and dimes, yo los llamo los five and dimes. "assimilated," ese dio mucho, porque salió en un buen momento donde todo el mundo estaba buscando la definición, you know. Y la poesía estaba caliente, y cuando salió "asimilao" salió right at a very nice historical moment, it answered a lot of questions, you know? "AmeRícan" era el nuevo poema. El poema de la generación siempre ha sido "Puerto Rican Obiturary" de Pietri, but I had a funny feeling that the Americans didn't want to use the poem as the signature Puerto Rican poem, and they have to use a Puerto Rican poem, so "AmeRícan" was mild enough, tú me entiendes, you know what I mean, … hay un lenguaje ahí de protesta pero it's mild enough you know, where they can use it for the eighth grade, or the twelfth grade or they can use for the college. Salió en *Heath Anthology of American Literature,* y si sale ahí hay tres más que lo cogen, the candy store right. So it got picked up, it was a clever title. It wasn't like a love poem and it had all the races there, it's a good study poem. I didn't think it would be a hit. Ese es el que me trae el chavo, you know siempre hay un chequesito dos, tres veces o cinco veces al año, viene un chequesito de "AmeRícan" y ése fue un surprise.

We have two and a half million Puerto Ricans born here. I had to find a new word: Rican. There is a difference because not everybody is from New York. When I began to talk in schools and colleges and people started to ask, I titled one of my books *AmeRícan*: "I-am-a-Rican." American. But our literary language is still bound up with Nuyorican writing, even though we are AmeRícans. We are all caught up in the dichotomy of the Popular Party and the *jíbaro* who wants to be everything. It's the experience of the Commonwealth. We are a state, we are free, we are associated. There are many Puerto Ricans being born in Philadelphia, in Cleveland, in Hawaii, all over. In Hawaii, one percent of the population is Puerto Rican. They talk in Hawaiian, neither in English nor Spanish, and call themselves "Pokoliko." I realized that going through the nation it did not adapt the name, or itself to other kids growing up in other parts of the United States. It was hard for them to be Nuyoricans because it says Newyorkicans… That is how I invented AmeRícan, because it has American, it has "Am-a-Rican," and it is inclusive of the nation. Both, with the intention of solving the problem of the tonalities. I am always looking at that tension, So AmeRícan was an expansion of a Nuyorican. We are supposed to define tonalities, so other people can fit into them. I saw the problems to create linguistic models, so they could define themselves, I did it through "asimilao;" I am not assimilated, I am "asi-mi-lado." Asimilado is different from assimilated. A un lado, it tries to solve issues in other people's perspectives. The Nuyorican to me is a school, a lifestyle now, just like hip-hop, which became a lifestyle. So Nuyorican is a lifestyle, a school of thought, not a "Rican," it's a way of making expressions. It is an important school because throughout the world to that connection of first language inside the second language, the connection that we make with the languages is the most famous connection in the world right now.

Mainstream Ethics

In *Mainstream Ethics* [1988] I was calling myself "mainstream" and that is a very dangerous title. But I began with "lady liberty," which is in English- this book goes from English, to Spanglish, to Spanish, and I end it with "conciencia," which is my Latin Americanization:

> te hablo porque puedo hablar
> tengo la confianza que entiendes
> mi genocidio mi pesadilla
> mi esclavitud mis cadenzas invisibles mis libertades falsas
> te digo que nuestra gente duerme. (1988: 49)

In other words, I end with the voice of Latin America and not the voice of my people from el barrio hispano. The voice of Latin America had to emerge in the end; that's mainstream. It's in Spanish and in English and both worlds live in my *Enclave*.

Mixturao

El primer título de *Mixturao* [2008] era "Continental" porque era la transición de *La carreta* a *Enclave* a *AmeRícan* a *Mainstream*. Entonces, pues, el proceso natural era "Continental" que era inglés y español, palabra en inglés, palabra en español y palabra hemisférica porque hay un poema, dos poemas, ahí se refiere al hemisferio, hay tres y cada sección tiene uno. Pero, el mixture con el "ao" yo quiero que me pongan *Mixturao* para cuando el americano lo lea ya con la r sabe que es mixture, entonces el "ao" que es el negro y es indígena, se mezcla a la nueva literatura, nuevas conexiones de lenguaje que se está reconsiderado, reconstruido en el occidente por la gente de la reconquista. So el "ao", me interesaba el "ao", pero tuve que meter el "mixture" para cuando el mexicano lo vea no se confunda. Yo quería ponerle una "e" y al lado del "ao." Pero, continental no tenía la negreza específica. I'm open minded to these kinds of things. Los últimos dos años yo estoy empujando el "mixturao", en una obra de teatro, en como ocho programas que ya he metido en mi curriculao diferentes cosas so ya la gente se está aprendiendo la palabra, pero no la he empujao. Pero el nombre original del libro era "Continental" porque it's a more natural transition from *AmeRícan, Mainstream,* to be mainstream you have to be continental y el dicho de la misma palabra en español y en inglés es uno de los requisitos de la poesía bilingüe y tiene que adaptarse a los dos idiomas, a las dos lenguas, porque viene, surge de ahí, no surge del español ni surge de inglés, surge de ese mixturao, de ese gran lenguaje mixto que es un lenguaje internacional porque todas las lenguas de todos los países de los colonialized countries de Europa, todo está en bilingüe porque es parte del lenguaje de África o del Caribe, mezclar con el lenguaje europeo. Es un poema bilingüe, hay un poema bilingüe en todas las colonias y residentes de Europa. La misma gente como en Francia, Alemania, el mismo spanglish, el spanglish de nosotros es el más avanzado. El Nuyorican is the most advanced spanglish. It's the most advanced acá en los Estados Unidos porque nosotros, unlike the Chicanos y los Mexicans usamos el negro. And unlike the Dominicans que no usan el negro. Como los chicanos, los mexicanos que están más en lo indígena y no adaptan tanto al negro. El cubano que no está con lo negro y está con lo indio. Y el puertorriqueño tiene una buena mezcla, so a los europeos les gusta estudiar nuestro lenguaje porque tiene raza. Tiene diferentes mixtures of urban United States. Yo sé que es una contribución lingüística de nosotros a la comunidad literaria mundial. So, espanglish no es un lenguaje típico o prototípico exclusivamente de los Estados Unidos. Existe en otros lenguajes, en otros lugares y está en esas comunidades, está en el mismo desarrollo lingüístico que nosotros. So, no estamos aislados porque tenemos que conectarnos a esos experimentos, ¿cuántos lenguajes no tienen los indígenas? ¿Hay cien dialectos en el continente, dirías tú?

Este experimento de espanglish nosotros debemos darle el aprecio de que lo hemos desarrollado mucho más que otros, pero no es exclusivamente Estados Unidos, estoy consciente de ese desarrollo. Y las veces que he ido a Europa para verme con lingüistas y todo eso, he notado que lo que están metiéndose bien profundo, conocen las raíces de mi literatura.

Entonces también por necesidad, había que tener también un poema muy bueno de los mexicanos,. "Southwest border trucos," porque ésa es la raza mayor. No es la mía, y esos son los más que compran libros. ¿Tú sabías que las mujeres mexicanas o chicanas son muy buenas con la literatura puertorriqueña y la estudian? Entonces, por ley tenía que tener un poema mexicano, so eso no es porque viene de mí, aunque vino de mí, porque yo tuve esa experiencia, es necesidad. Tener un poema mexicano bueno que me guste a mí aunque no le guste a nadie. Después que me guste a mí, yo te digo, yo le saco el sabor, de una manera u otra y tenía que tener un poema mexicano, tenía que. Es que realmente me encanta el momento, sí yo por obligación tenía que escribir el mexicano yo estaba buscando el momento, you know, para expresarlo. Es una búsqueda política, es una búsqueda, ¿no? No es por obligación, sí tengo que escribirlo, pero también tengo que buscarlo. Entonces, yo estoy cinco meses buscando el momento, you know, hay búsqueda.

En mi poesía, yo tenía que answer a González, que vivió en el exilio en México, José Luis González, un gran escritor puertorriqueño, que fue el primero que me enseñó a mí, cuando yo leí la historia de él, "En el fondo del caño hay un negrito" [1997b], yo me volví escritor, right there. I read it, and I became a writer. Entonces la semana después que yo leí eso, fue que escribí mi primer poema después de perder la vista, una semana después, o dos semanas después que yo leí ese cuento y yo tenía que escribirle a José Luis González; tenía que escribirle porque había contradicciones, you know, con él, pero también fue una fuente de creatividad, ese poema yo lo escribí después de que se me fue la vista y se llama "spanglish carta." Es una conexión con el Papote del primer poema que yo escribí y I had to write to him, eso yo lo escribí cuando perdí la vista. Y "patriota" es otro poema. Tú sabes, los libros míos tienen que tener la inconveniencia de la revolución puertorriqueña metida en algunos de los textos porque es parte de mi desarrollo, parte de mi cultura y también porque es la izquierda la que ayuda a vender libros y a mantener la literatura, no sólo bilingüe. Los bilingües están vendiendo los libros para las classrooms. Hay los centros de literatura, los centros de libros, los centros de poesía, son ellos los que mantienen esa parte de la cultura y yo por necesidad y también por aprecio intelectual es que yo he tenido que escribirle a ese grupo, so la militancia existe en esos libros, esos poemas de militancia, yo los escribí después de ciego, y por necesidad. El otro poema que escribí fue pues el poema de "callejerismos" porque me faltaba un personaje de esos callejeros; yo tengo ciertas voces, ciertos personajes que me salen muy bien y ahí es donde me sale el español, este, coloquial. You know, el español que he mantenido de una manera u otra y tipos de personajes de calle pero con valor, creo yo que tienen valor, y ese poema tuve yo que escribirlo después de perder la vista. El resto de *Mixturao* ya tenía la cáscara.

So, la poesía del *Mixturao* la hacía en el 2005 con excepción de poemas que yo tenía que escribir, no porque, vinieron de mi mente, sino porque era necesario. El libro de poesía tiene que tener un balance de diferentes cosas y pues los balances míos son con un español de la calle, de voz, de personajes, y tiene que tener el spanglish porque es la poesía del dinero, no es el inglés, ni el español, spanglish es el que te trae los chavos, porque ahí es donde está la interacción y donde están los movimientos, la creatividad y donde está la gente que son revolucionarios o independent thinkers o que quieren cambiar el sistema, you know. Entonces, ahí es donde está la creatividad, you know, intelectual. Está en spanglish, so, por ley hay que tener spanglish, entonces el inglés porque tengo que por ley definirme en este sistema, so hay un balance en la poesía que he escrito para crear el balance de los libros míos que siempre tienen el español puro, el inglés puro y el bilingüe. Hay un nuevo lenguaje, un "mixturao", que es diferente al bilingüe, que es más hemisférico. So, ese poema yo lo creé, igual con "Sur Americano", lo que es criollo latino, tuve que escribirlo. "Tesis de Negreza," ya lo había escrito, yo ya tenía la cáscara. Eso fue un estudio que hizo un profesor Víctor Manuel Vega que me dio los nombres. Entonces yo usé la canción de Cortijo, "Mataron al negro bembón", de Bobby Capó. Usé toda la letra de la canción y usé la terminología de este muchacho que fue por toda América buscando esta terminología de los negros y si ya tenía esas dos cosas entonces creé una guaracha, una nueva canción encima de la canción, fue un poema bilingüe pero de español y negro, pero no bilingüe de spanish and english, pero tiene esa mezcla y entonces tenía que escribir el poema "Bilingüe." Tenía que escribir ese poema y el concepto era usar una canción. Me gusta la cáscara de usar canciones en español y meterle el inglés encima de las letras, eso es una buena interacción, tejiendo y me encanta ese poema. Yo lo escribí, lo tenía que escribir pero usé la canción de Sylvia Rexach "Olas y arena" y no me salían las letras y lo que hice fue un estudio de las líneas de mis poemas y saqué letras de líneas, de previous poemas. Hice un estudio de lo que quería sacar y usé la poesía de previous libros, porque uno de los trucos que se hace en *Mixturao*, hay líneas de previas colecciones porque así los mantengo y le doy crédito abajo porque así mantengo los otros libros en el presente momento de los libros de ahora, ese es un truco que estoy haciendo.

V. El Teatro

Yo hice trabajo teatral en el año 1972 hasta 1988 cuando se rompieron los movimientos teatrales; algunos se cayeron, otros se rompieron y otros se hundieron. Entonces me envolví en esa vida bohemia, pero no era de calle. Era, you know, hay un movimiento muy bueno en el Lower East Side y yo nunca me he movido del Lower East Side. I discovered early that there is so much wealth of characters and attitudes in poetry. There are so many different styles of talk that characters inspire me to write. I always tell people that the two most developed organs are the mouth and the ears. I've had twelve plays produced. Some of them are: *Piñones* (1979), a musical with ten songs about Roberto Clemente's accident in Piñones; *La chefa* (1981), *Base of soul in Heaven's Café* (1987), *Becoming Garcia, AmeRícan* (1981), *King of Cans* (2001, 2012), *The Spark* (2006), *'77 PR Chicago Riot* (2007) and *Bandera a Bandera* (2008). I tend to write characters and situations. The characters of the poems spiritually push me to create the drama of the theatre. The poem gives me the characters and the drama follows them. Keep in mind that I had a very good schooling with The Teatro Cuatro. I was the head of the Shakespeare Festival Latino. I worked with the Festival for five years. Since I was so secure with poetry, the theatre became an experimentation with actors. The openness of the theatre allowed actors to go and get experience from the street, using our own intelligence and research. I was able to write from a collective perspective. So theatre was easy for me. I like the whole idea of working with people to create movements. Also, I had an excellent man who cared for my body of work: Woody King, Jr., under whom I was a director of Hispanic Theatre for five years. Through him, in my workshops, I had three plays produced with my students. The plays had a six-week run. I had a Black American person who committed himself to the body of work of a Puerto Rican writer.

Fui uno de los primeros poetas de acá que se adaptó al trabajo de Latino American writting, teatro popular. I used to like that, estaba centralizado en la comunidad de donde yo vivía y de allí surgieron cinco movimientos de teatro a la misma vez y yo estaba metido en los cinco. ¿Tú sabes? De una manera u otra en Nueva York, en el Lower East Side. En cada teatro yo tenía diferentes papeles. En uno, era el escritor, en otro, era el director, en otro era él que buscaba el dinero, tú sabes. Me ubiqué en el teatro Nuyorican, y pasé al teatro cultural, al teatro de jazz de acá y en todos tenía una base o enseñaba o estaba vinculado a los movimientos. You know.

There have been four poems that became plays. I pay very close attention to those poems of mine that define characters, sometimes a character is defined in such a totality that it gives me the fusion to create a play. I just finished researching the play *The Spark,* and it took me to train the actors in Chicago. Then I made them go further in the investigation of what happened in 1966 this Puerto Rican riot, then after I had gathered all the information, I could not write it. I had to write the poem of it first ... as a poem gives me the sketch. After writing the poem I found all the moods, the life of poems are so connected to conciseness... poetry was meant to be short novels, or novels in short lived prose. So the concentration of it gave me the attitude. The poems gave me the attitude, gave me the character definition, and when it comes in plays I develop the characters that express the attitude of those lines. So I am always very careful, especially when I am writing character poems. I am focusing on the history, the form that I could transport into something else, so there is definitely a connection. The tension is that. When I write theater, I write everything without the characters, actually I'm always writing poetry until I break down the characters. I write them as a poem, and then I go back and look at it and who says what, and then it gets broken down. So there is always tension in my dramatic characters, because I am always writing as if they were poetry. So the poetic text is always in tension inside the dramatic text, not like the dramatic one. Poetry is always defining the characters. However in the dramatic text, each line is always reflected so that there are people talking in each line, each line has a person talking, as opposed to poetry that you live it as it is, as it comes out, there is not restriction of voice. But in the dramatic text, each line is a direction, has to be in accordance with somebody expressing, so it is more restrictive because of what you can do with it.

VI. Language

Politically, I have gotten to the point that with my four or five books, I can read an hour in Spanish and an hour in Black. Being Puerto Rican gives me the totality of having a universal mission to talk to different groups at different times. And the fact that I do it in Spanish and English allows me to talk to the entire continent. Listen to my images and you will see that I'm a continental person. Spanish is a major language spoken in the continent; English is a dominant language of the society in which I live. For the countries of the New World, my two guns are the major languages, Spanish and English. Being an oral poet binds me to other oral poets and historically to all the great poets and poems of the world. Oral poetry is an art that is still alive. It is a tradition of Europeans and Africans who used to tell stories. By talking my poems, it binds me spiritually and morally not only to the presence of many nations but to a poetic chain of historical importance. Being a declamador binds me historically; being a Rican, it binds me to my people in their clash with society. It gives me the "bilinguality" of being able to absorb the contradictions of different form, the Blackness with the "colloquialness" of my people and the formality of Spanish and the tensions that arise in urban society. I'm a Nuyorican but I never call myself a Nuyorican. People call me a Nuyorican, and I accept it totally. Some people don't want to accept new terminologies. I believe we have cinco gorras; we wear the Hispano hat which answers to Latin America; we wear the Caribbean hat which binds us to Blackness; we wear the Nuyorican hat which binds us to the present society; we wear a Puerto Rican hat which binds us to our country, Puerto Rico; and we wear the Latino one which binds us to this nation. We wear all those hats. In the meantime, it is my responsibility, as effectively as I can, to let the voices of my people, at any moment, integrate into me and I just give it back to them the way they give it to me. Somebody asked me who's in your poem? There are a thousand people in every syllable. And I definitely believe the mirror imagery of giving a voice back to the people, because the people give me the voice, they give me the characters, they give me the moment and the reason for being. I'm lucky that I am able to give it back to them. So my objective is to give it right back to them. I know a couple of things. One, there are no Puerto Ricans anymore who don't understand English. I don't care who they are—they may not want to speak it but they understand it. Two, there is an accepted cordiality that when you do speak Spanglish, it's funny. Three, there is a very warm bonding between parents of the 2nd generation and the grandchildren of the 4th generation. And more than anyone else, we have resolved that problem. Que el nieto sea el roquero más grande del mundo y que se vista con el beebop. Lo que importa es si es buena gente. There is no problem at all with that. We have a great ability for allowing integration, experimentation, and keeping a certain basic to ourselves without going through too many changes. In that way, the Puerto Rican persona is, I consider an advanced person in society, in the humanistic category, in the social category, and in the political category, in terms of dealing with people, and in the spiritual category, in terms of accepting people. The Puerto Rican persona is very broad and he allows experimentation without a lot of psychological hang-ups. He is very broad natured and I think here's where our artistic totality lies; artistically we are very broad.

I know I have been called code switching, and I am very respectful of all the terminologies and in the laboratory of my thinking, it really represents the reality. I am an archeologist de lo que oigo en la acera, en la cocina, en el cuarto, el social club, en la esquina y en realidad lo consider como se dice code switching, y yo lo veo como se vive ahí mismo en el momento, la quick definition of whether it's in Spanish or in English or it is bilingual... The only way I can do this is by respecting the moment... Este momento en español, eso es lo que sale, pero hay otro momento en que es en inglés, y hay otro que es bilingüe, entonces yo no lo estoy haciendo en code switching, lo estoy hacienda en una definición del momento, la realidad mía es que yo no puedo existir exclusivamente en inglés o español. Los libros míos siempre son matemáticamente it comes in denominations, 50 percent straight English, no Spanish. 20 percent straight Spanish, no English. And the rest bilingual, or Spanglish, as a difference. Ahora estoy experimentando con *Mixturao*, que es más amplio que el Spanglish, el bilingüe es más serio. Por ejemplo un poema bilingüe mío es cuando yo cojo una canción como "Migration", que tiene la canción "En mi Viejo San Juan" hasta arriba y le meto mi español o mi Spanglish a un texto que ya está escrito con español y entonces es un poquito más serio en el lenguaje, Spanglish es el verbal, lo conmovido, lo exótico... Spanish es el español, porque es el lenguaje más grande del hemisferio. Hay 16 países que tienen el español, solamente siete países hablan inglés.

También ese sonido de la gente mía que, por ejemplo, me encanta el poema "Spanglish" pero no sé si lo he terminado pero porque creo que lo puedo terminar...

pues estoy creando Spanglish
bi-cultural systems
scientific lexicographical
inter-textual integrations
for Spanglish is two expressions
existentially wired
it is two dominant languages
continentaly abrazándose
in coloquial combates
en las aceras del soil
del imperio yanqui, Spanglish emerges
control pandillaje
sobre territorio bi-lingual
las novelas mexicanas
controladas en la sala
por mi madre y mi abuela
mixed with radio hip-hop
cocina cuchifrito lore
down the stairs to the immigrant migrant
nasal mispronouncement
inside the social club recordando
el ayer borinquen corrido
into the Spanglish street corner
tex-mex farándula reggaetón
into the standard english classrooms
with computer technicality. (2008a: 26)

So in all of my poems I discover that "spanglish is literaly perfect / spanglish is ethnically snobbish / spanglish is cara-holy inteligencia." Now, tú sabes yo corro ahí el gammet, ¿no? Right, so, pero no me gusta el terminar, porque estoy usando poetry of the past como te digo ese tiene un ejemplo que "literally perfect" and "ethnically snobbish", es un poema "intelectual." Pero me encanta eso porque es la poesía mía. Sometimes I write in English and sometimes Spanish. It depends. You have to select language according to theme. I am cataloged as a Nuyorican writer because of the school of writing I belong to. I write in two languages, and so I have the possibility of writing in either one. I can control both and mix them. All the possibilities of blending two languages are at the disposition of our bilingualism. I have to make a decision according to the colloquiality of the moment.

Yo no soy silly para solamente estar creando, si soy un Boricua, exclusivamente en inglés, no vale, no no cabe en ningún sentido... Aunque viví solamente 4 años en la escuela de Puerto Rico siempre fue mi deber de meterle el español, yo lo veía como el español criollo, formal, el español gramático... Me encanta el español... Ahora, yo considero que cuando yo blend the best in español with the best en inglés, I put it together, hay una cosa exquisita... El inglés tiene unos sentimientos que el español no tiene, y el español tiene unos sentimientos que el inglés no tiene, y entonces combinándolos los dos a veces me salen unos capullos de alegría, un amor más amplio que los dos idiomas separados, aunque se llama code switching. Lo consider como una forma artística, y los europeos lo ven así también, porque son multilingual... Aquí aún estamos obsesionados con la bastardization, los europeos viven con y por y en los lenguajes, es una sociedad multilingual, ahí viene la entrada y el peso, es una visión más amplia, no como aquí que es más estricta... Ir a Europa me ha salvado a tener una visión mucho más amplia, aquí la visión es más estricta con la definición del idioma. He amado en las visitas en Europa el concepto del lenguaje.

We learned throughout the years... Puerto Rico always had a very revolutionary nationalist independence straining and political history, and that was already a background for us. Resistance was part of it, but we did not have those many armed movements, armed revolts. Because it did not seem feasible or possible to have an armed revolt to liberate Puerto Rico, it's a mental and political decision that has to be made...The black movement gave us a sense of transforming el discurso. It gave us an attitude and a mood by which to negotiate and fight inside of the United States movement, it gave us a manner and a capacity to use language, to learn the systems, and it gave us the tonality. We speak in Black English, not in Southern English... I wonder, what is American English?... But we adapted the rhythm of the black mood in our talk... It also helped us to look at America and define America in a whole different perspective than we used to do in the island. Blackness gave us the language... It is a negotiated thing. Yes, I'm writing in English and the pieces are there. I feel I wanted to be able to say that I've done it already; I could do intellectual America pretty well. It may not be in the best written form, but I want to have an hour of poetry for everybody and be successful. People would say: "Hey! That's pretty good!" I want to be one of the boys, a respected boy. I think I've achieved that. Now I just need to expand the English.

I have no problems; I don't' pay any attention to the tension [with island writers]. As far as I'm concerned, I don't experience any tension in Puerto Rico. In that respect, Puerto Rican writers from Puerto Rico cannot come to the United States and be Puerto Ricans. The spectrum of the United States, as a nation, includes Chicanos, Latinos, Hispanos, Cubans, Mexicans... They cannot come into communities and be totally successful. They really can't; they can't come and talk to the masses, to twenty million Latinos of this nation. I can do that. I can go into any barrio, whether it be Chicano or Cuban or Puerto Rican. The broadness of my experience as a Puerto Rican here has allowed my work to be successful. I could do an hour's work or two hour recital to these people and be totally inclusive about their attitudes and ideas and be totally accepted; that's what I have tried to do in the United States, to be accepted by all the communities as a poet and be loved. The Puerto Rican consciousness has developed, and I give that credit to my people; they've really branched out in a humanistic way which allows us to communicate. If I go to Puerto Rico, I would probably stay Negroid because yo soy un negro de Puerto Rico. I happen to believe that I, with my Negroid poetry, can live in Puerto Rico, en cualquier esquina, you know. You have to have your protections. In cualquier sitio I can say:

> retumba el pasado presente prosa poesía
> retumba el calor sudor vaivenes de cuero
> salpicando mares olor tambor prieto quemao
> orgullos cadereando acentos al español
> conspiración engransando ritmos pleneros
> a la lengua española pa ponerle sabor.
> pero que retumba en la tumba resbalando
> pico pico tun tun de pasa áfrica se pierde
> en puerto rico tirando pasos richos a los santos
> carcando al uno dos en tres por cuatro
> que alientan los versos exaltan los salmos
> despierta la clave chupando las cañas
> pracutú-piriquín-prucú-tembandeando
> el secreto máximo: que luis palés matos
> también era grifo africano guillao de castellano.

Y por allí, palante. I have my spiritual protections going to Puerto Rico and tú puedes decir lo que tú quieras. Pero si tú te paras conmigo para recitar y me paro en cualquier lado, verás que quedo bien con mi pueblo y los portorros sin duda. My answer is that it doesn't apply to me, and I also know for a fact that it doesn't apply to people like Pedro Pietri. If Pedro goes to Puerto Rico, en cualquier nivel, intelectual y espiritualmente, y él no recita en español, people love him. And one of the things that's good to know is that at this point historically the English and the Spanish are not the question. The attitude of the English is what is important. Fortunately and unfortunately, my nation is bilingual. The people are into the English and into the Spanish, and if you do it right, no matter what language, it's fine. My second thesis is that Spanish is not an issue in this country; Spanish is the most grounded language in this country. No hay problema con el español. For every five Nuyoricans who are born speaking "Spanglish," there're ten Dominicans that come and bring the Spanish over; and there're twenty-five salvadoreños that bring it over. Spanish is constantly being reinforced so there's no danger of Spanish being lost in this country. Eso no es un problema. El español categorically is the most developed literary language in the continent, in the hemisphere, probably in the world. The reality of Spanish is not that it is being tumbao, just because of certain migrational experiences and all of that. Yo entiendo que the only good Spanish is the atom bomb y eso es una cosa pero correcta. What we need is the interaction to understand the experiences of people, to understand the experience of migration. Now being a Nuyorican, one of the things that I"ve noticed is that the world is in a bilingual tension: the Africans in Europe, the Turkish in Germany. There are movements from mother country to urban centers in conquering countries and it is not isolated to Puerto Rico. As Nuyoricans, we have captured the political and linguistic changes. People are looking for a Spanish or an English or a German point of view. But if you think about it, Europe tends to be multilingual. America isolates itself in the English only, and it wants to control biocenosis. You can't do that—it's a stupid move. It's exercising bigotry. But the broad world isn't looking at it that way; the linguistic tension exists everywhere in the world and the Nuyorican element of it, prestigiously, has grown in many ways. I'm not saying that's the only school of Puerto Rican writing, I'm not saying that I know, but, I'm saying that there's nothing Puerto Rico can do about bilingualism. It's a fact of life and a fact of world movement. That's the way I see it.

In terms of Puerto Rico, I personally think that the linguistics that have come out of there marks one of the more authentic integrations of language in Latin American Spanish. The vocabulary of the Puerto Rican repertoire in the last twenty-five years has achieved an incredible amount of openness in identifying the indigenous, the black, and the Spanish groups of languages. It has been respectful of Latin American literature, respectful of the Puerto Rican Diaspora, of the Puerto Rican identity and very open to English suggestiveness and brilliance. Puerto Rican writing has included jazz, has included black American literature. They have developed a patois, integrated linguistics. I do have problems with some thinkers and monolinguals who are opposed to the linguistic vernacular of our people: the ones who have problems with the way we talk. Those who study only books because they don't have time to talk to anybody. They spend all their time analyzing and categorizing language and not practicing it. They are boring extremists; perfumed educators, consumers of classical seventeenth-century Spanish, racist monolinguists, stuck-up Spanish-only speakers, nihilist philosophers, and misguided revolutionaries. I especially admire the women writers in Puerto Rico. Ana Lydia Vega is a great synthesizer of language. She's a national treasure. She's the ultimate sancocho. She should be on the pedestal of the Ateneo Puertorriqueño and of the Institute of Puerto Rican Culture (ICP); she should be in La Fortaleza selling Puerto Rican literature to the world.

In Spanish we have created many new words indigenous to Blacks. We have added our own dialects. Besides nineteen countries speak Spanish in the Americas. Why should I have to limit myself to English only when Spanish is the dominant hemispheric language? Bilingualism is not only between English and Spanish; it's a universal situation. It may refer to urban English in Spanish form. It's not the Spanish from the Antilles; it's a Spanish with an English tonality, with an English spirituality, it's a Spanish urbanized. A lot of young writers are into it because they have to deal with a school situation, but they want to deal with a home situation and a community situation. It's an accent in English, it's an accent in Spanish, it is Spanish with an English accent and with urban black tonalities. There is nothing creative about my poems. Everything is structured so that nadie me joda. As of 1992, I have published 198 poems: 60 percent of the poems are totally in English, 20 percent of them are totally in Spanglish, and the remaining 20 percent I write in total Spanish. I knew politically I had to do that. I like the Spanish language, but I have to look for a balance. I'm not saying that I'm the best writer, but politically, I have not been criticized. If I say I cover my angles, you know why, porque la comunidad puertorriqueña es la comunidad más bochinchosa en el seno del mundo. If I don't please all of them, me jodo. I'm in trouble because they'll find some fault por qué tú no hiciste esto y por qué tú no hiciste lo otro. So politically I have to write Spanish and English to cover all the grounds of my people. No quiero pleito con la gente mía.

VII. Nuyorican is Universal

Politically speaking, I would never write a book of poems in one language or the other; it doesn't work with the balance of the way my people as a whole refer to themselves. I always say I'm a Puerto Rican poet, I want to be able to recite where my people are, which is not only in Spanish or English but both. That's my criteria for being a universal poet. I like the way the Europeans define me. I don't like the way the Puerto Ricans define me. They try to place me in certain structures. I'm never monolingual because I write in Spanish and English and in Spanglish. To be Nuyorican is also a return. This is not our problem exclusively. It's a universal problem. The Dominicans have it; the Latin Americans have it; the Africans who go to France and England have it. They have to adapt. The Nuyorican is a displacement. It has to do with people from native countries having to come to mother countries and adapt to them. So the Nuyorican is not a phenomenon of the Puerto Ricans in New York and the Puerto Ricans on the island. It's a worldwide phenomenon. I want to reaffirm that, first of all, I'm becoming a poet, not a Puerto Rican poet or a Nuyorican poet. The way I have structured these 198 pieces of solid sweat have qualified me to be a poet. As a Puerto Rican, tengo cinco gorras. There is no way that I could reach my Puerto Rican popularity totally in Spanish, so I don't consider Spanish as being the totality of being Puerto Rican. English is another reality. I love the language, and I need to use it. Another reality is the colloquial, everyday, linguistic patterns of code switching which I find brilliantly exciting and which many have accepted as a normal way of life. There are several universal components in my work. Primarily, the respect for the word, the fact that there is such a thing as respetar las palabras that you put on a text to represent you, because once you write them they represent other things, it's not only for yourself. I noticed that about ten, fifteen of the poems that I have written have become universally affected or accepted by other cultures... You don't write only for yourself, once you put in on paper it does not belong to you. Many people can pick it up and treat it in many forms, so I am very respectful of the form that I put in print.

VIII. Loss of Sight

Después de *Mainstream Ethics*, en el año 1987, cuando yo terminé mi trabajo con el teatro cuatro, tuve como siete años de una vida bastante bohemia y estaba en definiciones alcohólicas y tomaba mucha cerveza. Fui cervecero. Nunca me gustó la bebida ni tampoco las drogas. Pero era un vicio bastante vanidoso, desde la mañana hasta la noche tuve muchas intranquilidades. Siempre he tenido un sitio donde quedarme en el Lower East Side porque es mi base. You know, entonces yo me ajusté bastante después de julio 4 de 2004 cuando se me fue la vista. Después de un proceso de siete meses, cuando yo estaba en la Universidad de Connecticut recitando un noviembre del 2003, en ese momento hubo un agujito que se me metió en los ojos, you know. Entonces yo estuve seis meses de loco, you know perdiendo la vista, en denial. Me volví loco... pero vivía tranquilo. Estaba con la bebida pero después del 2002, en el 2001 estaba más tranquilo y centralizado, y recogiendo material y escribiendo y ayudando. Una doctora me lo dijo en 1984, que tenía diabetes. Me lo dijo y yo no le hice caso. Mis amigos me lo dijeron. Y yo antes leía con esos glasses que uno compra por $1.80 o $2.50, en the drug store. Yo leía con ésos y nunca tuve problemas. Pero eso vino bien ligero, la pérdida de la vista. Bueno, fue una fatalidad personal con mi orgullo. Eso fue una ignorancia, yo lo he notado. Yo esperé hasta que se me fueron las retinas. Entonces pues, cuando se apagó la luz totalmente, ahí fue cuando se murió Celia Cruz y mi hermana fue la que entró al funeral parlor a vestirla y ponerle la peluca y la ropa, la misma ropa. Fueron dos vestidos, uno para Nueva York y otro para cuando se fue para Miami. Entonces yo tuve el privilegio de llevar a mi hermana a Campbell Funeral Parlor. Cuando el cuerpo de ella estaba allí esperando a mi hermana que trabajaba con el funeral guy para prepararla y ahí fue cuando me vino la transformación y ahí fue donde yo escribí el poema, desde el espíritu de ella pero nunca salió para afuera. Se llama "La guarachera del mundo." Entonces eso ocurrió a la misma vez cuando se me iba la vista. Yo estuve un año escondido escribiendo la obra. No está publicada pero yo la quería escribir, era para sanarme, ¿no? I had to write something in the darkness. Yo empecé a escribir long hand y ahí fue donde empecé a reinventarme. I've done a pretty good job in the last three years. Me he reinventado bastante.

    Tuve una transición de poesía a obra teatral porque yo era un taipiador de dos dedos. Cuando yo perdí la vista yo no podía taipear porque nunca aprendí. Entonces, este trabajo de poesías que yo lo hacía muy exacto, también me he dado cuenta que me encanta también. No pude escribir poesía así, tuve que aprender de nuevo el sistema de Word documents y los otros sistemas de ayudarme con la vista. Yo fui a la escuela y todo pero mi trabajo mental estaba más adelantado y me adapté a trabajar con gente que me oye la voz y me taipean, de voz a dedo. Y esa transición hizo que se me hiciera más fácil desarrollar personajes or do other kinds of writing that I used to not like more than poesía porque la poesía es más personal. Either you have to write it or create it out of your own personal self, el personaje a maquinilla o a papel y perder la vista a trabajar con otra gente se me salían, se me salen, los personajes mucho más ligero que la poesía. En *Mixturao* hay unos cuantos que pasaron después, pero ya como tenía la cáscara los pude trabajar porque ya tenía la tesis del poema. So, I had the thesis of the poem already written so, it was easy to work it with other people porque ya estaban creados. Like, por ejemplo, yo estoy trabajando un poema ahora mismo por mi visita a Edinburgo, es un poema sobre el Río pero tenía que buscar una técnica para escribir el poema que me ayudara a advance my writing. So, la técnica es buscar las líneas de gente y escribir encima de las líneas, so ese es el trabajo mío en los últimos dos meses yo he conseguido como treinta líneas del Río. You know, entonces, ya las tengo así, so ya tengo el metro pero hay gente pintando encima de ellas porque quiero honrar que estoy aquí en [la frontera] el hemisferio que nunca he estado en mi vida mirando al continente que me interesa mucho. So, ese es mi poema que estoy escribiendo y espero tenerlo para navidades porque es un regalo no sólo para los estudiantes que me ayudaron, sino que hay un montón de gente que me están dando líneas pero ese trabajo es técnico porque estoy usando las líneas de otra gente y conectando las frases, es un trabajo colectivo. A mí que me encanta el trabajo colectivo, yo vine de eso.

    No es fácil dictar los poemas a otra persona. No es fácil, no. No, I can't do it. No, es un acto más personal. Tiene que salir del soul al papel o al typewriter

¿no? So, al trabajar con gente pues son los personajes los que nacen, they come out real quick. Los personajes están desarrollando todas esas ideas, ideas en general, es trabajo educativo. Todos esos géneros, pero, la poesía es difícil para uno trabajarla con otra persona en el concepto de la creación. So, me afinqué a estudiar y rehacer trabajos que ya había escrito y afinarlos. Por eso saqué este libro *Mixturao* [2008], porque es una compilación de cómo siete u ocho años que ya había dedicado yo a esto. Ahora estoy aprendiendo a escribir de nuevo by long hand pero es que yo ya estoy tan acostumbrado a tener gente, que, tengo que descontaminarme de ese proceso y no es fácil. So, la obra de teatro es mi libertad y mi outlet. Pero, lo bueno mío era que yo siempre escribía dos obras de teatro y un libro. So, yo siempre estaba en el teatro. Yo siempre hacía esa transición porque, it's hard to get a lot of published books, pero los míos han sido reprinted a lot, you know, tan siquiera cada año hay doce o quince lecturas. Algunas que yo forzo. Algunas que yo exijo. Es una búsqueda, es un hustle, un guiso.

IX. Tato Hoy
El Tato de hoy, está bastante bien. Cuando crucé el puente a México con José Luis Martínez y me entró esa cosa de la cosecha y le estuve chavando la vida hasta que finalmente escribimos juntos en seis meses la propuesta para Cosecha Voices y reorganizamos un currículum académico. Nos imponemos un currículum académico con una nueva conexión entre un programa comunitario y un departamento y le sacamos jugo para poder ayudar a educar a los muchachos migrantes—una sección de la populación no solamente de aquí, porque ésta es una población central de la cosecha, pero también una institución y una comunidad académica que produce muchos educadores, especialmente en las escuelas públicas y hemos podido en seis meses imponernos en la cultura académica y yo considero eso ya una hazaña. Yo considero eso una hazaña y lo estamos llevando a ahí, al grano, eso es un movimiento histórico y una revolución. Estoy contento con la cosecha so, al mismo tiempo estoy haciendo el proyecto de Chicago que es la comunidad productiva puertorriqueña más grande de Estados Unidos. La más productiva y la más culturalmente desarrollada en términos políticos y la más revolucionaria y me han aceptado a mí como el dramaturgo en residencia. Yo voy allí todos los años, saco un grupo de jóvenes, les enseño el teatro, saco una nueva obra para la parada, la parada termina con mi obra. Ya el año que viene "Bandera, bandera"

está programada, ahora tengo que escribirla. Y el libro, que ahora estoy moviéndome con Kanellos [publisher of Arte Público Press], con este al lado, que estoy esperando a ver si meto sal y pimienta a la mente de él y le meto una nueva idea para sacar más dinero. Estoy en buena compañía, so aquí no hay fraude. Aquí hay progreso intelectual so, tengo buenos ayudantes, la gente me está rebuscando de una manera diferente, me he puesto en firmes pies en el ceno de América.

— V —

POEMS

i am a wise latina

i am a wise latina
nuyorican daughter of boricuas
interpreting legal decisions
from its purest constitutional framework
amended by congressional laws
adopted with states' clauses.
i am a wise latina
circuiting words in statutes
reviewing precedence
strictly defining issues at hand.
thank you president obama
for your trust and privilege.

i am a wise latina
nuyorican daughter of boricuas
emerging from bronx projects/caserios
from deep-rooted modest poverty
los de abajo' the down trodden.
i am a wise latinal
learning from tug\gut to top gun
intelligent maneuvers
educated from catholic spellman to twice ivy leaguer.
i am a wise latina
serious pensadora
cojeme miedo
be prepared to defend your legal argument
i am a wise latina
at my confirmation hearing me atacaron
they accused me of short sightedness
of being enraged and angry.
i am a wise latina
me atacaron.
intimidated me with a row of firemen
accusing me of negating
their civil rights.

i am a wise latina
i contested with discipline and truth
i contested with intelligence and candor
i contested with reverence and love of my constitution
i contested by not tipping favoritism to any issue.
i am a wise latina
with my family at hand
a supportive force on my behalf
i'm now confirmed with the
highest historical puerto rican achievement.
i'm a wise latina
sentenced to life-time serving
as jurist, judge sonia sotomayor,
at the united states supreme court

guarachera del mundo

"salsera del mundo, guarachera cubana,
caridad ochunera, azúcar carnaval"

      negreza mundo, madrina alegría
      madama pinareña, reina bembas colora...

      compañera sencilla, mojito su sazón,
      corte majestuosa, su imperial galante,
      pedro knight, mi cabecita de algodón...

      rumbera coquetera, exótica taconera,
      ramillete de accesorios, flamboyante vestuarios,
      tumbao de travesuras, que le den candela...

      espelucada extravagancia, espectáculo quimbamba,
      aplausos, adulaciones, exaltaciones a su reinado,
      celia cruz majestad entrega humildes gracias, AZÚCAR...

      sonera toda poderosa, diva máxima absoluta,
      leyenda musical y a tu lado, lennon, presley, moré,
      gardel, sinatra, ellington y mi hermano puente el rey...

      inspiraba con sus claves, con sus ritmos, con sus bailes,
      adueñados las cantamos, las integramos, las vivimos, imitamos,
      histórica fruta-voz sembrada, quimbara quim bamba...

celebrada las potencias celestiales,	salsera del mundo,
capilladas en su cuba estrella galardón,	guarachera cubana
antillana embajadora mundial humana	caridad ochunera
peregrinadora guarapo salsa de melao	azúcar carnaval
contra el cáncer batallastes ayudastes	

      banderines continentales ondeaban sus almas,
      sol caliente muchedumbre, lloraban, cantaban,
      esperaban sus entradas, a saludar tus cofres,

paciencia, honor, orgullo, templo de adoradores,
llegaron al féretro de tu paz y tu descanso...

vestimenta elegancia, soñando casi viva en su transición,
las penas se van cantando, magnética energía me dio
el señor, y lo transplantó a mi público corazón...

ahora canto en dos universos
ahora canto en dos reinados,
sacudiendo mis bembas infinitas
navegando para siempre, luz y alegría
dos vidas de carnaval, AZÚCAR.

piri

piri thomas
suavecito
vaya
allá
ya
va
su camino
esPIRItu   esPIRItous, cheverote, grandote su destino

poet, playwright, novelist, storyteller, filmmaker par excellence
from 1928 to 2011 serving us justice with the written flow
he had the flow, the low, the owl and the wolf in palabras.

piri
thomas
suavecito
vaya
alla
ya
va
su camino
esPIRItu   esPIRItous, cheverote, grandote su destino

asPIRIna
asPIRIng
desPIRItu

piri thomas
suavecito
vaya
allá
ya
va
su camino
esPIRItu   esPIRItous, cheverote, grandote su destino

empirical to arms with our own written destino
espíritu
insPIRIng and consPIRIng to make us sabios

piri thomas
suavecito
vaya
allá
ya
va
su camino
esPIRItu   esPIRItous, cheverote, grandote su destino

metemPIRIc: beyond or outside the field of experience
reinsPIRIted, andaba como un sacerdote
reinsPIRIting las calles down on these streets se abren palabras
sPIRItual meaning sus pasos they opened the waves like moses

piri thomas
suavecito
vaya
allá
ya
va
su camino
esPIRItu   esPIRItous, cheverote, grandote su destino

he walked like a sacerdote.
the streets opened up with a new found resource
a hemorrhage of expressions emerging from tenements feresqurecitas,
maduritas
literary rain fire through your black
negrito, you opened up the street possibilities
and we emerged like rioters from the jungle

piri thomas
suavecito

vaya
allá
ya
va
su camino
esPIRItu   esPIRItous, cheverote, grandote su destino

a lo negrito, you shouted liberation lingo uniting our movement of 500 years

aged on the cotton plantation
recogiendo cotton fruits off the thorn cut blades
was the same as the main broadway factoría where we cut the cotton by piece
work
the bushels eran los mimos
nothing has changed

piri thomas
suavecito
vaya
allá
ya
va
 su camino
esPIRItu   esPIRItous, cheverote, grandote su destino

un negro from the island, arturo schomburg, revolutionized the research of black studies
and a negro from manhattan, Piri Thomas, revolutionized
the projections of our screaming thoughts

piri no era un uncle tom, no era un tío tomás

he was and is the late 20th century embodiment
workshops, jails, institutions, teaching us to take the mind

click it!
click it!

empty that mother into the baseline paper
and fill it up, llénala with blood ink
brain child of your intimate pensamientos
panama hat, priestly garment, sensual, sexual, seductive sorcerer,
esPIRItual, smoother esPIRItoso, musician of magical palabras

gracias piri thomas
nobility, puetro rican black man for all

piri thomas
suavecito
vaya
allá
ya
va
su camino
esPIRItu   esPIRItous, cheverote, grandote su destino

piri thomas
suavecito
vaya
allá
ya
va
su camino
esPIRItu   esPIRItous, cheverote, grandote su destino

this-curso (epistle para un sabio)

professor frank bonilla
armed with profundo integrity of pensamientos
honing his academic excellence.

frank
community strategist for empowerment
utilizing métodos en mesa colectiva,
escudriñando, recovering
puerto rican historical documents
organizing institution builders.

bonilla
all the upcoming intellectuals,
community activists, izquierdistas-leftists,
students clamoring to join forces with centro de estudios
puertorriqueños led by his humble presence.

frank
university maestro, calificador of many writing disciplines,
from theses to book proposals
with the genuine respect for learned evaluation.

bonilla
defender against collegiate racism.
vocabularist, sociologist.
silk-smooth orator conferenciante.

professor frank bonilla
we left his office, scratching our cabezas remarking,
"e/se bonilla tiene tremenda plasta
cómo es posible that
we shouted, fought and engaged
in multiple desacuerdos sacando uñas
y ese frank, no se le paraban los pelos."

frank
i was facing this frightful moment of being called into his office
"óyeme tato, I hand you this published document,
our most important centro publication,
published in daedalus, using the title of your book,
la carreta made a u turn, as our entire document.
daedalus is a journal of intellectual americana."
i read the forty-page document.
i was being introduced to mainstream america and
baptized by this cra/de of writers, which also expanded
the writings of dr. juan flores.

dr. bonilla
the best callejerismo chatter that i ever heard
on a bus, towards a protest march in connecticut,
an elder pa/trio/ta de la vieja guardia
commenting, "mira, yo no estoy
de acuerdo que el frank bonilla se retire del centro.
ese hombre frank, tú lo ves ahí, ten cuidao, él es un apache.
el tiene una cueva, y adentro está un tigere.
no lo molesten mucho, él te puede salir de atrás p'alante, y darte
un boricua bimbazo de inteligencia que te puede mandar
hasta freírte tus fundillos."

bonilla
un sabio, deep alma
frank, mi amigo, un caballero
at his residence, he took his time to read my entire manuscript.
his remarks were hemispheric esencia in the study
of my puerto rican thoughts.
entonces, frank me enseñó, he taught me the values
of the written word, this majestic scholar imprinted in me
the necessity to impose our will to create institutions
like the library and the archives so to be developed so they
 can last a lifetime.
when i enter the evelina lópez antonetti centro library
i think of... lifetime.

after a round of vino and bocadillos
 i left his home. i walked the glorious riverside drive
i understood bonilla's brilliant academic/community mission.
óyeme dr. frank bonilla, gracias, compañero!
los ángeles celestiales rascándose los cascos, adivinando
¡qué diablo!
se va a inventar el frank ese, con su próximo scholarly atrevimiento.

339

—V—
DRAMA

King of Cans
EL REY DE LAS LATAS—REDEEMING SOULS IN EL BARRIO

King of Cans is a one act play with seventeen scenes that was originally written in 2001 and, produced and performed that same year at The Red Carpet Theater of Taíno Towers in El Barrio.[1] In 2012, Laviera re-wrote the play into a musical and this version was also performed at the Red Carpet Theater on July 15th, 22nd, and 29th of 2012. After Laviera became homeless in 2010, the community rallied together to find him a place to live, and Taíno Towers became his home. Laviera, then, took to reviving The Red Carpet Theater as a community space. Unfortunately, Laviera was not able to attend the first two performances, of July 15th and 22nd due to an emergency hospitalization. Laviera poured his heart, soul, and the little finances he had into the musical. He tried to charm the doctors into letting him attend the performance with the promise he would return to the hospital. They declined his wish, but he was able to be present for the performance on the 29th. Upon his death, the Executive Director of Taíno Towers, María Cruz, declared that the theatre was to be renovated and renamed the Tato Laviera Theater. A version of the play was published in the *Afro-Hispanic Review* (Laviera 2012).

As Laviera stated in his promotional materials,[2] this musical production of *King of Cans* tells the story of a group of can pickers of Spanish Harlem. Using prose and song they reflect on the circumstances that led to their homelessness and their journey towards redemption. Laviera's play touches on the issues of social justice, cultural identity, provides a face to the invisible can pickers and recognizes the value of work. The play also weaves a love story into the daily lives of the characters. It offers a surrealistic view of a cesspool where the main character, Latero, conducts his can business operation.

This re-staging of *King of Cans* featured a talented cast of actors including Sunilda Reyes as Subway Miss Can; original cast member Gary Cruz as Latero; actor/musician Eddie Condé as The Champ; Jorge Quevedo as The Brain; Rafael Morales as Narco Cop; and finally actor/comedian Arnold Acevedo as Reverend Sidewalk. Due to logistical issues the role of Your Highness was eliminated at the last minute. However, her part is kept here as Laviera originally wrote it. The production team consisted of set design/

costumes by artist Manny Vega; set construction by Josué Colón; costumes by Olga Ayala; Tech design by Eddie Pagán; and hair and makeup by Ruth Laviera Sánchez. *King of Cans* was made possible by Director Evelyn Carrillo, Executive Producer María Cruz, and Musical Director Maestro Sergio Rivera. The musicians included Papo Pepín (percussion), Al Acosta (sax and flute), Sergio Rivera, Gilberto Colón Jr. and Ely (piano), Roberto Rodríguez and Aníbal Martínez (trumpets), Willie Cintrón, Orlando Marín Jr, Rubén Rodríguez, Bernie Minosos, Bert Castro, and Sergio Laros (bass), and vocalist Cita Rodríguez.[3]

STEPHANIE ALVAREZ

NOTES

[1] The original 2001 version can be found at the Centro de Estudios Puertorriqueños archives. Jacqueline Lazú provides an insightful essay on the 2001 version of the play in this book.

[2] See: https://www.facebook.com/events/466951286649406/?ref=52&source=1/.

[3] The version presented here is an edited version of the 2012 musical production. It was reformatted for the purpose of publication. All attempts were made to maintain the integrity of the work.

King of Cans
EL REY DE LAS LATAS—REDEEMING SOULS IN EL BARRIO

CHARACTERS

LATERO.—A beer alcoholic. A veteran haunted by the ghost of his past. A natural leader. A visionary.

CHAMP.—A coke snorter. He tends to speak after the nose sniffle sound. Speaks with addict's diction. He is an ex-boxer and carries that stance. Ready to pounce at a moment's notice.

REVERAND SIDEWALK.—An excommunicated minister. He is an alcoholic and an adulterer searching for redemption.

THE BRAIN.—A well educated heroin addict. Well read. Takes pill after pill, which he concocts from a laboratory in his high tech carton bed. He never walks (transports himself on a piece of wooden casters or drags himself around). He has an abnormally large cabeza, you could almost see his brain. He is constantly scribbling on pieces of paper.

YOUR HIGHNESS.—Ex-madam. A strong woman. She is afflicted with asthma. She has a limp or walking impediment. She uses inhalers which sounds like an air pump (sound effect). She carries around a money machine and a picture of her dead daughter, Pamela, on a huge button on her costume.

SUBWAY MISS CAN.—Ex-beauty queen. Still in her youth. Strong and proud. Hides a tragic past and because of that she has a nervousness about her. Her hands are constantly in motion making points or tapping beats. She is a chain smoker.

NARCO COP.—An undercover rogue cop. Mysterious presence. Tough and versatile, a man of many faces. Sharp dresser.

ALL THE CHARACTERS WITH THE EXCEPTION OF NARCO COP ARE HOMELESS AND LIVE IN LAS CALLES OF SPANISH HARLEM.

SCENE 1

MUSICAL OVERTURE TO THE SONG "WE ARE WORKERS! WORKFORCE!" SOFT FADE ON EACH CHARACTER AS THEY JOIN THE SONG. THE SIX HOMELESS CHARACTERS ARE SEEN INDIVIDUALLY PICKING CANS AND GOING THROUGH TRASH AT NIGHT. NARCO COP IS ALMOST ALWAYS IN LAS SOMBRAS, OBSERVANDO. NIGHTTIME IMAGES OF DESERTED EAST HARLEM

STREETS ARE PROJECTED ON THE SCREEN, JUXTAPOSED WITH IMAGES OF NYC HOMELESS PEOPLE.

SONG #1

"*We Are Workers Workforce*" - CAST

"We are workers! Workforce!

We are workers! Workforce!

A whole day's work, five hundred cans,

six hours, forty blocks, a dollar an hour,

self-employed. Who would believe we are

homeless bums, homeless bums?

We are workers! Workforce!"

THE SCENE ENDS WITH URBAN SOUND EFFECTS OF THE START OF A NEW DAY, AS THE CHARACTERS PACK IT UP FOR THE NIGHT AND WALK UPSTAGE AND FADE INTO THE DARK. SUBWAY MISS CAN, YOUR HIGHNESS AND LATERO REMAIN ONSTAGE. THE STAGE FADES TO BLACK AS THE FINAL IMAGE REVEALS THE DAWN OF A NEW DAY.

SCENE 2

SUBWAY MISS CAN AND YOUR HIGHNESS HAVE A CONVERSATION. LATERO IS OFF BY HIMSELF WITH A SOFT LIGHT.

SUBWAY MISS CAN.—What's wrong with Latero?

YOUR HIGHNESS.—Pressure. Un ataque.

SUBWAY MISS CAN.—What to do?

YOUR HIGHNESS.—Let's keep him busy. I'll call my padrino, Walter Mercado. [SHE SPEAKS ON A CELL PHONE] Óyeme padrino, Walter, my godson está craqueao. His whole cuerpo from top to bottom, ¡hablando con los muertos!

LATERO.—Oh my god, but the human element and its capacity to solve with nothing is the ultimate challenge!

YOUR HIGHNESS.—[STILL ON CELL PHONE] Te digo m'ijo, nervous twitching in all directions is some kind of reacción nerviosa. Give me a prognostication! Padrino, espera un minuto. [SPEAKS TO LATERO] You got me working como esclava morena, bag lady, vendedora de cuchifritos, recogiendo latas, jodedora, assistant bailadora, recepcionista, and I'm not wearing these high heels. Who do you think I am, the Statue of Liberty? [BACK TO CELL PHONE] What's his problema? Bulequera, o bellaquera, that's bilingual for horny, yes you're right. Four years without a woman, how do I know? I listen to him over the phone.

LATERO.—But no Dr. Mental. No medication. I want it to come from within. Cold turkey.

YOUR HIGHNESS.—Métete Viagra brother, hasta por las nalgas.

SUBWAY MISS CAN.—How vulgar!

YOUR HIGHNESS.—Nalgas is acceptable Spanish. Why don't you do him a favor?

SUBWAY MISS CAN.—What?

YOUR HIGHNESS.—He needs, you know, no seas mala, llévatelo contigo pa' la cama.

SUBWAY MISS CAN.—I don't know what you mean.

YOUR HIGHNESS.—He's sick, you know enfermito. He has a bilingual condition.

SUBWAY MISS CAN.—What condition?

YOUR HIGHNESS.—Medical. QUINOSAYLAYPARAY

SUBWAY MISS CAN.—QUININOSAYLA what language is that?

YOUR HIGHNESS.—En español, la manguera está agota', o la longaniza está floja. In Spanglish lack of plátano or soft morcilla and in English quinosayleparay.

SUBWAY MISS CAN.—You're disgusting. [SPEAKS TO LATERO] She has no class! ¡Qué cafre!

LATERO.—She's our eyes and ears.

YOUR HIGNESS.—It's coming, the explosion, the exercise. Busca la palangana pónganse sun glasses. ¿Quién sabe la medida? Let's hear fresco language. Let's talk fresco language, sí papito chulo, right there, right after faster, que faster, ligerito, así, así, no, sí, no sí, cinco segundos para, mete la macana, mierda, break a leg.

LUZ EN CORO PÚBLICO [SINGS]

SONG #2

"*King of Cans!*"—SUBWAY MISS CAN/YOUR HIGHNESS/ LATERO

Ponte la gorra, ¡Latero!
Put on your hat, King of Cans!
Ponte la gorra, ¡Latero!
Put on your hat, King of Cans!
Rey de las latas, garbage cans
in New York City homeless king, su majestad
put on your hat, King of Cans!
Vendedor of illusions, business man de los pobres.
Put on your hat, King of Cans!

[MUSICAL BREAK, THEY DANCE]

Rey de las Latas, King of Cans!
Orándole a los santos,
Rey de las Latas, King of Cans!
Potencia suplicando,
Rey de las Latas, King of Cans!
Dios todo poderoso a ti te pido,
Rey de las Latas, King of Cans!
¡Qué ayude a los afligidos,
Rey de las Latas, King of Cans!
The homeless living in corners,
Rey de la Latas, King of Cans!
Misery in every border,
Rey de las Latas, King of Cans!
King of Cans! Aquí viene la obra,
King of Cans! Analyze el mensaje
King of Cans! Cuando ande por la calles,
King of Cans! When you walk down the streets,
King of Cans! You're not better than nadie,
King of Cans! you're not better than nadie,
King of Cans! ponte la gorra, Latero!,
put on your hat, King of Cans!

BLACKOUT

SCENE 3

LATERO INTRODUCES THE CHARACTERS AND AS HE NAMES EACH ONE A SOFT LIGHT FADES ON AND WE SEE THEM IN THEIR INDIVIDUAL HABITATS/SPACE/SETS THROUGHOUT THE STAGE. LATERO IS STANDING CENTER STAGE. THERE IS A TRASH CAN FILLED WITH GARBAGE TO HIS RIGHT, SLIGHTLY DOWNSTAGE. WHITE SPOT WASHES OVER HIM/TRASH CAN SYNCHRONIZED WITH A SOFT SOUND EFFECT; WHISH.

LATERO.—We are twentieth-century workfare jobless recipients, moonlighting in the sun as can pickers, a job invented by national and state laws designed to recycle aluminum cans to return to the consumer, acid laden gastric inflammation, pituitary glands, coca diet rite, godsons of artificially-flavored malignant indigestions somewhere down the line of a cancerous cell...

LATERO INTRODUCES THE BRAIN AND REMAINING CHARACTERS WITH THE FLOURISH OF A CIRCUS RING LEADER.
LIGHTS/SOUND EFFECTS
(TECHNICAL/COMPUTER NOISES, OUT OF SYNC).
THE BRAIN IS IN HIS CARTON BED/HOME: COMPUTER, BOOKS, MAP, A FISHING POLE. LATERO CONTINUES...

We collect cans in outdoor facilities, congested putrid residues, our hands shelving themselves, opening plastic bags, never knowing what to encounter...

LIGHTS/SOUND EFFECT (MONEY SOUNDS).
YOUR HIGHNESS, SITTING IN AN OLD ANTIQUE CHAIR/ THRONE DECORATED WITH MONEY RELATED ICONOGRAPHY. SHE IS KNITTING CANS AND THERE IS A PENNY MACHINE AND A BOX FILLED WITH FIFTY-PENNY ROLLS BY HER FEET. LATERO CONTINUES AS HE RUMMAGES THROUGH TRASH CAN TO HIS DOWNSTAGE RIGHT REVEALING THE DIFFERENT OBJECTS HE DESCRIBES.

Several times a day we touch evil rituals, slit throats of dead chickens, tongues of poisoned rats salivating on my index finger, smells of month old rotten food next to pamper's diarrhea, dry blood infectious diseases, hypodermic needles tissued with heroine water, drop blood hazardous waste materials, but we cannot use rubber gloves: they undermine our daily profit.

LIGHTS/SOUND EFFECTS
(RECYCLING MACHINE/BOXING MATCH)
THE CHAMP IS SURROUNDED BY MANY GARBAGE CANS,
HE IS COLLECTING AT A RECORD PACE. NARCO COP IS
RIGHT BEHIND HIM QUIETLY OBSERVING IN A MENACING
STANCE. LATERO CONTINUES.

We are twentieth-century pickers of cans moonlighting during the day as lateros, making it big in America. Someday, I, LATERO, might become experienced enough to offer technical assistance to other lateros. I am thinking of publishing my own "Guide to Latero Collecting" and founding a latero's union to offer mental and dental benefits so that I can FINALLY kiss.

LIGHTS/SOUND EFFECTS (SUBWAY/BEAUTY PAGENT)
SUBWAY MISS CAN SKATES OR DANCES BEAUTIFULLY AROUND
GARBAGE CANS MAGICALLY. LATERO CONTINUES

We are twentieth-century workers moonlighting at night as pickers of cans. We are considered some kind of experts.

LIGHTS/SOUND EFFECTS (CHURCH SERVICE/NOISY BAR)
REVEREND SIDEWALK IS SEEN WALKING AROUND SEVERAL
GARBAGE CANS STUDIOUSLY CHOOSING WHICH CAN TO
SELECT. HE SELECTS A GARBAGE CAN WITH A PLASTIC BAG
FULL OF CANS. LATERO CONTINUES.

Experts at collecting cans during Fifth Avenue parades. We have read in so many guides to success that in order to get rich, to make it big, we have to sacrifice ourselves by digging deeper and deeper into the extra can margin of profit.

KING OF CANS

LATERO PICKS CAN OUT OF BOTTOM OF TRASH CAN AND CRUMPLES IT IN HIS HAND.

We are on our way up the opportunistic ladder of success. In ten years, we will quit welfare to become legitimate businessmen. I will soon become a latero executive with corporate conglomerate intents. So...

SCENE 4

THE PLAYERS GATHER IN A SEMI-CIRCLE. THEY SIT ON PILES OF NEWSPAPERS TIED WITH TWINE. A MEETING IS ABOUT TO TAKE PLACE.

REVEREND SIDEWALK.—Let's pray to the Almighty.

CAST—Amen!

SONG # 3

"Nowhere To Go"—CAST.—CHORUS.

"Nowhere to go

no, no, no, no, no, no

nowhere to go"

YOUR HIGHNESS.—As Sergeant in Arms of the Executive Committee of Latas, Inc., I call this meeting to order.

THE CHAMP.—We're aching all over!

THE BRAIN.—Benefits! What about our benefits?

LATERO.—We wrote a proposal to The People's Church requesting a health unit to visit our premises.

SUBWAY MISS CAN.—We have to put more pressure.

CAST.—CHORUS

"Nowhere to go

no, no, no, no, no, no

nowhere to go"

REVEREND SIDEWALK.—My stomach and my liver, my intestines and my vessels, I have changed from blood to wine, I need a gallon a day, a gallon a day. Where can I go for help?

SUBWAY MISS CAN.—Go to the hospital's emergency room.

REVEREND SIDEWALK.—It was closed down yesterday.

CAST—CHORUS

"Nowhere to go

no, no, no, no, no, no

nowhere to go"

LATERO.—As soon as we get organizational certification.

THE CHAMP.—It better come fast! I viciously snort heroine mixed with cocaine bottled in crack vials, a stew of substances parading constantly through my nose. Where can I get help?

SUBWAY MISS CAN.—Go to the homeless substance abuse center.

THE CHAMP.—They have a five hundred person waiting list.

CAST.—CHORUS

"Nowhere to go

no, no, no, no, no, no

nowhere to go"

LATERO.—If we work hard for the rest of the year we might save enough pennies.

YOUR HIGHNESS.—Pennies, are you crazy? I'm suffering from deep rashes, street infected hypertension, swollen legs from diabetes. I'm afraid of needles insulation. Where can I go for help?

SUBWAY MISS CAN.—Go to the clinic on the Lower East Side.

YOUR HIGHNESS.—The appointment takes six months.

CAST.—CHORUS

"Nowhere to go

no, no, no, no, no, no

nowhere to go"

THE BRAIN.—Nowhere to go is right. I can't move from my carton bed; green pills, blue pills, red pills, white pills, once a minute, ten an hour, twenty a day, two hundred per week. That's all I do, take pills. Is there any place I can go?

CAST.—Brother, you're a terminal case, brother, you're a terminal case, terminal case, terminal case, brother!

THE CHAMP.—What about you, Latero?

CAST.—Oh we know, he's addicted to the can.

LATERO.—Budwiser, 16 ounce, 12 ounce, 8 ounce, six-pack, ten-pack, picnic pack for breakfast, lunch and dinner; beer an extension of me.

CAST.—Go to the A.A.

LATERO.—My A.A. is the local bodega.

THE CHAMP.—So far we have a lot of ailments and solutions. What productive actions are we gonna take Mr. Chairman?

LATERO.—Let's send Reverend Sidewalk to The People's Church next door.

YOUR HIGHNESS.—We want affirmative immediate action!

REVEREND SIDEWALK.—This meeting is adjourned.

THE BRAIN.—I second the motion, too much pain in this meeting.

LATERO.—If we keep our work up. We'll prevail. I have hundreds of ideas for programming.

LIGHTS

FILM SEQUENCE #1. "SYMPTOMS OF THEIR DEPRESSION"

BLACKOUT

FILM SEQUENCE #2. "FLASHBACK SCENE YOUR HIGHNESS"

SCENE 5

LATERO.—I am a twentieth-century...

YOUR HIGHNESS.—You're a twentieth-century fool, Latero.

LATERO.—[REMINISCING] Subway Miss Can, What a knockout!

YOUR HIGHNESS.—[REACTS JEALOUSLY] I wouldn't touch that Subway Miss Can even if she was sprayed with a disinfectant bomb.

LATERO.—Oh Your Highness, you know she's my sweetest pie.

YOUR HIGHNESS.—She's just out to conquer your penis, pennies. She was the biggest highway in the Hudson River. They called her tractor trailer.

LATERO.—She's the Executive Director of Latas Inc. You're just jealous cause I have the hots for her, not you. Say the truth.

YOUR HIGHNESS.—I'm only interested in money, in getting out of this church lot, and moving into a fifth-class hotel, and re-capturing my social security benefits. I have no time to be thinking about how you make dumb decisions by naming her to run your so-called empire.

LATERO.—We do perform good services, and you are the company's comptroller, you run the purse strings, Your Highness.

YOUR HIGHNESS.—You live an illusive dream, as if you were Donald Trump.

LATERO.—I'm better than Donald Trump. I get 2 percent of all my deals.

YOUR HIGHNESS.—Oh sure, one penny per can.

LATERO.—We began buying 500 cans per night.

YOUR HIGHNESS.—A mere 25 dollars for all that work. That's gross. All we net is 5 measly dollars.

LATERO.—500 pennies gross. 100 pennies net. Our currency is pennies. Plus, our business has grown 1000 percent. We now can facilitate 5000 cans a night.

YOUR HIGHNESS.—I don't like this part of the operation. It's the losing end of the business. Five thousand pennies is fifty dollars for all this pain. We gotta clean the cans, the people in the block are complaining of all these shady characters coming into the neighborhood. I'm telling you that our daily operation is much more profitable, and furthermore, I don't get much sleep!

LATERO.—You're wrong. We make money. At least 50 pennies on each worker per day, for sitting here. You know why? Because those homeless can pickers are proud to tell the world they are employees of Latas Inc., that they are part of a workforce, that they collect a pay. It's for their pride, for their integrity. It is to maintain hope, that's why many of them are honest workers. Plus, our additional incentives, bonus for best salesperson of the month.

YOUR HIGHNESS.—Sure, you give away our hard earned profit.

LATERO.—You're jealous because I have the hots for Miss Subway Can.

YOUR HIGHNESS.—Sure, then how come you've never kissed her, I know why.

LATERO.—You don't know why.

SCENE 6

SUBWAY MISS CAN APPROACHES. SHE HAS A PRIVATE CONVERSATION WITH LATERO. YOUR HIGHNESS IS EAVESDROPPING.

SUBWAY MISS CAN.—[CHAIN SMOKING] Where's my ring?

LATERO.—It's all invested in my business.

SUBWAY MISS CAN.—You're still undecided, ah! It's been four years. All I want is a public kiss and a ring. I'm the laughing stock of all the street corners.

LATERO.—I have the nightly payroll prepared for our workers. Please do the rounds. I have hired a new driver from the Spanish social club to take you to The Champ who will pay the daily salary to all our workers. Let's work diligently and fast. I'm only paying gasoline by the gallon. I'm paying the driver by the minute.

SUBWAY MISS CAN.—Don't change the subject.

LATERO.—I'm not changing the subject. We're a growing company, Latas Inc. Its future; its success; our daily street can collecting project; our high-rise project; our night project—we are a growing company, and you're its Executive Director.

SUBWAY MISS CAN.—Don't butter me up. We should at least have a decent room to live in every night. And you know it's not to have a sexual relationship. Don't you think it's your duty to provide a safe resting place for your girlfriend?

LATERO.—We have to invest every single penny into our business. That's the financial road to progress and success. That's the way empires are created.

SUBWAY MISS CAN.—I'm not getting any benefits for cooperating with you.

LATERO.—Of course you are, we're developing an organization, Latas lnc., a workforce for the downtrodden. We're developing a model of how to integrate homeless people, how to organize them. Society will take notice. Our efforts might lead to us owning our cycling plant, commercials, consultancies, 60 minutes, Hollywood, and then we will have everything! I'll quit welfare! I'll be corporate! We'll be a conglomerate!

SUBWAY MISS CAN.—I'm not waiting too much longer. The Champ, who pays all your workers is courting me and is talking bad about you.

LATERO.—Oh don't worry about The Champ. The Champ works for me.

SUBWAY MISS CAN.—If I were you, I'd worry about The Champ, for more reasons than one. I'll do the payroll rounds today.

YOUR HIGHNESS HANDS THE PAYROLL ENVELOPES TO SUBWAY MISS CAN. SHE EXITS. YOUR HIGHNESS WHO HAS BEEN LISTENING ALL ALONG REACTS TO HER EXIT.

YOUR HIGHNESS.—I told you Latero, now she's courting The Champ.

LATERO.—Oh, Your Highness, I'm not listening to you. Subway Miss Can is my sweetest pie.

SCENE 7

LATERO WALKS TO THE CARTON BED. THE BRAIN IS ASLEEP, ALMOST AS IF HE WERE OVERDOSING.

THE BRAIN.—Oh, Oh, there he comes. I don't feel like writing tonight. I'm going to divert him.

LATERO.—Wake up, The Brain!

THE BRAIN.—I'm drugged until eternity.

LATERO.—But this is our designated normal time to speak, once a day, at our prescribed time. We have an understanding. You have a responsibility to our organization. You said you can only give one hour a day and this is the hour.

THE BRAIN.—I can't even lift up my mouth. But I've been working on this super pill for your quenoseleparay.

LATERO.—[PUTS HIS HAND ON HIS CROTCH] I don't take any pills. There's absolutely nothing wrong with me.

THE BRAIN.—This pill can make your crotch as big as the heavens.

LATERO.—Listen, I need you, concentrate, think, just lie down, think.

THE BRAIN.—I got the pill that will release you to open up Subway Miss Can's chastity belt. You can fly her up to the sky.

LATERO.—[ONCE AGAIN HE PLACES HIS HANDS ON HIS CROTCH] You're getting off of the subject. Don't deviate from me. Think. This is our hour.

THE BRAIN.—Can't it wait until tomorrow?

LATERO.—You don't wait for creativity.

THE BRAIN.—I'll give you everything tomorrow. I'll give you two hours tomorrow.

LATERO.—Get up, man!

THE BRAIN.—Ok, I'll turn on the tape. You talk to the machine. Tell me what you want. I'll write later.

LATERO.—Ok.

THE BRAIN.—[TURNS ON THE TAPE RECORDER] Begin.

LATERO.—What I think is our ultimate potential is if the Coca-Cola Bottling Company will establish and support us as a modern urban homeless can center in the middle of this city.

THE BRAIN.—Regional Office Metropolitan Center.

LATERO.—What, I don't understand.

THE BRAIN.—Just talk, go ahead, I'm taking notes.

LATERO.—Urban can centers.

THE BRAIN.—Doesn't work.

LATERO.—What doesn't work?

THE BRAIN.—Why would the Coca-Cola Bottling Company aid other companies? Most of our cans are beer cans, not soda pops.

LATERO.—For supremacy.

THE BRAIN.—Supremacy?

LATERO.—For the homeless, for the environment, for the cause.

THE BRAIN.—I see what you mean.

LATERO.—We want to be self-employed.

THE BRAIN.—What do you mean?

LATERO.—To hire our corporation.

THE BRAIN.—Can pickers?

LATERO.—Jobs, workers.

THE BRAIN.—There's no profit.

LATERO.—There must be an angle.

THE BRAIN.—No angles in picking cans.

LATERO.—The human angle, public relations.

THE BRIAN.—Public relations?

LATERO.—Guaranteeing jobs, subsidizing my 25 cents an hour per worker salary.

THE BRAIN.—There's no profit.

LATERO.—Let them do a commercial.

THE BRAIN.—Everything you're saying is too complicated. I'm full of pills. We're not a corporation.

LATERO.—So let them pay our workers directly.

THE BRAIN.—We're a phantom force. No documentation. They'll think we're a farce!

LATERO.—We're not a farce, and you're not living up to your expectations. I'm totally disappointed with your comments. I expect a total proposal on my ideas, which you have taped in your recorder, tomorrow.

THE BRAIN.—Ok, Ok. I'm just full of pills. I'm drugged until eternity.

BLACKOUT

FILM SEQUENCE #3. FLASHBACK THE CHAMP

SCENE 8

SUBWAY MISS CAN.—Here's fifty envelopes for the workers in the field.

THE CHAMP.—Have you been thinking about our plans?

SUBWAY MISS CAN.—I have no plans.

THE CHAMP.—I've been waiting and saving for you, for that one day when you go on a I date with me.

SUBWAY MISS CAN.—Save but don't wait.

THE CHAMP.—Latero does not yearn for you.

SUBWAY MISS CAN.—He's an honorable man.

THE CHAMP.—He does not kiss you. How long has it been?

SUBWAY MISS CAN.—Four years.

FILM SEQUENCE #4
FLASHBACK SCENE SUBWAY MISS CAN

SONG #4

"One Kiss"—SUBWAY MISS CAN

"I was found
in the streets,
left for dead,
abused by many
men in caves
in parks, raped
by many lives
as alley cats.
He found me,
assisted me,
gave me life,
never touched me,
never kissed me.
I'm ready to resume

my passion life.
Nobody has touched me
since, I want
to begin with one
kiss, one kiss,
one kiss, from him.
All that I want is one kiss.
Guaracha
Han pasado cuatro años
desde que yo lo conocí.
Mi negro respetado, mi amigo
y yo también ya mucho lo quería.
Lo llevaba en mi memoria,
lo llevaba hasta la gloria
y anhelaba ese día
que él sus besos a mí
me los daría.
Y llegó, por fin pasó
una mañana melodía.
Por fin, por fin, por fin.
Él quería mi beso,
mi beso, mi beso,
dulce melodía.
Ese negrito quería que yo
le diera mi beso."

LIGHT CHANGE

THE CHAMP IS IN THE SAME PLACE HE WAS WHEN THEIR CONVERSATION STARTED BUT IN A FREEZE. FOLLOWING HER SONG SHE CONTINUES CONVERSATION WITH THE CHAMP.

THE CHAMP.—I think Latero is gay, he likes men.
SUBWAY MISS CAN.—You must be crazy!
THE CHAMP.—He's never kissed you.
SUBWAY MISS CAN.—I'll wait for him forever.

THE CHAMP.—You've grown so beautifully, our can picking Queen. You're the talk of our jungle streets, all I ask is one date with me, what's wrong with that? A night on the town. I'll close my shop for you. Ask Latero if he'll take time for you. All I ask is one date with you. All I ask is to have one date with you.

SUBWAY MISS CAN.—Ok. I'll have one date with you. But Latero will know.

THE CHAMP.—I want him to know. I want the whole world to know. Let him compete for your love. A little competition will do him well.

SUBWAY MISS CAN.—I don't love you. I never will.

THE CHAMP.—All I want is to be your friend. All I want is to be your friend. To be your friend. Your friend. Friend. Friend.

SUBWAY MISS CAN EXITS. LIGHT CHANGE.

SCENE 9

IMAGE OF BROADWAY STREET FROM PERSPECTIVE OF A TRASH CAN. NARCO COP SPEAKS TO THE CHAMP.

NARCO COP.—You're still after her but you'll never get her. She's in love with the President.

THE CHAMP.—One day I'll destroy him.

NARCO COP.—You can't. We'll blow our cover.

THE CHAMP.—I can run the organization. I can be President.

NARCO COP.—You don't have any charisma. You're a public relations disaster.

THE CHAMP.—Look, Narco Cop, I'm the champion can picker of all New York.

NARCO COP.—You're the champion, the boxer, but Latero is the promoter, your Don King, you see what I mean?

THE CHAMP.—I hate his guts. He's never even picked up a can. I'll bet you he's a fugitive from justice.

NARCO COP.—So are you. What's the point? Nobody is examining anybody's character or handing out the housekeeping seal of approval in the jungles of your streets.

THE CHAMP.—I want to find out his name, his real identity.

NARCO COP.—Look, don't be a chump. We're making a lot of money. We're smuggling drugs in empty cans. If they catch any of our runners, the authorities will blame Latero. Your hands will be clean.

THE CHAMP.—When will I get my share of the loot?

KING OF CANS   **360**

NARCO COP.—Look, if I give you the money, everybody is going to start asking questions. You must stay underground. When we make enough money, we'll both split to the Caribbean and live happily ever after.

THE CHAMP.—How can I know you're not going to double cross me?

NARCO COP.—I'm a crooked cop, not a slime ball. We'll take a picture together of our daily routine; putting the cocaine in Coca-Cola cans, delivering to twenty street corners. Street sellers taking the coke, delivering it to thousands of New Yorkers, smokers and snorters. The sellers then placing the money in Pepsi-Cola cans, our runners picking them up from our designated garbage cans. We collect the monies and live happily ever after.

THE CHAMP.—I need money to seduce Subway Miss Can.

NARCO COP.—I'll tell you what. I'll arrange a rendezvous, dinner, hotel, etc., tomorrow. One hundred dollar gift certificate at Plymouth store, and here's two hundred bucks for your entertainment pleasure.

THE CHAMP.—Will you do something else?

NARCO COP.—What?

THE CHAMP.—I want to find out Latero's real name, here are his fingerprints. (HANDS him the PLASTIC BAG with scrap paper he took from Latero).

NARCO COP.—I'll run a check on him.

THE CHAMP.—Yeah! Let's develop a dossier on him, just to make absolutely sure we can attack him.

BLACKOUT

SCENE 10

WE SEE LATERO INVOLVED IN AN ARGUMENT.
ONLY LATERO IS SEEN.

LATERO.—Go ahead Reverend Sidewalk and Your Highness. Pack it in! I refuse to be lackey for lily-white institutions to be paraded and photographed in chic wine and cheese cocktail parties of the high tech Teflon class!

REVEREND SIDEWALK.—You should accept the proposal. Your Highness has a right to a warm bed.

LATERO.—[LATERO TURNS AROUND AND SEES SUBWAY MISS CAN] Are you part of this conspiracy?

SUBWAY MISS CAN.—What conspiracy?

LATERO.—To have us join a lily white network.

SUBWAY MISS CAN.—I'll never leave Latas Inc. under any circumstances.

LATERO.—And what's this dating business with The Champ?

SUBWAY MISS CAN.—Just a friendly date.

LATERO.—He's been after you for years. He wants to undermine me. He's probably the main dude behind this movement Subway Miss Can.

SUBWAY MISS CAN.—Would you kiss me?

LATERO.—I'll kiss you when everything is right.

SUBWAY MISS CAN.—Take time off tomorrow.

LATERO .—With all this mutiny going on?

SUBWAY MISS CAN. -When do I become a priority in your life?

LATERO.—You've always been a priority.

SUBWAY MISS CAN.—When will you look at me with lover's eyes?

LATERO.—I look at you with human eyes, with the dreams of my achievements, with an honest culmination of what I'm searching for, Subway Miss Can, and when that moment comes, I'll knock at your door. You're it for me. You're part of my illusion, can you understand?

MUSICAL INTERLUDE TO THE SONG

SONG #5

"Enter Nuestro Mundo"—LATERO/SUBWAY MISS CAN
"I wish to clear my mind
to find elucidation.
I don't know what I'm after.
I don't know what I want.

To be met face to face
in business negotiations.
To have them come right down
cause I have firm foundations.

There's something I believe
something I believe,

come and enter nuestro mundo.
The last is first.
Come and enter nuestro mundo.
The last is base.
Come and enter nuestro mundo.
They will come down.
Come and enter nuestro mundo.
I have the magic.
Come and enter nuestro mundo.
Enter nuestro mundo.
Enter nuestro mundo."

SINGING STOPS, MUSIC CONTINUES. THE CHAMP IS OBSERVING. SUBWAY MISS CAN IS IN A ROMANTIC STATE

SUBWAY MISS CAN.—One Kiss...

LATERO.—If only I could.

SUBWAY MISS CAN.—Just once, come and enter mi mundo, enter my world.

LATERO.—If only I could.

SUBWAY MISS CAN.—We could offer each other support, affection.

LATERO.—If only I could.

SUBWAY MISS CAN.—Release me from these cadenas.

LATERO.—If only I could.

THE CHAMP.—Come to me, Subway Miss Can! Your king has no man! Tu rey no tiene hombre!

LATERO.—[LATERO IS STARTLED AND ALARMED]. The Champ, I have war blood on my hands!

THE CHAMP.—So bring them to me, so I could jab splash your bloody face.

WE HEAR AND WE WITNESS THE INNER SCREAM OF SUBWAY MISS CAN. THE MEN ARE STARTLED. THE LIGHTS ARE DIMMED.

SCENE 11

STREET SCENES OF EAST HARLEM DURING THE DAY. A SIGN WHICH SAYS LATAS INC. WE BUY CANS, CAN BOUTIQUE, MAIL BOXES, GENERAL SERVICES CHECK CASHING, LATERO BEGINS WITH ANNOUNCING HIS NEW BUSINESS OPERATION AS HE'S SEEN THROWING PENNIES INTO YOUR HIGHNESS'S CHAIR. THE BRAIN IS BY HIS CARTON BED WRITING A PROPOSAL WHILE LOOKING AT A POLITICAL MAP.

LATERO.—We sell cans, can boutique, mail boxes, general services, cash checking. We're making a lot of pennies. You're the man, The Brain!

THE BRAIN.—Voter.

LATERO.—That was a stroke of genius!

THE BRAIN.—Registration.

LATERO.—Mailboxes, instant can pickers.

THE BRAIN.—Elections.

LATERO.—Check cashing.

THE BRAIN.—Campaign.

LATERO.—Who needs to sell cans at night. Reverend Sidewalk, Your Highness, Subway Miss Can, and you were right!

THE BRAIN.—Empowerment.

LATERO.—Let The Champ have the night! I'm becoming a profitable day entrepreneur. I'm glad I'm listening to my Executive Committee. They gave me excellent advice. Our profits have increased one thousand percent. Pretty soon, our main currency might be in nickels rather than pennies!

THE BRAIN.—You're right, you're right, but for God's sake, please let me finish my political proposal.

LATERO.—What political proposal?

BLACKOUT.

IMAGE OF A SIGN THAT SAYS LATAS INC. COMMUNITY OUTREACH. REVEREND SIDEWALK AND YOUR HIGHNESS WITH TELEPHONES AND DESKS. CONVERSATION BETWEEN REVEREND SIDEWALK AND YOUR HIGHNESS IN THEIR NEW OFFICES

YOUR HIGHNESS.—You're messing up, Sidewalk.

REVEREND SIDEWALK.—I'm only drinking two gallons a day.

YOUR HIGHNESS.—I'm not losing my warm bed because of you.

REVEREND SIDEWALK.—Don't act so high and almighty. You're the one who used to run a whore house, got gypped by the IRS, and thrown into the streets to rot.

YOUR HIGHNESS.—What does my past have to do with your irresponsibility, your slurred speech, and your falling all over yourself when funding sources are evaluating our premises? You no good wino of the lowest ranks. You're fired. Go back to the tent and rot in your miserable sea of cheap sour wine. I hope you drown in fifth rate grape juice. Why don't you reform and go back to being a reverend and stop feeling sorry for yourself, you no good bum. You were not wrongfully accused by your congregation, like you're always moaning and groaning about.

BLACKOUT

FLASHBACK SCENE. STAINED GLASS WINDOW IMAGE. LIGHTS ON A PREACHER ENTERING CENTER STAGE WITH HIS WIFE.

PREACHER.—Welcome on this Sunday to our Bowery church congregation. My wife Loretta and I are proud to welcome the new minister for our youth, Reverend Sidewalk!

LIGHTS ON REVEREND SIDEWALK ENTERING WITH A BIBLE PREPARING HIS SPEECH FOR THE CONGREGATION BEING ASSEMBLED AS THEY SCREAM "HALLELUJAH!" THE PASTOR GOES TO THE CORNER IN THE BACKGROUND. LORETTA, HIS WIFE, STAYS UP FRONT TO PRAY WITH REVEREND SIDEWALK. DURING THE PRAYER, LORETTA IS SEEN MAKING LOVE GESTURES TO REVEREND SIDEWALK. THE PASTOR BEGINS TO SLAM HIS FIST AGAINST THE WALL. TOWARDS THE END OF THE PRAYER, LORETTA IS CLINGING TO THE LEGS OF REVEREND SIDEWALK AND PORTRAYING AMOUROUS INTENTIONS. SHE HAS BEEN MOVED BY THE SPEECH. SHE IS SEEN FALLING HEAD OVER HEELS. THE PASTOR SLAMS HIS FIST AGAINST THE WALL REPEATEDLY.

REVEREND SIDEWALK—God bless sister Sarah, she dreamt of Jesus drinking a glass of water with her and said Sister Sarah. Then she woke up and we all know Sister Sarah's struggles. Yes, the Lord comes down in strange ways. Praise the Lord, hallelujah. ¡Gloria a Dios for our Puerto Rican congregation! There's a message for Sister Sarah and to all of you sinners of the bottle; don't let the evil ways of Satan drive you down the gypsy road, invite you to the wine cooler bedroom of the devil. Do not be tempted, for Jesus came to sister Sarah to bring down a message; brothers and sisters to get high, yes, stoned with the Almighty. To get blasted, yes, blasted with the Savior. To get intoxicated, yes, intoxicated with Jesus. ¡Praise the lord, aleluiah, gloria a Dios for our Spanish speaking congregation! Nothing is more enlightening than to drink the life of Jesus. One water drink, is all you need. One drink, to see the after world. One drink, to feeeel goooooood inside, one drink. Brothers and sisters, aleluiah, praise the Lord, ¡gloria a Dios for our Nuyorican congregation! Pick up the pages of the Bible and get yourself drunk all the way up to salvation. Thumbs up to that sweet wine taste of Jesus, yes sir! Let's raise our chalices to the Lord's words. Yes sir, aleluiah. Let's gobble up the champagne toast of salvation. Yes sir, hallelujah. Drink Jesus, we say yes drink Jesus, we say yes drink Jesus. We all say yes, Jesus is the road to eternal freedom. Come, everyone, together, let's say hallelujah, gloria a Dios!

THE CONGREGATION ATTACKS REVEREND SIDEWALK WITH THEIR WORDS AS THEY CLOSE IN ON HIM.

CONGREGATION.—(CAST). We are accusing you of stealing money from the youth! We are accusing you of adultery! Accusing you of impersonating a reverend! Accusing you of laziness! Accusing you of wrath! Greed! We're accusing you of envy! Gluttony! Lust! Pride! You're out of here! Pa'fuera! Out of here! Pa'fuera! Pa'fuera! Pa'fuera!

THE CONGREGATION IS PUSHING REVEREND SIDEWALK OFF OF THE STAGE.

FLASHBACK ENDS.

LIGHTS BACK ON YOUR HIGHNESS.

YOUR HIGHNESS—Sidewalk! Go sleep out there in the cesspool! You don't belong inside of the church! You don't qualify to be a homeless counselor anymore! [REVEREND SIDEWALK IS THROWN OUT INTO THE STREETS]

SONG # 6

"Wrongfully Accused"—REVEREND SIDEWALK & CAST. (SING AS A LITANY)

"I'm an ex-reverend community minister.
    Chorus

Wrongfully accused
REVEREND SIDEWALK
of sleeping with the
pastor's wife, and
expelled from my ministry.
Chorus
Wrongfully accused.
REVEREND SIDEWALK
     Embarrassing the legacy
         of my father's call.
              Chorus
                   Wrongfully accused.
                   REVEREND SIDEWALK
                        I find myself a fugitive

from God, whom I had served.
Chorus
Wrongfully accused.
REVEREND SIDEWALK
Now God is my bottle.
Chorus
Wrongfully accused.
REVEREND SIDEWALK
God and I are out to
prove my Innocence.
Chorus
Wrongfully accused.
REVEREND SIDEWALK
The elder established minister
and his wife were jealous of
my ministry and my spiritual appeal.
Chorus
Wrongfully accused.
REVEREND SIDEWALK
God and I in bottle are out to
prove my innocence,
Chorus

Wrongfully accused.
REVEREND SIDEWALK
My innocence, my innocence,
my innocence.
Chorus
Wrongfully accused."

SONG ENDS. LIGHTS CHANGE.
REVEREND SIDEWALK IS ALONE WITH A BLANKET AND PILLOW.
HE CALLS OUT TO LATERO.

LATERO.—What's wrong, Reverend Sidewalk?
REVEREND SIDEWALK.—Your Highness threw me out of my warm bed.
LATERO.—Well, don't worry, your street bed is still in the same place. Maybe you can resolve your differences tomorrow.
REVEREND SIDEWALK.—I want to protest against my church.
LATERO.—Don't worry Reverend Sidewalk, we all have a history that we want to forget.

FILM SEQUENCE #5. LATERO'S FLASHBACK SCENE

LATERO.—The shock left me emotionally paralyzed. I have not been able to feel intimacy to softly caress anybody ever since. No puedo tocar. All of me is in a constant luto. My body is dead. When I returned I could not find any peace. Only the streets and the brew, the beer, la cerveza of all types, all shapes...the beer is my woman, Reverend Sidewalk! Just like the wine is your mistress. I have 1000 deaths parading in my head, Reverend Sidewalk! All of us have a past we want to forget. But I love you, Reverend Sidewalk. I love you and admire you, Reverend Sidewalk.

BLACK OUT

SCENE 12

LIGHT/IMAGE

THE CHAMP NOW RUNS THE LATAS INC., NIGHT PROGRAM. THERE'S TWO COCA-COLA GARBAGE CANS AT HIS COUNTER WHICH HE HAS HEAVILY FORTIFIED ALMOST LIKE A SAFE.

CONVERSATION BETWEEN NARCO COP AND THE CHAMP, EXCHANGING MONEY AND COCAINE. THE BRAIN IS TAKING SECRET PHOTOS FROM HIS CARTON BED.

NARCO COP.—Be careful, The Champ.

THE CHAMP.—Don't worry, Narco Cop.

NARCO COP.—Be very discreet.

THE CHAMP.—Look at the specially made garbage cans.

NARCO COP.—More people are looking at us now.

THE CHAMP.—We're working from inside the tent, now it's better for us, a more central location.

NARCO COP LEAVES. THE CHAMP CONTINUES TO SNORT ALL KINDS OF SUBSTANCES AT A RECORD PACE. THE MORE HE TAKES, THE MORE HE CANNOT PRODUCE A HIGH, HE'S FRUSTRATED. SUBWAY MISS CAN ENTERS. SHE'S BEAUTIFULLY DRESSED. SPEAKS WITH THE CHAMP.

SUBWAY MISS CAN.—What about our date?

THE CHAMP.—Date, oh I forgot!

SUBWAY MISS CAN.—I'm glad you forgot. I wouldn't have gone out with you anyway. You look like a total embarrassment.

SUBWAY MISS CAN LEAVES THE CHAMP, AND IS SUMMONED BY THE BRAIN WHO IS ALSO HIGH.

THE BRAIN.—Oh, Subway Miss Can ...

SUBWAY MISS CAN.—Yes.

THE BRAIN.—Will you take this role of film to be processed?

SUBWAY MISS CAN.—What kinds of pictures are they? You and The Champ getting bombed!

THE BRAIN.—Surprise! Surprise!

SUBWAY MISS CAN EXITS. THE CHAMP AND THE BRAIN SPEAK BY THE CARTON BED.

THE CHAMP.—I can't get it on today. Juice up these substances.

WE SEE THE BRAIN AND THE CHAMP CONCOCTING A SMALL KETTLE OF SUBSTANCES AND GETTING HIGH DURING THE FOLLOWING CONVERSATION.

THE CHAMP.—Tell me something about yourself.

THE BRAIN.—[IMAGES AND PANTOMIME]. I was abandoned at the church adopted into a home for boys institutionalized in a retard warehouse. Because I liked experimenting with electrical appliances they, gave me shock treatments and then millions of medications and one day the State threw me out into the streets with no counseling and no protection. Tell me something about yourself. [THE BRAIN SECRETLY TAPES THE CONVERSATION]

THE CHAMP.—Somebody's busting up my operation.

THE BRAIN.—What operation?

THE CHAMP.—They are arresting my runners.

THE BRAIN.—Runners?

THE CHAMP.—I have twelve garbage cans in crucial corners selling cocaine, collecting monies. I'm in this with Narco Cop.

THE BRAIN.—You think Narco Cop is double crossing you?

THE CHAMP.—He's my equal partner.

THE BRAIN.—What's your deal with Narco Cop?

THE CHAMP.—Money in escrow.

THE BRAIN.—Why?

THE CHAMP.—Narco Cop believes that in our coke on coke operation, I have to remain a can picker, be cool. He has an account with a fictitious name.

THE BRAIN.—Whose signature?

THE CHAMP.—His signature.

THE BRAIN.—You're crazy!

THE CHAMP.—I'm following instructions.

THE BRAIN.—You know what's going down? You're being set up. Narco Cop is your middleman, and he happens to be the law, that means that if you don't have solid evidence implicating him, he could have you arrested and leave you out in the cold.

THE CHAMP.—How could he when he's the leader of the ring?

THE BRAIN.—He's the criminal, and he's the law. He's got both hands under his belt.

You have none.

THE CHAMP.—[PAUSE] Oh, oh, I see what you mean.

THE BRAIN.—Yeah!

SCENE 13

NARCO COP IS SEEN BY THE COKE CANS TALKING ON A CELL PHONE AS HE NERVOUSLY OBSERVES THE CHAMP WITH THE BRAIN.

NARCO COP.—Yeah, Sergeant. I got a mole, with a big transplant, an operation you'd never believe involving can-pickers. I'll keep you informed. Yeah, Sergeant. I know I'm on probation. You think I'll do anything stupid? [THE CHAMP APPROACHES]

THE CHAMP.—Here's the rest of the money.

NARCO COP.—You've been hanging out with that creep, The Brain.

THE CHAMP.—Just shooting the breeze.

NARCO COP.—About what?

THE CHAMP.—Life.

NARCO COP.—What about the tape recorder? He was taping your conversation, you fool. I saw it with my own eyes. Don't take any chances! [HANDS HIM A GIGANTIC HYPODERMIC NEEDLE] Pluck him.

THE CHAMP.—But ...

NARCO COP.—Get the tape!

THE CHAMP SPEAKS TO THE BRAIN FROM THE COKE CANS. REVEREND SIDEWALK IS FAST ASLEEP IN ONE CORNER.

THE CHAMP.—Hey. I got something good for you.

THE BRAIN.—Is it what I think?

THE CHAMP.—Pure divinity bombarded for your personal pleasure. Come and get it!

THE BRAIN CRAWLS FROM THE CARTON BED TO COKE CAN SAFE.

THE BRAIN.—Give it to me.

THE CHAMP.—I'll give it to you, all right!

THE CHAMP PUSHES A GIGANTIC HYPORDERMIC NEEDLE INTO THE BRAIN

THE CHAMP.—That's for taping our conversation you, traitor!

THE CHAMP TAKES THE CASSETTE FROM THE BRAIN'S RECORDER AND EXITS. REVEREND SIDEWALK SEEMS TO OPEN HIS EYES. THE BRAIN IN OBVIOUS PAIN AND CONVULSING CRAWLS BACK TO THE CARTON BED, WRITES A MESSAGE ON A PIECE OF SCRAP PAPER, HE TAKES THE PROPOSAL AND PUTS IT IN HIS POCKET, MOANS AND CRAWLS INTO THE SOUP KETTLE, PUTS THE HAND WITH THE MESSAGE HE WROTE INTO THE BOILING POT AND SCREAMS. LATERO COMES TO AID THE BRAIN. HE KNEELS BY HIS SIDE AND CRADLES HIS HEAD.

THE BRAIN.—Do it for me, please do it for me.

LATERO.—What is it?

THE BRAIN.—Win the election.

LATERO.—What election?

THE BRAIN.—Here's my proposal.

THE BRAIN.—Cremate my body.

LATERO.—I promise.

THE BRAIN.—Spread my ashes throughout this lot.

LATERO.—I promise.

THE BRAIN.—Here's my winning proposal.

LATERO.—What's in it?

THE BRAIN.—Politics.

LATERO.—Politics?

THE BRAIN.—Yes, politics. You can win the County Committee seat in this community. Win for me! Promise!

LATERO.—I promise .

THE BRAIN GOES INTO CONVULSIVE FITS. DIES. HER HIGHNESS AND SUBWAY MISS CAN APPEAR DRESSED IN BLACK AND CARRYING A WHITE SHROUD AND A WHITE SUIT. THEY KNEEL BY THE BRAIN AND WASH HIS BODY, CHANGE HIS CLOTHES AND WRAP HIM IN THE SHROUD. LATERO HELPS THEM. HE IS CARRIED BY LATERO INTO THE CREMATION SITE. A RED SPOT IS CAST OVER CENTER STAGE. A FIRE IS PROJECTED ONTO THE SCREEN UPSTAGE. THE LIGHT CENTER STAGE FADES FROM RED TO BLUE TO WHITE. THE PROJECTION FADES FROM FIRE TO CLOUDS. THE BRAIN EMERGES FROM THE SHROUD, DRAPES IT ACROSS HIS SHOULDERS AND WALKS TOWARD THE PROJECTION OF CLOUDS RAISING HIS HANDS IN THE AIR AS IF RECEIVING AN EMBRACE. THE WHITE LIGHT GETS BRIGHTER AND SLOWLY FADES ALONG WITH PROJECTION. THE BRAIN EXITS. THE CAST ASSEMBLES DOWNSTAGE BEFORE REVEREND SIDEWALK, WHO IS HOLDING AN URN WITH THE BRAIN'S ASHES, PLACES IT IN FRONT OF THE PULPIT AND DELIVERS HIS EULOGY. THE SPEECH SLOWLY CRESCENDOS AS REVEREND SIDEWALK STARTS TO REALIZE THE ERROR OF HIS WAYS IN HIS OWN WORDS AND BEGINS A "BAPTISM OF RENEWAL" BY REMOVING HIS WINE TANK AND ATUENDO BY THE END OF THE EULOGY.

REVEREND SIDEWALK.—There are no scruples in this city. There is no everyday ethics. The only ethics is the desperate moment. People live for the instance. Life's principles around these parts is to eat, sleep, drink and to survive the hour, to make it into the night. Yesterday, today, tomorrow is to nobody's consequence. There's no planning, ambition, projection. Everybody's friend is everybody's enemy. There are no scruples in the law or civil comportment. Don't expect compassion. Everybody's too busy searching for the freebie, the handout. Everybody is exclusively for themselves. Desperation is the instant sadness. Devoured in every suffering step is a violent tragedy, Calvary crosses hopelessness, desperation, brains in ill health, bodies sick, souls bleeding incessantly. Expect everything good and everything bad at the same time. In this world there's nobody to be blamed for anything, nobody's looking, nobody's policing, enter it, sleep one night anywhere, close your eyes my dear, The Brain, and rest in peace in the forever of your amen.

SONG #7.—CAST
"Help, help society, help."
"Help, help society, help.

Help, help society, help
because we are a reflection of you
Help help society, help.
Help help society, help,
because we are a reflection of you.

Is deepness our demise?
Is hopelessness our depression?
To live outlawed like that
in front of your reflection?
To sleep in cold
to thirst in stomach pains
to be constantly exposed
to many danger's hell.

You are also to blame
for this: the crimes, the
drugs, infectious diseases.
You led the sick from state
to streets skyscrapers rise,
communities at risk.

Please just don't walk
on by, take action, fight
oppression. Injustices prevail.
Unite, shout out, society
at attention against the
legislature.
Our motto should be one,
against homelessness,
our nation."

END OF SONG. BLACKOUT

SCENE 14

LIGHTS. LATERO IS SEEN READING A PROPOSAL.

LATERO.—Let's campaign.

REVEREND SIDEWALK.—Let's at least go over this proposal.

LATERO.—County Committee, what's that?

REVEREND SIDEWALK.—A nonpaying political party position. The lowest elective rank usually reserved for Community Block Captains.

LATERO.—How do we get on the ballot?

REVEREND SIDEWALK.—You run in the local democratic primary.

LATERO.—Your Highness, tell The People's Church that I'll go work for them if they get me on the ballot. [TO REVEREND SIDEWALK] Who should be Campaign Manager?

REVEREND SIDEWALK.—Daily operations, Subway Miss Can.

LATERO—Voter registration drive?

REVEREND SIDEWALK.—Mailboxes registration, Your Highness.

LATERO.—What's a pollster?

YOUR HIGHNESS.— A person who recruits the mailbox homeless people to register, sign petitions, and vote the day of the elections.

REVEREND SIDEWALK—How do you know about that?

YOUR HIGHNESS—I've always been smarter than you about everything.

LATERO—According to the proposal, The Brain says, "Follow all my instructions."

IMAGE OF THE PROPOSAL USC. THE BRAIN'S GHOST APPEARS DRESSED IN WHITE AND WITH A LASER POINTER HE FOLLOWS THE ACTORS WORDS ON THE SCREEN AS THEY READ FROM THE PROPOSAL DURING THE FOLLOWING SCENE.

SUBWAY MISS CAN.—People who receive their mail at our address...

YOUR HIGHNESS.—Thirty three and three quarter St. Church Lane, New York City...

REVEREND SIDEWALK.—Should be registered to vote, then we take those registrations personally to the Board of Elections...

SUBWAY MISS CAN.—To make sure they don't get lost.

REVEREND SIDEWALK.—In addition we make Xerox copies...

LATERO.—That The Brain was a son of a bitch!

YOUR HIGHNESS.—Don't interrupt. Let's keep reading.

SUBWAY MISS CAN.—The can pickers sign the petitions when they come to pick up their mail.

YOUR HIGHNESS.—And the same people ...

LATERO.—I got it! The Brain means that we have the power to win in some democratic primary in New York City with the 380 mail boxes in our lot.

LATERO.—Let's go for it. I'm declaring my candidacy for County Committee for the City of New York!

BLACKOUT

SCENE 15

IMAGE OF A CAMPAIGN ORGANIZING SLOGAN. LATERO SPEAKS TO YOUR HIGHNESS WHO IS CLEANING THE BRAIN'S SOUP KETTLE, WHILE GETTING DRESSED IN A SUIT AND TIE.

LATERO.—How much do I have in savings?

YOUR HIGHNESS.—You're not spending a single penny on this campaign.

LATERO.—How much do I have to spend to win?

YOUR HIGHNESS.—Your personal savings are untouchable.

LATERO.—I want to guarantee my victory. I want to win. I want to gain respectability around here.

YOUR HIGHNESS.—Let the people vote. Haven't we done enough?

LATERO.—I want to win by any means necessary.

YOUR HIGHNESS.—Your money is being saved in two accounts. One is for a six-month rent, on a fifth class welfare hotel, paid in advance, as your Christmas gift for your so-called Subway Miss Can.

LATERO.—And the other?

YOUR HIGHNESS.—Your own personal account amounts to seventy eight thousand pennies, and you're definitely not spending that money! Remember, your goal was to save one hundred thousand pennies, your own personal fortune.

LATERO.—You figure it out. You budget my fortune into this campaign.

YOUR HIGHNESS.—Oh sure! You want me to budget exactly seven hundred and eighty dollars!

LATERO.—Seventy eight thousand pennies! I want the budget in pennies, not dollars! I want you to deal in thousands of pennies, not hundreds of dollars.

YOUR HIGHNESS.—You and your pennies structure.

LATERO.—Coffee, sandwiches for registration, petition, for voting, after voting.

YOUR HIGHNESS.—OK. OK. Let me take out my pad. You're crazy, you know that.

LATERO.—How much for the registration drive?

YOUR HIGHNESS.—Eighteen thousand pennies.

LATERO.—Petitions?

YOUR HIGHNESS.—Eighteen thousand pennies.

LATERO.—The morning of the elections?

YOUR HIGHNESS.—Eighteen thousand pennies.

LATERO.—And the celebration?

YOUR HIGHNESS.—Eighteen thousand pennies.

LATERO.—We need petty cash.

YOUR HIGHNESS.—Six thousand pennies. You are now broke.

LATERO.—Oh come on, Your Highness. You're the Campaign Chairman of everything. You figure it out. If we win the election, it will be a feather on your cap, a feather in The People's Church cap. I'm the candidate, go to the pulpit. I just want to hand out palm cards. I feel like a politician! Let's win for the Brain!

YOUR HIGHNESS.—Sure. I have to spend a fortune and a mint!

LATERO EXITS. YOUR HIGHNESS FINDS A NOTE AT BOTTOM OF THE KETTLE SHE HAS BEEN CLEANING. SUBWAY MISS CAN ENTERS.

YOUR HIGHNESS.—I found this note at the bottom of The Brain's soup kettle.

SUBWAY MISS CAN.—What does it say?

YOUR HIGHNESS.—P, dash, dash S, dash N.

SUBWAY MISS CAN.—There are letters missing.

YOUR HIGHNESS.—Eaten by the soup.

SUBWAY MISS CAN.—At the bottom of the kettle.

YOUR HIGHNESS.—Whose message?

SUBWAY MISS CAN.—The Brain.

YOUR HIGHNESS.—The Brain?

SUBWAY MISS CAN.—He died.

YOUR HIGHNESS.—With his hand inside the soup kettle.

SUBWAY MISS CAN.—He hated soup.

YOUR HIGHNESS.—So?

SUBWAY MISS CAN.—So?

YOUR HIGHNESS.—There's something fishy.

SUBWAY MISS CAN.—Well then, let's go fishing.

THEY PUT ON DETECTIVE HATS AND TAKE OUT MAGNIFYING GLASSES.

YOUR HIGHNESS.—Let's solve the puzzle.

SUBWAY MISS CAN.—P, dash, dash S, dash N

YOUR HIGHNESS.—Let's begin with word possibilities.

SUBWAY MISS CAN.—Let's begin at the end.

YOUR HIGHNESS.—Vowels

SUBWAY MISS CAN.—San, Sen, Sin, Son, Sun

YOUR HIGHNESS.—P something, something San. That's out, it sounds Japanese.

SUBWAY MISS CAN.—P something, something Sen. That's out, it sounds like Buddhist.

YOUR HIGHNESS.—P something, something Sin. No, that The Brain was always in Sin.

SUBWAY MISS CAN.—P, something, something Son.

YOUR HIGHNESS.—P, something, something Son.

SUBWAY MISS CAN.—Poison! He was poisoned!

YOUR HIGHNESS.—By whom?

SUBWAY MISS CAN.—Let's talk to The Reverend.

YOUR HIGHNESS.—Yeah! He was around that night, dead drunk!

SUBWAY MISS CAN.—Perhaps, he can give us clues.

YOUR HIGHNESS.—Hey, that was pretty good!

THEY CROSS THEIR ARMS TOGETHER, IMPROVISING A SONG ON THE FOLLOWING

YOUR HIGHNESS/SUBWAY MISS CAN.—P, something, something Son!

REVEREND SIDEWALK ENTERS DRESSED IN WHITE. HE SEES THE LADIES AND APPROACHES. THE CHAMP IS SECRETLY LISTENING

SUBWAY MISS CAN.—Reverend!

REVEREND SIDEWALK.—Rejuvenated, non-Alcoholic seeking a hearing before the Church Council in order to restore my ministerial rights!

YOUR HIGHNESS—Reverend!

REVEREND SIDEWALK.—Becoming a decent outstanding citizen once again!

SUBWAY MISS CAN.—Reverend!

REVEREND SIDEWALK.—Oh, the Brain, his death was my liberation, Yes, Lord, thank the Brain!

YOUR HIGHNESS.—Now you're becoming a non-person, from non-person to non-person, selfish people like you never change, rich or poor.

REVEREND SIDEWALK.—I will no longer tolerate your devilish insults, I am becoming a man of the cloth, respect my profession!

YOUR HIGHNESS—Your profession, my foot!

SUBWAY MISS CAN.—Reverend, the night The Brain died, do you remember seeing anything?

REVEREND SIDEWALK.—I have no recollection.

YOUR HIGHNESS.—Sure, you were dead drunk, out to pasture, blacked out!

REVEREND SIDEWALK.—I've never blacked out!

YOUR HIGHNESS.—Then answer our questions.

SUBWAY MISS CAN.—What was going on?

REVEREND SIDEWALK.—All I know is that he was mixing those chemicals with The Champ. The Champ left to talk with Narco Cop. The Champ came back and then The Brain was crawling to the kettle. No he first crawled to his carton bed, wrote something, then he crawled to the soup kettle. He put his hand in the hot boiling soup, screamed himself to death. Latero came, picked him up in his arms. The Brain had died, and like I said, his death was my liberation!

YOUR HIGHNESS.—The Brain was poisoned.
SUBWAY MISS CAN.—Conspiracy...
YOUR HIGHNESS.—The Champ, the Narco Cop.
SUBWAY MISS CAN.—The Brain knew something.
REVEREND SIDEWALK.—Yeah, as a matter of fact, I remember seeing The Champ and Narco Cop arguing by those cans before...
YOUR HIGHNESS—Before what?
REVEREND SIDEWALK.—Before The Champ approached The Brain.
YOUR HIGHNESS.—Those cans...
REVEREND SIDEWALK.—I'll check his bed...
YOUR HIGHNESS.—We'll check the cans.
SUBWAY MISS CAN.—Wait a minute, the photos!
YOUR HIGHNESS.—What photos?
SUBWAY MISS CAN.—The night the Brain died, he gave me a roll of film.
REVEREND SIDEWALK.—Where are the pictures?
SUBWAY MISS CAN.—Inside my desk. And he said surprise! surprise!

BLACKOUT

SCENE 16

LIGHTS. THE CHAMP SPEAKS TO NARCO COP BY THE COKE CANS

THE CHAMP.—They got evidence.
NARCO COP.—What evidence?
THE CHAMP.—Pictures, soup messages, taped conversations.
NARCO COP.—Of what?
THE CHAMP.—Of you and me, exchanging money and drugs, of me talking about our operations.
NARCO COP.—Who took the pictures? Who taped the conversations? And what the hell is a soup message?
THE CHAMP.—The Brain did it all, and he threw a note into the kettle.
NARCO COP.—You crazy fool. I should have never trusted you.
THE CHAMP.—What are we gonna do?
NARCO COP.—You're gonna do nothing. Sit here. Don't move! Wait for my

instructions! Do you hear me?

NARCO COPS WHISTLES AND A POLICEMAN APPEARS
AND PUTS CUFFS ON THE CHAMP, WHO STRUGGLES
BEFORE BEING HANDCUFFED.
BLACKOUT
NARCO COP ENTERS THE LOT. SPEAKS TO LATERO

NARCO COP.—Arrest him! You're wanted by the Guatemalan authorities for subversive activities against their government.

SONG #8:

"It Hits You All At Once"—LATERO/NARCO COP/ POLICEMAN/CAST
"You are about to be served.
When the law hits you
it hits you all at once.
When the law hits you
it hits you all at once.
hits you all at once
hits you all at once
all at once at once"

NARCO AND POLICEMAN.—You're charged with mail fraud! Importing cans! Resisting arrest! Tax fraud! Selling drugs! Extortion! Voter's fraud! Illegal address! Impersonating a politician! Forfeiting signatures! You're busted, busted, busted. You're busted.

LIGHT CHANGE
REVEREND SIDEWALK NEGOTIATES WITH NARCO COP

REVEREND SIDEWALK.—Do I have something for you?

NARCO COP.—Pictures, soup messages, tape recordings; I can always say it was part of a sting operation.

REVEREND SIDEWALK.—Deal!

NARCO COP.—Deal. Now where's the evidence?

REVEREND SIDEWALK.—Oh no, the evidence will be given to you after the arraignment and court appearance. I give you my word of honor.

NARCO COP.—If you double cross me.

REVEREND SIDEWALK.—After the arraignment and court hearing... That's the deal. Make sure you drop the trumped up charges, Sir.

NARCO COP LEAVES WITH LATERO AS PRISONER. LATERO LOOKS AT REVEREND SIDEWALK WITH LOOK OF BEWILDERMENT. REVEREND SIDEWALK PULLS HIM ASIDE

REVEREND SIDEWALK.—Don't say anything. Don't talk. Everything is all right, son. Just keep dignified. Just keep quiet. Don't talk.

POLICEMAN HAS THE CHAMP IN HANDCUFFS. NARCO COP WALKS TO THE CHAMP

NARCO COP.—You fool! You traitor!

THE CHAMP.—You no good bastard!

NARCO COP.—Who do you think you are?

THE CHAMP.—You never intended to treat me as an equal partner.

NARCO COP.—Who do you think you are you no good piece of shit? Did you actually think I was your equal, you slimy son of a bitch?

THE CHAMP.—What percentage were you planning to give me?

NARCO COP.—You twentieth-first century citizen of nobody. You addicted mother fucker. You degenerate homeless bum. You non-card carrying fuck. You represent nothing in life. This is your fuck'n destiny.

NARCO COP PULLS OUT A GIANT REVOLVER

THE CHAMP.—Don't kill me man. Don't give me nothing. Just let me live!

NARCO COP.—I'm taking this revolver, and I'm pulling the trigger into your head, aimed at your soul.

THE CHAMP.—I'll never squeal on you. I'll disappear. Just give me car fare.

NARCO COP.—I'm pulling this trigger in your mouth because I'm the power, and I'm the law and because you're nothing but shit in this society.

THE CHAMP.—You're shit yourself.

NARCO COP.—I'm pulling this trigger because you don't exist.

THE CHAMP.—You're yellow, let me loose. My body against your bullets and I'll get to you.

NARCO COP.—Why should I let you touch me, you inferior scum? Nobody will care about whether you fucking die, you're not an entity or an opinion.

THE CHAMP.—Go ahead, pull the trigger. Get it over with, at least come closer so that I can have the opportunity to spit in your face.

NARCO COP.—Nobody will give a damn about how you appear in public. I'm killing you to liberate you, because you're a threat to me, you slimy bastard. I'm killing you because I don't want scum like you ruining the family name of three generations of cops.

THE CHAMP TRIES TO DODGE THE BULLETS "BOXING" AT THEM WITH CUFFED HANDS

Take this shot. [SHOOTS] Take this bullet. Take this assassination. Take this act. Take this finger. You're lucky the law has killed you dead [SHOOTS] with an authoritative bullet. Rot in the forever of no life.

SHOOTS, BLOWS SMOKE. THE CHAMP SPITS WAD AT HIS FACE.

BLACK OUT

FILM SEQUENCE #6. LATERO DETOXES IN JAIL. DESPOJO ESPIRITUAL.

SCENE 17

THE TWO WOMEN ARE BY A COSTUME RACK

SUBWAY MISS CAN.—Where do we get clothes?

YOUR HIGHNESS.—At the Hollywood Theatrical Costume Department.

THE WOMEN BEGIN TO GET DRESSED NEXT TO A COAT RACK WITH MANY COSTUMES.

SUBWAY MISS CAN.—Let's go to Saks. I've got a little money, you know.

YOUR HIGHNESS.—Why should we? Here we can get dressed in any character we want.

SUBWAY MISS CAN.—Why don't we buy something, instead of renting? Let's go to Orchard Street.

YOUR HIGHNESS.—It's better here, child. We can't get dressed in Bloomingdales.

SUBWAY MISS CAN.—Why don't we go to Plymouth?

YOUR HIGHNESS.—That's a working woman's store. Here I can find the biggest most beautifully, outrageous hat in the world. A hat so bad that the Baptist ministry will be singing hallelujah, praise to God, as I walk down the judge's aisle.

SUBWAY MISS CAN.—With all these charges going on, wouldn't you think if we overdress they'll really think we're drug dealers or something?

YOUR HIGHNESS.—You have a point. We better Xerox a big copy of this daily rental receipt.

SUBWAY MISS CAN.—I guess we have a right to appear with our best before the judge.

YOUR HIGHNESS.—Honey, let's demonstrate, let's talk, and let's get dressed to seduce the judge. [TRIES TO WALK ON HER HEELS]

SUBWAY MISS CAN.—What's your problem?

YOUR HIGHNESS.—Honey, I have not worn any tacos since they busted me in my joint ten years ago?

SUBWAY MISS CAN.—Here try these.

YOUR HIGHNESS.—How can anybody walk on these Caribbean pogo sticks?

SUBWAY MISS CAN.—You'll get used to it.

HELPS YOUR HIGHNESS TO WALK

YOUR HIGHNESS.—Thank you.

SUBWAY MISS CAN.—Let me ask you a question? Is there anything about Latero's dreams that can really become a financial reality?

YOUR HIGHNESS.—When someone better than Latero presents himself, I'll seriously weigh the options. But for now, we have an elected official we have to protect.

SUBWAY MISS CAN.—You look beautiful!

YOUR HIGHNESS.—You're a knockout yourself!

SUBWAY MISS CAN.—Let's set an example.

YOUR HIGHNESS.—Forget an example...

SONG #9

"Let's demonstrate!"—BEGINS TO SING, SUBWAY MISS CAN JOINS IN
"Let's demonstrate!
Let's talk! Let's get
dressed to seduce the judge. Let's
demonstrate! Let's talk! We're dressed
to seduce the judge."

SUBWAY MISS CAN AND YOUR HIGHNESS HUG.
BLACKOUT
IMAGES OF PROTESTORS OUTSIDE A COURTHOUSE. YOUR HIGHNESS, SUBWAY MISS CAN AND REVEREND SIDEWALK APPEAR BEFORE THE JUDGE.

YOUR HIGHNESS.—Do you know what's going on out there your Honor? Do you know what's going on out there? It's not a pretty picture.

SUBWAY MISS CAN.—Not a pretty picture at all. It's a disease that's going on, an epidemic, there's total breakdown out there.

REVEREND SIDEWALK.—Outlaws, people who are mentally sick, people who don't belong in the streets, people who need treatment. Men...

SUBWAY MISS CAN.—And women who have lost their self-esteem, who live by the instant, people who steal, hurt and rape each other.

YOUR HIGHNESS.—People who are rotting from ailments, human beings with every imaginable disease, tuberculosis, aids, cancer.

REVEREND SIDEWALK.—Men and women who are violent against each other, there's no shelter, people who live and die in carton boxes, who wrap themselves in garbage piles, who warm the hard core cement, creating instant blanket tents framed by all their worldly belongings.

YOUR HIGHNESS.—People who are out there, sleeping as if they were dead, promoting outdoor tombs, one after the other, hundreds, thousands, forming a chain of human misery, a colony of despair, and there're so many of us, that society has been immunized to our problem.

SUBWAY MISS CAN.—We're dealing with an epidemic of runaway proportions, and it gets worse, and worse, and worse.

REVEREND SIDEWALK.—Our independent community organization of can pickers, all of us homeless set out to give a message of positivity by winning an election proposed by one of our founders, The Brain.

SUBWAY MISS CAN.—You know what we did to win the County Committee of Election District Number Seven of Assembly District Number Eight?

YOUR HIGHNESS.—The people who voted for Latero are in extreme need of services. We paid them one hundred cents to register and one hundred cents to vote.

REVEREND SIDEWALK.—As homeless people we invested a small penny fortune on 368 people which was the margin of victory we needed to win the election.

YOUR HIGHNESS.—Mr. Latero had been saving to buy a ring and rent a fifth class hotel for his girlfriend.

SUBWAY MISS CAN.—But he had made an election promise. He became a viable candidate. He developed a campaign organization, and a strategy, invested seventy-three thousand pennies in his campaign.

REVEREND SIDEWALK.—And we fed the homeless after they voted and we are proud of it.

SUBWAY MISS CAN.—So arrest all of us, the downtrodden, for attempting to make an effort to participate in the democratic process.

THE VOICE OF THE LAW IS HEARD. FLASHING LIGHT.

JUDGE'S VOICE.—This case is dismissed. Release the prisoner. Release this defendant. Dismiss all the charges. This case is a disgrace. Una desgracia.

CHEERS ARE HEARD. EVERYONE SHARES HUGS AND CONGRATULATES EACH OTHER.

BLACKOUT

IMAGES OF PEOPLE OF COLOR BEING RELEASED FROM PRISON, HANDS BEING LIBERATED FROM HANDCUFFS. URBAN SOUNDS START TO MIX IN WITH MUSIC FOR THE FINALE. LATERO IS CENTER STAGE LIKE IN THE BEGINNING OF THE PIECE. THE CAST IS AROUND HIM. MULTI-MEDIA BARRAGE OF SOUNDS AND IMAGES MIX IN WITH THE SONG, RISING IN CRESCENDO AND SPEEDING UNTIL THE FINAL MOMENT.

YOUR HIGHNESS.—Let's celebrate! Let's go to the social club! This is a wonderful day! Let's all dance!

REVEREND SIDEWALK.—¡Si! ¡Vamos a bailar! Can I have the pleasure, madam?

YOUR HIGHNESS.—Today I will even dance with you, Reverend Sidewalk!

EVERYONE BEGINS TO DANCE. THEY EXCHANGE PARTNERS.

SONG #10
"Dancing"—CAST
"dancing
we achieved victory
dancing
Latero is free – dignity
dancing
Can-pickers in style
dancing
silk and gold and high-tech french
dancing
alla italiana modern dressed
dancing
in latino modern dress
dancing
moving it, feeling it,
living it, holding it,
live and disco music dancing hips
that swing
dancing
curves expanding, dancing
the coro is chanting, dancing
turns entangling, dancing
sonero attacking, dancing
percussion bombarding, dancing
brass reacting, dancing
steps are snapping
dancing
música, música, música, música
música, música, música, música

clave-clave, clap, clap, clap
coro pueblo, clave que clave, clave la llave

clave-clave, clap, clap, clap
coro pueblo
la siento, mi madre, el ritmo en clave

clave-clave, clap, clap, clap
coro pueblo
la canto, la bailo, la música en clave
clave-clave, clap, clap, clap
coro pueblo
clave que clave, clave que clave

clave-clave, clap, clap, clap
coro pueblo
el ritmo en mis manos
el snap de tu llave

clave-clave, clap, clap, clap
coro pueblo

te bailo, vacilo,
todito tus ritmos
clave-clave, clap, clap, clap
coro pueblo
dancing
everything touching
dancing
bodies integrating
dancing
climaxing and sweating
dancing
the night is wild

dancing

no sense of time

dancing

salsa society

dancing

and we danced the night away

dancing

and we danced the night away

dancing

and we danced the night away

dancing

and we danced the night away

dancing

the night away

dancing

the night away

dancing

away, away, away, away, away

dancing"

CROWD (CAST).—Beso! Beso! Beso! Kiss! Kiss! Kiss!

LATERO AND SUBWAY MISS CAN ARE WALKING SLOWLY TOWARDS EACH OTHER. SUBWAY MISS CAN RELEASES HER CHASTITY BELT IN THE AIR AS THE CROWD CONTINUES THE CHANT "BESO, BESO, BESO." SUBWAY MISS CAN AND LATERO MEET AT CENTER STAGE, THEY KISS, PASSIONATE KISS, GLORIOUS KISS

SLOW BLACK OUT. SILENT PAUSE. IMAGE OF A HOMELESS CAN PICKER. URBAN SOUNDS AND MUSIC FROM PLAY AS ACTORES COME OUT FOR THEIR CURTAIN CALL. LIGHTS OPEN UP. CURTAIN CALL. ROLL CREDITS.

BLACKOUT

FIN OF PLAY

WORKS CITED

Adkins, Karen C. 2002. The real dirt: Gossip and feminist epistemology. *Social Epistemology* 16(3): 215–32.
Adorno, Theodor. 1974. Lyric poetry and society. *Telos* 20: 56–71.
Algarín, Miguel. 1975. Nuyorican Language. In *Nuyorican Poetry: An Anthology of Puerto Rican Words and Feelings*, eds. Miguel Algarín and Miguel Piñero. New York: William Morrow.
―――. 1981. Nuyorican literature. *MELUS* 8(2): 89–92.
―――. 1987. Nuyorican Aesthetics [1981]. In *Images and Identities: The Puerto Rican in Two World Contexts*, ed. Asela Rodríguez de Laguna. 161–3. New Brunswick, NJ: Transaction.
―――. 1994. The Sidewalk of High Art. In *Aloud: Voices from the Nuyorican Poets Café*, eds. Miguel Algarín and Bob Holman. 3–28. New York: Henry Holt.
Algarín, Miguel and Bob Holman, eds. 1994. *Aloud: Voices from the Nuyorican Poets Café*. New York: Henry Holt.
Algarín, Miguel and Miguel Piñero, eds. 1975. *Nuyorican Poetry: An Anthology of Puerto Rican Words and Feelings*. New York: William Morrow.
Alvarez, Stephanie. 2006. ¡¿Qué, qué?!—Transculturación and Tato Laviera's Spanglish poetics. *CENTRO: Journal of the Center for Puerto Rican Studies* 18(2): 25–47.
―――. 2013. Evaluating the role of the Spanish Department in the education of U.S. Latin@ students: Un testimonio. *Journal of Latinos and Education* 12(2): 131–51.
Alvarez, Stephanie, Juan Flores, and William Luis. 2010. Tato Madera Smith. *Afro-Hispanic Review* 29(1): 7–8.
Alvarez, Stephanie, William Luis and Edna Ochoa. 2010. Crossing y tejiendo borders: Conversación multilingüe con Tato Laviera. *CENTRO: Journal of the Center for Puerto Rican Studies* 22(2): 34–49.
American Diabetes Association. n.d. Diabetes Basics: Type 2. Accessed 7 November 2009. http://www.diabetes.org/diabetes-basics/type-2/.
Anderson, Benedict. 1996 [1991]. *Imagined Communities: Reflections on the Origin and Spread of Nationalism*. Rev. ed. New York: Verso.
Andrade, Oswald de. 1928. Manifesto antropófago. *Revista de Antropofagia* 1(1): 3–7.
Andújar Persinal, Carlos. 1997. *La presencia negra en Santo Domingo*. Santo Domingo: Ediciones UAPA.
Anzaldúa, Gloria. 1987. *Borderlands/La Frontera: The New Mestiza*. San Francisco: Aunt Lute.
―――. 1999. *Borderlands/La Frontera: The New Mestiza*. 2nd ed. Intro. Sonia Saldívar-Hull. San Francisco: Aunt Lute Books.
Aparicio, Frances. 1988. La vida es un Spanglish disparatero: Bilingualism in Nuyorican Poetry. In *European Perspectives on Hispanic Literature in the United States*, ed. Genevieve Fabre. 147–60. Houston: Arte Público Press.

_____. 1993. Viejas rumbas, rumbos nuevos: el discurso musical en *La Carreta Made a U-Turn*. *Revista de Estudios Hispánicos* 20: 209–20.

_____. 1993. From Ethnicity to Multiculturalism: An Historical Overview of Puerto Rican Literature in the United States. In *Handbook of Hispanic Cultures: Literature and Art*, eds. Nicolas Kanellos and Claudio Esteva Fabregat. 19–39. Houston: Arte Público Press.

_____. 1998. Tato Laviera. In *The Heath Anthology of American Literature*. Volume 2, 3rd Edition. General editor Paul Lauter. 3076–7. Boston: Houghton Mifflin.

Aparicio, Frances R. and Susana Chavez-Silverman, eds. 1997. *Tropicalizations. Transcultural Representations of Latinidad*. Hanover, NH: University Press of New England.

Báez, Josefina. 2000. *Dominicanish*. New York: Ayombe.

Bhabha, Homi. 1994. *The Location of Culture*. New York: Routledge.

Barnet, Miguel. 1966. *Biografía de un cimarrón*. México, DF: Siglo XXI Editores.

Barradas, Efraín. 1980. Introducción. In *Herejes y mitificadores: muestra de poesía puertorriqueña en los Estados Unidos*, eds. Efraín Barradas y Rafael Rodríguez. 11–30. Río Piedras, Puerto Rico: Ediciones Huracán.

Barthes, Roland. 1972 [1957]. *Mythologies*. Trans. Jonathan Cape. New York: Hill and Wang.

_____. 1975. *The Pleasure of the Text*. New York: Hill and Wang.

_____. 1977. *Roland Barthes*. Trans. Richard Howard. New York: Hill and Wang.

Benítez Rojo, Antonio. 1998. *La isla que se repite*. Barcelona: Editorial Casiopea.

Berghom, Jennifer L. 2009. The power of the pen. Migrant students find their voices during writing workshop. *The Monitor* [McAllen, TX] 26 March: 1B, 8B.

Beverley, John. 1993. *Against Literature*. Minneapolis: University of Minnesota Press.

Beverley, John and Marc Zimmerman. 1990. *Literature and Politics in the Central American Revolutions*. Austin: University of Texas Press.

Binder, Wolfgang. 1985. Introduction to *AmeRícan*. In *AmeRícan*. Houston: Arte Público Press.

Blackmer Reyes, Kathryn and Julia E. Curry Rodríguez. 2012. Testimonio: Origins, terms, and resources. *Equity and Excellence in Education* 45(3): 525–38.

Blanco, Tomás. 1985 [1948]. *El prejuicio racial en Puerto Rico*. Río Piedras, Puerto Rico: Ediciones Huracán.

Bloch, Ernst. 1988. *The Utopian Function of Art and Literature*. Ed. and Intro. Jack Zipes. Trans. Frank Mecklenburg and Jack Zipes. Cambridge, MA: MIT Press.

Bost, Suzanne. 2010. *Encarnación: Illness and Body Politics in Chicana Feminist Literature*. New York: Fordham University Press.

Brecht, Bertolt. 1966. Mother Courage and Her Children; a Chronicle of the Thirty Years' War. In *Evergreen Black Cat Book*, ed. Eric Bentley. New York: Grove.

_____. 1992 [1964]. *Brecht on Theatre: The Development of an Aesthetic*. Ed. and Trans. John Willett. New York: Hill and Wang.

Bowdre, Paul H., Jr. 1971. Eye Dialect as a Literary Device. In *A Various Language: Perspectives on American Dialects*, ed. Juanita V. Williamson and Virginia M. Burke. 178–9. New York: Holt, Rinehart & Winston.

Bruce-Novoa. 1990. *Retrospace: Collected Essays on Chicano Literature*. Houston: Arte Público Press.

Burgos, Jr., Adrián. 2007. *Playing America's Game: Baseball, Latinos, and the Color Line*. Berkeley: University of California Press.

Cabanillas, Francisco. 2004. Tato Laviera. In *Latino and Latina Writers*, Vol. 2., ed. Alan West-Durán. 895–904. New York: Charles Scribner's Sons.

Campbell, Susan M. 2002. Interview with Tato Laviera. 8 August.

———. 2007. Nuyorican Poetry, Tactics for Local Resistance. In *Spanish and Empire*, eds. Nelsy Echávez-Solano, and Kenya C. Dworkin y Méndez. 117–38. Nashville: Vanderbilt University Press.

Carpentier, Alejo. 1967 [1949]. *El reino de este mundo*. Santiago de Chile: Editorial Universitaria.

Caruana, Louis. 2000. *Holism and the Understanding of Science: Integrating the Analytical, Historical and Sociological*. Aldershot, England: Ashgate.

Center For Puerto Rican Studies. nd. Biography. In Pedro Pietri Papers, Archives of the Puerto Rican Diaspora. New York: Hunter College.

Cepeda, Palmira. 2013. Personal email communication with Stephanie Alvarez. 31 July.

———. nd. Mi testimonio. www.utpa.edu/cosechavoices/.

Chabram-Dernersesian, Angie and Adela de la Torre. 2008. *Speaking from the Body: Latinas on Health and Culture*. Tucson: University of Arizona Press.

Chapman, Francisco. 2002. *Race, Identity and Myth in the Spanish Speaking Caribbean: Essays on Biculturalism as a Contested Terrain of Difference*. New York: Chapman and Associates.

Cisneros, Sandra. 2002. *Caramelo*. New York: Alfred A. Knopf.

Cohen Minnick, Lisa. 2004. *Dialect and Dichotomy: Literary Representations of African American Speech*. Tuscaloosa: University of Alabama Press.

Colón, David. 2001. Other Latino poetic method. *Cultural Critique* 47: 265–86.

Córdova, Nathaniel L. 2005. In his image and likeness: The Puerto Rican *jíbaro* as political icon. *CENTRO: Journal of the Center for Puerto Rican Studies* 17(5): 170–91.

Cortes, Félix, Angelo Falcón and Juan Flores. 1976. The cultural expression of Puerto Ricans in New York: A theoretical perspective and critical review. *Latin American Perspectives* 3: 117–50.

Craige, Betty Jean. 1992. *Laying the Ladder Down: The Emergence of Cultural Holism*. Amherst: University of Massachusetts Press.

Crawford, James. 1992. *Language Loyalties: A Source Book on the Official English Only Controversy*. Chicago: University of Chicago Press.

cummings, e.e. 1994. next to of course god america i [1926]. In *100 Selected Poems*. New York: Grove Press.

Davis, Paul A. 1979. The Black man and the Caribbean as seen by Nicolas Guillén and Luis Palés Matos. *Caribbean Quarterly* 25: 72–9.

De Certeau, Michel. 1994. *The Practice of Everyday Life*. Trans. Steven Rendall. Berkeley: University of California Press.

———. Walking in the City. In *The Cultural Studies Reader*, ed. Simon During. London: Routledge, 1993. 151–61.

de Granda, Germán. 1994. El proceso de koineización en el período inicial de desarollo del español de América. In *El español de América en el siglo XVI*, ed. Jens Ludke. 87–108. Frankfurt and Madrid: Vervuert and Iberoamericana.

DeFilippis, James. and Peter North. 2004. The Emanicipatory Community? Place, Politics and Collective Action in Cities. In *The Emancipatory City? Paradoxes and Possibilities*, ed. Loretta Lees. 72–87. London: Sage Publications.

DeGrave, Analisa. 2003. Heterodox Utopias: Defying Impossibility in Latin American Poetry. Ph.D. dissertation, University of Wisconsin-Madison.

———. 2007. Ecoliterature and dystopia: Gardens and topos in modern Latin American poetry. *Confluencia: Revista Hispánica de Cultura y Literatura* 22(2): 89–104.

Delgado Bernal, Dolores. 1998. Using a Chicana feminist epistemology in educational research. *Harvard Educational Review* 68(4): 555–82

———. 2002. Critical race theory, Latino critical theory, and critical raced-gendered epistemologies: Recognizing students of color as holders and creators of knowledge. *Qualitative Inquiry* 8(1): 105–26.

Delgado Bernal, Dolores, Rebeca Burciaga, and Judith Flores Carmona. 2012. Chicana/Latina testimonios: Mapping the methodological, pedagogical, and political. *Equity and Excellence in Education* 45(3): 363–72.

Deleuze, Gilles and Felix Guattari. 1986. *Kafka: Toward a Minor Literature*. Trad. Dana Polan. Minneapolis: University of Minnesota Press.

Díaz, Junot. 2007. *The Brief Wondrous Life of Oscar Wao*. New York: Riverhead Books.

Díaz Quiñones, Arcadio. 1976. *Conversación con José Luis González*. Río Piedras, Puerto Rico: Ediciones Huracán.

———. 1982. *El almuerzo en la hierba (Lloréns Torres, Palés Matos, René Marqués)*. Río Piedras, PuertoRico: Ediciones Huracán.

———. 1985. Introducción. Tomas Blanco: Racismo, Historia, Esclavitud. In *El prejuicio racial en Puerto Rico*. 3rd Ed. Río Piedras, Puerto Rico: Ediciones Huracán.

———. 1993. *La memoria rota*. Río Piedras, Puerto Rico: Huracán.

———. 2000. *El arte de bregar: ensayos*. San Juan: Ediciones Callejón.

Domínguez Miguela, Antonia. 2003. 'Kalahari' or the Afro-Caribbean Connection: Luis Palés Matos's *Tuntún de pasa y grifería* and Tato Laviera's *La Carreta Made a U-Turn*. AMERICAN@ 1(1). Accesed 24 May 2005 fromhttp://www.uhu.es/hum676/FIRST%20ISSUE.htm/.

Donne, John. 2001. From Devotions Upon Emergent Occasions [1624]. In *The Complete Poetry and Selected Prose of John Donne*, ed. Charles M. Coffin. 414. New York: Modern Library.

Du Bois, W.E.B. 1903. *Souls of Black Folk*. Chicago: A.C. McClurg & Co.

Elder, Arlene E. 1990. Preliminaries: Folklore and orature. *MELUS* 16(1): 1–3.

Esteves, Sandra María. 1981. A Julia y a mi. In *Yerba Buena*. Greenfield Center, NY: Greenfield Review Press.

———. 1994. Not Neither. In *Stone on Stone/ Piedra Sobre Piedra*, ed. Zoe Anglesey. 60. Seattle: Open Hand.

Fadlon, Judith. 2005. *Negotiating the Holistic Turn: The Domestication of Alternative Medicine*. Albany, NY: SUNY Press.

Fernández Olmos, Marguerite and Lizabeth Paravisin-Gebert. 2003. *Creole Religions of the Caribbean: An Introduction from Vodou and Santería to Obeah and Espiritismo*. New York: New York Univeristy Press.

Flores, Juan. 1981. Introduction to *Enclave*. In *Enclave*. 5–7. Houston: Arte Público Press.

———. 1985. "Que assimilated, brother, yo soy asimilao": The structuring of Puerto Rican identity in the U.S. *Journal of Ethnic Studies* 13(1): 1–16.

———. 1993. *Divided Borders: Essays on Puerto Rican Identity*. Houston: Arte Público Press.

———. 2000. *From Bomba to Hip-Hop: Puerto Rican Culture and Latino Identity*. New York: Columbia University Press.

———. 2000. Broken English Memories. Languages of the Transcolony. In *Postcolonial Theory and the United States: Race, Ethnicity, and Literature*, eds. Amritjit Singh and Peter Schmidt. 338–48. Jackson: University Press of Mississippi.

———. 2009. *The Diaspora Strikes Back: Caribeño Tales of Learning and Turning*. New York: Routledge.

Flores, Juan. John Attinasi and Pedro Pedraza. 1981. *La Carreta Made a U-Turn*: Puerto Rican language and culture in the United States. *Daedalus* 110(2): 193–217.

Flores, Juan and George Yúdice. 1993. Living Borders/Buscando América: Languages of Latino Self Formation. In *Divided Borders: Essays on Puerto Rican Identity*. 199–224. Houston: Arte Público Press.

Fodor, Jerry and Ernest Lepore. 1992. *Holism: A Shopper's Guide*. Cambridge, MA: Blackwell.

Folsom, Ed. 1994. *Walt Whitman's Native Representation*. Cambridge: Cambridge University Press.

Fox, Aaron A. 2004. Real *Country: Music and Language in Working-Class Culture*. Durham, NC: Duke University Press.

Franco, Franklin J. 1998. *Los negros, los mulatos y la nación dominicana*. Ninth edition. Santo Domingo: n.p.

Frank, Arthur. 1995. *The Wounded Storyteller: Body, Illness, and Ethics*. Chicago: University of Chicago Press.

Freire, Paulo. 1993 [1970]. *Pedagogy of the Oppressed*. Trans. Myra Bergman Ramos. New York: Continuum.

García-Peña, Lorgia. 2008a. Dominicanidad in Contra (Diction): Marginality, Migration, and the Narration of a Dominican National Identity. Ph.D. dissertation, University of Michigan.

———. 2008b. Performing identity, language, and resistance: A study of Josefina Báez's *Dominicanish*. *Wadabagei: A Journal of the Caribbean and Its Diaspora* 11(3): 28–45.

Gates, Henry Louis, Jr. 1988. *The Signifying Monkey: A Theory of African-American Literary Criticism*. New York: Oxford University Press.

Ginsberg, Allen. 2004a. America. In *Twentieth-Century American Poetry*, ed. Dana Gioia, David Mason and Meg Schoerke. 647–8. New York: McGraw-Hill.

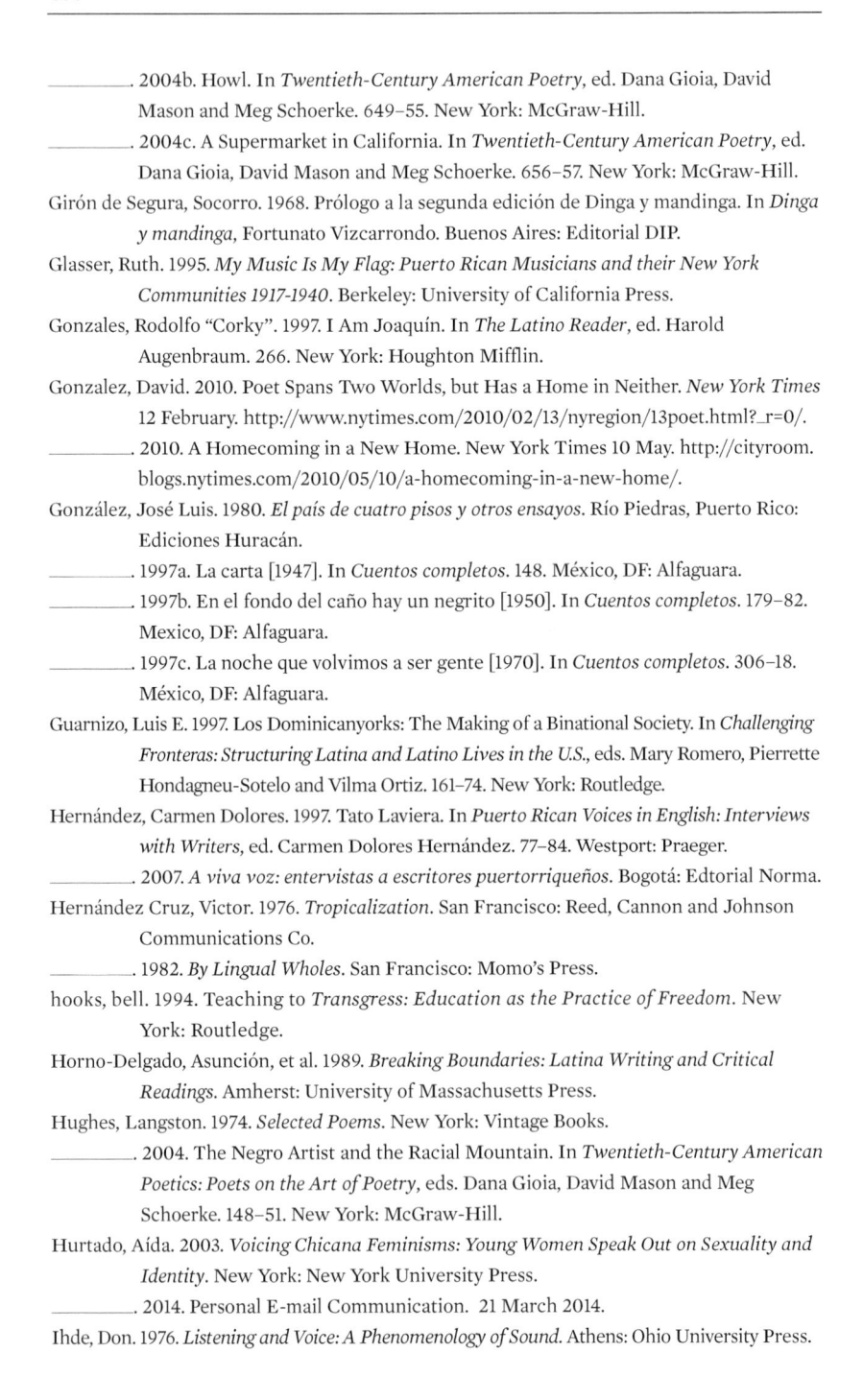

———. 2004b. Howl. In *Twentieth-Century American Poetry*, ed. Dana Gioia, David Mason and Meg Schoerke. 649–55. New York: McGraw-Hill.

———. 2004c. A Supermarket in California. In *Twentieth-Century American Poetry*, ed. Dana Gioia, David Mason and Meg Schoerke. 656–57. New York: McGraw-Hill.

Girón de Segura, Socorro. 1968. Prólogo a la segunda edición de Dinga y mandinga. In *Dinga y mandinga*, Fortunato Vizcarrondo. Buenos Aires: Editorial DIP.

Glasser, Ruth. 1995. *My Music Is My Flag: Puerto Rican Musicians and their New York Communities 1917-1940*. Berkeley: University of California Press.

Gonzales, Rodolfo "Corky". 1997. I Am Joaquín. In *The Latino Reader*, ed. Harold Augenbraum. 266. New York: Houghton Mifflin.

Gonzalez, David. 2010. Poet Spans Two Worlds, but Has a Home in Neither. *New York Times* 12 February. http://www.nytimes.com/2010/02/13/nyregion/13poet.html?_r=0/.

———. 2010. A Homecoming in a New Home. New York Times 10 May. http://cityroom.blogs.nytimes.com/2010/05/10/a-homecoming-in-a-new-home/.

González, José Luis. 1980. *El país de cuatro pisos y otros ensayos*. Río Piedras, Puerto Rico: Ediciones Huracán.

———. 1997a. La carta [1947]. In *Cuentos completos*. 148. México, DF: Alfaguara.

———. 1997b. En el fondo del caño hay un negrito [1950]. In *Cuentos completos*. 179–82. Mexico, DF: Alfaguara.

———. 1997c. La noche que volvimos a ser gente [1970]. In *Cuentos completos*. 306–18. México, DF: Alfaguara.

Guarnizo, Luis E. 1997. Los Dominicanyorks: The Making of a Binational Society. In *Challenging Fronteras: Structuring Latina and Latino Lives in the U.S.*, eds. Mary Romero, Pierrette Hondagneu-Sotelo and Vilma Ortiz. 161–74. New York: Routledge.

Hernández, Carmen Dolores. 1997. Tato Laviera. In *Puerto Rican Voices in English: Interviews with Writers*, ed. Carmen Dolores Hernández. 77–84. Westport: Praeger.

———. 2007. *A viva voz: entrevistas a escritores puertorriqueños*. Bogotá: Edtorial Norma.

Hernández Cruz, Victor. 1976. *Tropicalization*. San Francisco: Reed, Cannon and Johnson Communications Co.

———. 1982. *By Lingual Wholes*. San Francisco: Momo's Press.

hooks, bell. 1994. Teaching to *Transgress: Education as the Practice of Freedom*. New York: Routledge.

Horno-Delgado, Asunción, et al. 1989. *Breaking Boundaries: Latina Writing and Critical Readings*. Amherst: University of Massachusetts Press.

Hughes, Langston. 1974. *Selected Poems*. New York: Vintage Books.

———. 2004. The Negro Artist and the Racial Mountain. In *Twentieth-Century American Poetics: Poets on the Art of Poetry*, eds. Dana Gioia, David Mason and Meg Schoerke. 148–51. New York: McGraw-Hill.

Hurtado, Aída. 2003. *Voicing Chicana Feminisms: Young Women Speak Out on Sexuality and Identity*. New York: New York University Press.

———. 2014. Personal E-mail Communication. 21 March 2014.

Ihde, Don. 1976. *Listening and Voice: A Phenomenology of Sound*. Athens: Ohio University Press.

Ives, Sumner. 1971. A Theory of Literary Dialect. In A *Various Language: Perspectives on American Dialects*, ed. Juanita V. Williamson and Virginia M. Burke. 145–77. New York: Holt, Rinehart & Winston.

Jackson, Richard L. 1975. Black phobia and the white aesthetic in Spanish American literature. *Hispania* 58: 467–80.

Jackson, Tony E. 2006. The de-composition of writing in *A Passage to India*. *Journal of Modern Literature* 29(3): 1–18.

Johnson, Robert D. 2004. *The Politics of Healing: Histories of Alternative Medicine in Twentieth-Century North America*. New York: Routledge.

Juan Boria. Portal Oficial del Estado Libre Asociado de Puerto Rico. Accessed 17 November 2004. http://www.gobierno.pr/GPRPortal/Inicio/ Informacion GeneralYTurismo/PersonajesIlustres/Meses/febrero/Juan+Boria.htm/.

Kanellos, Nicolas. 1979. Foreword. *La Carreta Made a U-Turn*. Houston: Arte Público Press.

———. 1986. Canto y declamación en la poesía nuyoriqueña. *Confluencia* 1(1): 102–6.

———. Introduction. 1988. *Mainstream Ethics (ética corriente)*. 3–4. Houston: Arte Público Press.

Kumar, Amitava. 2000. *Passport Photos*. Berkeley: University of California Press.

Kumar, Krishan. 2000. Utopia and Anti-Utopia in the Twentieth Century. In *Utopia: The Search for the Ideal Society in the Western World*, ed. Gregory Claeys, Roland Schaer and Lyman Tower Sargent. 251–67. New York: New York Public Library/Oxford University Press.

La Fountain-Stokes, Lawrence. 2009. *Queer Ricans: Cultures and Sexualities in the Diaspora*. Minneapolis: University of Minnesota Press.

The Latina Feminist Group. 2001. Telling to Live: Latina Feminist Testimonios. Durham, NC: Duke University Press.

Laviera, Tato. 1979. *La Carreta Made a U-Turn*. Gary, IN: Arte Público Press.

———. 1981. *Enclave*. Houston: Arte Público Press.

———. 1985. *AmeRícan*. Houston: Arte Público Público.

———. 1988. *Mainstream Ethics (ética corriente)*. Houston: Arte Público Press.

———. 1989. *Olú Clemente*. In *Nuevos Pasos: Chicano and Puerto Rican Drama*, eds. Nicolás Kanellos and Jorge A. Huerta. Houston. Arte Público Press.

———. 1997. my graduation speech. In *The Latino Reader*, ed. Harold Augenbraum. 379. New York: Hughton Mifflin Company.

———. 2001. *King of Cans*. Unpublished manuscript.

———. 2006a. nideaquínideallá. *Afro-Hispanic Review* 25(2): 173–5.

———. 2006b. Selections from *Mixturao* Review. *Afro-Hispanic Review* 25(2): 173–90.

———. 2006c. The Spark. *Afro-Hispanic Review* 25(2): 191–210.

———. 2007. '77 Chicago Riot. *Afro-Hispanic Review* 26(2): 145–84.

———. 2008a. *Mixturao and Other Poems*. Houston: Arte Público Press.

———. 2008b. *Bandera a Bandera*. *Afro-Hispanic Review* 27(2): 165–226.

———. 2010. *El Barrio: A Novel* (Selections). *Afro-Hispanic Review* 29(1): 207–20.

———. 2012. *The King of Cans*. *Afro-Hispanic Review* 31(1): 189–232.
Lazú, Jacqueline. 2008. Interview with Efraín Nazario. 29 August.
Lienhard, Martín. 1991. *La voz y su huella: escritura y conflicto étnico-social en América Latina 1492–1988*. Serie Rama. Hanover: Ediciones del Norte.
Lipsky, John M. 1994. *Latin American Spanish*. New York: Longman Publishing Group.
———. 2008. *A History of Afro-Hispanic Language: Five Centuries, Five Continents*. New York: Cambridge University Press.
López, Belinda. 2009. Mi testimonio. www.utpa.edu/cosechavoices/.
———. 2013. Personal email communication with Stephanie Alvarez. 31 July.
López, Edrik. 2005. Nuyorican spaces: Mapping identity in a poetic geography. *CENTRO: Journal of the Center for Puerto Rican Studies* 17(1): 202–19.
Luis, William. 1992. From New York to the world: An interview with Tato Laviera. *Callaloo: A Journal of African-American and African Arts and Letters* 15(4): 1022–33.
———. 1997. *Dance Between Two Cultures: Latino Caribbean Literature Written in the United States*. Nashville: Vanderbilt University Press.
———. 2008a. Tato Laviera: Mix(ing) t(hro)u(gh)ou(t). In *Mixturao and Other Poems*. ix–xxi. Houston: Arte Público Press.
———. 2009. Afro-Latino Identity and the Poetry of Tato Laviera. *Review: Literature and the Arts of the Americas* 78.42(1): 31–41.
———, ed. 2013. *Looking Out, Looking In: Anthology of Latino Poetry*. Houston: Arte Público Press.
McAlister, Alfred L. Cheryl L. Perry and Guy S. Parcel. 2008. How Individuals, Environments, and Health Behaviors Interact: Social Cognitive Theory. In *Health Behavior and Health Education: Theory, Research, Practice*. 4th Edition, eds. Karen Glanz, Barbara K. Rimer and K. Viswanath. 169–88. San Francisco: Jossey Bass.
Makoni, Sinfree and Alastair Pennycook. 2005. Disinventing and (re)constituting languages. *Critical Inquiry in Language Studies* 2: 137–56.
Maldonado, Adál. 2004. *Out of Focus Nuyoricans*. Cambridge, MA: David Rockefeller Center for Latin American Studies at Harvard University
Mansur, Mónica. 1973. *La poesía negrista*. México, DF: Ediciones Era.
Margolick, David. 2007. Penny Foolish. *New York Times* 11. Accessed from http://www.nytimes.com/2007/02/11/opinion/11margolick.html/.
Maristany, Hiram. 1983. Young Lords Party: 1969–1975. *Caribe* 7(4): 17.
Marqués, René. 1991 [1953]. *La carreta: drama en tres actos*. Río Piedras, Puerto Rico: Editorial Cultural.
———. 1981. *Cuentos puertorriqueños de hoy*. Río Piedras, Puerto Rico: Editorial Cultural
Marre, Jeremy. 1979. *Salsa: Latin Pop Music in the Cities*. Videotape. Harcourt Films.
Martín Barbero, Jesús. 1993. *Communication Culture and Hegemony: From the Media to Mediation*. Trans. Elizabeth Fox and Robert A. White. London: Sage Press.
Martín-Rodríguez, Manuel M. 1999. A sense of (dis)place(ment): Tato Laviera's AmeRícan identity. *Monographic Review* 15: 262–72.

Martínez, Glenn. 2008. Interview with Tato Laviera. 2 November. Edinburg, Texas.

Martínez Diente, Pablo. 2006. "Words without border": A bilingual conversation with Tato Laviera. *Afro-Hispanic Review* 25(2): 151–8.

Marvasti, Amir B. 2003. *Being Homeless: Textual and Narrative Constructions*. Lanham, MD: Lexington Books.

Marzán, Julio. 1995. The poetry and antipoetry of Luis Palés Matos: From canciones to tuntunes. *Callaloo* 18(2): 506–23.

Méndez, Danny. 2012. *Narratives of Migration and Displacement in Dominican Literature*. New York: Routledge.

Mercer, Kobena. 2005. Diaspora Aesthetics and Visual Culture. In *Black Cultural Traffic*, eds. Harry Justin Elam and Kennell Jackson. 141–61. Ann Arbor: University of Michigan Press.

Miahle, Pierre Toussaint Fréderic. c. 1855. *Album pintoresco de la isla de Cuba*. La Habana: B. May y Ca.

Mignolo, Walter. 2000. *Local Histories/Global Designs: Coloniality, Subaltern Knowledges, and Border Thinking*. Princeton, NJ: Princeton University Press.

Mohr, Nicholasa. 1987. Puerto Rican writers in the United States, Puerto Rican writers in Puerto Rico: A separation beyond language. *The Americas Review* 15(2): 87–92.

Moll, Luis C., Cathy Amanti, Deborah Neff and Norma Gonzalez. 1992. Funds of knowledge for teaching: Using a qualitative approach to connect homes and classrooms. *Qualitative Issues in Educational Research* 31(2): 132–41.

Moraga, Cherríe. 1981. Theory in the Flesh. In *This Bridge Called My Back: Writings by Radical Women of Color*, eds. Cherríe Moraga and Gloria Anzaldúa. 23. New York: Kitchen Table/Women of Color Press.

Morales, Ed. 2002. *Living in Spanglish: The Search for Latino Identity in America*. New York: St. Martin's.

Morris, Tracie. 1994. Morenita. In *Aloud: Voices from the Nuyorican Poets Café*, eds. Miguel Algarín and Bob Holman. 102–6. New York: Henry Holt.

Muñoz, Ana. 2013. Personal email communication with Stephanie Alvarez. 31 July.

Muñoz, José Esteban. 1999. *Disidentifications: Queers of Color and the Performance of Politics*. Minneapolis: University of Minnesota Press.

Muñoz Marín, Luis. 1974. The Pamphlet. In *Borinquen: An Anthology of Puerto Rican Literature*. Trans. Barry Luby. Ed. María Teresa Babín and Stan Steiner. 199. New York: Knopf.

———. 2004 [1920]. Panfleto. In *Literatura puertorriqueña del siglo XX: antología*, ed. Mercedes López-Baralt. 721. San Juan: La Editorial de la Universidad de Puerto Rico.

National Diabetes Education Program. 2008. The Diabetes Epidemic among Hispanics/Latinos. Accessed 7 Novermber 2009. http://ndep.nih.gov/media/FS_HispLatino_Eng.pdf/.

Navarro Tomás, Tomás. 1950. *Manual de pronunciación española*. Madrid: Publicaciones de la Revista de Filología Española.

Negrón-Muntaner, Frances. 1997. English Only Jamás but Spanish Only Cuidado: Language and Nationalism in Contemporary Puerto Rico. In *Puerto Rican Jam: Rethinking Colonialism and Nationalism*, eds. Frances Negrón-Muntaner and Ramón Grosfoguel. 257–85. Minneapolis: University of Minnesota Press.

Nelson, Dale. 1996. The Political Behavior of New York Puerto Ricans: Assimilation or Survival? In *Historical Perspectives on Puerto Rican Survival in the United States*, eds. Clara Rodriguez and Virginia Sánchez Korrol. 109–29. Princeton, NJ: Markus Wiener Publishers.

Neruda, Pablo. 1924. *Veinte poemas de amor y una canción desesperada*. Santiago de Chile: Nascimiento.

———. 1966. *Los versos del capitán: poemas de amor*. Buenos Aires: Editorial Losada.

———. 1990. *Canto general*. Ed. Enrico Mario Santí. Madrid: Cátedra.

Noel, Tomás Urayoán. 2008. NYPR Blues: Experimentalism, Performance, and the Articulation of Diaspora in Nuyorican Poetry. Ph.D. dissertation, New York University.

———. 2011. Counter/Public Address: Nuyorican Poetries in the Slam Era. *Latino Studies* 9(1): 38–61.

Noll, Volker. 2005. Reflexiones sobre el llamado andalucismo del español de América. In *El español de América: aspectos teóricos, particularidades, contactos*, eds. Volker Noll, Klaus Zimmermann e Ingrid Neumann-Holzschuh. 95–112. Madrid and Frankfurt: Iberoamericana/Vervuet.

Nuyorican Poets Cafe. nd. Accessed 1 June 2008. http://www.nuyorican.org/AboutUs / AboutUs.html/.

Ochoa, Edna. 2009. Tato Laviera: un poeta puertorriqueño en Nueva York. *Archipiélago* 64: 31–3.

Office of Minority Health. n.d. Diabetes and Hispanic Americans. Accessed 7 November 2009. http://minorityhealth.hhs.gov/templates/content.aspx?ID=3324/.

Omi, Michael and Howard Winant. 1994. *Racial Formation in the United States: From the 1960s to the 1990s*. New York: Routledge.

Ong, Walter. 1982. *Orality and Literacy: The Technologizing of the Word*. London: TJ Press Ltd.

Ortiz, Fernando. 1985. *Nuevo catauro de cubanismos*. La Habana: Editorial de Ciencias Sociales.

———. 1995 [1940]. *Cuban Counterpoint, Tobacco and Sugar*. Trans. Harriet de Onís. Introduction Bronislaw Malinowski. Prologue Herminio Portell Vilá. New Introduction Fernando Coronil. Durham, NC: Duke University Press.

Pabón, Carlos. 2002. La imposible lengua apropiada. In *Nación postmortem: ensayos sobre los tiempos de insoportable ambigüedad*. 89–103. San Juan: Ediciones Callejón.

Palés Matos, Luis. 1978. *Poesía completa y prosa selecta*. Ed. Margot Arce. Caracas: Ayacucho.

———. 1995 [1937]. *Tuntún de pasa y grifería y otros poemas*. Edited by Trinidad Barrera. Madrid: Anaya & Mario Muchnik.

Paredes, Américo. 1991. *Between Two Worlds*. Houston: Arte Público Press.

———. 1994. *The Hammon and the Beans and Other Stories*. Houston: Arte Público Press.

Parkin, David and Stanley Ulijaszek. 2007. *Holistic Anthropology: Emergence and Convergence*. New York: Berghahn.
Pedreira, Antonio S. 1969 [1934]. *Insularismo*. Río Piedras, Puerto Rico: Editorial Edil.
Perdomo, Willie. 1996. *Where a Nickel Costs a Dime*. New York: W. W. Norton.
———. 2002. *Visiting Langston*. Illustrations by Bryan Collier. New York: Henry Holt.
———. 2003. *Smoking Lovely*. New York: Rattapallax Press.
Pérez, Norma. 2013. Personal email communication with Stephanie Alvarez. 31 July.
Pérez-Firmat, Gustavo. 1995. *Bilingual Blues*. Tempe: Bilingual Press/Editorial Bilingue.
———. 2003. *Tongue Ties: Logo-Eroticism in Anglo-Hispanic Literature*. New York: Palgrave Macmillan.
Pinch, Trevor and Bijsterneld, K. 2004. Sound studies: New technologies and music. *Social Studies of Science* 34(5): 635–48.
Piñero, Miguel. 1985. *La Bodega Sold Dreams*. Houston: Arte Público Press.
Pizarro, Marcos. 2005. *Chicanas and Chicanos in School: Racial Profiling, Identity Battles, and Empowerment*. Austin: University of Texas Press.
Poe, Edgar Allan. 2000. The Bells [1849]. In *Complete Poems*, ed. Thomas Olive Mabbott. 429. Champaign: University of Illinois Press.
Pradeau, Jean-François. 2000. Plato's Atlantis: The True Utopia. In *Utopia: The Search for the Ideal Society in the Western World*, ed. Gregory Claeys, Roland Schaer and Lyman Tower Sargent. 83–91. New York: New York Public Library/Oxford University Press.
Pratt, Mary Louise. 1977. *Toward a Speech Act Theory of Literary Discourse*. Bloomington: Indiana University Press.
———. 1988. *Imperial Eyes: Travel Writing and Transculturation*. 2nd ed. New York: Routledge
Rama, Ángel. 1984. *La ciudad letrada*. Hanover, NH: Ediciones del Norte.
Ramos Rosado, Marie E. 1999. *La mujer negra en la literatura puertorriqueña: Cuentística del setenta*. San Juan: La Editorial, Universidad de Puerto Rico.
Rauline, Véronique and Tato Laviera. 1998. Tato Laviera's Nuyorican Poetry: The Choice of Bilingualism. In *Strategies of Difference in Modern Poetry*, ed. Pierre Lagayette. 146–63. Madison, NJ: Fairleigh Dickinson University Press.
Reyna, Roberto. 2013. Personal email communication with Stephanie Alvarez. 1 August.
Rivera, Raquel Z. 2003. *New York Ricans from the Hip Hop Zone*. New York: Palgrave Macmillan.
Rivera-Servera, Ramón. 2000. Apartarte/Casarte (review). *Theatre Journal* 52(1): 110–12.
———. 2002. A Dominican York in Andhra. In *Caribbean Dance: From Abakuá to Zouk: How Movement Shapes Identity*, ed. Susanna Sloat, 152–61. Gainesville: University Press of Florida.
Rivero Marín, Rosanna. 2004. *Janus Identities and Forked Tongues. Two Caribbean Writers in the United States*. New York: Peter Lang.
Rodó, José Enrique. 1971 [1900]. *Ariel*. Ed. Emilio Gascó Contell. Salamanca, España: Anaya.
Rodríguez-Morazzani, Roberto P. 1996. Beyond the rainbow: Mapping the discourse on Puerto Ricans and race. *CENTRO: Journal of the Center for Puerto Rican Studies* 8(1–2): 150–69.

Rose, Tricia. 1994. *Black Noise: Rap Music and Black Culture in Contemporary America*. Middletown, CT: Wesleyan University Press.

Rothenberg, Daniel. 1998. *With These Hands. The Hidden World of Migrant Farmworkers Today*. New York: Harcourt Brace and Company.

Rothstein, Jules M. 1998. Editor's note: Of weddings and baseball. *Physical Therapy Journal September*. Accessed 7 May 2005. http://www.ptjournal.org/Sept98/Ednote.cfm/.

Rysman, Alexander. 1977. How the 'gossip' became a woman. *Journal of Communication* 27(1): 176–80.

Salamaca, Annabel. 2013. Personal email communication with Stephanie Alvarez. 9 August.

Sánchez, Luis Rafael. 1997. La gente de color. In *No llores por nosotros, Puerto Rico*. 19–30. Hanover, NH: Ediciones del Norte.

Sandoval, Art. 2009. Interview with Tato Laviera. University of Texas Public Relations, Edinburg, Texas. 4 December.

Sandoval, Chela. 2000. *Methodology of the Oppressed*. Minneapolis: University of Minnesota Press.

Santos Febres, Mayra. 1991. *Anamú y manigua*. Río Piedras, Puerto Rico: Editorial La iguana dorada.

———. 1996. *Pez de vidrio*. Río Piedras: Ediciones Huracán.

———. 2005. *Sobre piel y papel*. San Juan: Ediciones Callejón.

Sargent, Lyman Tower. 2000. Utopian Traditions: Themes and Variations. In *Utopia: The Search for the Ideal Society in the Western World*, ed. Gregory Claeys, Roland Schaer and Lyman Tower Sargent. 8–17. New York: New York Public Library/ Oxford University Press.

Sargent Thomas J. and François R. Velde. 2002. *The Big Problem of Small Change*. Princeton, NJ: Princeton University Press.

SNL. n.d. *The SNL Archives*. http://snl.jt.org/char.php?i=98/.

———. 1979. *Saturday Night Live* Transcripts. Season 5: Episode 6. http://snltranscripts.jt.org/79/79fupdate.phtml/.

Schafer, R. Murray. 1977. *The Tuning of the World*. New York: Alfred A. Knopf.

Schneider, Steven. 2009. Conversation with Tato Laviera. 18 August.

Schneirov, Matthew and Jonathan David Geczik. 2004. Beyond the Culture Wars: The Politics of Alternative Health. In *The Politics of Healing: Histories of Alternative Medicine in Twentieth-Century North America*, ed. Robert D. Jonston. 245–56. New York: Routledge.

Seco González, Carlos. 2010. 'If You Know Your History' Celtic FC and Irish Rebel Songs:Identity Formation and Politics. In *'To Banish Ghost and Goblin' New Essays on Irish Culture*, eds. David Clark and Rubén Jarazo Álvarez. 149–58. Oleiros La Coruña, Spain: Netbiblo SL.

Smith, Marc and Mark Eleveld, eds. 2003. *The Spoken Word Revolution: Slam, Hip Hop, and the Poetry of a New Generation*. Naperville, IL: Sourcebooks MediaFusion.

Solis, Sylvia. 2009. Cosecha Voices: Toward a Transcultural Pedagogy. Master's thesis, University of Texas-Pan American.

Sommer, Doris. 1999. *Proceed with Caution, When Engaged by Minority Writing in the Americas*. Cambridge, MA: Harvard University Press.
Soto-Crespo, Ramón E. 2009. *Mainland Passage: The Cultural Anomaly of Puerto Rico*. Minneapolis: University of Minnesota Press.
Spivak, Gayatri. 1993. *Outside in the Teaching Machine*. London: Routledge.
Spurr, David. 1966. *The Rhetoric of the Empire: Colonial Discourse in Journalism, Travel Writing, and Imperial Administration*. Durham, NC: Duke University Press.
Sued Badillo, Jalil and Ángel López Cantos. 1986. *Puerto Rico negro*. Río Piedras, Puerto Rico: Editorial Cultural.
Thomason, Sarah G. 2001. *Language Contact*. Washington, D.C.: Georgetown University Press.
Thompson, Becky. 2002. Multiracial feminism: Recasting the chronology of second wave. Feminism. *Feminist Studies* 28(2): 337–60.
Thornborrow, Joanna and Deborah Morris. 2004. Gossip as strategy: The management of talk about others on reality TV show *Big Brother*. *Journal of Sociolinguistics* 8(2): 246–71.
Torres, Andrés. 1995. *Between Melting Pot and Mosaic: African Americans and Puerto Ricans in The New York Political Economy*. Philadelphia: Temple University Press.
Valdés Fallis, Guadalupe. 1976. Code-switching in bilingual Chicano poetry. *Hipania* 59(4): 877–86.
Valenzuela, Angela. 1999. *Subtractive Schooling: U.S.-Mexican Youth and the Politics of Caring*. Albany: State University of New York Press.
Vásquez, Manuel. 1998. An AmeRícan Lesson in Bilingual Poetic Cha-cha. *Chimes*. Grand Rapids, Michigan: Calvin College, 16 October.
Vega, Ana Lydia. 1981. Pollito Chicken. In *Vírgenes y mártires*. Río Piedras, Puerto Rico: Antillana.
Vidales, Raúl. 1991. Dimensión utópica de la liberación. In *La utopía en América*. 47–75. México, DF: Universidad Nacional Autónoma de México.
Volex, E. 1997. Testimonial Writing. In *Encyclopedia of Latin American Literature* [E-reader version], ed Verity Smith. London: Fitzroy Dearborn. http://ezhost.utpa.edu:3895/ehost/ebookviewer/ebook/bmxlYmtfXzg5MjVfX0FO0?sid=c94076e4-9578-4e8b-9e42-4bd52fd86eb1@sessionmgr4003&vid=1&format=EB&rid=1/.
Waldron, John. 2008. Tato Laviera's Parody of *La Carreta*: Reworking a Tradition of Docility. In *Writing Of(f) the Hyphen: New Critical Perspectives on the Literature of the Puerto Rican Diaspora*, eds. Carmen H. Rivera and José L. Torres-Padilla. 221–36. Seattle: University of Washington Press.
Whitman, Walt. 1964. *Whitman: Prose Works 1892, Volume II*, ed. Floyd Stovall. New York: New York University Press.
―――. 1965. *Leaves of Grass: Comprehensive Reader's Edition*, ed. Harold W. Blodgett and Sculley Bradley. New York: New York University Press.
―――. 1987. *An American Primer by Walt Whitman*, ed. Horace Traubel. Stevens Point, WI.: Holy Cow Press.
―――. 1998. *Walt Whitman: An Encyclopedia*, eds. J.R. LeMaster and Donald D. Kummings. New York: Garland Publishing.

Whorton, James C. 2004. From Cultism to CAM: Alternative Medicine in the Twentieth Century. In *The Politics of Healing: Histories of Alternative Medicine in Twentieth-Century North America*, ed. Robert D. Johnston. 272-289. New York: Routledge.

Young, Marion. 1990. *Justice and the Politics of Difference*. Princeton, NJ: Princeton University Press.

Zenón Cruz, Isabelo. 1975. *Narciso descubre su trasero. El negro en la cultura puertorriqueña*. Humacao, Puerto Rico: Ediciones Furidi.

Zentella, Ana Celia. 1997. *Growing Up Bilingual: Puerto Rican Children in New York*. Malden, MA: Blackwell.

Zuñiga, Johanna. 2013. Personal email communication with Stephanie Alvarez. 31 July.

CONTRIBUTORS

STEPHANIE ALVAREZ (smalvarezm@utpa.edu) is Assistant Professor of Spanish and Director of Mexican American Studies and at The University of Texas-Pan American. She is the recipient of the American Association of Hispanics in Higher Education's Outstanding Latina/o Faculty in Higher Education Award (2011) and The University of Texas Board of Regents' Outstanding Teaching Award (2009). She is co-founder with Tato Laviera and José Martínez of Cosecha Voices: Documenting the Lives of Migrant Farmworker Students. Cosecha Voices aims to empower migrant farmworker students by creating a space in which they develop and perform their own written and digital *testimonios*. She is the author of several essays on and the confluence of Latin@ identity, language, literature, culture, education and empowerment in various edited books and journals such as Hispania, Journal of Latinos and Education and *CENTRO: Journal of the Center for Puerto Rican Studies*, among others.

FRANCES R. APARICIO (frances-aparicio@northwestern.edu) is Director of the Latina and Latino Studies Program and Professor in the Department of Spanish and Portuguese at Northwestern University. Author of the award-winning *Listening to Salsa* (1998), she has published extensively on Latino/a cultural identities through popular culture, music, gender politics, literature and poetry, and language and bilingualism. She is currently writing a book on Intralatinos/as in Chicago, individuals who are of two or more Latin American national heritages in the social framework of Latinidades.

SUSAN M. CAMPBELL (camp0189@umn.edu) is a Contract Professor in the Foreign Languages Department at University of Genoa, Italy. She has published several articles on Latin American literature and culture, focusing mainly on Latinos in the U.S. She is a professor of translation and works as a translator from Spanish, French and Italian into English. She has a Ph.D. from University of Minnesota in Hispanic and Luso-Brazilian Literatures and Linguistics. Her doctoral dissertation, "Nuyorican Resistance: Fame and Anonymity from Civil Rights Collapse to the Global Era" focused mainly on the work of Tato Laviera.

ANALISA DEGRAVE (degravae@uwec.edu) received her Ph.D. and M.A. in Spanish at the University of Wisconsin-Madison and her B.A. in Spanish and History at Gustavus Adolphus College. She is an associate professor of Spanish and the Director of Latin American Studies at the University of Wisconsin-Eau Claire where she teaches Spanish, Latin American literature and courses in Latin American Studies. DeGrave's areas of interest include Latin American and Latino poetry, utopian studies, and ecoliterature.

ANTONIA DOMÍNGUEZ MIGUELA (andomi.es@gmail.com) is assistant professor of English at the University of Huelva. She is the author of *Esa imagen que en mi espejo se detiene: La herencia femenina en la narrativa de Latinas en Estados Unidos* (2001), and *Pasajes de ida y vuelta: Narrativa puertorriqueña en Estados Unidos* (2005) and has published a number of articles in volumes, and journals on Latino/a writing and culture. Her current research interests are U.S. Puerto Rican Narrative and ethnic women's writing. American and Latino poetry, utopian studies, and ecoliterature.

JUAN FLORES (juan.flores@nyu.edu) is Professor in the Department of Social and Cultural Analysis at New York University. Affiliated with the Latino Studies Program, his main scholarly interests include Puerto Rican and Latina/o culture, diaspora and transnational communities, social and cultural theory, and the Afro-Latino experience in the United States. Flores' books include *Poetry in East Germany, The Insular Vision, Divided Borders: Essays on Puerto Rican Identity, La venganza de Cortijo, From Bomba To Hip-Hop: Puerto Rican Culture and Latino Identity, The Diaspora Strikes Back*, and *Bugalú y otros guisos*. He is the translator of *Memoirs of Bernardo Vega and Cortijo's Wake* by Edgardo Rodríguez Juliá, and co-editor of *On Edge: The Crisis of Latin American Culture*, the *Companion to Latino Studies*, and the *Afro-Latino Reader*. He was awarded the Casa de las Américas Prize in 1979 for *The Insular Vision* and in 2009 for *Bugalú y otros guisos*, and the Latino Legacy Award from the Smithsonian Institution in 2008. Flores lectures widely, serves on a range of editorial and advisory boards, and is a founder of the Afrolatin@ Forum.

LAWRENCE LA FOUNTAIN-STOKES (lawrlafo@umich.edu) is Director of the Latina/o Studies Program and Associate Professor of American Culture, Romance Languages and Literatures, and Women's Studies at the University of Michigan, Ann Arbor. Born and raised in Puerto Rico, he received his A.B. from Harvard (1991) and M.A. and Ph.D. from Columbia. He is author of *Queer Ricans: Cultures and Sexualities in the Diaspora* (2009), *Uñas pintadas de azul/ Blue Fingernails* (2009), and *Abolición del pato* (2013). He co-edited an issue of *CENTRO Journal on Puerto Rican Queer Sexualities* (Spring 2007) and is currently working on a book titled "Translocas and Transmachas: Trans Diasporic Puerto Rican Drag."

JACQUELINE LAZÚ (jlazu@depaul.edu) is an Associate Professor of Modern Languages and Director of the Community Service Studies Program at DePaul University. She earned her B.A at Dartmouth College and M.A. and Ph.D. from Stanford University in Spanish. Her research interests include Caribbean and Latino Literature and culture, cultural theory, theater, aesthetics and politics. Recent projects include "Poeta en el Paseo: Tato Laviera's Chicago Plays," and "Apocalypse, Femininity and Postcolonial Aesthetics in Nuyorican Theater: José Rivera's Revolutionary Millenarianism."

EDRIK LÓPEZ (elopez@fairfield.edu) is an Assistant Professor of English at Fairfield University in Connecticut. He received his Ph.D. from the University of California at Berkeley in 2009. He teaches courses in American Poetry, Literary Theory, Ethnic Literature, and Literature of the Americas.

WILLIAM LUIS (william.luis@vanderbilt.edu) is the Gertrude Conaway Vanderbilt Professor of Spanish at Vanderbilt University. He is the author of numerous books, including *Literary Bondage: Slavery in Cuban Narrative* (1991), *Dance Between Two Cultures* (1997), and *Looking Out, Looking In: Anthology of Latino Poetry* (2013). Luis is the recipient of a Guggenheim Fellowship in 2012. He is the Director of Vanderbilt's Latino and Latina Studies Program and Editor of the *Afro-Hispanic Review*. Born and raised in New York City of a Chinese father and an Afro-Cuban mother, Luis is widely regarded as a leading authority on Latin American, Caribbean, Afro-Hispanic, and Latino U.S. literatures.

GLENN MARTINEZ (martinez.474@osu.edu) is Professor of Hispanic Linguistics at The Ohio State University. He is author of *Mexican Americans and Language: Del dicho al hecho* (2006), co-editor of *Recovering the U.S. Hispanic Linguistic Heritage* (2008) and author of dozens of articles in the areas of sociolinguistics, language policy, and language teaching. His current research focuses on language, health, and health care in Latino communities in the United States.

JOSÉ LUIS MARTÍNEZ (martinez.joselm@gmail.com) is a Ph.D. student in the Chicano/Latino Studies Program at Michigan State University. His research interests include examining the theoretical and pedagogical frameworks that inform the postsecondary education of children from migrant farm working families. He has worked in migrant education, both in K-12 and higher education, to expand postsecondary opportunities for migrant students. He has also coordinated and directed multiple university programs at various institutions of higher education. He is co-founder with Tato Laviera and Stephanie Alvarez of Cosecha Voices: Documenting the Lives of Migrant Farmworker Students.

ISRAEL REYES (Israel.Reyes@dartmouth.edu) is an Associate Professor of Spanish and Portuguese at Dartmouth College. He teaches and conducts research on Latin American, Puerto Rican, and U.S. Latina/o literature and culture. His publications include his 2005 book, *Humor and the Eccentric Text in Puerto Rican Literature*, published by University Press of Florida, and scholarly articles on Judith Ortiz Cofer, Lalo Alcaraz, Nemesio Canales, Cristina García, Ana Lydia Vega, and Manuel Ramos Otero. He is currently working on a book manuscript titled "Transcultural Enterprises: Diaspora and Economic Imaginaries in Hispanic Caribbean Literature."

STEVEN P. SCHNEIDER (schneiders@utpa.edu) is a poet, critic, and professor of English at the University of Texas-Pan American, where he serves as Director of New Programs and Special Projects in the College of Arts and Humanities. He is the author of three books of poetry, *Borderlines: Drawing Border Lives* (2010), a collaborative effort with his artist wife, Reefka Schneider, *Unexpected Guests* (2008), and *Prairie Air Show* (2000). He is the author and editor of several scholarly books, including The Contemporary Narrative Poem: Critical Crosscurrents (2012), a collection of ten essays on the contemporary American narrative poem.

MARITZA STANCHICH (mstanchich@gmail.com) is a Professor of English at University of Puerto Rico, Río Piedras, where she teaches Caribbean, Latina/o and U.S. Literatures, and serves in the Academic Senate. She has published on William Faulkner; literature of the Puerto Rican diaspora, currently the focus of a book manuscript, and the UPR crisis. She previously worked as an award-winning journalist, and her recent columns for *The Huffington Post* and *New York Times* helped bring international attention to the crisis in Puerto Rico. As an activist, she has supported academic unionization at University of California and at UPR, among other movements.

Index

A

77 PR Chicago Riot xv, xlvii, xlix, 311
African heritage 246, 261, 267, 273, 275-7, 280
africanize 263
Afro-Caribbean vi, xxiii, li, 5, 9-10, 15-7, 19, 27-9, 38, 124, 132, 140, 189, 190, 193, 244, 245, 254, 258-62, 264, 266-76, 278, 280, 281, 282, 393
Afro-Caribbean music 9, 16, 124, 193, 245, 271
Afro-Diasporic 241-2, 244, 248, 255
Afro-Hispanic Review iv, xv, 342, 390, 396-7, 398, 408
Afro-Latino xix, 42, 240, 397, 407
Afro-Puerto Rican xix, 5, 36-7, 125, 149, 241
Afro-Spanglish 37-8
Algarín, Miguel xix, xxxv, xxxvi, xxxix, 87, 196, 241-4, 255-6, 283, 297, 305, 390, 398
Alvarez, Stephanie iii-vi, ix, xi, xxxv-i, xlix, lxi-iii, 37-8, 120, 124, 141, 150-1, 177, 191, 204, 207, 210, 224-5, 233, 277, 282, 288, 289, 343, 390, 392, 397-8, 400, 401, 403, 406, 409
AmeRícan i, iii-v, xi-iii, xv, xxxi, xlvii, l, liii, 5, 7, 9, 11, 13, 15-7, 19, 23, 25, 27, 29, 31, 33-5, 37, 39, 41, 43, 47, 49, 51, 53, 55, 57, 59, 67, 69, 71, 73, 75, 77, 79-80, 82-121, 124-38, 141, 143, 145, 147-51, 153, 159, 161, 163, 165, 167, 169, 171, 173, 177, 179, 181, 183, 185, 189, 191, 193, 195, 197, 198-9, 201, 205, 207, 209, 211, 213, 215, 217, 219, 221, 223, 225, 227, 229, 231, 233, 235, 241, 243, 244-7, 249, 251, 253, 255, 259, 261, 263, 265, 267-9, 271, 273-5, 277, 279, 281-3, 289, 291, 293, 295, 297, 299, 301-3, 305-9, 311, 313, 315, 317, 319, 321, 323, 327, 329, 331, 333, 335, 337, 343, 345, 347, 349, 351, 353, 355, 357, 359, 361, 363, 365, 367, 369, 371, 373, 375, 377, 379
AmeRícan (play) xlvii, 311
Anzaldúa, Gloria xi, lii, 46, 51, 56-7, 59-60, 113, 136, 390, 398
  Borderlands/La Frontera xi, 46, 57, 59, 390
Arte Público Press 125, 303, 324, 390-1, 394, 396-7, 399-400
arts poetica xxv
assimilation 22-5, 32-3, 35, 39, 89, 91, 98, 109-12, 115-6, 119, 138, 191, 270
  asimilao 20, 33, 35-7, 39, 40, 91, 108-13, 115, 116, 119, 244, 306

B

Babalao xxxix, xl
Báez, Anthony 78
Báez, Josefina vi, li-ii, 240, 249, 253, 394

Bandera a Bandera xv, xlvii, 311, 396
Barbero, Jesús Martín 66, 68, 79, 397
Barradas, Efraín 82, 391
Barthes, Roland 46, 54, 146, 391
Base of soul in Heaven's Café xlvii, 311
Becoming Garcia xlvii, 311
Benítez Rojo, Antonio 266, 282, 391
bilingualism 54, 66, 161, 177-8, 190, 316, 319, 406
  bilingües 17, 299, 308-10, 314, 411
Black aesthetics 261
Black urban speech 276
blindness xxxv, xli, 4, 171, 176, 214, 216
bomba xxiii, 5, 19, 27, 53, 87, 149, 196, 241-3, 256, 264, 267, 276-7, 292, 295
Boria, Juan 140, 246, 266, 282, 297, 305, 396
branching out 33-5, 90-1, 101, 106, 113-4, 118, 119, 121, 244
Brandon, Jorge xxiv-v, 242, 255, 273, 282, 297

C

calque 49-1, 161
Caribbean 5, 9-10, 15, 16, 17, 19, 27-9, 34, 35, 38, 40, 42, 124, 132, 140, 145, 152,
    189-90, 193, 240-6, 248, 250, 254-5, 258, 259, 260-8, 280-3, 295, 301, 313,
    360, 383, 392-4, 397, 400, 408-10
Caribbean heritage 29, 267, 269-70, 272, 274, 278
Carpentier, Alejo xlii
Chicago 4, 33, 35, 133, 171, 198, 252, 256, 311–2, 323, 392-4, 396, 406, 408
Chicana/o literature 24, 30, 59, 209–10
Cisneros, Sandra lii, 46-8, 50, 51, 57-9, 392
  Caramelo 47-8, 50-1, 57, 392
Civil Rights 66-8, 70, 72-4, 76, 78-80, 167, 406
code-switching 48, 110, 118, 124, 189, 191
Colón, Jesús 141, 255
communities 10, 13, 33, 42, 51, 56, 60-1, 75, 85, 88, 90, 98, 104, 108, 114, 119, 152,
    158-60, 165, 167, 168, 171-3, 177, 185, 213, 267, 280, 288, 317, 373
  homeless community 173
  imagined community 121, 173
  Puerto Ricans communities 173
Cortijo, Rafael xxxii, 290, 292, 310, 407
Cruz, Celia xxxvii, xl, lxv–i, 15, 61, 290, 321

D

Daedalus 22–3, 33, 394
de Burgos, Julia 74, 241
diabetes xii, xv, xxxv, lii–iii, 4, 171, 176,–7, 181–6, 321, 351, 390
Diabetic Sugar Slam 176, 184–6
diaspora xxix, liii–iv, 4, 7, 10, 18, 33, 37, 101, 140–2, 145, 148–53, 162, 200, 407, 410
diasporic 33, 37, 49, 120, 140, 150, 153, 188–92, 198–200, 240, 249, 251
Díaz Quiñones, Arcadio 148–9, 151, 152, 261, 282, 393
Dominican Republic xxxix, 241, 243, 251–2, 256
Dominican York 240, 400
Doña Gabriela 24, 26, 303–4
Du Bois, W.E.B. 51, 393

E

Edinburgo Poet's Café 228
El Barrio (novel) xlvii
El Nuevo Día 150, 153, 224
Enclave xv, xxiv–vi, 5, 19, 34, 72, 75, 77, 79, 80, 141, 193, 196, 197, 198, 244, 246, 270, 274, 276, 280, 282, 297, 304, 307, 394, 396
Espada, Martín 141
espanglish 46, 48, 50, 52, 54, 56, 58, 60, 308, 309
Esteves, Sandra María xxii, xxvi, xxxv, xxxvii, 22, 74, 83, 145, 242, 243, 255, 297
eye dialect 41, 42, 43

F

familia 208, 211, 223, 292
feminism 66, 67, 70, 71, 72, 73, 76, 78, 79, 80, 402
Flores, Juan v, xxxv–i, xli, li–ii, lxii, 5, 22–3, 33, 36, 83, 85, 89–91, 101, 106, 112, 118, 120–1, 124–5, 127, 129, 141–2, 147, 151, 153, 191, 197, 201, 205, 223, 244, 256, 267, 269, 271, 282, 292, 300, 390, 392, 393, 394, 407
Free Associated State 29, 49, 140
Ginsberg, Allen liii, 125, 137, 138, 394
Gonzales, Corky 52
González, José Luis v, xxxvii, liii–iv, 27, 125, 140, 141, 149, 150, 151, 152, 153, 243, 266, 309, 393, 395, 401
gossip 8-9, 11-3, 15-6, 19, 69, 89, 197, 256, 273, 401
  chisme 11, 15
  radio bemba 11
gufeo 162, 174
Guillén, Nicolás 73, 241, 243, 281, 282, 296, 392

H

healing 8, 19, 59, 152, 180-1, 193-5, 200, 221-2
health promotion 176-7, 181-2, 185-6
Here We Come xlvii
Hernández, Carmen Dolores 22, 153, 160, 170, 241, 246, 255, 266, 270, 282, 288, 292, 395
Hernández Cruz, Víctor 22, 255, 270, 282, 395
Hinojosa, Rolando 296
hip-hop 240, 307, 315
Hispanic Caribbean 240-3, 255, 262, 409
holistic approach 188-9, 193, 198, 200
homeless 158-9, 163-4, 166, 167-8, 171-3, 342, 345, 347, 351, 353-6, 365, 374, 381, 384-5
Hughes, Langston xxiv, liii, 55, 125, 131-3, 136-8, 240, 247, 255, 395

I, J, K

interlingual liv, 116, 140, 190-2, 196, 199, 200
jíbaro 24, 27, 129, 138, 141, 146-9, 261, 267, 292, 302, 306, 392
Kanellos, Nicolás 4, 5, 324
King of Cans vi, xv, xlv, xlvii, xlix, lii, lv, 158, 160-1, 163, 166-9, 172-4, 311, 342-4, 346, 347, 396, 397

L

La Carreta xv, xxviii, 4, 16-7, 22-7, 31, 34, 80, 125, 141-2, 149, 160, 177, 191-2, 195, 244-5, 269, 270, 272, 274, 279, 282, 288, 293, 295, 300, 302-4, 391, 393-4, 396, 402
La Carreta Made a U-Turn xi, xv-i, xxv-i, xxix, xlix, 4, 16, 22, 23, 26, 27, 31, 34, 80, 125, 141, 142, 149, 160, 177, 244, 245, 269, 270, 272, 274, 279, 282, 288, 293, 295, 300, 303
La Carreta Made a U-Turn: Puerto Rican Language and Culture in the United States (essay) 23, 125
La chefa 311
La Fountain-Stokes, Lawrence 142, 240, 396, 408
Latinas/os 6, 7, 13, 17, 37, 61, 129-30, 176, 181, 240, 242, 244-6, 248-50, 252, 254-6, 270, 278, 406, 407
Laviera Aesthetics xvii-ii, xix, xxi-iii, xxv-i, xxxiii-iv, xlix
Laviera, poems
  "against muñoz pamphleteering" 29, 142, 145
  "AmeRícan" v, xi, 82-3, 86-9, 95, 112-4, 116-7, 119, 124, 126, 128, 130, 132, 134, 136, 138, 189, 197-8, 274, 306
  "angelito's eulogy in anger" 304

"a sensitive bolero in transformation" xx, xxi, xxiii, 160
"asimilao" 36, 39, 40, 91, 109-13, 115-6, 306-7
"ay bendito" 10, 11, 273
"bilingüe" 17
"bomba para siempre" 19
"brava" xi, 13-4, 135-6, 279
"callejerismos" 12, 14, 310
"Carpetas in Your Dossier" 78, 79
"chinese" 100
"Consignas in Brutality" 78
"el moreno puertorriqueño (a three way warning poem)" xviii, xxv, 28
"enchulá" 69
"english" 91, 101, 104, 106-8, 112
"esquina dude" xi, 134-6, 274
"felipe luciano i miss you in africa" xix, 245, 273
"homenaje a don luis palés matos" xxv, 246, 297
"intellectual" 91-3, 96, 98, 108, 302
"jamaican" 34
"jesús papote" xxvi, xxxii, xxxiv, xxxix, xlii–iv, xlvi, 52, 141, 193, 195, 304
"jorge brandon" xxv
"juan boria" xxv, 246
"juana bochisme" xi, xxv, 10-1, 69, 197
"just before the kiss" 72-5, 301, 302, 413
"lady liberty" xxii, 307
"machista" xii, 72, 73
"migración" 17, 154
"m'ija" 13, 135-6, 274
"Militant" 78, 79
"Mixturao" 43, 161, 179, 181, 186, 308, 310
"my graduation speech" xi, xvii, 26, 31, 151, 177-8, 191, 278, 300, 306
"negrito" 268, 291, 301, 302
"nideaquínideallá," 82-3, 85-7, 90, 98, 112, 119, 199, 200
"nuyorican" 91, 101, 104, 106-8, 112
"olga pecho" 69
"para ti, mundo bravo" xvi, xxix, 195, 288
"patriota" 309
"penetration (to sandra esteves/julia de burgos)" 72, 74
"santa bárbara" xix, xxxix, 272
"savorings, from piñones to loíza" 246, 272
"something I heard" 29, 146
"sonero mayor" 17
"Spanglish Carta" 78, 150

"spanish," 91, 101, 104-8, 112
"standards" 73-4, 301-2
"the africa in pedro morejón" xix, xxiii, 28, 243, 273, 278
"the american dollar symbol" 28
"the last song of neruda" xx, xxiii
"the nuevo rumbón" xii, xiv, 16, 124, 192, 245, 269
"the salsa of bethesda fountain" xii, xxiii, 27, 295
"tito madera smith" xxiv, xxvi, xxxv, 33, 37, 276
"vaya carnal" 35
Laviera (Sánchez), Ruth ix, xv, xxxvii–xliii, xlv, lv, lx, lxvi, 290
Levins Morales, Aurora 141, 149
Lower East Side 162, 168-9, 205, 241, 301, 311-2, 321, 351
Luis, William iii–vi, ix, xiii, xv, xviii, xxxiv, xxxvi, xlix, l, liii, lv, lix, lxii, lxvi, 5, 27, 29, 30, 73, 75-7, 87-9, 101, 119-21, 125, 140-1, 148-50, 152-3, 161-2, 171, 178, 204, 208, 210, 211, 213, 225, 228, 233, 241, 243, 246, 249, 258-60, 262, 264, 266-74, 276, 278, 280-2, 288, 289, 297, 309, 323, 390, 392–3, 395, 397-9, 401, 408-9

M

machismo 71, 72, 74, 298
Mainstream Ethics xv, xxii, 70, 77, 80, 178, 180, 244, 282, 303, 307, 321, 396
Maldonado, Adál 61, 169, 397
Marqués, René xv, xxviii, xxix, 23-4, 32, 124-5, 141-2, 245, 269, 272-3, 302-3, 393
Martínez Diente, Pablo 192, 198, 288, 398
Melting Pot 108, 402
mestizaje 17, 188-90, 198, 200, 259, 280
mestizo 16, 190-1
migrant farm worker 206-9, 211-3, 215, 221, 225, 229, 406
migration 6, 22-6, 29, 30, 34, 141, 146-7, 190, 241, 254, 258, 267-9, 318
  Puerto Rican migration 30, 34, 269
Mixturao xv, 4-6, 17, 37, 43, 52, 67, 74, 77, 121, 141, 150, 161-2, 177-9, 181, 186, 224, 303, 307-8, 310, 311, 314, 322-3, 396-7
Mohr, Nicolasa 120, 398
Moraga, Cherrie 221, 398
mulata 70, 73, 261-2
mulatta/o 16, 151, 260, 261-2, 266–7, 279, 281
multiethnic 240
multilingual 181, 245, 279, 316, 318
Muñoz Marín, Luis v, liii, 29–30, 140-8, 151, 153, 213
  "El Panfleto" 142, 145, 146

N

Negrista movement xviii, 140, 266
Neruda, Pablo xx
Nuyorican xix, xx, xxv-i, xlvi, xlix, l-i, liii-iv, lxi, lxiii, 13, 17, 23-7, 31-3, 35, 39, 42, 52, 61, 66-70, 72, 74-6, 78-9, 82, 83-5, 87, 89, 95-6, 105-7, 113, 118-20, 124-6, 132, 140, 142, 145, 158-63, 167-9, 171, 173-4, 188-93, 195-201, 212-13, 224, 240-5, 249, 254, 256, 258-9, 267, 269, 270, 273-4, 283, 288, 293, 297, 304-8, 312-3, 315, 318-20, 365, 390, 392, 397-400, 406, 408, 413-4
Black Nuyorican 89
Nuyorican culture 76, 197
Nuyorican poets xix, xx, 87, 145, 168, 171, 190, 240-1, 244, 259, 267
Nuyorican writer 140, 160, 315
Nuyorican Poets Cafe xlvi, xlix, 168, 241, 242, 399

O

Ochoa, Edna 210-1, 215, 233, 288-90, 399
Olú Clemente xlvi
Operation Bootstrap xxix, 29, 141, 147
oral tradition 5, 270-1, 273-4, 276
  declamador 246, 292, 297, 313
Ortiz Cofer, Judith xxix, 278, 409
Ortiz, Fernando xxix, xlvi, li, 37, 121
Otheguy, Ricardo 41-3
oxcart 23, 25-7, 29, 269

P

Palero xxxix, xl
Palés Matos, Luis vi, xviii, xix, xxiv-vi, l, lii, 27, 38, 73, 140, 148-9, 241, 243, 246, 258-8, 280-3, 297, 392-3, 398-9
Paredes, Américo 59, 399
Perdomo, Willie vi, li, lii, 240, 247-9, 254-6, 400
Pérez Firmat, Gustavo 47, 55
performance 4, 6-8, 10-1, 97, 120, 140, 142, 149, 151, 154, 160-1, 166, 169, 185, 209-12, 215, 221-2, 229, 240, 242, 244, 249, 252, 297, 342
Pietri, Pedro 22-3, 26, 61, 145, 169, 242, 255, 318, 392
  Puerto Rican Obituary 23
Piñero, Miguel xvi, xix, lii, 145, 168-9, 241-2, 255, 297, 305, 390, 400
Piñones xlvi, 311
Piri Thomas 26, 247, 255, 334
plena xxiii, 5, 27, 87, 89, 115, 125, 130, 138, 241, 246, 267, 273, 276, 281, 292, 295

Pollito Chicken 49, 51, 402
Popular Democratic Party 146, 147
Puerto Rican literature 258, 319
Puerto Ricans in New York City 13, 75

R, S, T

Río Grande Valley xii, 204, 205, 211, 225
Rivera, Ismael xii, xxiii, xxxii, 17, 18, 243, 273, 290
Santiago, Esmeralda 141, 149
Soto, Pedro Juan 27, 125
Sound Theory 7
Sound Studies 7, 8, 9, 20
Spanglish 13, 31, 37-8, 40, 46-9, 51-3, 55-61, 78, 88-90, 117, 124, 135, 150, 190-3, 197-8, 204, 225, 241, 243, 254, 269, 270, 272, 278, 307, 313-15, 318, 320, 346, 390, 398
synchretism 17, 245
Taino Towers xxxvii, xxxviii, xlvi, 342
testimonio ix, liv, 209, 210, 213, 223-4, 231, 288-90, 392, 397, 414
The Spark xv, xlvii, xlix, 311, 312, 396
transculturation 17, 37-8, 58, 121, 124, 192, 276, 277

U, V, W, Y, Z

University of Texas—Pan American (UTPA) xii, xiii, 204, 206, 225, 230, 232
Vega, Ana Lydia 49, 266, 319, 409
Whitman, Walt l, li, liii, 101-3, 125-30, 137-8, 241, 394, 402
Young Lords 72, 397
Zentella, Ana Celia 42, 43, 247, 403
Zimmerman, Marc 88, 391